In Pursuit of Knowledge

IN PURSUIT OF KNOWLEDGE

Black Women and Educational Activism
in Antebellum America

KABRIA BAUMGARTNER

New York University Press

NEW YORK

NEW YORK UNIVERSITY PRESS
New York
www.nyupress.org

Paperback edition published 2022.

References to Internet websites (URLs) were accurate at the time of writing. Neither the author nor New York University Press is responsible for URLs that may have expired or changed since the manuscript was prepared.

Library of Congress Cataloging in Publication Data

Names: Baumgartner, Kabria, 1982– author.
Title: In pursuit of knowledge : black women and educational activism in
    antebellum America / Kabria Baumgartner.
Description: New York : New York University Press, [2019] | Includes
    bibliographical references and index. | Summary: "'In Pursuit of
    Knowledge' explores Black women and educational activism in Antebellum
    America"— Provided by publisher.
Identifiers: LCCN 2019009450 | ISBN 9781479823116 (cloth) |
    ISBN 9781479816729 (paperback) | ISBN 9781479802579 (consumer ebook) |
    ISBN 9781479871377 (library ebook)
Subjects: LCSH: African American women educators—History—19th century. |
    African American women political activists—History—19th century. |
    African Americans—Education—History—19th century. | African
    Americans—Social conditions—19th century. | United States—Race
    relations—History—19th century.
Classification: LCC LC2741 .B38 2019 | DDC 371.829/96073—dc23
LC record available at https://lccn.loc.gov/2019009450

New York University Press books are printed on acid-free paper, and their binding materials are chosen for strength and durability. We strive to use environmentally responsible suppliers and materials to the greatest extent possible in publishing our books.

Manufactured in the United States of America

10 9 8 7 6 5 4 3 2

Also available as an ebook

For Ella and Maya

Contents

List of Figures   xi

Introduction: Purposeful Womanhood   1

PART I. WHAT OUR MINDS HAVE LONG DESIRED

1   Prayer and Protest at the Canterbury Female Seminary   13
2   Race and Reform at the Young Ladies' Domestic Seminary   46
3   Women Teachers in New York City   79

PART II. GOD PROTECT THE RIGHT

4   Race, Gender, and the American High School   107
5   Black Girlhood and Equal School Rights   142
6   Character Education and the Antebellum Classroom   177

Conclusion: Going Forward   205

Acknowledgments   209

Appendix A. List of Black Students at the Canterbury
Female Seminary in Connecticut   215

Appendix B. List of Black Students at the Young
Ladies' Domestic Seminary in New York   217

Appendix C. List of Black Families in the Northeast   219

Appendix D. Physical Attacks on Black Schools
in the Northeast, 1830–1845   223

Notes   225

Index   277

About the Author   287

Figures

I.1.   "Colored Scholars Excluded from Schools"   3

1.1.   Sarah Harris   15

1.2.   Prudence Crandall   17

1.3.   "Colored Schools Broken Up in the Free States"   44

2.1.   Hiram Huntington Kellogg   47

2.2.   Joanna Turpin Howard   63

2.3.   Serena deGrasse's painting   69

3.1.   Rosetta Morrison's school advertisement   90

4.1.   Sarah Parker Remond   119

4.2.   Petition of Eunice Ross   137

5.1.   William Cooper Nell   148

5.2.   Edwin F. Howard   162

5.3.   J. Imogen Howard   171

5.4.   Adeline T. Howard   173

5.5.   Edwin Clarence Howard   175

6.1.   Friendship album of Mary Anne Dickerson   185

6.2.   Charlotte Forten   199

IN PURSUIT OF KNOWLEDGE

Introduction: Purposeful Womanhood

In the spring of 1833, twenty young African American women trekked to the Canterbury Female Seminary located in the town of Canterbury, Connecticut. They were overjoyed to partake in this opportunity for advanced schooling. But white Canterbury residents were far from joyful; in fact, they sought to drive these young women out of the town. After seventeen months of continuous harassment, abuse, and even violence, white residents got their wish as the Canterbury Female Seminary closed in September 1834. This incident marked yet another unfortunate case of northern racist violence, but it was more than that too: it reveals a larger, more complex story of African American girls and women in pursuit of knowledge in nineteenth-century America.

The controversy surrounding the Canterbury Female Seminary galvanized African American women activists, who penned essays on the value of education, set their sights on building schools, and entered the teaching profession. Sarah Mapps Douglass, an African American teacher and school proprietor in Philadelphia, was certain that education opened a path to civil rights and economic betterment. In a public letter, she offered a powerful motto to guide African American girls and women: "Be courageous; put your trust in the God of the oppressed; and go forward!"[1] In her estimation, educated and pious African American girls and women ought to live their lives with a sense of purpose.

In Pursuit of Knowledge examines the educational activism of Douglass and other African American women and girls living in the antebellum Northeast. "Activism" is broadly defined here to capture the forms of mobilization and resistance sometimes overlooked in histories that rely on more formal definitions. Few of the African American girls and women discussed in this book have been heralded as educational activists, and yet, as the following chapters will show, they engaged in concerted efforts to procure advanced schooling (beyond the primary level) and teaching opportunities for themselves and their communities.[2] African American girls and women from working- and middle-class families used their resources and networks to establish schools that welcomed *all* students, regardless of race and class.[3] These brave young women did not and could not simply go to school or teach; they had to engage in conscious, vigorous, and sustained acts of defiance and protest in their quest for an education. An African American mother trying to enroll her children in school was performing an act of protest (Figure I.1); an African American girl daring to rise to the top of her class affirmed that black intelligence was real and material; and an African American female teacher guiding African American children flouted exclusionary school laws. Rather than reading these acts of protest as disparate and singular, I read them as continuous and dynamic, becoming more and more organized and formal by midcentury.[4]

Students and teachers like Sarah Harris, Mary E. Miles, Serena deGrasse, Rosetta Morrison, Sarah Parker Remond, Susan Paul, Sarah Mapps Douglass, Charlotte Forten, and others were educational activists—each a pioneer and forerunner in her own way. Collectively they pushed for racial (and often gender) inclusion at a time when many white Americans considered the very idea of a multiracial democracy to be contrary to the good of the nation. Eschewing a strict division between public and private spheres, these African American women activists viewed the schoolhouse as both an extension of the home and a defining civic space.[5] They framed their argument for educational inclusion as a matter of equality and rights—hence this book's use of the phrase "equal school rights" to describe their efforts.

During the nineteenth century, schools became sites of production—to make Americans, to turn poor white boys into ministers, or to prepare white women for civic life. The historian Hilary Moss describes public schools of this period as "an Americanizing agent, an institution whose central purpose was to fuse children from all religions and ethnicities into a single American citizenry."[6] Yet African American children were routinely excluded from this nationalist pedagogical project because they were viewed as noncitizens. Similarly, proponents of women's education endorsed female seminaries as places to train women to contribute to

FIGURE I.1. "Colored Scholars Excluded from Schools." This illustration from the *American Anti-Slavery Almanac* (1839) depicts a man apparently barring an African American mother from leading her children into a schoolhouse. Author's collection.

civil society but rarely felt the need to specify "only white women," so implicit was the understanding that African American women would be excluded.[7] The education of white men, women, and children thus flourished as schooling became increasingly bound up with social, political, and cultural obligations. African Americans, however, were considered unworthy of such responsibilities. A process of racialization was embedded within the very notions of childhood, womanhood, manhood, education, and citizenship.

Despite—and, perhaps even more intensely, *because* of—this exclusion, African American girls and women had educational ambitions that framed their very sense of womanhood. The historian Erica Armstrong Dunbar finds that many middle-class African American women in Philadelphia and New York City proved their respectability by their appearance, conduct, and education.[8] Respectability signified moral excellence and contributed to a larger activist strategy to uplift the race.[9] The scholar Linda Perkins argues that African American women were encouraged to become educated to promote this ideology of racial uplift.[10] My book seeks to expand upon these narratives of respectability and racial uplift by tracing their specific meaning and impact in the nineteenth-century fight for equal school rights and by locating African American girls and women as actors in their own stories. I argue for a framework that puts African American girls and women at the center by viewing their actions collectively, not just individually, and by analyzing their ideas, words, and experiences as the valuable historical records they are.[11]

What emerges is the significance of another idea shaping African American women's actions—not just the well-documented demand for respectability but also the related yet distinct call for *purpose*. Purpose held different meanings for different people; for some, it meant proselytizing, pursuing meaningful work, expanding the mind, and leading a respectable life. Both men and women used the term, as did whites and African Americans. In fact, some white women teachers in the antebellum era linked their Christian faith to a notion of usefulness.[12] To the historian Thomas Woody, "social usefulness" rationalized white women's education, particularly at female seminaries.[13] But the racial and gender oppression under which African American women struggled gave purpose—and *purposeful womanhood* more specifically—a different meaning. African American women talked about leading a purposeful life not simply to rationalize their access to advanced schooling but to motivate more young women to value themselves and to do something of value in a world that failed to recognize them as valuable.

A purposeful woman was resilient, enterprising, and active—a proud seeker of knowledge. Though the ideology of purposeful womanhood came with some restrictions, it still offered a more capacious definition of domesticity, piety, and activism since it was specific to the experiences, actions, words, and thoughts of African American girls and women in a way that the ideology of the cult of domesticity, with its racial entanglements, never could be. Purposeful womanhood afforded African American girls and women the opportunity to study, to write, and to pursue knowledge—as activists, educators, community members, leaders, and, most of all, human beings.

African American women activists articulated this idea of the purposeful woman at literary societies, where members talked about being models to their families and communities; at female seminaries, where students learned to be resilient and to ignore racial abuse; and even on the lecture circuit, where lecturers stressed intellectual vitality. In a speech on women's intellectual improvement, Elizabeth Jennings Sr., an African American homemaker, declared that women had a duty to "make ourselves useful," to persevere in their quest for knowledge, and to engage in civic life.[14] Hence embodying purposefulness was a way to resist white supremacy and to challenge racialized myths that denied African American girls and women virtue, will, and intellect. More important, it was a way to navigate and be in the world. Purposefulness was a proud articulation of self and community, an assertion of humanity, and a statement of African American girls' and women's raison d'être. African American girls and women worked to become what *they* wanted to be, despite the oppressive and hostile conditions of the antebellum North.

Any pretense that the antebellum North shone like a beacon of liberty for free blacks has been shattered by historians writing about northern black activism.[15] In particular, the Northeast, which includes six New England states plus New York, New Jersey, and Pennsylvania, counted a little over 122,000 free blacks in 1830. By then, slavery was all but extinct in the region, but white supremacy thrived nationwide, leaving free blacks in a precarious position, to say the least. If not by law, then by custom, African American women, men, and children experienced disenfranchisement, racial discrimination in public accommodations, and economic insecurity. Facing this reality, free blacks established their own institutions, formed activist networks, and participated in reform movements from temperance and abolition to education.

The subject of African American women's education in the United States often focuses on a single institution, Oberlin College, which adopted a policy to admit students, regardless of sex and race, in 1835. That same year James Bradley became the first African American man to attend Oberlin, and a year later Elizabeth Latta was probably the first African American woman to do so. Oberlin was indeed an important educational destination, so much so that some African American families moved to the area. For instance, Blanche V. Harris received her early education at public schools in Monroe, Michigan, before her family relocated to the town of Oberlin so that she and her siblings could attend the college.[16] This college, as the historian Carol Lasser rightfully points out, was the "only institution of higher education in the [antebellum] United States to offer collegiate-level training to African American women."[17]

But all roads did not lead to Oberlin College. In fact, the African American student population at Oberlin remained small, hovering around 4 to 5 percent of the total between 1840 and 1860.[18] And most African American women students enrolled there hailed from the South and Midwest, not the Northeast.[19] No doubt distance and, relatedly, cost were overriding factors. Maritcha Lyons, an African American teacher in New York, later reflected that she might have attended Oberlin, but for several reasons she changed her mind, including the "long distance—for so it was then—between myself and home [in New York]."[20] An exclusive focus on Oberlin ignores the African American girls and women in the Northeast who were educational activists before Oberlin College even began accepting African American students.

In addition to studies on Oberlin College, historians have explored the development of African American schools and literary societies, probed the rise of white opposition to African American education, and examined the struggle over racial segregation in public education, but none of this scholarship, with few exceptions, engages women or gender.[21] Yet scholars of African American women's history have shown that the everyday work of African American women influenced family, community life, and public culture in the nineteenth century.[22] *In Pursuit of Knowledge* writes African American girls and women back into the history of early American education while also enlarging the scholarship on northern black activism. Exploring the dimensions of African American women's educational experiences demonstrates that both race and gender shaped the struggle for equal school rights in the Northeast.

Indeed the quest for educational inclusion and equal school rights was one strand within the broader movement among African Americans for genuine freedom and equality. Sarah Mapps Douglass rejected repeated attempts by many whites to exclude African Americans from the body politic. She vowed to help build a truly democratic and multi-racial republic, one child at a time. "Our enemies know that education will elevate us to an equality with themselves. We also know, that it is of more importance to us than gold," she declared.[23] Her sentiments echoed those of David Walker, an African American activist who accused many whites of being deathly afraid of black elevation. No matter the enemy, African Americans would battle for equality, rights, and inclusion, with education as their weapon.[24]

Three major tenets characterized African American women's educational activism: eradicating prejudice and promoting Christian love, training African American women and men to be educator-activists who would fight for civil rights, and cultivating moral and intellectual character in children and youth. Instilling moral and intellectual character in children and youth meant abiding by a biblical version of morality that stressed care, kindness, and God's love. This perspective shaped what children and youth studied in the classroom, whether it was English grammar, botany, geography, or French. It was thought that pursuing knowledge could dramatically augment the effectiveness of African American claims for freedom, civil rights, and human dignity. In other words, education was more than just a path to literacy; it was a force multiplier allowing African American men, women, and children to live their purpose.[25]

Examining African American women's education makes it clear that racial and gender discrimination in public and private schools was not just local but hyperlocal. Local customs and rules determined how public, and sometimes private, schools were built, constituted, and maintained. Moreover local customs might actually be temporary. In Salem, Massachusetts, for example, the school committee initiated a policy of racial school discrimination in 1834, but at least one public grammar school did not enforce that policy, and African American students were schooled alongside white students. Salem was not an outlier, as other towns and cities, including Providence, Rhode Island, operated in like manner. Policies that shaped private and public schools in the Northeast were not fixed, and gradual changes to the composition of the student body could occur within the system of public education.

Public education was in its early stages of systematization at the turn of the century. Many towns and cities in the region had a common, or public, primary school, which offered a basic education in reading, writing, and arithmetic; some grammar schools, which provided more advanced study; and occasionally a public high school, which some educational reformers referred to as "democracy's college" for its egalitarian ethos and advanced curriculum.[26] Educational divisions, however—like primary school and high school—did not exist in the same way as in today's schools. Hence I examine private seminaries along with public high schools for three reasons: First, young African American women and their families did not confine their educational quest to one town but actually crisscrossed urban areas and rural communities to attend various types of schools. Second, only during the nineteenth century did the public high school gradually begin to overtake the private seminary as the preferred institution for advanced study.[27] Third, this gradual shift coincided with a discursive turn among African American activists, wherein the fight for educational opportunity at private seminaries gave way to a demand for equal school rights at public high schools.

The stories that we can tell about African American women are definitely shaped by the archive. This book draws from a rich set of records that concern African American women's experiences but are not always written by African American women themselves. Like other historians faced with the fragmented nature of the archive, I have carefully read into and interpreted archival silences and absences to provide a glimpse into the lives of African American women in the distant and not-so-distant past.[28] I highlight sources such as diaries, letters, and essays produced by young African American women that offer insights into their learning, schooling, and teaching. Untapped archival and digital collections at repositories in Ohio, Connecticut, and Massachusetts as well as genealogical records document the family history of some of these women (appendix C).[29] And I have mined other archival materials, such as school catalogues, annual reports from antislavery organizations, court records, and petitions to reconstruct broader debates about race, gender, and education and to make African American girls and women—and their desire to learn—visible and palpable.[30]

Building on Bettina Aptheker's concept of "pivoting the center," this study also considers the meaning of solidarity and alliance within the larger struggle for African American education in the early nineteenth century.[31] To that end, I pull in the observations of African American and white male abolitionists who supported young women, including Theodore S. Wright, William Cooper Nell, and William Lloyd Garrison; white school founders such as Prudence Crandall and Hiram Huntington Kellogg; and white teachers at private female seminaries and public high schools such as Elizabeth Everett and William Dodge, among others. By admitting African American girls as students, by treating them as equals in the classroom, and by empowering them to raise their voices, these abolitionists, school founders, and teachers powerfully contributed to African American women's schooling and learning.

In Pursuit of Knowledge unfolds in two overlapping parts, each comprising three chapters. Part I traces educational opportunity at private female seminaries. Chapter 1 follows the young African American women at the Canterbury Female Seminary. Nineteen-year-old Sarah Harris and others were met with hostility from white residents but responded by adopting and practicing an ethic of Christian love, a distinct form of social protest. Sarah and her peers named prejudice and other forms of wrongdoing anti-Christian, while also advocating for peaceful and loving communities inclusive of African Americans.[32] Chapter 2 opens with fifteen-year-old Mary E. Miles fleeing the Canterbury Female Seminary and arriving at the Young Ladies' Domestic Seminary in Clinton, New York. Founded in 1833 by Hiram Huntington Kellogg, a white Presbyterian minister and abolitionist, this seminary linked academic study in physics and botany with manual labor such as washing and cooking. Unlike the Canterbury Female Seminary, Kellogg's seminary thrived as African American and white women students lived, worked, studied, and prayed together. These young women learned that prosocial behavior actually informed social reform initiatives. Chapter 3 offers a glimpse into the life of Rosetta Morrison, who attended the Young Ladies' Domestic Seminary before embarking upon a short-lived teaching career in New York City. Rosetta benefited from an emerging local network of African American women teacher-activists who worked alongside African American men. Teaching and mothering not only constituted service to the race but also offered one way to lead a purposeful life. Telling Rosetta's story enlarges the archive on African American women's educational activism in New York City.

Part II explores the pursuit of educational justice in Massachusetts public schools. Though some African American families in the Northeast availed themselves of private schools, these institutions were capricious and undependable. Hence African American families took advantage of the expansion of public school systems in the Northeast, especially in Massachusetts, a leader in antebellum educational movements. Chapter 4 recognizes young African American women who turned Massachusetts public high schools into a battleground for equal school rights. Sarah Parker Remond and Eunice Ross were denied access to the public high schools in Salem and Nantucket, respectively, despite their strong qualifications. They both worked with allies to launch a campaign to end racial exclusion in public schools.[33] Chapter 5 chronicles the twenty-year struggle for equal school rights in the city of Boston. African American activists and their allies engaged in a range of protest strategies, from boycotts to lawsuits, in order to abolish racially exclusive public schools. In the process, the African American girl became an icon for educational justice. Chapter 6 examines the pedagogy of African American women teachers in Boston and Philadelphia, such as Susan Paul, Sarah Mapps Douglass, and Charlotte Forten. Analyzing didactic fiction alongside newspaper advertisements and antislavery correspondence, the chapter imagines the antebellum classroom with an African American woman teacher. Faith, activism, and commitment to character education united these teachers and their practices.

To overlook African American girls and women as educational activists in early America is to ignore their insights and perspectives, especially concerning race and gender. Fully aware that education was far from a panacea, African American women insisted nonetheless on its centrality for black achievement, opportunity, and civil rights. They, along with their allies, wished to blaze a path for themselves and the next generation.[34] Chronicling their struggles, *In Pursuit of Knowledge* addresses an essential human question: What does it mean to live a purposeful life? To seek learning and to grow, some African American women might respond. But would they be welcomed into the classroom, or would they be debarred? Would they be harassed by adversaries, or could they learn in peace? These purposeful young women never knew what awaited them. But they went forward anyway.

PART I

What Our Minds Have Long Desired

1 / Prayer and Protest at the Canterbury Female Seminary

On a walk around the village green of Canterbury, nineteen-year-old Sarah Harris (Figure 1.1) might have spied the large, two-story, Federal-style building that housed the Canterbury Female Boarding School. She and her family had recently moved to the area. Her father, William Montflora Harris, born in the West Indies, emigrated to the United States, likely during the Haitian Revolution. He settled in Norwich, Connecticut; married Sally Prentice, who was of Mohegan and European descent; and raised eleven children.[1] In January 1832 he purchased a farm in Canterbury, which dates the family's arrival at that village. About seventy free blacks resided in Canterbury in 1830, constituting less than 4 percent of the village's population.

Sarah and her siblings likely received their early education at Sunday schools.[2] They may have gone to the public primary schools in Canterbury too, which, like some other small towns and villages in Connecticut, allowed African American and white children to attend together. In urban areas such as Hartford, however, public primary schools were racially segregated. In any case, a boarding school was different. Operated by Prudence Crandall, a white Quaker woman, the Canterbury Female Boarding School enrolled twenty young, middle-class and elite white women from the Windham County area. The Board of Visitors, an eight-member, all-white, all-male board consisting of lawyers and politicians, praised Prudence's teaching.[3] The young female students enjoyed their experiences; years later, two former students reminisced about "the many pleasant moons we have spent together under the chesnut [sic] tree studying our definitions."[4] While these young women studied English grammar, natural and moral philosophy, and music and drawing, among other subjects, Sarah labored as a servant in the house of her white neighbor Jedediah Shepherd.[5]

But in September 1832, only eight months after arriving in Canterbury, an ambitious Sarah asked for admission to Prudence Crandall's all-white school. Her goal, she explained, was to get "a little more learning, enough to teach colored children."[6] What inspired Sarah to reject servitude and push for advanced study? We cannot know for sure, but possibly a recent lecture had inspired her. That same month, Maria W. Stewart, an African American lecturer, delivered a speech about servitude at Franklin Hall in Boston, which was later printed in the *Liberator*, an antislavery newspaper edited by the white abolitionist William Lloyd Garrison. Stewart asserted that African Americans "ha[d] dragged out a miserable existence of servitude from the cradle to the grave."[7] Perhaps her words resonated with Sarah, a servant herself, and also a reader of the *Liberator*. Sarah's father and her brother, Charles, both circulated the newspaper, and Sarah once described it as a "welcome visiter [sic]" in her home.[8] Sarah's rather modest personal goal—to acquire enough learning "to teach colored children"—thus suggests not simply a personal ambition but also a communal mission to see free blacks move beyond a position of servitude.

Prudence weighed Sarah's request carefully.[9] She suspected some of her white students might bristle at the idea of attending classes with a young African American woman, but Sarah's earnestness prevailed. "If I was injured on her account I would bear it," Prudence resolved, and she agreed to admit Sarah.[10] And bear it she did, for Sarah's admission completely unsettled the village of Canterbury. The parents of the white students held a meeting with Prudence and demanded that she dismiss "the nigger girl."[11] When they threatened to withdraw their daughters, Prudence pushed back, reopening the school in April 1833 exclusively for African American girls and women. Now the school's stated purpose was to train young African American women as teachers.[12]

This reconstituted female seminary faced bitter opposition from white residents such as Andrew T. Judson, a Connecticut state attorney and politician who fervently supported the American Colonization Society, an organization founded in 1816 to resettle African Americans in Liberia. Hence the very idea of educating young African American women instead of young white women—not to mention devoting an

FIGURE 1.1. Sarah Harris (1812–1878) was the first African American student to desegregate the Canterbury Female Boarding School in Connecticut in 1832. The controversy surrounding her admission led to the establishment of the Canterbury Female Seminary for African American girls and women in April 1833. Sarah later married George Fayerweather and settled in Kingston, Rhode Island. Courtesy of the Prudence Crandall Museum. Canterbury, CT.

entire school to the task in the United States—conflicted with Judson's colonizationist views. Opposition from white residents intensified over a seventeen-month period, with verbal threats, legal action, and finally violence, which led to the school's abrupt closure in September 1834.[13]

How did African American girls and women individually and collectively contest this escalation of white opposition and racism in Canterbury? Writings from several students at the seminary published in the antislavery press provide a glimpse into their thoughts and actions. These writings, consisting of speeches and letters, cite scripture, praise God, and highlight the power of Christian love. Canterbury's African American students evoked and implemented an ethic of Christian love, which included biblical principles to "love God" and "love thy neighbor." This ethic was neither meek nor militant but rather, I argue, an act of social protest. Just as historians have analyzed moral suasion and other ideologies as foundational tactics in antebellum social movements, so too must we recuperate African American women's self-developed ethic of Christian love.[14]

Perhaps most remarkable is that these young women espoused an ethic of Christian love amid the looming threat of violence. Instead of citing biblical passages from Exodus, commonly referenced by African American ministers, these women turned to the Gospel of Mark, the Letter to the Romans, and the Book of John—scriptures emphasizing love that enabled them to argue for inclusion and belonging. Time was of the essence since they wanted to remain at Prudence's school. These students bound their communal project of learning with an appeal to the minds and hearts of the white Christian men of Canterbury. They decried white wrongdoing, all the while urging their opponents to do right: to love. In turning to a discourse that counseled compassion for the very people trying to thwart them, these young women transformed the seminary into a significant site for African American women's activism.[15]

Before Prudence Crandall (Figure 1.2) established her all-white boarding school, the Rhode Island native had attended the New England Friends School, a well-known Quaker boarding school in Providence. There she met classmate Abby Kelley, later a staunch antislavery and woman's rights activist. Prudence decried the sinfulness of slavery but had yet to identify the struggle for African American education as part of her own mission. She later admitted that she had been "entirely ignorant" of the experiences of northern free blacks. Before coming to Canterbury, she had lived in nearby Plainfield, Connecticut, where she ran a school for young white women. Impressed with her initiative,

FIGURE 1.2. This portrait of Prudence Crandall
(1803–1890) was painted by Francis Alexander
in 1834. Prudence was a white abolitionist from
Rhode Island and the proprietor of the Canterbury
Female Seminary in Connecticut. Courtesy of
the Division of Rare and Manuscript Collections,
Cornell University Library.

training, and curricular emphasis on literature and writing, some Canterbury citizens, including Judson, recruited her to establish a school for young white women in the area. Samuel Hough, a white factory owner, loaned her the money to buy the school building, and the school opened in 1831.[16]

The Canterbury Female Boarding School fit firmly within the tradition of the female seminary movement. This movement began in the Revolutionary era as leading white intellectuals, including Benjamin Rush and Judith Sargent Murray, raised concerns about the twin goals of forming the national character and developing a unified citizenry.

These concerns helped to accelerate support for widespread schooling of both young white men and women at colleges and seminaries, respectively. In 1787 Rush, a white physician, political leader, and educator in Philadelphia, delivered a speech, "Thoughts upon Female Education," at the Young Ladies' Academy. He proposed a curriculum of English language and grammar, writing, bookkeeping, geography, and history to "prepare [women] for the duties of social and domestic life."[17] This proposal stressed the usefulness of a woman's advanced learning to manage household affairs, to influence her husband, to promote the well-being of her family, and to engage in intellectual conversation. Rush and other leaders cast women as central actors in stabilizing the nation and seminaries as sites of meaning-making and cultural production.[18]

From 1790 to 1860 more than 350 female seminaries and academies were founded in the United States.[19] Almira Hart Lincoln Phelps, a white female educator and writer, observed in 1837 that seminaries were "institutions of a permanent and elevated character" that were "fast multiplying" across the nation.[20] While a few poor and working-class white female students received tuition scholarships, most of the students who attended female seminaries were twelve- to eighteen-year-old young white women from middle-class and elite families who could afford the tuition and room and board.[21] Hence only a small percentage of the population could actually avail themselves of these institutions. The historian Margaret Nash asserts that female seminaries "played an [important] role in class formation and consolidation."[22] For instance, material conditions and cultural values like self-improvement and morality defined middle-class status and were often reinforced at seminaries and academies.[23]

Nineteenth-century educational advocates argued that both white men and women possessed intellectual abilities in need of refinement, even though these groups would occupy different roles in the nation. The rationale for women's pursuit of advanced education focused on notions of usefulness and intellectual growth, with gender ideology an important but not singular consideration. To be sure, proponents of female seminaries such as Rush emphasized that educated women would make good wives and mothers.[24] The explosion of religious revivalism and the emergence of the market revolution further stimulated the growth of female seminaries, and the seminary movement would soon become a watershed in the history of white women's education.[25]

But like other educational movements of the day, the female seminary movement did not serve African American girls and women, a fact that angered many African American activists and their allies. In 1830 the free black population in the United States stood at 300,000, with over 40 percent located in the free states and territories of the North.[26] Whether in urban areas or small towns, African Americans confronted discrimination, and the schoolhouse was no exception. Some public schools barred African American children from attending. Only a small number of African American men were admitted to colleges and universities. The female seminary fared no better. A letter on women's education, signed by a person named Matilda and featured in *Freedom's Journal*, the first African American newspaper, simultaneously praised the emerging national dialogue claiming that the mind had no sex while lamenting the fact that racial prejudice qualified the dialogue. "We possess not the advantages with those of our sex whose skins are not colored like our own," Matilda declared.[27] As the national dialogue went, the mind had no sex, but it certainly had a race.[28]

Female seminaries endorsed a racialized and gendered model of republican citizenship; an unspoken requirement for admission was whiteness, apparently even before sex.[29] For example, the Albany Female Seminary in New York enrolled both young white women and "small [white] boys."[30] In the early nineteenth century, coeducation at seminaries and academies was not unusual, but racial integration was.[31] Hence white women applicants to seminaries and academies such as Bradford Academy in Massachusetts had to be ladies of "good character"—a seemingly amorphous category with specifically racialized assumptions about who did and did not qualify.[32] So when white women attended these seminaries, they inhabited predominantly white female spaces.[33]

Though called a boarding school, Prudence Crandall's school was, for all intents and purposes, a female seminary.[34] Female seminaries typically offered a three-year course of study in English language and literature, reading and composition, arithmetic, geography, history, natural and moral philosophy, and botany, as well as electives such as drawing and music. William Russell, an instructor of reading at a Massachusetts-area female seminary, extolled the virtues of this standard curriculum, which would enable a woman to "acquit herself aright, to whatever social duty she may be justly called."[35] The female seminary was thus an academically rigorous environment, and the Canterbury Female Boarding School offered all of these subjects and even added chemistry, astronomy, rhetoric, and French.

In these white female spaces, racial hierarchies and boundaries were implicitly, if not explicitly, observed and maintained, especially when it came to socializing. Mary Eckert, a young white woman from a well-to-do family, penned a letter to her parents while at her aunt's female boarding school in Washington, Pennsylvania. Mary noted the planned lecture tour by Reverend John B. Pinney, a white Presbyterian missionary who worked as an agent for the American Colonization Society. Mary recounted hearing "a lady ask . . . why our blacks should not be educated and taken into company with the whites, that she would like to see them taken into our parties." Though it is unclear where Mary was when she heard the question, her sentiments were made clear when she recorded her thoughts on the matter: "I think that's carrying the joke rather too far."[36] The question of whether African Americans should even be permitted at parties aside, Mary's description of their mere presence in white spaces as a "joke" is revealing.

The very rationale for white women's education made the presence of African American women at female seminaries precarious, at best. As the historian Mary Kelley argues, the female seminary encouraged young white women to "chart the nation's course."[37] An African American woman attending a seminary demonstrated her desire and ability to improve her mind and lead a purposeful life. And allowing her to attend a seminary affirmed her legitimate inclusion within the broader project of nation-building, which conflicted with racial ideologies that refused African Americans an equal place in the nation, let alone recognized their ability to contribute to it. An African American woman's desire for learning, as well as her capacity to learn, was thus summarily dismissed.

Nevertheless African American families invested in and cared deeply about their children's learning. When Prudence Crandall decided to open a seminary for African American girls, she visited the homes of African American families who "seemed to feel much for the education of their children."[38] With an introduction from Garrison in hand, she traveled to Providence, where she met Elizabeth Hall Hammond, a free, middle-class African American widow with two daughters, Ann Eliza and Sarah Lloyd, who showed interest in attending a female seminary.[39] Elizabeth introduced Prudence to other black families as well as white abolitionists, including George William Benson, a leather and wool merchant in Providence, and his brother, Henry E. Benson, an agent for the *Liberator*. The Benson brothers, who helped to establish the Providence Anti-Slavery Society, had ties to the Brooklyn, Connecticut, community, where their father, George Benson, settled the family in 1824. Esther Baldwin, a young white woman from Canterbury who attended the Norwich Female Academy, wrote to her sisters, one of whom had attended

Prudence's boarding school, "The blacks [in Norwich] talk about Miss Crandall's academy."[40] The network of free black New England families from Providence to Norwich was abuzz over this new African American female seminary.

Grace Lanson, a seventeen-year-old African American indentured servant from New Haven, Connecticut, had apparently learned of the Canterbury Female Seminary. She labored at the Litchfield, Connecticut, residence of Benjamin Tallmadge, a white politician and military officer who had served with George Washington in the American Revolution. In August 1833 Grace ran away, and Tallmadge placed an advertisement in the *Columbian Register* reporting her escape and explaining as her reason for fleeing "to attend some new boarding school."[41] Whether she ever reached the Canterbury Female Seminary, returned to the Tallmadge residence, or remained missing is unknown. On the one hand, Tallmadge's advertisement registered white anxiety about African American women's education: Grace forfeited her indenture to attend school; on the other hand, it reveals that at least one African American girl put herself at great risk to pursue knowledge.

Very few institutions existed in early 1830s Connecticut for African American children and youth seeking advanced study. In the first decade of the nineteenth century, the town of Colchester earmarked funds to build a school for formerly enslaved children. A unique educational initiative, this school, located adjacent to the prestigious Bacon Academy, welcomed approximately forty African American children.[42] Prince Saunders, a mixed-race man from New England, taught at the school while taking courses in Latin and Greek at Bacon Academy. Such an arrangement was an early example of the hyperlocal nature of schools. Indeed, there appears to have been no recorded objections to Saunders's presence at Bacon Academy or the existence of a school for African American children, for that matter. This school did, however, close in 1840. Prudence's African American female seminary was thus truly one of a kind.

When Prudence shifted her school's female student body from white to African American, her decision was so politically significant—and, to some, dangerous and offensive—precisely because it affirmed African American women's capacity for and pursuit of learning. As Prudence traveled the eastern seaboard, personally meeting with prospective female scholars, the *Liberator* carried an advertisement for the school. It resembled the old advertisement for her all-white boarding school, except for two key differences: rhetoric was no longer listed as a course offering, and black and white abolitionists replaced white town leaders in the list of boosters. The advertisement was less a recruitment tool than a declaration in support of African American women's learning.[43] It represented the seminary's aim to show that young African American women were refined and elegant ladies, with a right to learn and the potential to excel at it.

Of the fifteen male boosters who acted as references for the seminary, at least six were African American, including three New York City clergymen, Peter Williams, Theodore S. Wright, and Samuel Cornish; two Philadelphia businessmen, James Forten and Joseph Cassey; and one Connecticut clergyman, Jehiel Beman. In addition to commending this educational endeavor, these boosters vouched for Prudence as a teacher and helped to recruit students. Cornish boldly claimed, "Every measure for the thorough and proper education of colored females is a blow aimed directly at slavery. As such it is felt by slave-holders at the south, and their friends and abettors at the north."[44]

African American female enrollment at the seminary was small at first but steadily increased. In April 1833 Prudence had only "two boarders and one day scholar," Sarah Harris and likely the Hammond sisters.[45] A month later as many as thirteen African American girls and women had enrolled, including Sarah's younger sister, Mary.[46] Another sibling pair were the Glasko sisters from Griswold, Connecticut: twenty-two-year-old Eliza and thirteen-year-old Miranda, the daughters of Isaac Glasko, a successful blacksmith, and his wife, Lucy Brayton Glasko.[47] Fourteen-year-old Mary E. Miles, who grew up in a Quaker family in Rhode Island, also attended the seminary.[48] Sixteen-year-old Theodosia deGrasse came from a fairly well-known family in New York. Her father, George, was a Hindu man born in Calcutta and adopted by the white French admiral Count de Grasse; George deGrasse petitioned for U.S. citizenship, which was granted in 1804. Theodosia's mother, Maria, was probably a mixed-race woman descended from Abram Jansen Van Salee, the son of a Moroccan woman and Jan Jansen Van Haarlem, a Dutchman.[49] During the seventeen-month period that the seminary remained open, as many as twenty-five students may have passed through its doors.

While some of the students at the seminary came from middle-class and elite free black families who could afford the $25 tuition per quarter, others did not. Fifteen-year-old Harriet Rosetta Lanson performed domestic work at the school to offset her tuition costs. Adopted by Simeon Jocelyn, a white pastor from Connecticut and an engraver by trade, Harriet attended both public primary and Sabbath schools and was particularly interested in studying the Bible. Jocelyn noted that Harriet possessed a "love of study and habits of observation."[50] At least one student from New York was supported financially not by her mother but by a former slave woman whom she knew. Another student's father was a former slave. One editorialist pointed to the diverse backgrounds of these young women as proof of their ambition: "Where can we find such thirsting for knowledge among our white population?"[51]

Whether learning from their teachers or each other, these girls and women were knowledge seekers. One anonymous student dispelled the myth of black intellectual apathy while also calling attention to African American women's collective ambition in an address delivered on behalf of her peers who had finally "begun to enjoy what our minds have long desired; viz. the advantages of a good education."[52] At the Canterbury Female Seminary, African American female scholars proved that their minds were neither weak nor empty and, within an openly hostile local environment, asserted an educated identity that defied racist antebellum stereotypes.

African American women's education gained broader public attention thanks to Prudence's seminary, as African American women activists praised the students who had enrolled and encouraged more to attend. Under the penname Zillah, Sarah Mapps Douglass published a letter in the antislavery newspaper *Emancipator* urging young African American women "who *promised* to become Miss Crandall's pupils, to go forward."[53] Her public letter may have been inspired by her own advocacy of women's education, not to mention that her cousin, Elizabeth Douglass Bustill, may well have attended the seminary.[54] In her letter, Douglass asked prospective students to be active, courageous, and resilient—essentially, to be purposeful women. The very act of pursuing advanced study was a form of activism that opened up new opportunities. She did not deny the challenges ahead; rather she counseled the students to endure the inevitable "insults, wounds, and oppressive acts" for the sake of an education.[55]

Just as African American religious and political associations became sites of abolitionist protest, so too did educational institutions.[56] Four white abolitionists taught at this seminary, including Prudence's sister, Almira; Samuel J. May, a minister and educational reformer in Connecticut; and William Burleigh, the brother of Charles Burleigh, a journalist and abolitionist, from nearby Plainfield. May believed that "education is one of the primal, fundamental rights of all the children of men," a declaration that must have felt empowering to students.[57] Teachers and students conversed on subjects such as religion and slavery, making it a vibrant, intellectual, and politically engaging space. In an essay published in the *Liberator*, one student described slavery as an "awful, heaven-daring sin" and condemned slaveholders and their defenders for contradicting both God's will and biblical teachings.[58]

Given the wide age range of students, spanning some thirteen years, Prudence may have adopted the monitorial system, a popular instructional method developed by Joseph Lancaster, a white British-born educator. This method arranged for older, typically more advanced students to teach younger, less advanced students.[59] At Canterbury older students could have also taught younger ones about the principles of the radical abolition movement, which included ending slavery and promoting racial equality.

Regardless of the specific pedagogical method employed, Christian teachings were the glue that held the curriculum together. Though the school did not advertise biblical instruction, Prudence opened and closed the school day with prayer.[60] Moreover she and her students attended church services, welcomed preachers at the schoolhouse, and learned and quoted from scripture in their addresses, published writings, and private letters. Some students, among them Harriet Rosetta Lanson, actually experienced their conversion at the seminary.[61] Far from being a spiritual layer that supplemented the scholarship, Christianity was inextricably woven into the school's pedagogical mission. Through their studies, these young African American women gained knowledge of their own dignity and that of the word of God. In other words, they experienced God's love as righteous, intellectual human beings.

Prudence both facilitated and participated in female interracial solidarity and collective action at the seminary. As one student observed in an article for the *Liberator*, there was a strong sense of community at the school: "Love and union seems [sic] to bind our little circle in the bonds of sisterly affection." The student reminded her classmates that they had been "adorned with virtue and modesty," and now was their moment to "pursue every thing that will bring respect to ourselves, and honor to our friends who labor so much for our welfare." Nothing was ever just an individual pursuit; rather students and faculty alike saw themselves as contributing to a greater good and a broader purpose.[62]

This effort to educate African American women had many implications for radical abolitionists who were committed to African American education in the antebellum North. At the First Annual Convention of the Free People of Color at Wesleyan Church in Philadelphia, in June 1831, Simeon Jocelyn and five other white abolitionists, including William Lloyd Garrison, proposed to establish a manual labor college for African American men in New Haven, the first college of its kind in the nation. For Garrison, this initiative was crucial to racial uplift: "It can be, and *must be*, accomplished."[63] However, both elite and working-class white New Haven residents rejected the proposal, citing fear of economic competition, incongruity with the aims of the American Colonization Society, and an overall revulsion at the presence of African Americans. The weight of opposition, at times violent, in New Haven did not lead proponents to abandon the project immediately; however, they explored the possibility of opening the college in a different location, but nothing ever came of that.

Historians rightfully cite a fear of economic competition to explain white opposition to the manual labor college initiative, but such an explanation fails to account for white opposition to an African American female seminary. Educated African American men aimed to compete with white men in the labor market for skilled jobs. Arguably African American women did not pose such an economic threat to white women, or men for that matter, since an educated woman's role was not intended to be in the public sphere. The goal of women's education, in the words of Leonard Worcester, a white principal of the Newark Young Ladies' Institute in New Jersey, was to make women "fit companions for educated men" and "qualified to educate their children," thus forming "individual and national character."[64] Worcester's reasoning followed that of Benjamin Rush. Likewise, Samuel Young, a New York state senator, suggested that "no universal agent of civilization exists, but our mothers."[65] Educated women, if anything, would not compete for jobs and should have been less threatening.

Nevertheless African American education, whether pursued by men or women, was rooted in the broader project of achieving black civil rights, which did threaten social and racial hierarchies, thus angering white opponents. After all, servants might relinquish their post, as Sarah Harris and Grace Lanson had done. Moreover racialized dimensions of white opposition were still informed by gender. The scholar Mary Kelley argues that the curriculum at female academies "schooled [women] for *social* leadership" and as "makers of public opinion." This distinctive social role within civil society "informed the subjectivities [of female] students," as Kelley notes, but also protected and ensconced white girlhood in the female seminary until marriage. The female seminary movement helped to shape the very notion of the ideal woman; it reinforced the assumption that she was a white, middle-class or elite, educated, and nurturing wife and mother. Including young African American women in the female seminary movement threatened to overstep racial boundaries, but such a move insisted, too, on the students' status *as women* capable of striving for the same idealized femininity.[66]

The failure of the manual labor college initiative in New Haven was, in Garrison's words, "a bad precedent" with potentially devastating consequences. Another educational failure in the region might sound the death knell for the entire project of African American education. "If we suffer the school to be put down in Canterbury," Garrison wrote, "other places will partake of the panic, and also prevent its introduction in their vicinity." Opposition was contagious and imitative. Garrison's predictions revealed the uphill struggle that African Americans and their allies faced in pursuit of educational opportunity. No gain could be taken for granted, and no setback could be assumed to be minor. Hence Garrison's injunction: "Miss [Crandall] must be sustained at all hazards."[67]

For Canterbury residents who opposed her seminary, Prudence's project amounted to a kind of betrayal—a betrayal that, ironically, stood directly across the street from the home of Andrew T. Judson, one of the very men who had recruited Prudence to open a boarding school for young white women. Judson quickly became a leading opponent of the African American seminary, organizing town meetings, proposing resolutions, and rebuking Prudence. At the first town meeting, on March 9, 1833, Samuel J. May and Arnold Buffum, de facto trustees of the new seminary, represented Prudence since she could not attend on account of her gender. Their presence, later joined by Henry E. Benson, infuriated residents who viewed abolitionists as interlopers. All of those who spoke at the meeting condemned the seminary except for George S. White, a white Episcopal minister and émigré, who rebutted Judson's inflammatory claims. Still, the townspeople voted in favor of numerous resolutions opposing the seminary. One associated the abolitionist-backed seminary with the town's demise—a claim that, according to May, stirred up a frenzy among the townspeople "that a dire calamity was impending over them."[68] Given the hostile environment, neither May nor Buffum said anything during the meeting, but afterward May spoke out, defending Prudence and her students. Judson and others organized yet another town meeting, where further resolutions were passed to remove the seminary once and for all. These resolutions, however, did not stop Prudence.

The sequence of Prudence's decision-making here is important. At first, she sought only to admit Sarah Harris to her all-white boarding school. However, the parents of the white female students, and likely some of the white female students themselves, could not accept an African American girl as a classmate. If they had hoped to discourage Prudence, they failed. For it was only after this that Prudence decided to establish a seminary specifically for African American girls and women, which meant reconstituting her student body. In a private conversation, May told Judson exactly that: "If you and your neighbors in Canterbury had quietly consented that Sarah Harris, whom you *knew* to be a bright good girl, should enjoy the privilege she so eagerly sought, this momentous conflict would not have arisen in your village."[69] Judson, however, saw no place for free blacks in the United States, let alone at a female seminary across the road from his house, and surely not at the expense of white women.

Judson and another of Prudence's opponents, Rufus Adams, a lawyer and justice of the peace, raised two other key objections to the seminary that revolved around Prudence's alleged misconduct. First, Judson and Adams condemned the "the manner in which Miss C. effected the change in her school," which they deemed "very objectionable." Judson averred that Prudence had disregarded her "fellow-citizens," the same citizens who had recruited her from nearby Plainfield, by failing to inform them of her plan. Second, Prudence had "forced upon" Canterbury this "evil" school, without so much as a discussion. These objections soon gave way to racist explanations, threats, and legal maneuvers, all intended to shut down the seminary.[70]

One of Judson's first lines of attack was to recapitulate oppressive ideologies that called into question the character of African American girls and women. Through the press, Judson stated quite clearly why he and others objected to the presence of young African American women in and around Canterbury: "[Their] characters and habits might be various and unknown to us, thereby rendering insecure, the persons, property, and reputations of our own citizens."[71] This objection, framed as a deeply held concern, evoked the racist and sexist ideologies that placed African American women outside of True Womanhood.[72] Never mind that Sarah Harris, described by Prudence as "the daughter of honorable parents," was known to Judson and other residents, or that some of the scholars at the seminary came from middle-class and elite free black families.[73] To opponents, all these scholars were "foreigners" whose illegitimate demand for education had established "a black seminary to the exclusion of a white one," rendering the entire (white) community insecure.[74]

Just as slaveholders suggested that literacy would spoil a slave, so too did colonizationists marshal a form of false benevolence to argue that schooling African American women would ruin their lives. One anonymous writer, who claimed to be a colonizationist, wrote a letter to the editor of the *Norwich Republican* denouncing African American education and defending Canterbury opponents. The Canterbury Female Seminary, in the words of this writer, offered a "pernicious" kind of education in which African American women learned about "their own dignity and consequence" in a nation where they would "be met with spontaneous, unconquerable aversion of the white to the black." The argument acknowledged only part of the seminary's teachings. Prudence did affirm African American women's respectability; she and her students believed that prejudice could be conquered by young women armed with education and thus empowered to advance themselves and their communities as they fought for their civil rights. In the writer's estimation, however, the educational outcome would not be winning black rights or even, as some abolitionists predicted, a weakening of racial prejudice, but instead would leave African American women "angry" and "sink [them] into degradation and infamy." This writer revealed his unwillingness to *see* educated and empowered African American women.[75]

By allying herself with her African American female scholars, Prudence forced, albeit briefly, a conversation about the virulence of racial prejudice in the North. She described white racism as "inveterate" and "the strongest, if not the only chain that bound those heavy burdens on the wretched slaves," thus linking slavery and racial prejudice. This injustice motivated her to establish the Canterbury Female Seminary, whose mission was to "fit and prepare teachers for the people of color."[76] Preparing women for the teaching profession at female seminaries was hardly a new endeavor, though it had, until then, been one mostly reserved for white women. For instance, Ipswich Female Academy, founded in 1828 and run by Zilpah Grant, graduated twenty-seven female students between 1829 and 1830, all but two of whom immediately became teachers.[77] Prudence's words and actions thus forced her opponents to confront their prejudices. One editorialist confessed, "Will it be said that this is prejudice?—Be it so."[78]

Prudence also faced sexist attacks, further demonstrating that white opposition was intimately tied to constructions of manhood and womanhood. Opponents smeared her, painting her as a crook who transformed her school only to make money, and as a champion of racial mixing. One editorialist from the *United States Telegraph* suggested that getting the "young lady [Prudence] a husband" would surely lure her away from her experiment—implying that Prudence suffered from her lack of a husband and was not genuinely committed to educating African American women.[79] Judson went even further, accusing her of "step[ping] out of the hallowed precincts of female propriety" by betraying her original mandate and refusing men's demands to return to it. Prudence's opponents sought to reset the racial and gender order she had upset, restoring white women to their subordinate status to white men (and African American women excluded altogether).[80]

Opponents of the seminary employed various means to force its demise. Ann Eliza Hammond, the sixteen-year-old African American woman from Providence whose mother introduced Prudence to other families, became the first out-of-state student at the school. The sheriff of Windham County served a warrant, signed by Rufus Adams, against Ann Eliza, citing the Act for the Admission of Inhabitants in Towns, an eighteenth-century Connecticut law allowing local government officials to deport any nonresident in the state. If the person did not leave, he or she had to pay a fine of $1.67 per week, and if the person had not paid the fine and had not left after ten days, he or she was to be "whipped on the naked body not exceeding ten stripes."[81] The warrant was meant to put Ann Eliza in her place and also to put her *out*: out of Canterbury or, if colonizationists had their wish, out of the United States altogether. May advised Ann Eliza to "bear meekly the punishment, if they should in their madness inflict it; knowing that every blow they should strike her would resound throughout the land, if not over the whole civilized world, and call out an expression of indignation before which Mr. Judson and his associates would quail." May need not have worried: Ann Eliza was "ready for the emergency" and responded to the challenge "with the spirit of a martyr."[82] However, Prudence disagreed with May's idea about how to handle legal violence and refused to put Ann Eliza in harm's way. Instead she decided to pay the first fine, which ended the matter.[83] May's depiction of a courageous Ann Eliza coupled with Judson's "madness" prompted abolitionists to ask publicly, "Who are the savages now?"[84] The Act for the Admission of Inhabitants in Towns echoed larger systems of violence against black bodies, particularly the African slave trade and slavery itself.

Some of Prudence's students reacted to the sexist and violent attacks with both anger and sadness, though these emotions did not endure.

Most viewed white opposition as a sign that white Canterbury residents needed Christian love. Harriet Rosetta Lanson wrote home to her adoptive guardian expressing dismay that she and her classmates were barred from attending the Congregational church in the village and had to travel to one in Packersville. But instead of dwelling on the inconvenience, Lanson pledged "to consecrate [to God] the little knowledge [she had] to his service."[85] Similarly, another student reminded her classmates that Prudence had taught them "not to indulge in angry feelings towards [their] enemies." Quoting scripture on forgiveness (Romans 12:20) and loving one's enemy (Luke 6:28), the student urged steadfast adherence to Christian principles of love and peace. She exhorted her classmates, "Feel at peace with all men; for we all know this is the spirit of the Christian, and this we must possess to support us through the trials we are called upon to pass in this life."[86] No matter what, Christian scriptures best governed human actions and behaviors, especially during trying times.

A strong commitment to Christian love did not preclude these young women from labeling the actions of white Canterbury residents unrighteous. As Christian women, they could, according to scripture (Romans 12:9), "abhor what is evil." That evil was racial prejudice. In her address the same student explained, "We as a body, my dear school-mates . . . know . . . it is the prejudice the whites have against us that causes us to labor under so many disadvantages." After all, African Americans' pursuit of knowledge had actually inflamed prejudice and provoked white violence. This student stated matter-of-factly, "White people . . . put *every* obstacle they can in our way to prevent our rising to an equal."[87] She recognized the pattern of systematic oppression that inhibited black advancement. Her observations were valid: George Benson overheard one opponent confess that if the Canterbury Female Seminary flourished, then free blacks in Canterbury "would begin to look up and claim an equality with the whites."[88] Clearly the very idea of an educated African American woman terrified some residents. Racial prejudice was the disease that had to be named and cured precisely by fighting for African American education.

At the same time that Prudence's students criticized their white opponents, however, the most radical dimension of their invocation of Christian love was its insistence that African Americans belonged to a universal Christian family. In a separate address, an anonymous student linked Christian love to the fight for racial equality. In the Christian imagination, this student explained, God was the father of humankind, which certainly included African Americans, and thus African

Americans and whites shared a "common father." Racial prejudice, then, made little sense, and *all* good Christians had an obligation to fight it. This student encouraged civic action and implored the public to "obey the voice of duty" and follow the example of the few like Prudence, who "stepped from within the shadow of prejudice, and [were] now pleading [African Americans'] cause, in the midst of persecution, with great success."[89] This student's remarks evoked radical abolitionist ideology. As the historian Paul Goodman argued, radical abolitionists were "serious Christians [who] grounded their belief in human equality in faith."[90] They took seriously the biblical verse "God hath made of one blood all nations of men" (Acts 17:26). The fight for black equality and freedom was both a Christian duty and a national cause.

Students' public writings sought to teach white Canterbury residents to be civil and moral, stressing Christian axioms of loving one's neighbor and the Golden Rule. "If all were taught to love their neighbors as themselves, to do to others as they would be done unto, there would be no disposition to repeat the crime of him who slew his brother," reflected one student.[91] By recasting the biblical story of Cain and Abel as one of kinship relations instead of racial marking, this student attributed the conflict and violence in Canterbury to an absence of Christian love. The emphasis on Christian love implied neither submission nor complacency; rather it represented the potential for change. If Canterbury residents actually practiced a law of love, they would not and could not continue their course of action to destroy the Canterbury Female Seminary. These young women were students, but they were also teachers, showing whites how to behave civilly.

By invoking the ethic of Christian love, these young women proved that religious beliefs and values were central to their lives. They relied on this ethic to provoke a kind of resigned acceptance from white Canterbury residents who would then allow the seminary to exist. A more combative response, in all likelihood, would not have benefited the cause. Opponents near and far, not just slaveholders, regularly assailed the character of African American women and men, deeming them unworthy, inferior, and even dangerous, especially after Nat Turner's rebellion in 1831. While these young women might have agreed with a radical activist like David Walker, who warned that the perpetuation of slavery would result in violence, they articulated no such sentiments in their writings. Rather an ethic of Christian love prevailed, becoming an important mode for African American women's public self-expression and civic engagement.

White women abolitionists also espoused an ethic of Christian love to highlight the bonds of sisterhood. Frances Whipple, an abolitionist from Rhode Island, wrote a poem lauding Prudence's heroism while imploring *all* women to help each other, for "God loveth all alike."[92] Likewise, an anonymously authored appeal, published in the *Female Advocate*, a moral reform newspaper, argued that the Canterbury affair concerned *every* American woman. Potentially any woman, this columnist suggested, could be thrown "into prison, for seeking female improvement and elevation." This appeal urged women to band together and join the struggle for women's education. It closed by encouraging women to be "vigilant . . . [and] active," like the biblical figure Esther, in order to "save [the] country." Education was about good character as well as intellectual improvement, which would be useful in the domestic realm and beyond.[93]

This seemingly local controversy over African American women's education triggered a statewide initiative to curb free blacks seeking education. Canterbury opponents abandoned their plan to arrest students for violating old Connecticut laws and instead drafted and pushed through the Connecticut General Assembly an addendum to the Act for the Admission of Inhabitants in Towns that targeted African Americans from other states. This addendum stated that the migration of African Americans to Connecticut "injured" the state and its citizens, and it forbade the establishment of "any school, academy, or literary institution, for the instruction or education of colored persons who are not inhabitants of this state . . . without the consent, in writing . . . of the civil authority."[94] This so-called Black Law resembled legislation passed in various southern states that had outlawed the instruction of African Americans, free and enslaved. For instance, a Virginia law of 1819 prohibited enslaved African Americans, and those associated with them, from meeting for the purpose of "teaching them reading or writing."[95] The Virginia legislature later amended this antiliteracy law to include free blacks and mulattoes along with enslaved African Americans.[96] Both the Virginia and the Connecticut law targeted specific sites of learning, whether the school or the church, and restricted black access to teaching and learning overall. With the help of Phillip Pearl, a white state senator from Hampton whose daughter had attended Prudence's first, white female boarding school in Canterbury, the Connecticut law passed, effectively criminalizing the Canterbury Female Seminary.

In June 1833 Canterbury officials arrested Prudence and her younger sister, Almira, for violating the Black Law. The charges against Almira were dismissed since she was a minor; however, the charges against Prudence remained. Instead of posting bail in the amount of $150, she and her abolitionist supporters believed that her jailing in Brooklyn, the county seat, would shame Canterbury officials.[97] Throwing a white Quaker woman in jail might prove, at least according to May, "how bad, how wicked, how cruel" the Black Law was.[98] Prudence's students agreed. They regarded the law as "unrighteous," and they even sang a song comparing the biblical persecution and imprisonment of Paul and Silas to that of Prudence.[99] After Prudence had spent one night in jail, George Benson posted bond, and she was soon released.

Abolitionists used the press to rebuke Canterbury opponents and turn the myth of African savagery on its head. In bold print ran the headlines "More Barbarism" and "Savage Barbarity," attacking the white men of Canterbury who sought to destroy the seminary.[100] The *Liberator* labeled Prudence's imprisonment an act of "savage barbarity," the same term used earlier by an anonymous African American female student and by May to describe the threat of violence against Ann Eliza Hammond. Abolitionists surmised that the "persecution" that Prudence and her students endured resulted from the "genuine fruit of colonization principles and prejudices," a criticism of colonization as both primitive and racist.[101] Arthur Tappan, a wealthy white entrepreneur and brother of businessman Lewis Tappan, even bankrolled the creation of a newspaper, eventually called the *Unionist*, to "disabuse the public mind of the misrepresentations and falsehoods" about the Canterbury Female Seminary, Prudence Crandall, free black communities, and the radical abolition movement more broadly.[102] Abolitionists framed white Canterbury opponents as savage, thus turning upside down the myth of African savagery and, by extension, the rationale for racial prejudice and slavery.

Some New England journalists defended Judson by arguing that Prudence had sullied her own reputation and that of Canterbury in her over-ambitious and misguided effort to educate African American women. One unnamed writer regarded the entire project as "outlandish." This writer caricatured the students as "girls with black skins, wooly heads and flat noses," a far cry from "young ladies and little misses."[103] The *Rhode Island Republican* referred to Prudence as successful only in "[making] herself look ridiculous" by associating with "fanatical friends"—surely a reference to abolitionists—who rejected the notion that the Black Law was a "good and wholesome" measure to protect Canterbury and its residents from being "overrun" by African Americans.[104] Similarly the *New Hampshire Gazette* found Prudence's "overzealous [spirit] too much influenced by William Lloyd Garrison and Arthur Buffum," assuming that any agency on the part of a woman must be traceable to a man.[105]

The case of *State of Connecticut v. Prudence Crandall* began on August 23, 1833, in a Windham County courtroom in Brooklyn, Connecticut, with Judge Joseph Eaton of Plainfield presiding. Prudence pleaded not guilty. The prosecution, led by Jonathan A. Welch, a Windham County lawyer, with Judson and Ichabod Bulkley appointed as assistant prosecutors, alleged that Prudence taught and boarded African American students without first obtaining a license to do so, violating the Black Law. Arthur Tappan financed Prudence's legal defense, which included three distinguished white lawyers, William Ellsworth, Calvin Goddard, and Henry Strong.[106] Ellsworth, the lead defense attorney, Yale College graduate, and congressman, argued that the Black Law was unconstitutional because it denied African American citizens equal rights. Twelve white male jurors would decide the fate of Prudence and her seminary. This trial, Prudence's biographer Donald E. Williams Jr. contends, became "the first civil rights case in American history."[107]

Though Prudence was the defendant in this case, the prosecution figuratively put her students on trial with her. Contrary to how they had been characterized by Judson and others, however, they came across as educated and poised. In an effort to prove that Prudence had violated the Black Law, the prosecution called at least five African American female students, all nonresidents of Connecticut, to testify, including Theodosia deGrasse, Ann Elizabeth Wilder, Catharine Ann Weldon, Ann Peterson, and Ann Eliza Hammond.[108] All five invoked their constitutional right against self-incrimination and thus did not testify. Judson called another student, Eliza Glasko, to the stand, and she too refused. Judson argued that Eliza was in contempt of court for failing to "declare her knowledge in the matter" and thus should be jailed.[109] Judge Eaton agreed. The prosecution then spotted Mary Benson in the courtroom and compelled her to testify. Mary, a member of the Benson family of Brooklyn, Connecticut, was Prudence's friend and had helped her that fateful day that she had been arrested and jailed. As Donald E. Williams Jr. makes clear, legally she "had no constitutional basis on which to refuse to answer."[110] She testified that Prudence taught Ann Eliza of Providence, Rhode Island, a violation of the Black Law. On the heels of this testimony, Ellsworth advised Eliza Glasko to testify. She did so, recalling that she and her fellow schoolmates learned "reading, writing, grammar, [and] geography" and that "the scriptures were read and explained daily" at the school.[111] This depiction captured the eloquence and dignity of the students and portrayed the Canterbury Female Seminary as decidedly Christian, a picture that numerous supporters confirmed.[112] A reporter for the *Connecticut Courant* summed it up best: "Miss Crandall appeared at the bar of the court very interesting, and her pupils were inferior to no others, in their conduct, language and appearance."[113] After closing arguments, the jury deliberated for a few hours, but could not reach a verdict.

The date of the second trial came sooner than Prudence's defense team expected. Judson refiled charges against her, and the court set her trial date for October 3, 1833. This time, Judson and state attorney Chauncey Cleveland prosecuted the case with new evidence. Judson introduced the testimony of Mary Barber, a white servant who worked alongside Sarah Harris in Jedidiah Shephard's house. Mary presented a different version of the origins of the Canterbury Female Seminary; she alleged that Prudence convinced Sarah to postpone her engagement to George Fayerweather, a blacksmith, in order to attend the seminary. Donald E. Williams Jr. questions whether Judson and the prosecution influenced and perhaps even composed Mary's testimony so as to bring Prudence into disrepute.[114] Given Mary's subordinate status, had she been persuaded to give this testimony for the good of the cause of getting rid of the seminary? Or was she being truthful? Both Prudence and Sarah flatly denied her account. By November 1833 Sarah had left the Canterbury Female Seminary anyway and married Fayerweather. Still, Barber's testimony, which the prosecution likely leaked to the press before the second trial commenced, painted Prudence not as a Christian woman embodying a spirit of benevolence but as a schemer who had lied about her school and defied the conventions of womanhood by redirecting Sarah's goals. In turn, Barber's testimony stripped Sarah of any ambition, portraying her instead as pliable, perhaps even passive.

The actions of Chief Justice David Daggett, coupled with Judson's dogged determination, greatly influenced the outcome of the second trial. While in the first trial, the prosecution focused on Prudence's violation of the Black Law, in the second trial they resorted to racist scare tactics. Judson described the United States as a "nation of white men" who should "indulge that pride and honor." To combat a carefully calculated mission by abolitionists to end slavery and bring about race mixing, Judson framed the Black Law as an act of protection. He warned that Prudence's school and her association with abolitionists threatened that honor and could actually "work to dissolve the Union." Such an appeal may well have excited the jury despite Ellsworth's own impassioned speech.[115]

In both trials Ellsworth's line of defense actually affirmed the rights and protections of citizenship for African American women. In the first trial, he made an emotional appeal to the jury to support African American education by arguing that the Black Law would "extinguish the light of knowledge, would degrade those who are now degraded, and depress those who are now depressed." Another of the defense attorneys, Henry Strong, asked the jury to look directly at the young African American women in the courtroom and think about whether they were "worthy of being instructed." The request cast African American women in a position that departed from prevailing views about black womanhood, not to mention legal restrictions on black civil rights.[116]

In a moment of judicial activism, Judge Daggett settled the question about black citizenship by stating unequivocally, "Slaves, free blacks or Indians . . . are not citizens."[117] To support this conclusion, he quoted a renowned legal scholar, James Kent, chancellor of New York, who had written, "Free white persons and free colored persons of African blood did not participate equally with the whites in the exercise of civil and political rights."[118] Daggett, who had opposed the manual labor college in New Haven a year or so earlier, instructed the jury to come to a decision on this case based on the alleged fact that the Black Law was constitutional. After a short period of deliberation, the jury found Prudence Crandall guilty and the court ordered her to pay a fine as well as court costs. Most important, the ruling meant that she had to close her seminary. Ellsworth filed an appeal, to be heard in the next session of the Connecticut Supreme Court, in July 1834.

The arguments in the state supreme court case essentially pitted black civil rights against white male supremacy. On July 22, 1834, four Connecticut Supreme Court justices heard Crandall's appeal: Thomas S. Williams, Clark Bissell, Samuel Church, and Chief Justice Daggett, who opted not to recuse himself. Judson and Chauncey Cleveland asked the court to uphold the judgment of the lower court. Judson repeated his and Daggett's outright rejection of black citizenship, pointing to a lack of voting rights for African American men and the degraded condition and inferiority of African Americans in general. He also played on the fears of the white community, asserting that a victory for Prudence would amount to a surrender of the entire American nation. "I would appeal to this Court—to every American citizen," he avowed, "and say that America is ours—it belongs to a race of white men."[119] That this proclamation of white manhood emerged in a court of law where a white woman was convicted of educating African American women was no coincidence.

Judson used the courtroom to call on white men to close ranks and stop the radical abolition movement's threats to the racial and gender order. In their remarks, Judson and Cleveland essentially requested the affirmation of white male supremacy, of its institutions, and of the denial of black educational rights.

Ellsworth and Goddard sought to refute the lower court's verdict by arguing that the Black Law violated the Privileges and Immunities Clause in the U.S. Constitution. To make the case for African American citizenship, Ellsworth relied on a gendered construction of citizenship tied to black male military service and voting, which enabled him to assert normative ideas about race and gender. His entire defense was predicated on the contention that "a distinction found in color . . . is inconvenient and impracticable."[120] African Americans were thus *like* white Americans. An argument in favor of African American women's citizenship apart from African American men would have seemingly affirmed racial distinction. That is, as the historian Corinne Field explains, to "promote the equal rights of black women . . . would . . . suggest that . . . black people's capacities followed a different normative pattern than white people's maturation, thus giving credence to the idea of natural racial differences."[121] Nevertheless Ellsworth and Goddard took a radical stance when they defended the humanity, citizenship, and rights of African American women.[122]

African American women activists like Sarah Mapps Douglass and Maria W. Stewart defined citizenship in terms of Christian faith, national allegiance, and inclusion. They espoused what the historian Stephen Kantrowitz has termed a "citizenship of the heart," namely legal freedom, civil rights, and belonging.[123] Douglass claimed America as her home, vowing to "embrace her [America] the closer," despite the fact that it "unkindly strives to throw me from her bosom."[124] By late September 1833 Stewart had left the Boston lecture circuit, largely due to disapprobation from African American male leaders. She delivered an impassioned farewell address, celebrating and encouraging a kind of activism rooted in "godliness" and "peace."[125] Christian love was about people's relationship to one other and to God. Though Stewart and Douglass rarely invoked the word "citizen" in their writings, they shared this sentiment.

Likewise, Prudence prepared her students for active citizenship determined by knowledge and character, not sex or race. Indeed many politicians and educational reformers in early America linked education to democratic citizenship. Calvin Goddard put it plainly: the Black Law denied African Americans "of all opportunity to acquire that knowledge and those habits which [could] render them good citizens, useful to each other and their native country."[126] The assertion of black female citizenship by Prudence's legal team laid bare this crucial question: What constituted citizenship in early America, particularly for women and African Americans? Years later, in 1848, James Kent affirmed black citizenship, regardless of status, arguing that "the privilege of voting, and the legal capacity for office, are not essential to the character of a citizen."[127] Prudence, her allies, and students might have agreed: common humanity, peace, love, and forgiveness constituted good citizenship. African American female students at Canterbury possessed a desire for knowledge and acted in a loving way, which reflected their character. This stood in stark contrast to their detractors, who turned to acts of violence that ought to have thrown their own citizenship into question.

As the *Crandall* case wound its way through the court, African American women students continued to board at the school and attend classes. When Charles Stuart, a white Bermuda-born abolitionist, visited in June 1834, he observed that the school was "in a very flourishing and happy condition, although still occasionally subject to annoyance."[128] These annoyances were actually incidents of violence and harassment directed at Prudence Crandall as well as the school's teachers and students. That same month William Burleigh, one of the teachers, was assaulted with eggs; he was later arrested for violating the Black Law; and a one-pound stone was hurled through one of the school's windows, landing in a student's room.[129] Earlier that year, on January 28, a fire broke out at the seminary. No one was hurt, but Chauncey Cleveland charged Frederick Olney, an African American man who had performed odd jobs at the school, with arson. Three African American female students testified at Olney's trial; Maria Robinson, Amy Fenner, and Henrietta Bolt recounted his work at the schoolhouse, particularly on the day in question. Given the thin evidence in the case, Olney was found not guilty.[130]

Because Canterbury had proven to be an unwelcome site for her seminary, over a year earlier Prudence had contemplated a move to Reading, Massachusetts, and May had received a letter from the townspeople there, who were "willing to have [Prudence's] school established."[131] It is unclear why Prudence did not relocate her school there, but her personal life changed when she married Calvin Philleo, a widowed white Baptist minister from New York, on August 12, 1834. Calvin Philleo became increasingly involved in the seminary. First the couple tried to broker a deal to relocate the school to another part of Canterbury, but the local governing board ignored the offer. Prudence next set her sights on Philadelphia. Lydia White, cofounder of the Philadelphia Female Anti-Slavery Society and proprietor of a free labor goods business, had visited the Canterbury Female Seminary that August 1834 and may have alerted Prudence to the possibilities available in the City of Brotherly Love. Later that month Prudence and her husband traveled to Philadelphia, where they met with the activists James Forten, Charlotte Vandine Forten, and Lucretia Mott, among others.[132] During this visit, Prudence devised a plan to establish a school for black children and recruited fifty boys and girls.[133] The idea of an African American female seminary in Philadelphia apparently fell by the wayside. It may have been reasoned that focusing solely on African American women's education was too limited, especially when qualified teachers were needed to staff Philadelphia's black schools. Most critical at that moment was keeping the project of African American education alive. In the end, given Philadelphia's ongoing problems with racial violence in the summer of 1834, Prudence felt that relocating her school there was not a viable option.[134]

Meanwhile in Connecticut, the Canterbury controversy had ignited spirited debates about colonization and radical abolition among the inhabitants of Windham County. At its fourth annual meeting on July 4, 1834, the Windham County Colonization Society, which Judson attended, resolved to do more to spread colonization, including increasing the number of auxiliary societies. But it was the local antislavery movement that grew. The following month, the Anti-Slavery Society of Plainfield and its vicinity (including Canterbury) formed with forty-three members, a number that nearly tripled weeks later. A New England antislavery convention report claimed that "much alarm was manifested at [this] rapid spread of Abolitionism."[135]

On July 28, 1834, the Connecticut Supreme Court issued its decision in the *Crandall* case, voting three to one to dismiss the charges, thus overturning the lower court's ruling. Justice Williams wrote the majority opinion, citing a technicality, and Daggett was the lone dissenter. The inconclusive legal outcome of the case only fanned the flames. The *Vermont Chronicle* put it succinctly: "Mr. Judson and his associates must *endure* Miss Crandall's school till they can go through the whole process again—*at least*."[136]

The prospect of another trial coupled with the growth of the antislavery movement in Connecticut may well have pushed Prudence's opponents over the edge. Possibly responding to all that the Canterbury Female Seminary represented and the inconclusive legal outcome, a group of men attacked the school building in September 1834. They smashed most of the windows, leaving the building, in one anonymous student's words, "almost untenantable." This student remained grateful, though, that her "lot was no worse," which may mean that the men had not physically harmed her or any of her classmates.[137] That night Calvin Philleo went to Judson's house across the street from the school to tell him of the attack and to ask if anyone had witnessed anything, but Judson was dismissive. Feeling she had no choice, Prudence asked Samuel J. May to do what she could not: tell the students that the school had to close for their protection and safety. May later wrote of the events, "I felt ashamed of Canterbury, ashamed of Connecticut, ashamed of my country, ashamed of my color."[138]

Though their education was abruptly halted, these young African American women still championed Christian love. Not only were they steadfast in their faith in God and their love for each other, but they also remained committed to extending that love to their neighbors. After all, the Bible stated that love was a Christian principle (1 John 3:23). These women entered the school in love and parted in love, remembering the biblical definition of goodness (Romans 12:9). In a short essay, one student shared her memories of female friendship at the seminary, where "love was without dissimulation." She credited May with helping her to develop morally and intellectually. By embodying Christian values, he had taught her a lot about religion: "With him I saw religion, not merely adopted as an empty form, but a living, all-pervading principle of action. He lived like those who seek a better country: nor was his family devotion a cold pile of hypocrisy, on which the fire of God never descends. No, it was a place of communion with heaven." This student's reflection revealed her understanding of Christianity. On the one hand, Judson and other opponents favored prejudice, rage, and violence; they acted unjustly. On the other hand, May, Crandall, and her students believed in peace, thus upholding an ethic of Christian love.[139]

Years later this ethic of Christian love still governed the actions of some former students. One from Hartford, with the initials E.F., penned a temperance song that was sung at the Colored Temperance Convention in Middletown, Connecticut, in May 1836.[140] Harriet Rosetta Lanson vowed to devote her life to doing God's work. She joined the temperance movement and began to prepare for a career as a Sabbath school teacher. She gave speeches, most likely at church services, where she encouraged parents to guide children and youth. "Pour in the oil of counsel, and guide their tottering steps to tread the upward path to virtue," she urged.

Upon her death from consumption on November 8, 1835, Simeon Jocelyn remembered her as a faithful young Christian woman who sought to "kindle a love for virtue" among African American youth.[141] Her piety manifested in her commitment to her own education and that of others.[142]

Following Prudence's example, radical abolitionists began to develop educational initiatives for African American children and youth. In an 1841 letter to the editor of the *Philanthropist*, Davis Day, a young African American man who attended Oberlin College, linked moral and intellectual improvement to women's influence, arguing, "The elevation of our race, depends in a great degree upon the talents and education of our *females*." Day spoke of the critical need for educated African American teachers in black communities in Ohio; ignoring African American women's education undermined the struggle for black freedom.[143] The American Anti-Slavery Society, established in December 1833, passed resolutions that supported Prudence's "philanthropic efforts" in educating African American women, praised educational institutions that accepted African Americans, and condemned antiliteracy laws "which prevent or restrict the education of the people of color, bond or free." Jocelyn vowed to campaign to abolish these laws "more earnestly than corporeal slavery itself [because] ignorance enslaves the mind and tends to the ruin of the immortal soul."[144] African American education, for enslaved and free blacks, was understood as a multidimensional strategy for freedom.

In the mid-1830s a few white proprietors and abolitionists made concerted efforts to establish schools for African American women. Theodore Dwight Weld helped to build literary institutions in Cincinnati, Ohio, and planned to open a school for African American women that was to be led by Charlotte Lathrop, a young white woman from Connecticut.[145] Martha and Lucy Ball, two white abolitionist sisters, opened a school for African American women in Boston that taught "reading, writing, arithmetic, grammar, geography, &c. and . . . plain sewing, knitting, &c."[146] One of the African American teachers at that school was Julia Williams, who had studied at the Canterbury Female Seminary. She earned public praise for her excellent teaching and for her work in the Boston Female Anti-Slavery Society.[147] Another white woman taught African American women "spelling, reading, and writing, needle-work, &c." at the home of Peter Gray in Boston.[148] In 1834 Rebecca Buffum, the daughter of Arnold Buffum, founded a school in Philadelphia for young women "without regard to their complexion."[149] While these efforts advanced African American women's education to some extent, they lasted only a few years.

For African American women, teaching was central to racial uplift. Of the twelve or so young African American women who we know attended the Canterbury Female Seminary, at least six went on to become teachers: Ann Eliza Hammond, Elizabeth H. Smith, Julia Ward Williams, Miranda Glasko, Mary E. Miles, and Mary Harris. Upon her return to her home state of Rhode Island, Ann Eliza taught at the coeducational Providence English School for Colored Youth, operated by Reverend John W. Lewis.[150] Her classmate Elizabeth worked as a teacher and principal at the Meeting Street School in Providence.[151] Miranda taught at a school for African American children in New London, Connecticut, in the late 1830s.[152] Though it is difficult to assess whether and how Christian love figured in the work of these African American women teachers later in their lives, they were often remembered in obituaries and memorials as learned and virtuous Christian women who defended their communities.[153]

The Harris sisters too devoted themselves to a life of learning and activism. While many members of the Harris family remained in Canterbury, Sarah—the young woman who had moved to that village with her parents and siblings in 1832—and her husband, George Fayerweather, eventually settled in his native state of Rhode Island. She only briefly studied at Prudence's school before starting her own family and raising her children. Her daughter, Isabella, went to a high school in New Bedford, Massachusetts, and Sarah encouraged her, probably on more than one occasion, "Improve your time at school."[154] Sarah also remained active in the antislavery movement, corresponding with Garrison as well as attending lectures and abolitionist meetings throughout the Northeast.[155] Her sister, Mary Harris, married Pelleman Williams, an African American teacher, and they settled in New Haven, where Williams taught. Mary reared their three children and, like many free black women, worked occasionally as a domestic servant to supplement the household income.[156] In the post–Civil War era, the family moved to Louisiana, where Mary and her husband taught freed people.[157]

For Sarah Harris Fayerweather, the experience at Canterbury was politically and morally formative. At an antislavery meeting in the summer of 1862, Emma Whipple, Prudence's stepdaughter, met Sarah, who introduced herself as the "first colored scholar at Prudence Crandall's school," revealing her pride in the title. Emma described Sarah as "very intelligent and lady-like[,] well-informed in every movement relative to the removal of slavery." In their conversation, Sarah expressed "the warmest love and gratitude" for Prudence. She had even named one of her daughters Prudence, and she named one of her sons Charles Frederick Douglass.[158] Her activist ties only deepened over the years. Crandall and Sarah maintained a loving long-distance friendship, exchanging letters and remembering the activism of early allies. Sarah even traveled to Crandall's home in Kansas for a visit in 1877. A year later, Sarah passed away. The inscription on her gravestone reads, "Her's [sic] was a living example of obedience to faith, devotion to her children and a loving, tender interest in all."[159]

For seventeenth months, nearly two dozen young African American women had access to advanced schooling in Canterbury. African American and white abolitionists celebrated this milestone, but white residents were incensed. The black pursuit of knowledge provoked racialized and gendered forms of violence, which ranged from the threatened whipping of Ann Eliza Hammond to the eventual attack on the school building. Virulent white opposition arose out of a place of racism and sexism, anger at Prudence's decision to establish a new seminary that displaced white women, and anxiety about the status of African Americans in the nation. Prudence and her students characterized this violence as unchristian.

Amid this rising tide of violence, African American women and their allies mobilized. Maria W. Stewart, for instance, championed love, especially within the black community, just as Prudence's students espoused Christian love to persuade Canterbury residents to accept Prudence's educational project. This ethic of Christian love armed students with the discursive power to promote inclusion and equal treatment, at the schoolhouse and beyond. Alongside their abolitionist allies, these women resisted their dehumanization and devaluation through the pursuit, acquisition, and use of knowledge, insisting all the while that they themselves were valuable members of the community.

Moreover these students staked their claims to the category of woman. Just as middle-class and elite white women students learned to take on a distinctive social role, so too did African American women at this seminary develop a particular kind of social reform rooted in their Christian faith. These students also showed that they could play an influential role in their own communities, as both mothers *and* reformers. In doing so, they enacted their own idealized version of purposeful womanhood, one that required resilience and love.

SCHOOL FOR COLORED GIRLS

COLORED SCHOOLS BROKEN UP, IN THE FREE STATES.
When schools have been established for colored scholars, the law-makers and the mob have combined to destroy them;—as at Canterbury, Ct., at Canaan, N. H., Aug. 10, 1835, at Zanesville and Brown Co., Ohio, in 1836.

IMMEDIATE EMANCIPATION.

Aug. 1, 1834, 30,000 slaves were emancipated in Antigua. Without any apprenticeship, or system of preparation, preceding the act, the chains were broken at a stroke, and they all went out FREE! It is now four years since these 30,000 slaves were "turned loose" among 2,000 whites, their former masters. These masters fought against the emancipation bill with all their force and fury. They remonstrated with the British Government—conjured and threatened,—protested that emancipation would ruin the island, that the emancipated slaves would never work—would turn vagabonds, butcher the whites and flood the island with beggary and crime. Their strong beseechings availed as little as their threats, and croakings about ruin. The Emancipation Act, unintimidated by the bluster, traversed quietly through its successive stages up to the royal sanction, and became the law of the land. When the slaveholders of Antigua saw that abolition was *inevitable*, they at once resolved to substitute immediate, unconditional, and entire emancipation for the gradual process contemplated by the Act. Well, what has been the result? Read the following testimony of the very men who, but little more than four years ago, denounced and laughed to scorn the idea of abolishing slavery, and called it folly, fanaticism, and insanity. We quote from the work of Messrs. Thome and Kimball, lately published, the written testimony of many of the first men in Antigua,—some of whom were among the largest slaveholders before August, 1834. It proves, among other points, that

EMANCIPATED SLAVES ARE PEACEABLE.

TESTIMONY. "*There is no feeling of insecurity.* A stronger proof of this cannot be given than *the dispensing, within five months after emancipation, with the Christmas guards, which had been uninterruptedly kept up for nearly one hundred years*—during the whole time of slavery.

"I have *never head of any instance of revenge* for former injuries." *James Scotland, Sen. Esq.*

"Insurrection or revenge *is in no case dreaded.* My family go to sleep every night with the doors unlocked. There is not the *slightest* feeling of insecurity —quite the contrary. Property is more secure, *for all idea of insurrection is abolished forever*." *Hon. N. Nugent, Speaker of the House of Assembly.*

"There has been no instance of personal violence since freedom. I have not heard of a single case of even *meditated* revenge." *Dr. Daniell, member of the Council, and Attorney for six estates.*

"Emancipation has banished the *fear* of insurrections, incendiarism, &c." *Mr. Favey, Manager of Lavicount's.*

"I have never heard of an instance of violence or revenge on the part of the negroes." *Rev. Mr. Morrish, Moravian Missionary.*

FIGURE 1.3. "Colored Schools Broken Up in the Free States." This illustration from the *American Anti-Slavery Almanac* (1839) essentially reinterprets the violent attack on the Canterbury Female Seminary in 1834 and connects it to other attacks on African American schools that happened throughout the North, from Ohio to New Hampshire. Author's collection.

Five years after the closure of the Canterbury Female Seminary, an illustration in the *American Anti-Slavery Almanac* (1839) depicted a scene of a mob attacking a school for young African American women; the caption read, "Colored Schools Broken Up in the Free States" (Figure 1.3). In the illustration, a mob wields weapons and hurls rocks at the front of the "School for Colored Girls." A man holding a torch moves toward the side of the building, lunging at two African American women fleeing through the back door, with only a wooden gate separating them from the man. The illustration linked the attack on the Canterbury Female Seminary to similar incidents in Canaan, New Hampshire, and Brown County, Ohio, where "law-makers and the mob" conspired to destroy schools for African Americans.[160] What happened in Canterbury, then, was not unique; I estimate that violence had erupted in the antebellum North over African American education *at least* ten times (see appendix D).

African American activists, however, remained committed to women's education. Despite waves of white opposition, young African American women continued their educational quest. Four years after the Canterbury Female Seminary closed, one student, Mary E. Miles, found a place at a female seminary in Clinton, Oneida County, New York, a school that did not share the same fate as Prudence Crandall's school.

2 /   Race and Reform at the Young Ladies' Domestic Seminary

Fifteen-year-old Mary E. Miles fled the Canterbury Female Seminary in Connecticut sometime in September 1834. Harassment and violence at the hands of white Canterbury residents displaced her and twenty other young African American women. Nonetheless, in the short period of time that Mary studied at this school, she met young women whom she would come to know for a lifetime. And it was there that she met her indefatigable teacher Samuel J. May. Where Mary went immediately after leaving Canterbury and what she did remains uncertain; perhaps she went back home to Rhode Island. One fact is known: her educational quest did not end.

In the winter of 1838 nineteen-year-old Mary applied for admission to the Young Ladies' Domestic Seminary in Clinton, Oneida County, New York. Established in 1833 by Hiram Huntington Kellogg (Figure 2.1), this distinctive seminary combined academic study in reading and writing, physics, and botany with domestic work such as washing and cooking. Kellogg, a white Presbyterian minister and abolitionist, agreed to admit Mary. He also appealed to a wealthy white abolitionist named Gerrit Smith for financial support to offer reduced tuition to her and potentially other African American women. Finally Mary could take advantage of a new opportunity for rigorous study and intellectual and moral improvement. By the spring of 1839, a path had opened for other African American women to follow.

During its eight-year run, the Young Ladies' Domestic Seminary educated over five hundred women, including at least six African American

FIGURE 2.1. Hiram Huntington Kellogg (1803–1881) was a white abolitionist and proprietor of the Young Ladies' Domestic Seminary in Clinton, New York, and later the first president of Knox College in Illinois. Courtesy of Special Collections and Archives, Knox College Library.

women besides Mary E. Miles. These women transformed the all-white seminary into the first *racially integrated* female seminary in New York, if not in the entire North. The other six were twenty-two-year-old Margaret Morrison and her sister, twenty-one-year-old Rosetta Morrison, both from Connecticut; the Turpin sisters from New York, thirteen-year-old Joanna and twelve-year-old Lucretia; sixteen-year-old Serena deGrasse from New York; and twenty-year-old Ursula James from New York.[1] Unlike Prudence Crandall's Canterbury Female Seminary, this school operated for years even after African American women enrolled.[2]

Those involved in this remarkable educational endeavor included Kellogg and his fellow teachers, the abolitionists who supported the seminary, and the African American women students and their families who cast aside their reservations and embraced this opportunity. Indeed some black families initially may have held reservations about enrolling their daughters in the seminary because it had only recently welcomed African American students. These families had no doubt heard about what happened at Canterbury. What is more, Kellogg's seminary had a manual labor focus. In the mid-nineteenth century, domestic work in the Northeast had become increasingly racialized, and at first glance young African American women learning to perform manual labor might actually affirm their suitability as domestic servants.[3] At the Young Ladies' Domestic Seminary, however, *all* women performed manual labor and learned to relate this work to the prosperity of their families. It was a radical notion that young African American women would labor not in white households but in their own homes, caring for their own families.

This racially integrated female seminary invites a rereading of the cult of Christian domesticity as it shaped African American girls and women. Historians have noted that certain aspects of this ideology, such as "the notion of passivity," did not accord with African American women's lived experiences.[4] Consequently free black women advanced their own sense of womanhood, namely, the idea of the purposeful woman, which did not conflict with the mission of Kellogg's seminary. After all Kellogg's version of the cult of Christian domesticity and the idea of purposeful womanhood shared a common denominator: a belief in social reform. In other words, African American and white Christian women had a distinct role to play in social reform—in the home, the classroom, and the missionary field—and fighting for the rights of the oppressed did not contravene their feminine role. Furthermore the presence of young African American women at this seminary enabled Kellogg to theorize as well as actually demonstrate that the twin pillars of racial equality and black freedom constituted one kind of social reform. White women students were thrust into this reform initiative while young African American women students began to imagine different roles for themselves, as makers of their own home and as purposeful women, building strong communities.

Born on April 12, 1819, Mary Elizabeth Miles was raised in a Quaker household in Rhode Island, perhaps Providence. Her family may have been poor or working class since she required financial assistance to attend the Young Ladies' Domestic Seminary. Her obituary noted that, as a child, she had gained "a superior education," perhaps through tutoring, attending a Sabbath school, or enrolling at one of the Providence-area schools such as the African Union Meeting and School House, the Meeting Street School, or a Quaker school.[5] Teacher retention was a problem at the African Union Meeting and School House, so classes were sometimes irregular. The Meeting Street School, a public school for African American children, opened in 1828 and offered greater regularity. In any case, Mary's primary school education prepared her for advanced study at the Canterbury Female Seminary.

At Canterbury, Mary met May, who became a dear friend. He probably recommended her for admission to the Young Ladies' Domestic Seminary since he could vouch for her intelligence, character, and piety.[6] A proponent of African American women's education, he once asked the women's rights advocate and abolitionist Lucretia Mott to encourage female antislavery societies to "assist those ladies in different parts of the country who may be devoting or willing to devote themselves to the education of colored females."[7] When May ran the State Normal School in Lexington, Massachusetts, in the 1840s, he threatened to resign if the board refused to admit Mary. Years later he described her as an "estimable woman."[8] May was certainly an ally for those African American women like Mary seeking access to advanced schooling.

In fact abolitionist networks provided an important route for African American youth to gain access to academies, seminaries, and colleges. Abolitionists often introduced promising youth to school proprietors, usually via a letter extolling the character and intelligence of the student in question. For example, Peter Williams, one of the first African American men ordained as an Episcopal priest in the United States, proposed a plan to educate young African American men who could then "prove, that all that has been said about the inferiority of African intellect is false."[9] He focused on procuring a liberal education for three young men in particular: Alexander Crummell, James McCune Smith, and Serena's brother, Isaiah deGrasse, all of whom became intellectual leaders in the fight for racial equality. In the same way, abolitionists helped African American women enroll at female seminaries like Kellogg's.

The Young Ladies' Domestic Seminary was the first female seminary in the United States to combine manual labor with a liberal arts curriculum.[10] An editorialist summarized the unusual nature of this idea: "Manual Labor—Young Ladies!—What an odd association!—Who ever heard of such a thing!"[11] Yet the manual labor school movement had been growing. The white abolitionist Lewis Tappan, along with other reformers, organized the Society for Promoting Manual Labor in Literary Institutions in 1831 in New York City to "collect and diffuse information" to advance the manual labor system at schools, academies, and colleges nationally. Educational reformers soon raved about Kellogg's seminary for its attention to women's domestic learning. For example, the *American Annals of Education*, a journal edited by a Yale graduate named William C. Woodbridge, featured an article, probably written by Woodbridge, celebrating Kellogg's seminary for "enlarg[ing] the intellect of our female youth, without interrupting the formation of domestic character."[12]

The seminary enrolled between sixty and seventy white female students in any given term. Most students hailed from western New York, though a few called New England and even the Arkansas Territory home. As in most female seminaries of the day, students ranged in age from their early to late teens. For instance, twelve-year-old Annie M. Sykes, the eldest daughter of Orrin and Nancy Sykes from Clinton, studied at the seminary in 1833 before embarking upon what would become a successful career as a music teacher. Twenty-two-year-old Susan Elvina Lowe and her twenty-year-old sister, Julia Ann, enrolled in 1833. A few years later Susan and her husband, Augustus Wattles, became leading abolitionists in the Old Northwest. A classmate of the Lowe sisters was Elizabeth Everett, who was born on March 20, 1818, in Denbighshire, Wales, and settled with her parents and ten siblings in Remsen, New York. Everett would later teach at the seminary and develop a strong relationship with her African American women students.

Kellogg distinguished his seminary by welcoming young white women from poor and working-class as well as middle-class backgrounds. Though exact costs varied by region, a seminary education carried a high price tag. For example, at Ontario Female Seminary in Canandaigua, New York, a complete course of study plus board ran approximately $118 for the 1833–34 academic year of three terms, each approximately fourteen weeks long.[13] This amounted to about one-third of the annual income of a fully employed skilled artisan. In comparison, tuition and board at the Young Ladies' Domestic Seminary hovered around $110, but those expenses could be greatly reduced depending on how much domestic labor a young woman performed. Six categories characterized the manual labor system at Kellogg's seminary: housework, washing dishes, cooking, doing laundry, nursing, and sewing. This system enabled Kellogg to admit a socioeconomically diverse group of young women.[14]

Kellogg believed that democratizing women's access to advanced education reflected the larger social, economic, and cultural changes occurring in Oneida County. Settled in 1787 by Moses Foote, a Connecticut native, and seven other New England families, Clinton boasted rich farmland and attracted many more New Englanders. The historian Whitney Cross called this region of western New York the "Burned-Over District," seared by the fires of evangelical awakening.[15] Oneida County began as an agrarian settlement with a household economy strongly tied to family production, but by the 1830s much had changed with the rise of commerce and industry that moved production out of the home.[16]

Oneida County soon became an educational enclave. New Englanders established public primary schools and more advanced educational institutions from Whitesboro to Utica. In 1793 Samuel Kirkland, a white Presbyterian missionary to the Oneida Indians, opened the Hamilton-Oneida Academy to educate both white and Native American boys. In 1812 the academy was rechartered as Hamilton College, an institution that soon drifted from its interracial mission and admitted mostly white men. Other institutions established in the early nineteenth century were Clinton Liberal Institute, Clinton Grammar School, Miss Royce's Seminary, and the Young Ladies' Domestic Seminary.

Christian principles pervaded many female seminaries in the 1830s, and the Young Ladies' Domestic Seminary was no exception, especially given Kellogg's background. Born in Clinton on February 26, 1803, to Massachusetts transplants Susan and Aaron Kellogg, their son Hiram imbibed the strong spirit of Christian evangelicalism that had intoxicated the masses.[17] Educated in Clinton schools, he graduated from Hamilton College in 1822 and studied theology at Auburn Seminary, completing his degree in 1825. He then embarked upon a career as a Presbyterian minister, joining the white radical abolitionist, Theodore Dwight Weld, and others as a member of Charles Grandison Finney's Holy Band, which traveled throughout the Northeast to preach the word of God. In October 1829 Kellogg married Mary Gleason Chandler, a well-educated white woman from nearby Augusta, Oneida County.[18] After a period of failing health, he relinquished his career in preaching and chose a more settled existence as a school proprietor, in which he could combine his theological training with his views on women's education.

In the post-Revolutionary era, prescriptive literature, from advice manuals to conduct books, declared the home the most influential space for middle-class and elite white women. The home became, as the scholar Glenna Matthews concludes, a "potent symbol of integration at this time, valuable because it seemed to represent a haven of stability."[19] This ideology of Christian domesticity, as it was called, embraced essentializing arguments about the unique character of women, particularly concerning their suitability as teachers. For instance, Catherine Beecher, the white proprietor of the Hartford Female Seminary in Connecticut and later an educational theorist, argued that women possessed an innate capacity to nurture as well as a strong moral core to influence the next generation, making them natural teachers. Thus a solid education for women was vital not solely for individual gain but also to serve others.[20] Likewise Kellogg claimed that women were "better qualified by nature than the other sex. They better know how to secure the attention, confidence, and hearts of the young."[21] Beecher, Kellogg, and other educational reformers encouraged women to embrace and promote their authority in the home *and* in the classroom.

By invoking this ideology of Christian domesticity, Kellogg politicized the home and, along with it, the cause of women's education. Women's minds, he argued, had to be "highly cultivated" since their "chief responsibility [was] for forming the youthful character and moulding the infant mind."[22] He cited biblical passages, specifically an Old Testament passage from Proverbs:

> A wife of noble character who can find?
> She is worth far more than rubies.
> Her husband has full confidence in her
> and lacks nothing of value.
> She brings him good, not harm,
> all days of her life.[23]

Evangelical Protestants cited Proverbs 31 frequently in sermons, women's magazines, and popular literature. This image of the virtuous Christian housewife was firmly affixed within the ideology of Christian domesticity. To do right by God was to be an educated Christian woman who owed it to herself to imbibe the spirit of Christ and to be useful in the world by spreading God's word. To that end, a woman might proselytize as a missionary in Thailand, move to the western U.S. to teach primary school, participate in a female moral reform society, or be a devoted housewife and mother. Yet in Kellogg's estimation, women's education had suffered. Compared to young men, young women lacked access to affordable, permanent seminaries. Just as magazines, novels, and poems advanced this ideology, so too could a female seminary that made domestic labor a central curricular component. Such a school would demarcate female behavior and provide practical experience.

The cause of women's education was no less political among African American leaders. In fact women's pursuit of advanced schooling spurred debate. Lewis Woodson, an African American minister in Pittsburgh, Pennsylvania, was exasperated that teachers taught boys and girls the same subjects, such as arithmetic and geography, "without any regard to the duties of girls in after life [sic]." He wished to see girls learn needlework, drawing, and music, subjects categorized as "ornamental."[24] A related concern involved the eventual role that an educated African American woman would assume. Charles B. Ray, an African American abolitionist from New York and editor of the Colored American, stressed the importance of teaching a young woman about domestic economy because she would later assume the role of wife and mother.[25] Gender and racial politics thus intersected in these debates about what women should learn.

Charles B. Ray agreed with other educational reformers that an educated mother could strengthen the home and family. To that end, he supported advanced schooling for African American women, especially if it conformed to the ideology of Christian domesticity. Ray predicted that educated African American women would become "the wives of an enlightened mechanic, a store keeper, or a clerk."[26] Similarly, a columnist writing for the Palladium of Liberty, an Ohio-based newspaper edited by the African American abolitionist David Jenkins, named the domestic "circle where the most powerful influence of woman is exerted, that is, her heaven-ordained sphere—one to make it a home of delight, the blest place on earth."[27] For this columnist, separate spheres ideology empowered educated African American women and, by extension, the African American family.

In published writings, a few African American women framed the ideology of Christian domesticity as empowering. An editorialist from Philadelphia named Beatrice wrote in the Liberator that she relinquished "physical strength" and "moral courage" to men while upholding the "domestic circle" as an educated woman's domain.[28] Likewise Mary Still advised the African American woman to "be virtuous, pious and industrious, her feet abiding in her own house, ruleing [sic] her family as well."[29] Having been schooled in the art of domestic work, female homemakers could educate children and thus engender community uplift. According to James Forten Jr., son of Charlotte Vandine and James E.

Forten, a prominent African American abolitionist couple from Phila-delphia, domestic education was particularly powerful because children could learn in the home, an environment "free from the eye of hatred, and the pointed finger of scorn."[30] Thus the emphasis on the ideology of Christian domesticity at Kellogg's seminary appealed to both African Americans and whites, if for slightly different reasons.

Well aware of the social position that free African American women occupied, Mary E. Miles tried to enlighten abolitionists such as Gerrit Smith. Like many free African American women, she had to "contend with," in her words, "not only . . . prejudice against poverty, prejudice against color but prejudice against her sex." Her conscious expression of, what we might refer to today as, her intersectional identities signaled her social awareness and her determination. She revealed her drive for self-elevation, despite systems of prejudice—poverty, racism, and sexism. By writing a letter to Smith, she pleaded for him to "look into this mat-ter" and support African American women's education in the same way that he had supported African American men's education.[31] Perhaps she knew nothing of Smith's early donations to the Young Ladies' Domestic Seminary that directly supported her, but whatever the case, she shared her honest and earnest words, making him aware of the triple burden—race, gender, and class oppression—that poor and working-class African American women faced.

Mary was entering an area in upstate New York with an emerging abolition movement, a growing free black population, and expanding educational opportunities. In Oneida County the institution of slavery rose and fell rapidly at the turn of the nineteenth century.[32] The passage of the Gradual Emancipation Act in 1799, which freed enslaved African American children born after July 4, 1799, expanded free black com-munities in the area. While the overall population of Oneida County increased from 71,326 in 1830 to 85,310 in 1840, the African American population remained small, never rising above 1 percent during the nine-teenth century.[33] Still, free black communities emerged from the rubble of slavery to establish mutual aid societies, places of religious worship, schools, and antislavery organizations.

The 1830s was an incredible decade in the radical abolition move-ment: globally, with the abolition of slavery throughout the British Empire in 1833; nationally, with the establishment of the American Anti-Slavery Society, founded by William Lloyd Garrison in 1833; and locally, with the creation of numerous antislavery societies in New York. The white abolitionists Gerrit Smith, Alvan Stewart, and Beriah Green, among others, convened in October 1835 in Utica, New York, intending to launch an antislavery society. Their plan enraged white citizens like Joseph Kirkland, the city's mayor, and Chester Hayden, a judge. A mob tried to obstruct the convention, but Smith invited the antislavery activists, including Hiram Kellogg, to reconvene at a church in Peterboro. Smith then declared himself an abolitionist and established the New York State Anti-Slavery Society later that month, with Stewart as president.[34] Kellogg too joined the new organization, donated money to it, and acted as a delegate to the New York state antislavery conventions.[35] He knew Smith, who had served as a trustee of the Young Ladies' Domestic Seminary and sent his daughter, Elizabeth, to study there.

African American education in Oneida County gained some ground as free blacks and their allies built schools. In 1814 Eunice Camp opened a school for black children in Utica and later ran the Sunday Evening School for People of Color.[36] In 1834 Smith subsidized a manual labor school for African American men ages fourteen and older. One student noted in the *Vermont Chronicle* that the stakes were high: "The eyes of the whole community are upon us, and if our school should produce its desired effect, it will be the means of putting to silence many of our enemies . . . [and] those who have pretended that the blacks have neither ambition nor brain."[37] Smith exchanged letters with prominent African American leaders like Theodore S. Wright, who recommended prospective students. Around thirty young men enrolled, but Smith's school folded a year later.[38] Nearby, in Utica, schools for African American children existed, including Mrs. Maxon's School for Colored Children. An apparently successful school exhibition there led one spectator to declare that racial prejudice would cease "if whites would put themselves in a way of *knowing* more about colored people."[39] In 1840 Jermain Loguen opened a school for African American children in Utica, a place that he claimed "was in advance of the cities of the North in regard to freedom—and its anti-slavery attractions secured the residence of an intelligent and spirited colored population."[40] He knew all about the politics of freedom as he had escaped slavery in Tennessee at the age of twenty-one and moved to the Whitesboro area to attend the Oneida Institute, an abolitionist institution of higher education.[41]

Under the leadership of Beriah Green, the principle of racial egalitarianism governed Oneida Institute. Green, a white reformer and educator from Vermont, graduated from Middlebury College in 1819 and spent a year at Andover Theological Seminary. He relocated to Ohio to take up a professorship in sacred literature at Western Reserve College. There he cofounded the college's antislavery society, denounced the American Colonization Society, and championed the immediate abolition of slavery as well as racial equality. To Green, race was an artificial construction. "The arrangements of human society are artificial. Birth, complexion, place, a thousand things, which have nothing to do with constitutional character, or moral worth, have had a controlling influence on public sentiment," he argued.[42] In 1833 he took the helm at Oneida Institute after the retirement of George Washington Gale, who had established the institute to provide young men with academic and theological training to enter the ministry. Green sought to transform public sentiment about race, first by explaining its artificiality and then by promoting interracialism in the classroom.

Green posited that interracialism would beget peace and love, two values that local communities needed to thrive. While Green shared Gale's evangelical revivalism and enthusiasm for agricultural and mechanical arts, he also imagined Oneida Institute as an interracial abolitionist haven that promoted "fitness for public service."[43] Beginning in 1835, at least fourteen African American male students passed through the doors of this college, including a few who would go on to become well-known activists: Amos G. Beman, Alexander Crummell, Henry Highland Garnet, and John V. deGrasse, the brother of Serena and Isaiah deGrasse. Of this interracial student body, Green celebrated "the red sons of the Western forest, the sable sons of the sunny South [who] have here found a home together, and amidst their various tasks, manual and mental, have lived in peace and love with their pale-faced and blue-eyed brethren."[44] According to Green's biographer, Milton Sernett, Oneida Institute became "America's first truly interracial college," preceding Oberlin's enrollment of African Americans by more than a few years.[45] Green's vision of a multiracial community paved the way for a cadre of emerging African American male leaders.

Though the "Burned-Over District" had its fair share of radicals, white opposition to the abolition movement at times disturbed antislavery institutions in the area. During the 1835 mob attack at the antislavery convention in Utica, students had to secure Oneida Institute's buildings, lest the anti-abolition mob charged.[46] A year later David Wager, a white state senator from Utica, attempted to deny the college funding to which it was entitled. Green organized a protest rally that roused abolitionists and netted the college close to $5,000 in donations.[47] Wager's legislative attack had failed. *Friend of Man*, the New York State Anti-Slavery Society's weekly newspaper edited by William

Goodell, published an article alluding to the "most bitter and unrelenting hostility" visited upon this college.[48] For ten years Green and his
supporters blunted white hostility by using mass protest and calling
on abolitionist networks, thus prolonging the life of these model interracial institutions. However, crushing debt, more than anything else,
led to Oneida Institute's closure in 1844.

The antislavery circles that Hiram Kellogg frequented made the subject of African American education a central concern. In the wake of
the closure of the Canterbury Female Seminary, New York abolitionists
bemoaned the lack of advanced educational opportunities for young
African American women. Theodore S. Wright wrote to Smith about the
"unprincapalled [sic] people of Canterbury, Conn. [who] have at length
persecuted Miss Crandall's School out of existence."[49] No doubt Kellogg
also knew about the destruction of the school at Canterbury. Four years
later educational opportunities for African American girls and women
remained limited. For instance, Miss Whitehead's School for Young
Ladies of Color in New Bedford, Massachusetts, offered studies in the
"usual branches," which meant reading, writing, and grammar, along
with "plain and ornamental needle-work, Drawing and Painting."[50] This
school did not offer advanced subjects, such as chemistry, natural history, and French, that a female seminary did.

In fact the few seminaries in the Northeast that were open to African
American women in the mid-1830s were coeducational institutions run
by African American proprietors or, in rare cases, white proprietors. For
example, Daniel A. Payne, an African American minister and abolitionist, opened a coeducational seminary in June 1840 in Philadelphia that
offered higher education to both African Americans and whites. By the
following year a total of twenty-three students, ranging in age from six
to eighteen, were enrolled, some of whom studied grammar and geometry.[51] There is no indication that white youth attended. In Cass County,
Michigan, Benjamin F. Neely, a white Free Will Baptist minister from
Montpelier, Vermont, oversaw the Randalian Seminary, which had a
preparatory department and a higher "academical department" that
"cheerfully" accepted "young gentlemen and ladies of color."[52] The coeducational Phoenix High School for Colored Youth in New York City, run
by Frederic Jones and supported by David Ruggles and Samuel Cornish,
also won praise from activists.[53] Such seminaries and high schools promoted racial and gender inclusion as well as educational equity, but they
were often short-lived: Payne's seminary, Neely's seminary, and Phoenix
High School closed within a few years.

In all likelihood, less than a handful of female seminaries in the Northeast accepted African American women. Sarah Mapps Douglass, an African American educator and abolitionist, ran a well-respected female seminary in Philadelphia. In New York City a Miss Miller, perhaps Jane Miller, taught African American women.[54] Aside from these few opportunities, young African American women and their families wishing to enroll at a female seminary had to blaze their own path by applying to all-white female seminaries.

Intrigued by the mission of a seminary like Kellogg's, a young woman applied either by writing directly to the proprietor or asking a family friend to write on her behalf. This application process was similar at other female seminaries. A typical letter of application presented a student's deep interest in the institution; her desire to educate herself further for some putatively noble purpose, probably to teach in the West or become a missionary; and her background, qualifications, and references. Admission was not a foregone conclusion but required careful consideration.

When Kellogg received an inquiry from a prospective African American female student in the fall of 1838, he had to consider both the student's qualifications and his own inclination to welcome African American women into his seminary. In the mid- to late 1830s, student enrollment at the Young Ladies' Domestic Seminary held steady at around 120 students for each academic year.[55] After Kellogg reduced the student body from seventy students per term to about fifty, enrollment dipped to 106 students in the 1836–37 academic year.[56] This change occurred probably in response to the financial crisis following the Panic of 1837, when many seminaries and academies suffered decreased enrollments. Aside from the financial crisis, these numbers also reveal the sporadic rates of attendance for some young women, who might enroll one term and then leave the next. Despite enrollment dips and the rates of absence, the Young Ladies' Domestic Seminary appeared to be on fairly solid financial footing. Hence Kellogg's seminary could potentially crumble if he chose to accept African American women as students; irate parents might pull their daughters out of the seminary. The Crandall controversy made some white school proprietors wary. For example, a white school proprietor in the Northeast decided against admitting African American women, declaring, "It would break up my school; and I have neither pecuniary means nor physical strength to fight the battle."[57] Racial school integration was indeed a battle from which some white proprietors wittingly retreated.

The difficulties that Prudence Crandall faced in Canterbury in 1833 did not mean that Hiram Kellogg would share the same fate some five years later in Clinton. About a dozen white male Canterbury residents had recruited Prudence to establish a seminary. When she, as a white *female* proprietor, changed the composition of her student body, these residents leveled sexist attacks at her. In contrast, Kellogg was a white *male* proprietor who had established his seminary on his own accord and in his hometown. Moreover, compared to Crandall's first all-white boarding school, Kellogg's school boasted a larger student body that had already been exposed to abolitionist principles. The location of each institution also shaped how those respective communities regarded it: both were in villages with a small African American population, but Clinton had an abolitionist presence and a comparatively quieter colonizationist constituency.[58]

Furthermore Kellogg could point to the success of Oneida Institute, just five miles away. He could call on support from Green and his fellow abolitionists, if need be. The time to act was now. Just as Green's decision to open Oneida Institute to African American men was bold, so too was Hiram's decision to admit young African American women to the Young Ladies' Domestic Seminary.

Sometime in the fall of 1838 Mary E. Miles entered Kellogg's seminary. He agreed to subsidize her costs because "circumstances of indigence required a reduction of her expenses."[59] Once word circulated that a female seminary welcomed African American girls and women on equal terms, more African American women applied. The following semester, in May 1839, Kellogg admitted three more young women, who also received tuition reductions.

African American girls and women who attended this seminary advanced the concept of purposeful womanhood. For instance, twenty-year-old Ursula James from Watertown, New York, sought to attend Kellogg's seminary with the sole purpose of becoming a teacher and missionary. She had appealed to Squire Chase, a white Methodist missionary and agent of the American Colonization Society, for assistance. Chase believed that the Society would pay Ursula's tuition and he advised her to write to Kellogg for admission. Kellogg described Ursula as "a very interesting young woman" and discerned that she was "anxious to come into the Semy [*sic*]."[60] A purposeful Ursula was well aware of the reputation of Kellogg's seminary in training missionaries and teachers, which fit her goals.

A principled young woman, Ursula viewed the American Colonization Society as an enemy and refused their support.[61] Kellogg wrote to

Smith, "[Ursula] is not at all friendly to the colonization plan. She says she has never known much about it, but has always viewed it with disapprobation," a sentiment shared by many free blacks at the time.[62] As badly as she wished to attend a seminary and become a teacher and missionary, she would not compromise her values. Kellogg was sympathetic and admitted her without the Society's support; she planned to board with and work for Chase and his family to offset tuition costs, but according to Kellogg, this arrangement made her uneasy because Chase could not guarantee that he planned to stay in Clinton. In the end, Kellogg offered her reduced tuition, made possible in part by additional funds received ($100 in April 1839) from Smith, and she then entered the seminary.

Ursula soon met Margaret and Rosetta Morrison, who probably had arrived at the seminary some months earlier. Little is known about the Morrison family, but they lived in Hartford, Connecticut, a community with a rising free black middle class that promoted reform, respectability, and community.[63] Margaret, born in 1817, and Rosetta, born Maria in 1818, had an older brother, Abraham J. Morrison, and another sister, Elizabeth Morrison Foster. They were orphaned after their father, James, died, probably in the late 1830s. Margaret and her siblings had only limited opportunities for schooling. In the early 1800s an African American primary school existed in Hartford, though it had closed by the mid-1820s. In the early 1830s a public primary school was set up at the Talcott Street Church and at the African Methodist Episcopal Church.[64]

The Morrison sisters apparently had divergent childhood experiences. In 1827 nine-year-old Rosetta began laboring as a servant in the Rowland family household in Exeter, New Hampshire. Meanwhile Margaret had moved to Middletown, Connecticut, a growing commercial and shipping center with a small free black community of 211 in 1830, about 3 percent of the city's population. The single advantage that Rosetta had as a servant girl was that the Rowland family wished to educate her.

The white patriarch of the Rowland family was William F. Rowland, a Connecticut native who graduated from Dartmouth College before becoming pastor of the First Congregational Church in Exeter in 1790, a position he held for thirty-eight years.[65] He and his second wife, Ann, had four children: William, Mary, Sarah, and Theresa. A letter from Mary to her cousin Frances Bliss Rowland described Rosetta's arrival at the Rowland home:

> We have been without any girl or boy this summer excepting for
> now and then a day or two at intervals we have had a stupid girl and

exhausted our patience over her and let her go. We *cannot* get help of the right sort possibly unless we pay higher wages then [*sic*] we can afford. We had a day or two ago a little boy and a little girl added to our family in the capacity as *sarvents* [*sic*]—the damsel is a *genuine* blackey—She is nine years old and we take such a fancy to her we think of changing her name (Maria) to "Rosetta"—She is sprightly and we are more in love with her and if our patience is not spent soon we intend to educate her to suit us—as we have been so long destitute of *domestics* and as we have had far more than our usual company (a matter of course in such circumstances) I have lived in the kitchen. I never in all my life have been so closely confined at home as for the last months.[66]

To Mary, renaming Maria represented the family's feelings of approval, especially after experiencing difficulty securing a domestic servant. Yet the action also evoked the practice of renaming slaves, which occurred not only in the antebellum South but also in Puritan New England. The Rowlands viewed Maria as *theirs*, and renaming her represented their attempt to win her affinity and loyalty as well as encourage her hard work. In the antebellum era, common domestic tasks for a servant included cleaning, washing, and cooking, and Rosetta would later perform similar work at Kellogg's seminary. Female domestic servants often worked long hours, had little privacy, and remained isolated from friends and family.[67] In Rosetta's case, Exeter was over 150 miles from Hartford.

If Rosetta explored the town of Exeter, she probably saw very few African Americans. Exeter, the county seat of Rockingham County, a commercial center in New Hampshire, was home to the largest African American population in the state. That population, however, was still tiny, at around eighty people, less than 1 percent of the Exeter population in 1830. By then race relations in the town had grown tense. Rosetta may have heard about the mob that destroyed the house of Ben Jakes, an African American resident, that same year.[68] Or maybe she read local newspaper accounts in August 1835 when a mob dragged the building that housed Noyes Academy, an interracial and coeducational institution, into a swamp. There is no indication that Rosetta attended that school, though she may have gone to public schools in Exeter, which did enroll African American children.

Some towns and villages in antebellum New Hampshire tolerated the presence of African American children in public schools, more often because of particular circumstances than as any kind of radical sociopolitical statement. It proved too costly to organize public schools solely for so few African American children. In her semi-autobiographical novel, *Our Nig, or, Sketches from the Life of a Free Black*, Harriet E. Wilson, a mixed-race African American writer, depicted a public school in Milford, New Hampshire, that the novel's protagonist, Frado, attended. White children initially mistreated Frado because of her race (and gender), but the white female teacher, Miss Marsh, quickly corrected their behavior, modeling acceptance and love in her interactions with Frado. Soon Frado's white classmates began to accept her; eventually they even liked her.[69] But Frado's duties were to the abusive Bellmont family, so she attended school for only a few years. Likewise Rosetta's duties were to the Rowlands. Frado remained a servant until her eighteenth birthday; how long Rosetta remained a servant is unknown, but it could have been a similar duration.

The Turpin sisters, thirteen-year-old Joanna (Figure 2.2) and twelve-year-old Lucretia, probably joined Rosetta and Margaret at the Young Ladies' Domestic Seminary in April 1839. They lived in New Rochelle, Westchester County, New York, about 250 miles from Clinton. They had a younger brother, Joseph Henry Turpin, who later worked in Boston as a daguerreotypist, as well as a younger sister, Eliza.[70] Their mother, Adaline Leggett Turpin, hailed from New York. Their father, Joseph Thomas Turpin, had been enslaved by William Turpin, a white merchant from Charleston, South Carolina. William eventually emancipated his slaves, including Joseph, and joined the colonization movement. In a letter to former U.S. president Thomas Jefferson, William enclosed an antislavery pamphlet and encouraged Jefferson to free his slaves and induce them to move to Haiti.[71] When William moved to New York City in the mid-1820s, Joseph accompanied him. On January 21, 1835, William died at the age of eighty-one. In his will, he sought to aid African Americans as well as the antislavery movement, with donations to antislavery newspapers such as Garrison's *Liberator* and Benjamin Lundy's *Genius of Universal Emancipation*.[72] Judah Jackson, a free black girl, and her brother, Edward, received property, and William remunerated twenty-one of his former slaves, many still in South Carolina, for their labor. To his "faithful friend and freed black man," Joseph, William left one of the largest individual gifts: three properties in New York City valued at $60,000 to $70,000, a huge sum.[73]

Nearly eight months after this windfall, Joseph Turpin passed away at age forty. That August he had prepared his will, which his executors filed in October at the Surrogate Court for Westchester County. He made

FIGURE 2.2. This photograph of Joanna Turpin
Howard appeared as part of a feature on the Howard
family written by the African American writer Pauline
E. Hopkins and published in the *Colored American
Magazine* (1902). Courtesy of the James Weldon
Johnson Collection, Yale Collection of American Lit-
erature, Beinecke Rare Book and Manuscript Library,
Yale University.

provisions for his wife, her sister, Rosetta, and her mother, Tamer Leggett.
From rents collected on the properties in New York City, his wife was to
receive $500 per year for the rest of her life and an additional $200 "for
the support and education of each of [her] children till they shall arrive
to the age of fifteen years." Joseph wished for his daughters and his son to
receive a quality education. He did, however, allocate an additional $100
to his son until he turned twenty-one.[74] Perhaps this bequest hints at
cultural expectations that a young man should pursue a lucrative career,

which might require additional training, in order to be able to provide for a family. Though the Turpin children had lost their father, they knew that he wanted them to get an education.

On May 29, 1837, Adaline Turpin married Theodore S. Wright. Born in Providence, Rhode Island, in 1797, Wright had relocated to New York City with his family, where he enrolled at the first African Free School on Cliff Street. With support from DeWitt Clinton, governor of New York, Theodore earned admission to Princeton Theological Seminary in 1825; he graduated in 1828, making him the first African American man to graduate from a theological seminary in the United States. In 1829 he was ordained in Albany, New York, but tragedy struck when his first wife, Beneba, died after exposure to the elements while traveling on a racially segregated boat from New Brunswick to New York City.[75] Wright soon answered the call to a life of activism and religious service as he assumed the role of pastor of the First Colored Presbyterian Church in New York City in 1830; he served there until his death in 1847. He was a leading African American abolitionist and clergyman in the 1830s.[76]

Kellogg's seminary probably impressed the Wrights because it schooled girls and women in the liberal arts and Christian faith. The very first textbook listed in the seminary catalogue was the Bible. Kellogg, who taught physiology and led Bible study, preached to his students Christian values such as goodness and charity. When Wright served as an agent for the New England Anti-Slavery Society, he had traveled throughout the Northeast lecturing on Christian brotherhood and sisterhood, the wrongs of slavery and racial prejudice, and the benefits of educating African American children and youth. Wright's message about black educational access took on even deeper meaning now that he had four school-age stepchildren.

Arguably it was Wright who converted Kellogg to racial school integration. In fact black protest shaped the radical abolition movement, pushing more white antislavery activists to the immediate abolition of slavery and the recognition of African Americans as full and equal citizens of the United States.[77] On September 20, 1837, Wright delivered a provocative speech at the New York State Anti-Slavery Society convention wherein he described the collective feeling of sadness among African Americans that "not a single high school or female seminary in the land is open to our daughters."[78] Kellogg was probably in the audience to hear this lament; he was listed on the roll of delegates from Oneida County and even submitted a report on the success of a missionary, Marcia H. Smith, in the Sandwich Islands (Hawaii). Wright commanded this audience of antislavery activists to "annihilate in their own bosoms the cord of caste": "Let every man take his stand, burn out this prejudice, live it down, everywhere consider the colored man as a man . . . and the death-blow to slavery will be struck."[79] Shortly after this convention, Kellogg admitted Mary E. Miles to his seminary. Two years later he was teaching all of his students to "break over the laws of caste," as Wright had implored.[80] Kellogg believed that he and his students had a Christian duty to abolish racial prejudice and, if necessary, to cut ties with those who did not share this view.

Adaline Wright epitomized Christian womanhood through her religious work and community service.[81] Her daughters probably witnessed her selflessness, caring for infirm family members, and her strong religious faith, especially as she endured multiple stillbirths. On April 24, 1839, she passed away after a brief illness. Her daughters were either already at Kellogg's seminary or en route to it when they learned of their mother's death. In a postscript to his letter to Gerrit Smith, Kellogg wrote, "Bro Wright Daughters have both as we trust been wanted—they have been called home by the sickness of their mother whose death I've noticed in last weeks [sic] Emancipator."[82] One thousand people attended Adaline's funeral at her husband's church. Charles B. Ray wrote a long obituary in the Colored American honoring her as "a Christian, a faithful and affectionate wife, a tender and devoted mother, a beloved sister, and a sincere and confiding friend."[83] In a few years, the Turpin children had lost their mother and father, but they gained a stepfather and probably relied on distant kin, such as their grandmother. Joanna and Lucretia fulfilled their parents' wishes when they returned to the Young Ladies' Domestic Seminary.

Attending a female seminary coincided with a particular stage in a young woman's life. Serena Leonora deGrasse was sixteen years old—the ideal age to begin her education at a seminary. She may have had a younger sister, six-year-old Georgenia, whose name did not appear on the roster at the Young Ladies' Domestic Seminary;[84] perhaps she was too young to matriculate. The name of Serena's older sister, Theodosia, was not on the roster either, but Theodosia had attended the Canterbury Female Seminary in 1833. She could have enrolled at another institution in the intervening years, or perhaps she had already begun her teaching career. She might also have just met her future husband, Peter Vogelsang, Jr., whom she would marry in July 1840. Or maybe she did not wish to attend another female seminary after the trauma of what transpired at Canterbury—a story she surely shared with Serena, who could have heard it from Mary E. Miles at Kellogg's seminary.

The deGrasse family's racial background confused some community members. The Indian-born father, George, was Hindu. The mother, Maria van Salee deGrasse, was a mixed-race woman. They had at least seven children: Maria, Theodosia, Serena, Georgenia, Emma, Isaiah, and John.[85] Peter Williams described Isaiah as a "mixture of Asiatic and European with African blood," though an article at the time claimed that Isaiah had "no African blood in his veins."[86] These warring interpretations speak to the volatility of race and racial perception in antebellum America.

Nevertheless the deGrasse family allied themselves with the African American community and viewed themselves as African Americans. They lived in New York City's emerging free black community, where they became active members of religious organizations.[87] They joined St. Phillip's Church and participated in African American celebrations. During a public festival commemorating the abolition of slavery in the state of New York, according to one newspaper account, "a large company partook of a splendid dinner provided for the occasion by Geo. Degrass."[88] Maria was one of twenty-one women on the Board of Managers for the African Dorcas Association, a women's organization established in January 1828 that made garments for poor children. *Freedom's Journal*, a black newspaper that George circulated as an agent, noted that this charitable work brought "honour" to the African American community.[89] The participation of the deGrasse family in these institutions demonstrates their deep connection to and affiliation with African Americans.[90]

The deGrasse sons and daughters were well educated. Almost all of the children attended primary schools and went on to college and seminary. Maria, born in 1809 or 1810, likely attended one of the African Free Schools in New York and then taught at one beginning in May 1832. Isaiah, born in 1814, attended African Free School No. 1, and his composition defending the African race was published in *Freedom's Journal.* He attended Geneva College from 1834 to 1836 and then received a bachelor's degree from Newark College (now the University of Delaware) in 1836, making him the first black graduate of a public university. He was ordained as a deacon at St. Phillip's in 1838 and delivered lectures on Christianity for the Philomathean Society, a black literary organization. John, born in 1825, graduated from Bowdoin Medical College in Brunswick, Maine, in 1849, along with another African American student, Thomas J. White.[91]

While the subject of women's education had been neglected in the *Colored American*—Ray admitted as much—most abolitionists agreed that the struggle for black freedom and equality in the United States necessitated African American women's advanced schooling. Ray summarized the mission and curriculum of the Young Ladies' Domestic Seminary: to provide young women with the skills and knowledge necessary "to be educated an[d] refined; to possess all the attributes which constitute the lady."[92] When the seminary began to accept African American students in 1838, it filled the gap left by the Canterbury Female Seminary four years earlier. Abolitionists lauded the change, and the school continued to be advertised in antislavery and black newspapers.

A commitment to dismantling racial prejudice lay at the heart of the radical abolition movement, though it proved difficult to achieve. Far from running away from the challenge, Kellogg rose to it—and called on his students to do the same. In his original prospectus, he had described his wish to nurture a welcoming environment for young white women; he now argued that African American women students deserved the same opportunity and with "equal participation" with white students.[93]

Some opposition to the revamped seminary existed among white women students and the larger Oneida County community. Three white students withdrew from the school upon finding out that African American girls and women had been accepted.[94] Harriet Tenney, a white student from West Exeter, New York, noted that Kellogg "encountered much opposition on account of his firm adherence to principles which he considered of vital importance and of those the cause of human rights." The nature of this opposition is unclear, though some Clinton residents probably disagreed with Kellogg's new policy. Another white student, Catharine Clarke, from Sidney Plains, New York, told her brother, "[The] school [is] very good indeed though it is not thought to be as good as formerly by some." Her comment suggests that the seminary's reputation had suffered after Kellogg instituted a policy of racial equality. Yet despite such whispers of disrepute and some apparent opposition from Clinton residents, the seminary maintained steady enrollment.[95]

A typical day at the seminary in 1839 was demanding. Catharine Clarke outlined the schedule: a bell at 5:00 a.m. called students to rise; a half hour later all students attended "family worship," or the morning religious service; at 6:30 they ate breakfast and then washed their dishes; the bell rang again at 9:00 for the start of morning recitations; around 12:00 dinner was served; recitations resumed at 1:30; school ended around 5:00; there was a short tea break, and beginning at 6:30 students studied or worked; finally, the bell rang for bed at 9:45 p.m.[96] Myrtilla Miner, a twenty-four-year-old white woman from Hamilton, New York, noted in her description of the seminary that students "assemble[d] in the school room for family worship in the evening."[97] Miner would go on to establish a school for African American girls in Washington, D.C., in the 1850s. A student named Elizabeth, possibly Gerrit Smith's daughter, wrote to her friend Delia Fuller a full account of her three recitations (in Latin, algebra, and chemistry) and daily activities, echoing what other students described. Elizabeth asked her friend, "Now D which do you think has the most spare time[?]"[98]

Academically, students could choose from a variety of courses. Serena deGrasse took a drawing class, among others, and shared her drawings with her white peers (Figure 2.3). Catharine Clarke studied arithmetic, physics, and botany as well as a once-a-week astronomy course called Geography of the Heavens. Elizabeth Everett, a student teacher at the seminary in 1839, also took Geography of the Heavens along with "five daily recitations."[99] Catharine and Elizabeth were probably in their second and third year of study, respectively. Perhaps Mary and Rosetta shared the same recitations. Elizabeth's younger sister, twelve-year-old Jane, enrolled in the first-year course of study, which included classes in arithmetic, geography, and composition and the domestic task of washing dishes; given their age, the Turpin sisters may have taken the same classes and had the same domestic tasks. Kellogg selected popular textbooks for instruction, such as Paley's *Natural Theology*, Hedge's *Elements of Logick*, and Smellie's *Philosophy of Natural History*.[100] Louisa M. Gifford, Emily Kilbourn, and Maria C. Benham, along with three student assistants, composed the all-white faculty.

The Christian character of the school was evident in moments of sickness and, in rare cases, death. Teachers worked to maintain the general health and wellness of the students, but illness was unavoidable. When a student fell ill, teachers called upon a religious leader and a local physician. In November 1839 Elizabeth Everett described a few individual cases of sickness, including Margaret Morrison's: "One of the colored girls has been sick nearly all the term with an inflammation of the membrane between the abdomen and chest—(epigastrinn [sic] I think is the technical term)." This was probably the medical diagnosis of a physician who tended to Margaret. From her arrival to the moment that she got sick, Margaret could not have had much time to devote to her studies. Elizabeth doubted that Margaret would recover: "She had long been out of health previously to her present severe attack. She is we hope a pious girl though not a church member."[101]

Margaret died on December 20, 1839. Her obituary, likely written by Kellogg, attests to her piety and intellect. In her six months or so at the

FIGURE 2.3. Serena deGrasse painted this stone fruit, probably plums, in one of her classes at the Young Ladies' Domestic Seminary. Her classmate Lorain Knight Fenton had it in her possession for decades until she sent it to one of Serena's daughters in March 1880. Courtesy of the Moorland-Spingarn Research Center, Howard University.

Young Ladies' Domestic Seminary, she had grown close to her teachers and fellow students. Long a believer in Christ, she was baptized about a week before her death, making the seminary the site of her religious conversion. Though her life was short, her obituarist offered some solace by noting, "She is now removed to an institution, from which none are excluded for the color of their skin, and where, under the tuition of heavenly spirits, she will possess all that knowledge to which she here aspired."[102] Margaret's pursuit of knowledge was fleeting in the earthly realm, but this Christian rhetoric celebrated the heavenly world that nourished the mind, body, and soul of all God's children, no matter their race.

In all likelihood Margaret expected to live, study, and complete the full three-year course at Kellogg's seminary, for she carried all of her belongings with her to Clinton. Upon her death, her brother, Abraham, filed paperwork to claim her property, which amounted to about $20. Abraham, born around 1810, resided in New Milford, Connecticut, with his wife, Emeline, and their son, William.[103] He worked as a laborer and was active in the abolition and colored convention movements. We can only imagine how Margaret's siblings dealt with her death, especially Rosetta, who remained at the seminary for at least another year.

Though white and African American students may have felt some anxiety about this new interracial environment, social gatherings fostered a culture of Christian fellowship, helping students minimize their anxieties.[104] Such a party celebrating Mary Fowler took place on the evening of October 22, 1840. Fowler, a white alumna of the seminary who taught there, planned to marry Stephen Johnson; together, as missionaries, they would soon set sail to Thailand. Fowler's time at Clinton had prepared her for missionary work. Kellogg's wife, Mary, did not teach at the seminary because of familial obligations (she bore eleven children), but her obituary later noted that her "spirit of missions" influenced her own children and "that of others . . . who, from the Seminary at Clinton, went forth as Foreign missionaries to the heathen in Ceylon, India, Siam, Turkey, China, and the Sandwich Islands."[105] Mary Kellogg may well have inspired Fowler to engage in missionary work. The party provided a space for Rosetta and her classmates, who sang "The Missionary Farewell," a popular hymn written by the white minister Samuel F. Smith, to participate in patriotic performances of nationhood while exalting the missionary endeavor.[106]

Kellogg's leadership facilitated positive social interactions between African American and white students. He noted that those who previously felt "some reluctance in associating with young ladies of color, have found their reluctance to disappear."[107] Writing some sixty years later, a white alumna, Elizabeth Gridley, recalled that "the innovation [of African American women as students] scarcely produced a ripple in the even tenor of the school where the pupil boarders sat side by side with them, and the usual harmony prevailed."[108] Gridley's reminiscence might be overly generous, but it does show that white students were taught to accept African Americans as their peers.

African American and white women students learning from each other was a realization of Kellogg's vision of racial progress. Rosetta befriended Mary M. Addington, a young white woman from Utica, New York, who taught Rosetta how to play the pianoforte. In a letter to Frances Bliss Rowland, Rosetta described the scene: "If you should have happen to have been there, you might have thought it straing to see white, and coulerd, in the parlor to geather, without the least contrast." What was a familiar sight, if not downright ordinary, at Kellogg's seminary was strange, if not strictly forbidden, elsewhere. This moment of learning stood out for Rosetta because racial customs had been broken.

While some incidents of racism may have transpired at the seminary, compared to Connecticut and other places Rosetta visited, the Young Ladies' Domestic Seminary was a refuge from racial prejudice. In October 1840 she had recently returned from a visit to Connecticut, writing, "[I was struck by the] sting [of racial prejudice] . . . in my own native state among those I thought I loved most. But god forbid that I should not love all my friends." She did not elaborate on what had occurred, but the experience triggered in her feelings of pain and exasperation. She lamented, "Oh when will this monster sin prejudice be done away with."[109] Many discontented free blacks asked the same question.

The presence of African American girls and women diversified Kellogg's seminary and deepened its mission. The original curricular focus of training young Christian women in the art of domestic economy continued, but the school's mission expanded the moment African American women walked through the doors. Now the seminary became a site where one could learn and participate in social reform practices. Kellogg reported that white women students re-formed their racial attitudes when they found in African American women "persons of like passions with themselves, and whom they are happy to recognize as sisters."[110] In this way, the seminary's curriculum became both formal and informal, something taught in the classroom but also infused throughout the students' living space and daily lives.

For Hiram Kellogg, the fight for racial equality went hand-in-hand with Christian principles. When he declared that racial integration had "a decidedly happy" effect on both students and teachers, he rebutted claims from proslavery leaders and even colonizationists that whites and African Americans could never coexist. The students' age was crucial; Kellogg remained "convinced that in unsophisticated youth there is no prejudice against color." Racial prejudice was thus learned; if exposed to racial diversity at an early age, whites would accept African Americans as equals. John Everett, Elizabeth's brother, concurred: "White students, thus brought into daily contact with colored students on the basis of equality where any thing like prejudice is frowned upon, will learn to respect moral and intellectual worth equally whether found in white or black." Teaching whites the wrongs of racial prejudice while stressing

African American equality could help to resolve the problem of racial caste and, by extension, slavery.[111]

The ideology of Christian domesticity required a dutiful wife to curate a peaceful home, but she need not be bound *to* the home; rather she could participate in social reform work such as the abolition of slavery and the realization of racial equality. Kellogg modeled this careful balance for his students through field trips to antislavery meetings. Elizabeth Everett, for instance, wrote home to her parents describing the "Anti-Slavery conference and prayer meeting" she attended in November 1839. She left believing in the efficacy of these meetings, which welcomed all, even proslavery advocates: "If a proper spirit is manifested they will I think tend to do away [with] prejudice and perhaps win the hearts of opposers."[112] Rosetta reported that during her travels to the seminary, she and her companions, which included Mary Addington, the Turpin sisters, and probably more young women, met Kellogg and his family in Utica and "attended the Anti-Slavery convention during the day."[113] Perhaps they attended the New York State Anti-Slavery Society meeting on September 16, 1840, in Utica. In any case, this antislavery work was part of their studies; it was not incidental, but ongoing.

No sooner had young African American women settled in at the seminary than Kellogg contemplated leaving to join Knox Manual Labor College in Galesburg, Illinois. In 1835 he served on a steering committee, along with George Washington Gale and a few other white activists, investigating the prospect of purchasing land in Indiana or Illinois to build a religious, antislavery community, including an educational institution. Not long after, the committee oversaw the purchase of over ten thousand acres of land in western Illinois, which became the site of Knox Manual Labor College.[114] Chartered by the Illinois legislature in 1837, Knox aimed to train young men as "evangelical and able" ministers and to prepare young women as "help-meets [to the aforementioned ministers] . . . and instructors and guides of the rising generations."[115] Kellogg was named a trustee of the college and acted as a fundraising agent before he considered taking up the presidency. Knox would soon become one of the few colleges in the United States to accept men and women, regardless of race.[116]

Kellogg's decision to leave his seminary fractured African American women's tenuous bid for advanced education. He advertised in the *New York Evangelist* that he was selling two separate parcels: the hundred-acre farm surrounded by mature trees and manicured gardens, as well as the seminary building and a number of adjacent buildings on thirty acres.[117] The 1840 U.S. census recorded only twenty-five students at the Young Ladies' Domestic Seminary at the time, suggesting that some students had already withdrawn. For the second term of the year, which began in May, four African American women remained: three ages ten through twenty-three—probably Serena deGrasse, Joanna Turpin, and Lucretia Turpin—and one older student, probably Rosetta Morrison. Ursula James may have withdrawn for the term.[118]

News about the closure of the Young Ladies' Domestic Seminary dashed the hopes of African American leaders. George T. Downing, an African American activist and caterer from New York who had been courting Serena, sent a letter to Kellogg encouraging him to continue his seminary. Kellogg shared the contents of this letter with the entire student body, and a version of it may have appeared in the *Emancipator* in December 1839. In the letter published in the *Emancipator* and signed "D," the author directly addresses the newspaper's editor, Joshua Leavitt, stating, "All of your endeavors to raise the colored man must ultimately be fruitless unless we have educated females, and the only institution to which we can look with hope for them is the Young Ladies' Domestic Seminary at Clinton, all other doors being barred against the colored female." If the seminary closed, an important pathway to racial uplift would be closed.[119]

Downing outlined two reasons that Kellogg should remain at the Young Ladies' Domestic Seminary. First, the seminary was one of a kind.[120] Indeed Downing lobbied for the establishment of similar institutions of higher education, which helped define and strengthen a multiracial democracy. Second, it taught the valuable lesson of racial equality. An editorialist writing in the *Christian Reflector* made a similar point by declaring the value of Kellogg's seminary "in wearing away unfounded prejudices, and [producing] pleasant, scriptural equality where moral worth and Christian consistency are standards of excellence and superiority."[121] The closure of the Young Ladies' Domestic Seminary would not only reduce African American women's educational opportunities but also mark a major setback in the struggle for black freedom.[122]

Ultimately Kellogg sold the seminary to a group of Free Will Baptists, who elected to expand the student body and move away from manual labor and Christian domesticity. Clinton Seminary, as it was sometimes called, remained committed to racial equality and moral character, but its coeducational turn enabled young men and women, no matter their race, to pursue advanced learning together.[123] John J. Butler, a well-educated white preacher from New England, ran the institution, while Elizabeth Everett, who later married Butler, operated the Female Department.[124] Advertisements for the seminary appeared in antislavery newspapers, including the *Liberator* and *National Anti-Slavery Standard*. One editorialist commended Butler for continuing to democratize American higher education by offering "terms . . . so low that any one, male or female, desirous of obtaining an education, may, for a longer or shorter time, avail themselves of its privileges."[125] After attending Oneida Institute for one year, John V. deGrasse went to Clinton Seminary for two years before studying in France and later Maine.[126]

Before taking up the presidency at Knox Manual Labor College, Kellogg delivered a rousing and lengthy valedictory address celebrating the Christian community that he and his students built in Clinton. He began by reflecting upon his path from an itinerant minister to the proprietor of a successful female seminary, one that welcomed young women from various class and racial backgrounds. Discrimination, Kellogg asserted, whether against the poor or African Americans, was fundamentally unchristian. He hoped that he had imparted lifelong lessons to his students: to be useful and to denounce caste.[127]

Kellogg's farewell remarks urged young women to cling to the ideals of Christian faith and social reform. He recalled that he had never *asked* his all-white student body their opinion about admitting African American women; he simply regarded African American women as students and, in so doing, led by example, recording no moments of unkindness or discord. All of the women who graduated from his seminary, he declared, could boast a "well-cultivated mind and an improved heart" and a sense of how to be in the world.[128] He even reminded young women to *reduce* domestic tasks in order to devote more time to moral and mental improvement as well as social reform.

Emotions ran high as his words evoked, for some students, powerful memories about their teachers, as well as hopes for their own future. Speaking in imperatives, he directed his students, "Maintain a high regard for man, seek to ameliorate his condition and to improve his prospects. Especially cherish a lively regard for those who are suffering under the influence of oppression; seek to lighten their burdens—to soothe their anguish-stricken souls. Let the claims of the enslaved ever hold a high place in your hearts."[129] Even students who had transferred to other institutions praised his insights. For instance, Harriet Gates, a white student who had attended Kellogg's seminary before enrolling at nearby LeRoy Seminary, wrote, "Mr. Kellogg's valadictory [*sic*] [was] so good [and] practical. I shall keep it ever in remembrance."[130] An anonymous student mentioned, "[The great influence] of my dear teachers' counsels, instructions, and admonitions I feel still breathing over me." She now practiced their lessons in her own life: "[I exert] what little influence I have on the right side, as though it were felt by the whole world."[131]

Some of the young women seminary graduates looked back at their experience with feelings of nostalgia. Eliza D. Thomas, from Clinton, New York, apparently broke down in tears as she penned a letter to Elizabeth Everett: "How hard it is for me to part from you all with out any prospects of ever seeing you a gain in this world."[132] Clarissa M. Palmer must have kept up with her classmates' accomplishments because when she too wrote to Everett she celebrated the fact that her peers were "doing well for themselves as well as being useful to others." Palmer resided in Parish, New York, with her husband, a farmer. Yearning to continue her education, she asked Everett, "Do you think you would accept Mr. Palmer and myself as pupils at your Sem. next winter? We have thought some of attending. Mr. P would like to attend for the purpose of studying the languages."[133] We do not know whether the Palmers matriculated at the seminary, but Clarissa had heeded Kellogg's advice to continue her intellectual pursuits. Jennett Perkins Dickenson regarded her time at the seminary as a "precious precious privilege," one that enabled her to shed her identity as a "vain, and thoughtless girl." She reported to Everett that she had obtained a teaching position in Syracuse.[134] The content of these letters speaks to the powerful bonds these women forged at the seminary and their desire to ensure neither their friendships nor their learning would come to an end.

The strong emotional bonds cultivated between students and teachers existed even after the seminary closed. When Serena deGrasse left the seminary in April 1841, her beau, George T. Downing, picked her up. Upon arriving home, she got word that her twenty-seven-year-old brother, Isaiah, had passed away, a victim of yellow fever, in Jamaica, where he had been working as a missionary. Serena described to her former teacher, Elizabeth Everett, the sadness that blanketed their home: "The house and every thing around seemed desolate. Miss Everett I have lost a dear, dear brother." Serena's mother remained inconsolable. Serena lamented that she and her family did not even have the "real pleasure of seeing his grave." All that remained were memories and his personal effects. Isaiah was beloved by his family, friends, and community. His obituarist remembered him for "the zeal with which he filled the ministerial office—his fervid, impassioned eloquence."[135] In some ways Serena remembered her brother by writing about him to her teacher.

Fully embodying Christian faith was an ongoing effort for former students. Despite the deGrasse family's membership at St. Phillip's Episcopal Church, Isaiah's strong Christian convictions, and her own education at Kellogg's seminary, Serena's Christian conversion had not yet occurred. She recalled Everett's advice, which must have been religious in nature, because she apologized for not following it. She continued, "As such, I wish that I were a Christian. I have not experienced any change."[136] Though Christian instruction constituted a major part of the seminary curriculum, young women struggled with their faith. A year later, in May 1842, Serena wrote to Everett again about her recent marriage to Downing. She admitted that she still had not heeded her teacher's religious advice: "I am sorry to say that I have not become a Christian religious yet."[137] The very fact that she wrote about it twice demonstrates the impact of this ideology on her, especially in her new role as a wife and curator of her home.

Serena also exchanged letters with Mary E. Miles, who had moved to Philadelphia in 1841. Mary then returned to Massachusetts to attend the State Normal School in Lexington, which was under the leadership of Samuel J. May. In 1843 she graduated, an achievement that made her the first African American graduate from a public normal school. She taught at the Wilberforce School in Albany and the Cincinnati High School in Ohio while also participating in the abolition movement.[138] At an antislavery meeting in New York, she met Henry Bibb, a fugitive slave and abolitionist lecturer. They married in June 1848 in Dayton, Ohio, and settled in Detroit.[139] After the passage of the Fugitive Slave Law in 1850, the Bibbs moved to the village of Sandwich in Canada, where Mary operated her own private school while helping Henry run his newspaper, *Voice of the Fugitive*. Samuel J. May celebrated Mary for "devot[ing] herself, with great assiduity, to the instruction of the children of the fugitives."[140] Henry died at the age of thirty-nine in 1854. Mary continued operating her school, which she advertised in various antislavery newspapers, in an attempt to recruit African American students from the Northeast. Her school offered courses in common subjects such as arithmetic and grammar, but also contained some scientific study in physiology.[141] She later married Isaac N. Cary, and they settled in Windsor, Canada, before returning to Washington, D.C., where Mary passed away in 1881.[142]

Serena deGrasse, Joanna Turpin, Lucretia Turpin, Ursula James, Rosetta Morrison, and Mary Miles became lifelong friends. Rosetta and Ursula likely spent time with Serena, since she knew they were teaching in Brooklyn, New York, in the early 1840s. Serena noted that she saw Ursula "almost every day."[143] Joanna and Lucretia returned to New Rochelle but visited Serena at her home in New York in late summer 1841. Theodore S. Wright presided over the nuptials of Joanna and Edwin F. Howard, an African American barber and caterer from Boston, on February 22, 1844.[144] The Howards would become activists in the abolition movement and the campaign to desegregate Boston public schools in the 1850s. Nearly thirty years later, Serena and her husband, George, received an invitation from the Howards to celebrate their "silver wedding."[145]

In 1845 Lucretia married Thomas J. Bowers, an African American businessman and opera singer known as the "American Mario." For a while, the Bowers lived in Troy, New Yok, where Lucretia helped support the newspaper *Impartial Citizen* along with other African American women like Julia Ward Williams Garnet, a Canterbury Female Seminary alumna and the wife of Henry Highland Garnet. The Bowers later relocated to Philadelphia. In 1854 their daughter, Alice C., was born. She would go on to become a schoolteacher at the Friends' School for Colored Children in Philadelphia.[146] Alice's sudden death at the age of twenty-six crushed both Lucretia and Thomas. Three years after her death, Thomas published a sentimental poem, "To My Alice," in the *State Journal*.[147]

The presence of African American women at the Young Ladies' Domestic Seminary forced many white women students to bear witness to racial prejudice. Serena, Joanna, Lucretia, Ursula, and Mary corresponded with some of their white classmates over the years and even entertained them as visitors in their homes. Serena invited Elizabeth Everett to visit New York, especially if Everett were "found [fond] of variety."[148] It is not clear if she ever visited. Eliza D. Thomas did, though, and remarked, "The poor coulleard [sic] people find but few friends in these parts prejudice against color exists much stronger here than in Clinton."[149] Whether this comment reflected a conversation that Eliza had with her African American friends or was based on her own observations traveling throughout the Northeast, she nonetheless recognized that prejudice impacted the lives of African Americans. Moreover she appreciated how certain spaces—like a seminary—might become places of refuge.

The Young Ladies' Domestic Seminary was a pioneering institution of higher education, and the seven African American women who attended were pathbreakers who influenced many of their white female classmates. Positive social interactions allowed these women to nurture strong bonds and lasting friendships. The power of racially integrated institutions rested in their ability to educate all students while teaching white students, in particular, the importance of the twin pillars of racial equality and black freedom. These young Christian women proved that the fight against slavery and racism could be waged at the female seminary and similar educational institutions.

Hiram Kellogg sought to impart to his students the value of leading a useful life, denouncing inequality, and doing good in the world, all ideas that aligned with African American women's notion of purposeful womanhood.[150] Kellogg believed in the ideology of Christian domesticity, which often required women's passivity, but he endorsed women's activity in social reform, albeit confined to three areas: the missionary field, the classroom, and the home. Nevertheless African American women students at his seminary were purposeful, active, and educated; as wives and mothers they cultivated their own Christian homes, and as teachers they trained the rising generation in the values they learned at the Young Ladies' Domestic Seminary.

3 / Women Teachers in New York City

It was her last year at the Young Ladies' Domestic Seminary in Clinton, New York, and Rosetta Morrison was contemplating her future. She shared her thoughts with her "affectionate" friend, Francis Bliss Rowland, a young white woman from Windsor, Connecticut, whom she had met while a child servant in the Rowland family household in New Hampshire. The Free Will Baptists had agreed to take control of the Young Ladies' Domestic Seminary, and Rosetta had no plans to stay. She had to figure out the next step in her life. In a letter to Francis, she expressed optimism and uncertainty: "I do not know what will be come [*sic*] of me, but I trust I shall be taken care of."[1]

By April 1841, however, she had found her path: with help from her friend and classmate Ursula James, Rosetta opened a "select Primary School" for African American children in Brooklyn, New York.[2] Though the endeavor was a short-lived one—the school remained open for about eight months—Rosetta's experience reveals the existence of an emerging local network of African American women teacher-activists who worked alongside African American men. This supportive network enabled her to establish her school and enroll students; it also exposed her to key activist initiatives being pursued by teachers in the fight for equality and civil rights. Teachers such as Fanny Tompkins, Jane M. Vogelsang Forten, and Elizabeth Jennings, Jr., joined the abolition movement, supported black newspapers, and served in mutual aid and self-help organizations.

Despite this activism, the contributions of African American women remained overshadowed and undervalued by some male leaders. For instance, Alexander Crummell, an African American minister, concluded that in antebellum New York "the desire for learning was almost exclusively confined to colored *men*. There were a few young women in New York who thought of these higher things."[3] Crummell's remark appeared in a reprint of the collected writings of Maria W. Stewart, published in 1879. Perhaps in his desire to praise Stewart as an extraordinary African American woman—indeed the first American-born woman to speak in public on political issues, he dismissed the work of other, lesser-known educated African American women. Regardless, the continuous work of African American women teachers contradicted Crummell's shortsighted remark.

Quite a few African American women teachers in New York City funneled their ambition and activism into the field of education; some, like Rosetta, went so far as to build their own schools. That the schools were often short-lived does not detract from the women's commitment to education. For African American women, teaching constituted service to the race, or what I call race work.[4] Teachers shaped the community, tended to the intellectual and moral improvement of African American children and youth, and deepened their own knowledge.

Educational activism was ever present in Rosetta's life—as a student, a teacher, and then as a wife and mother. Her experiences later in life, however, demonstrate that her education could not shield her from personal hardships brought on by larger social, political, and legal forces. Though born free, Rosetta would be caught in the web of slavery, which tore her family apart.[5] Yet she taught her children the power of learning and the meaning of purpose; all four of her daughters went on to teach in New York City schools. Stories like Rosetta's reveal that teaching and mothering were two allied paths that afforded consciously chosen means of leading a purposeful life.

At the turn of the nineteenth century, the African American community in New York City was demographically diverse yet united by the will to realize self-definition and self-determination. Community leaders carved out an autonomous existence as the reality of legal freedom set in with the passage of the Gradual Emancipation Act of 1799, which emancipated enslaved children born after July 4, 1799. In 1800 the black population neared 6,000, with a little over half still enslaved.[6] By 1820 the black population stood at 10,886, with less than 1 percent enslaved. Religious institutions and organizations such as the Mother Zion African

Methodist Episcopal Church and the African Mutual Relief Society were founded. The historian Craig Steven Wilder argues that these distinctly African institutions were "communitarian and nationalistic."[7] As slavery faded, white racism and racial violence rose as a mechanism to curtail black civil rights and impede African American inclusion in civil society. African Americans strategized to overcome this opposition by mounting public protests and expanding educational opportunities.

In publications such as *Freedom's Journal* and in religious sermons, leaders argued that education could strengthen the moral and intellectual character of children, promote economic independence through the acquisition of skilled jobs, counter pernicious myths about black intellect, and aid African Americans in their claim for civil rights.[8] John Russwurm and Samuel Cornish used *Freedom's Journal* to tout "education [as] an object of the highest importance to the welfare of society."[9] Despite ever-growing white racism as well as the constraints on black life in the pre–Civil War era, African Americans remained optimistic about the great possibilities associated with education.

Likewise white leaders viewed schooling as a way to socialize children, especially as the rates of poverty and income disparity grew in New York City, along with an increase in immigration. With the church and some other social institutions in decline, the New York Common Council expanded charity schools through state funding. In 1805 the Free School Society, led by Thomas Eddy, a white Quaker philanthropist, established schools for poor children. In 1825 this private organization changed its name to the Public School Society and declared its intent to open up schools to all children and put an end to the appropriation of state funds to sectarian schools.[10] That same year, the Public School Society supported eleven schools and educated almost twenty thousand children. White children from working-class families dominated the schools run by the Public School Society; African American children, whether working class or elite, usually attended racially segregated schools.[11]

Some white philanthropists backed education because they believed it would improve African American life. For instance, the New York Manumission Society, an antislavery group founded by white men in 1785, opened the New York Free African School in 1787 to teach emancipated slaves to be "honest . . . quiet and orderly citizens" and to provide them with "knowledge of the means, whereby they may insure not only their happiness in the present, but in the world to come."[12] The school offered a basic English education, including reading, writing, arithmetic, geography, grammar, and moral improvement.[13] In its first year, the school enrolled forty-seven students, including girls and boys, ages five to fifteen, from working-class and middle-class backgrounds. As more African American parents wished to send their children to this school, plans were made to construct a new building and open more schools. By 1831 five African Free Schools had been established in New York City.[14] Although the elite white male leadership of the New York Manumission Society did not view African Americans as active agents in their own emancipation, the scholar Anna Mae Duane argues that African Free Schools became a "venue through which the marginalized [could] gain entry to the public sphere."[15]

More importantly, African American students themselves knew that their individual pursuit of schooling held the possibility for collective prosperity. In his valedictory speech in April 1822, fourteen-year-old Andrew R. Smith urged his classmates, "[Be] industrious and upright to make *respectable* members of society . . . and make such *use* of our learning as will prove a blessing to ourselves, and to the community."[16] Schooling was never a purely individual endeavor for African Americans; it had wider implications. *Freedom's Journal* even advertised on behalf of African Free Schools and promoted their agenda of teaching children to lead lives of "usefulness and respectability."[17] Both African American and white educational reformers constantly repeated these terms—industry, usefulness, and respectability—underscoring the nineteenth-century religious and educational discourse upon which schools were founded. These characteristics, it was promised, would lead to a life of enjoyment; for African Americans, the well-being of the community and the fight for civil rights depended on it.

African American male leaders made suffrage the dominant civil rights issue. Similar to other northern states such as Connecticut, most African Americans could not vote in New York because of status and property qualifications.[18] In 1821 New York State revised its constitution to grant suffrage to most white male citizens, while African American men had to own at least $250 in taxable property and meet strict residency requirements to be able to vote.[19] The African American male leaders Samuel Cornish, Philip A. Bell, Charles B. Ray, Theodore S. Wright, William P. Johnson, and Thomas Downing, among others, fought this discriminatory legislation by authoring petitions and writing missives.[20] These leaders were "groomed in a sociopolitical culture of manhood," as Craig Steven Wilder observes, and that might partly explain why the issue of suffrage predominated in New York.[21]

These leaders fused their activism on voting rights with the issue of education, arguing that schools taught African Americans the rights and

obligations associated with voting and citizenship. Hence the fight for universal male suffrage not only included petitioning and speechifying but also stressed the transformative power of schools. John Peterson, for instance, participated in organizational meetings on securing the franchise while also teaching African American youth. Peterson began teaching at African Free School No. 6 in 1832 and later became principal of Colored School No. 1. In 1841 he married Eliza Glasko, an alumna of the Canterbury Female Seminary.[22] Peterson, according to Walter B. Warren, a former student, taught him and his peers "uncompromising fearlessness, a love of truth . . . self-reliance and self-respect."[23] Peterson's colleague Prince Loveridge, a school agent and later a missionary to African American seamen, wrote in the *Colored American*, "Schools . . . will procure our enfranchisement."[24] Schooling could win other rights too, specifically the abolition of slavery and the elimination of racial prejudice.

As the scholar Carla Peterson has noted, however, the myopic focus on universal male suffrage "relegated [women] to the sidelines," no matter how inadvertently.[25] The struggle for suffrage was specifically, if implicitly, gendered that its exclusion of African American women was almost never named, let alone questioned. Nevertheless African American women themselves continued to carve out their own activist spaces, particularly in the field of education and community affairs. John Russwurm, the African American newspaper editor and abolitionist, confirmed that African American women had "engaged in the active duties of Societies" aimed at moral reform and charity.[26] No female organization received more praise in the black press than the African Dorcas Association, which benefited poor children at African Free Schools. *Freedom's Journal* urged men and women to actively support mutual aid societies.[27] Associational work coupled with personal ambition and a belief in community uplift likely inspired early African American women educators such as Maria M. deGrasse, Sarah Ennalls, Maria W. Stewart, and Fanny Tompkins.

Fanny Tompkins served her community as a career teacher in New York City schools. Though much about her early life and educational biography remain unknown, we do know that in 1833, as a twenty-three-year-old, she worked as an assistant teacher at African School No. 4.[28] A year later she was the only female teacher at African School No. 5 at 161 Duane Street, a position she held for two years before moving back to African School No. 4 in 1837.[29] There she taught nearly a hundred children per year. In September 1841 she took the helm of a private

African American seminary on Canal Street. Her advertisement for that school stressed the importance of teaching a diversity of subjects, from astronomy to history, in addition to "personal deportment and habits." By October 1841 thirty students had enrolled. Even though Charles B. Ray in the *Colored American* encouraged the community to support the seminary, it ultimately folded less than a year later, as did many private institutions in the nineteenth century.[30]

Fanny's career as a teacher continued nonetheless. Like many African American women teachers, she remained unmarried and wholly devoted to her educational work. In the 1840s she returned to public school teaching.[31] She taught at Colored School No. 1 and then Colored School No. 2, and, in the 1850s she supervised the Colored Evening School alongside John Peterson. The evening school welcomed women and men, boys and girls who worked during the day and attended arithmetic, reading, and writing classes in the evening.[32] Fanny also organized community events. In 1859, then the principal of the Female Department at Colored School No. 2, she hosted a benefit concert called "Oratorio of Joseph," led by her students, to support St. Philip's Episcopal Church.[33] Fanny's students included fourteen-year-old Harriet L. Vogelsang and sixteen-year-old Maria T. Vogelsang, the daughters of Peter Vogelsang Jr. and Theodosia deGrasse Vogelsang. In 1864 Fanny earned praise again for organizing an exhibition for Colored School No. 2 and preparing youth to deliver flawless recitations and beautiful music.[34] Upon her death on December 14, 1871, she had dedicated forty years of her life to teaching. Far from being anomalous, Fanny's career exemplified the experience of other African American women teachers.

Economic necessity and a desire for autonomy propelled some women into the teaching profession, while others were drawn to a culture of benevolence. Defined by scholars as a call to do good in the world, this culture of benevolence permeated American life, filling the pages of periodicals and novels and leading to the establishment of many charitable institutions. Education was seen as well-suited for women who could make the greatest impact, but the very few African American women who graduated from private schools and wished to pursue teaching careers lacked access to the same teaching networks enjoyed by white women. Indeed only a few African American women in the North entered the teaching profession in the pre–Civil War era, partly because of limited educational opportunities. White women, on the other hand, could take advantage of teaching recruitment networks at female seminaries like Emma Willard's Troy Female Seminary and Sarah Pierce's

Litchfield Female Academy. Hence white women came to dominate the teaching workforce during the nineteenth century, leading to what some scholars call the feminization of teaching.[35]

Geographical boundaries also encumbered prospective African American women teachers. While young, single white women traversed the United States to take teaching positions in the West and the South, young, single African American women worried about racial discrimination. On the northwestern frontier, the classroom, as Julie Roy Jeffrey argues, "presided over by a female teacher was offered as the means of civilizing the West." In the pre–Civil War era, the vast majority of these female teachers were white.[36] To teach in the South, a free black woman might need to obtain free papers to prove her status, lest she be classified as a slave. These papers, however, were difficult to obtain if one was born free, and such documentation proved meaningless anyway in the face of kidnapping. Rosetta Morrison completely ruled out a move to the South. "I cannot go where I have to get free papers, if I cannot live in free air, I do not wish to live at all," she declared. For free blacks, slavery was haunting and compromising. Rosetta wished to remain in the North, despite all of its flaws.[37]

With her job search focused in New York City, Rosetta probably relied on her classmates and her brother, Abraham J. Morrison, to tap into the network of African American activists who knew about teaching opportunities. Theodore S. Wright was one such person. When African Americans, both male and female, sought teaching positions, it was advantageous if one could mention the well-respected Wright, an alumnus of the first African Free School and a graduate of Princeton Theological Seminary.[38] Rosetta could have met Wright through Abraham, who was an activist in his own right. Or perhaps she met Wright when she traveled to the Young Ladies' Domestic Seminary in 1840 with the Turpin sisters, Wright's stepdaughters. Rosetta could not rely on the teaching networks of white women, but she could appeal to her own family connections and peer associations to realize her goals.

Rosetta's work as a teacher in the early 1840s was centered in Weeksville, Brooklyn, a burgeoning African American community. In 1835 Henry C. Thompson, an African American land investor, had bought thirty-two lots of land, which were later purchased by early Weeksville residents like James Weeks and his brother, Cesar; Samuel Anderson; and Francis P. Graham. Some of these early residents were born free, while others had been enslaved; some hailed from New York, while others came from Virginia and even the Caribbean; and some worked in skilled occupations or as professionals. Whatever their background, they all descended upon this area in eastern Brooklyn to form a community. The historian Judith Wellman argues that these early founders took an active role in social reform and, in doing so, "defined what was important to them—physical safety, education, economic self-sufficiency, and political determination."[39]

Strong religious and educational institutions, built by African American residents in Weeksville, boosted the community. The African Methodist Episcopal (AME) denomination spread throughout the North after Richard Allen, an African American minister, established the first AME Church in Philadelphia in 1816. Two years later a local group of African American worshippers, including Peter and Benjamin Croger, departed the biracial Sands Street Wesleyan Methodist Episcopal Church after repeated incidents of racism and incorporated the AME Church in Weeksville.[40] Like many African American churches in the antebellum era, Weeksville's AME Church served as both a house of worship and a meeting place for activists and reformers. For instance, Benjamin Croger and George Hogarth, a black AME deacon, among others, organized a temperance society.[41] Rosetta's school would thus be positioned in a building at the center of black institutional life in Weeksville.

In 1815 Peter Croger established a day and evening school for African American children at his home on James Street.[42] A year later Brooklyn common schools admitted African American students in the same schoolhouses as white children, but in separate classrooms. Primarily because of racial prejudice, African American students were eventually pushed out of these schools altogether. The African Woolman Benevolent Society, a mutual aid organization that supported widows and orphans, raised money to construct the Woolman Society Hall on Nassau Street; it would accommodate a school, later known as the Colored School of Brooklyn in Weeksville. In the 1830s George Hogarth taught there and also served as a trustee, along with Henry Brown and Sylvanus Smith.[43] At one school exhibition held at the AME Church on High Street in April 1836, thirty African American girls and boys, ranging in age from three to sixteen, read "dialogues, poems, and recitations . . . [and sung] hymns." For African American leaders, this exhibition demonstrated that African Americans "were [more] capable of receiving and retaining education than is generally accredited to them." Hogarth resigned from his teaching position in 1840 as he took on a larger role for the AME Church.[44]

Devoted teachers encouraged African American children and youth to be studious and diligent. Augustus Washington was one such teacher.

Hailing from Trenton, New Jersey, he taught at the Colored School of Brooklyn in the early 1840s. Washington received his early education at predominantly white schools; antislavery newspapers inspired him to deepen his study of history and literature; he then set his goal to "become a scholar, a teacher, and a useful man."[45] He ran a small school for African American children and then studied at Oneida Institute in New York before being recruited to teach at the Colored School of Brooklyn. During a school exhibition in August 1841, about forty children completed recitations in subjects ranging from geography to composition. An observer noted that "parents, who had never enjoyed the advantages of education, listen[ed] with delight and wonder to the attainment's [sic] of their own children."[46]

In late summer of 1841 Washington resigned his teaching position in order to advance his academic studies.[47] The three trustees of the Colored School of Brooklyn, George Hogarth, Henry Brown, and Sylvanus Smith, advertised in the Brooklyn Evening Star, seeking to hire a "competent colored male teacher." Perhaps recruiting an African American male teacher reflected a desire among leaders to retain men in the teaching profession, which was fast becoming dominated by women. Or maybe gendered beliefs about male leadership pushed the trustees to prefer a male teacher; the previous four teachers had been male. Possibly the local city government encouraged such a hire. The advertisement noted that applicants had to have the proper qualifications to "pass their inspections before the City Public School Inspectors."[48]

While some historians argue that the Colored School of Brooklyn was either independent or completely under African American control, the local city government had some influence prior to 1845, especially in terms of hiring qualified teachers. Though this school would not join the Brooklyn public school system until 1845, it still abided by Brooklyn common school laws. An 1835 law allowed a "Common Council . . . to appoint . . . in each district . . . three trustees of common schools, and for the whole city three inspectors and three commissioners of such schools."[49] Hence the Colored School of Brooklyn had three trustees who appear to have managed day-to-day affairs, while the public school inspectors oversaw funding and had input on administrative decisions such as hiring. In 1829, $1,100 was set aside for Brooklyn public schools, some of which the Colored School of Brooklyn received.[50] This arrangement may be an early example of shared governance of public schools.[51]

On April 26, 1841, Rosetta Morrison opened the Primary Select School of Brooklyn, apparently outside of the purview of common school laws and the local city government. It was located in the basement of the AME Church on High Street, so Weeksville now boasted two schools. Many of Weeksville's early residents were illiterate, but they were eager to secure educational opportunities for their children.[52] Quite a few students must have filed into Rosetta's classroom because she eventually contacted her friend and former classmate, Ursula James, to come and teach with her. By November 1841 upwards of seventy students were in attendance.[53] Rosetta's school represented what African American leaders and community members in Weeksville longed for: to champion the value of education and to express self-determination through their own institutions.[54]

Rosetta's decision to open a school for African American children displayed considerable ambition. The process by which she established the school must have been daunting, even given her references from African American male leaders. First, she had to secure a comfortable space to accommodate forty or fifty children, who would attend regularly. Then she had to recruit these children and hire an assistant teacher. Rosetta did that and more.[55] She visited Brooklyn-area African American families with children who might enroll at her school. Her educational background must have appealed to them, not simply because she had studied at a prestigious female seminary but also because doing so demonstrated her drive, hard work, and Christian piety, the same qualities that she promised to instill in their children.

Rosetta operated her school as a select school, most likely because the Colored School of Brooklyn already existed. A primary select school targeted younger students, while an ordinary select school might educate children as old as seventeen. A select school also charged tuition, usually in the range of $1 to $2 per quarter; for this reason it often appealed to slightly more well-to-do families. Sometimes it offered a more advanced curriculum. For instance, Timothy Read ran a select school for African American children and youth in New Haven, Connecticut, endorsed by Amos G. Beman, an African American minister. With tuition at 25 cents per week, the school offered a common English education, including subjects such as reading, spelling, grammar, geography, and arithmetic.[56] Rosetta's school offered the same subjects, though no mention was made about tuition in the advertisement.[57]

Private or tuition-based schools constituted an integral part of African American education in urban areas such as New York City. Of course, these institutions faced a continual struggle for funding. A few, though, managed to remain open, such as the New York Select Academy, run by

John Brown, and the St. Mark's School in Jamaica, Long Island, under the leadership of Samuel V. Berry, a New Jersey–born African American clergyman. Berry received his education at the Episcopal Theological Seminary before being ordained.[58] An unnamed benefactor donated money to the school, which opened in 1839 with courses in reading, writing, geography, and moral philosophy, among other subjects, and Berry promised, "Special attention will be paid to the moral and religious [Episcopalian] culture of the children."[59] Before his death, Isaiah deGrasse, brother of Theodosia and Serena, taught advanced science courses there. In 1841 St. Mark's became a boarding school for African American children, with male and female departments.[60] Tuition and room and board cost $18 per quarter, no small sum at the time. For context, African Americans looking to rent a room in New York City might pay $12 to $15 per quarter.[61] Private institutions were thus an option primarily for middle-class and wealthy African American families, and Rosetta could count on that.

An advertisement (Figure 3.1) for the Primary Select School of Brooklyn ran in the Colored American five times, from April to June 1841. The advertisement, which Rosetta likely wrote, mentioned that, in addition to offering a standard English curriculum, "particular attention [would] be paid to the morals and manners of the pupils intrusted [sic] to her care."[62] It was common for select school advertisements to make such promises. In 1833 a Miss Wilson taught at the select school for African American children at 33 Liberty Street in New York City, which advertised, "Every advantage may be expected which can result from an exact course of instruction and strict discipline."[63] Even for white children, both intellectual and moral improvement were central. When William Poe established a select school in Storrs, Ohio, he made sure to add, "Very special attention will be given to the moral and religious, as also to the intellectual culture of pupils."[64]

In November 1841 the Primary Select School of Brooklyn held an exhibition showcasing African American children as learners and thinkers. Between sixty and seventy students demonstrated their proficiency in reading, spelling, arithmetic and geography. An observer writing for the Colored American noted, "I was struck to witness the capacity of the infantile mind for the reception of knowledge in a short period, when under faithful tutelage." The audience apparently expressed gratitude upon seeing this great display of black intellectual achievement. Two African American clergymen addressed the exhibition audience, commending the children while also encouraging the public to continue to patronize the school.[65]

NOTICE.

MISS ROSETTA MORRISON will open a select Primary School for colored children, on Monday, 26th April, in the basement room of the Methodist Episcopal Church in High street, Brooklyn.

In connection with the branches usually taught in primary schools, particular attention will be paid to the morals and manners of the pupils intrusted to her care. Reference may be had of

Rev. T. S. Wright, No 1 White st., N. Y.
Rev. Charles B. Ray, Editor of Col. Am.
Mr. Wm. P. Johnson, 69 Leonard st.

FIGURE 3.1. Rosetta Morrison's Primary Select School of Brooklyn advertisement appeared in the *Colored American* newspaper on April 24, 1841. Courtesy of Gale Cengage Learning.

This school exhibition demonstrated that Rosetta and Ursula were purposeful women and masterful teachers. The same observer noted that the school was "entirely the result of female enterprize [*sic*] and effort [as] . . . Rosetta Morrison entered this field, a stranger, singlehanded, and alone, with an ardent desire of *usefulness* to her people." Could this observer have been Theodore S. Wright? He knew of Rosetta's "enterprising" personality and had helped her educational vision come to fruition. The remark about usefulness, or what I call purposefulness, is perhaps most revealing. The idea of purposefulness was evident in Rosetta's life, but it also circulated as a major tenet at her alma mater, the Young Ladies' Domestic Seminary, an institution that Wright knew very well thanks to his stepdaughters' enrollment there. In any case, George Hogarth attended the exhibition and "congratulated the ladies on the success of their enterprize [*sic*], and urg[ed] them to a continuance of their good work."[66] Rosetta and Ursula later welcomed other visitors to the school, one of whom called it a "very excellent private Seminary."[67]

Word of the success of Rosetta's school traveled around the community, eventually reaching the ears of her former classmate and friend Serena deGrasse. When Eliza D. Thomas, a white classmate at the Young Ladies' Domestic Seminary, visited Serena in New York City, she met Theodore S. Wright. Eliza recalled, "Mr. Wright informed me that Rosetta Morison [*sic*] has a very good school and is accomplishing a great deal of good."[68]

Serena later shared that news with her former teacher, Elizabeth Everett, but Elizabeth learned more from another former student, Maryette Barker from Madison, New York.[69] Maryette wrote that she "received a paper from Rosetta containing an interesting account of an exhibition of her school which ha[d] been held in Brooklyn."[70] If Rosetta's advertisements in the Colored American were not proof enough that she read and probably subscribed to this newspaper, Maryette's letter confirmed it. Clearly, Rosetta took pride in her achievements and wanted to share that with former classmates. With the Colored American in hand, Maryette read about Rosetta's school and perhaps perused the newspaper's headlines about local black convention meetings, the efficacy of petitioning, and the fight for the abolition of slavery.

Rosetta's purposefulness and apparent success triggered in Maryette feelings of inadequacy. Maryette did express genuine happiness for Rosetta: "I know not when I have heard any thing that has given me so much joy as to hear that her school is flourishing. I know she will be happy while she is doing so much good." As a teacher, Rosetta fulfilled the tenets of Christian domesticity that both she and Maryette had been taught. Maryette, however, had not yet figured out how to embody purposefulness in her life. She confessed to Elizabeth Everett, "When I hear that so many of the dear Seminary girls are engaged in teaching, or in doing good some other way, I feel reproved for my own useless life." It was no easy feat in the early nineteenth century for young women, white or African American, to chart their paths in life. Rosetta and Ursula, though, had found their purpose as teachers doing race work.[71]

To some historians, black schools that stressed both intellectual and moral culture, like the Primary Select School of Brooklyn, represented a larger discourse of respectability advocated by elite African American leaders and forced upon the black poor and working class.[72] But as the historian Erica Ball argues, respectability was but one "part of a larger process of self-transformation, an opportunity to become something better in the eyes of one's family, one's peers, and one's God."[73] In other words, teaching morality and conduct was not simply about social acceptance and belonging for African Americans, but also how to be purposeful in the world. As teachers, women like Rosetta and Ursula worked with children and youth to counter racist myths that dehumanized African Americans. They showed these children the importance of self-respect, persistence, industry, and community activism and, in doing so, claimed an activist space for themselves in the field of education.

The Primary Select School of Brooklyn closed its doors in December 1841. Why, especially if it had been flourishing and Rosetta herself derived purpose from teaching? The answer is that on December 8, 1841, Rosetta Morrison married Isaac Wright. Her eight-month teaching career was relatively short, just like that of many young women teachers during the pre–Civil War era. For instance, in 1845 the average teaching career of a female teacher in Massachusetts was 2.6 years; twelve years later the average in Wisconsin was 1.5 years.[74] Perhaps Rosetta no longer wanted to teach but sought to pursue other interests or thought teaching incompatible with married life or felt compelled to leave the teaching profession upon getting married. While prevailing social conventions, which were admittedly local, held that women teachers should be unmarried, most school boards had not placed legal restrictions on married women in the profession.[75]

Ursula James too appears to have relinquished her teaching career. In May 1842 Serena deGrasse Downing recounted that she saw Ursula almost daily, but that changed when Ursula planned to leave the following month for a place "so far away."[76] Perhaps Ursula had realized her goal to follow her brother into the missionary field in Africa. Wherever she went, she did not stay long; she was in Princeton, New Jersey, on May 25, 1843, to marry Samuel Johnson in a ceremony presided over by Theodore S. Wright.[77] Born in Long Island, Samuel was an African American porter and community leader. The couple had four children in the next six years, two of whom died in infancy.[78] Ursula passed away in December 1850 at thirty-one.

Before 1860 some African American women in New York City public schools continued teaching after they married.[79] Jane M. Vogelsang Forten and Elizabeth Jennings Jr. stand out as prime examples. Jane was a well-educated woman from New York City. The Vogelsang family enjoyed a fairly high social status as leading activists and founding members of African American institutions in New York. Peter Vogelsang Sr. hailed from St. Croix and worked as a businessman in the shipping industry; his wife, Maria Miller Vogelsang, was a Manhattan native and homemaker.[80] Jane's siblings included Peter Jr., a shipping clerk and abolitionist who married Theodosia deGrasse, of the prominent deGrasse family from New York City in 1840; Eliza, who married William H. Topp, a skilled African American tailor and abolitionist from Albany, New York, in 1842; and Thomas, a merchant sailor who married Rebecca Bishop, whose father, William, was from one of the twelve richest families in Annapolis, Maryland.[81] On January 13, 1839, Jane married

James Forten Jr., son of Charlotte Vandine and James E. Forten Sr., both notable abolitionists and members of Philadelphia's black elite.[82] Jane and James had one son, James Vogelsang Forten.[83]

Dire financial constraints, brought on by large debts accrued by her husband, prompted Jane to secure a teaching position to support her family. In 1849 she taught in the female department of Colored School No. 2 under the management of the Society for the Promotion of Education among Colored Children, an African American organization incorporated by the state legislature in 1847. The trustees of this organization included such well-known African American leaders as James McCune Smith, Charles L. Reason, and Charles B. Ray, all of whom Jane could count as friends.[84] Frederick Douglass, the famed African American abolitionist, visited the school and described Jane as a "lady of large attainments and . . . well qualified for her station."[85] By 1850 thirty-one-year-old Jane did not reside in the same household as James Jr. and their son; she boarded instead with the Esteve family, a well-to-do African American family in New York City.[86] A year later she hired attorney Lucien Birdseye to represent her in her complaint against her husband, probably to dissolve their marriage. In early 1852 Jane was slated to earn a yearly salary of $325, but that same year, on July 16, she passed away at thirty-three from consumption, the same disease that had claimed her mother's life in December 1839.[87] Jane was buried in Albany, in a plot owned by her brother-in-law William H. Topp.[88]

Elizabeth Jennings Jr., Jane's colleague, also had strong ties to the African American community, which allowed her to retain her teaching position as a married woman. Elizabeth was born in 1827 in New York City to free black parents, Elizabeth Sr. and Thomas L. Jennings. In addition to his activist work, Thomas ran a boardinghouse and worked as a cloth merchant. The younger Elizabeth had at least three brothers, James, William, and Thomas Jr., and at least one sister, Matilda. Her parents were proponents of education, so the Jennings children attended New York City public schools. The younger Elizabeth then climbed the teaching ranks, first working with Fanny Tompkins at Colored School No. 2, run by the Public School Society. A year later, in 1849, she taught at the same primary schools as Jane M. Vogelsang Forten. These schools eventually fell under the jurisdiction of the New York City Board of Education.

In addition to her lifelong work as an educator, Elizabeth fought against racial discrimination. In July 1855 she tried to board a horse-drawn trolley car, but the conductor dragged her out of the car. She sued the Third Avenue Railway Company, operator of the car. Her father, who had founded the Legal Rights Association, an African American civil rights group, helped Elizabeth contract Chester Arthur, who would become U.S. president in 1881, to represent her. Elizabeth won her case and was awarded $225 in damages. African American activists celebrated this civil rights victory, but there was no respite when it came to racism. In 1857 Elizabeth and Helen Appo had graduated from the Colored Normal School, but both women were ejected from the graduation ceremony at the Academy of Music because of their race. Abolitionist newspapers condemned these actions, calling it a "gross insult to their scholarship and their womanhood."[89] Despite these racist incidents, Elizabeth proved herself to be a formidable teacher; Frederick Douglass called her "the most learned of our female teachers in the city of New York."[90]

Unlike the Brooklyn School Board, the New York City School Board did not compel women teachers to vacate their teaching position upon marriage, but the issue was still up for debate well into the twentieth century. In fact, in 1884 the New York City Board of Education sought to amend its by-laws to read, "Should a female teacher marry, her place shall thereupon become vacant."[91] After marrying Charles Graham in 1860, Elizabeth Jennings, Jr., continued teaching at Colored School No. 5 in New York City until her retirement. With a teaching career spanning some thirty-five years, she was a talented and well-respected woman from an activist family.[92] The experiences of Elizabeth Jennings, Jr., and Jane M. Vogelsang Forten demonstrate that communities sometimes defied prevailing conventions concerning married women teachers. Unlike Jane and Elizabeth, Rosetta did not come from a prominent elite family with deep connections to community leaders.

Rosetta faced financial challenges later in life largely because of the status of her husband, Isaac, a fugitive slave. Born around 1817 in Virginia, he claimed at first that he had been born free, but he later admitted that he had been enslaved at birth before escaping to Philadelphia and eventually settling in New York.[93] A runaway slave advertisement described him as "5 feet 10 or 11 inches high, dark complexion, well made, full face, speaks quick, and very correctly for a negro."[94] The observation about his command of the English language suggests that he was intelligent and learned. Whether he immediately shared with Rosetta that he had been enslaved at birth is not clear, but she must have known that he was technically a fugitive slave, as his story became a cause célèbre among abolitionists when he and two free blacks were kidnapped as adults while living in the North.

In November 1837 Isaac, Robert Garrison, and Stephen Dickerson were working aboard the steamer *Newcastle* in the port of New York, earning "eighteen dollars for the first month, and twenty dollars afterwards." Four months into a trading voyage to the South, Thomas Lewis, a thief and murderer on the run, took the helm of the steamer from an ill Captain J. Dayton Wilson and sold all three men to Alexander Botts, a slave dealer who confined them at Harper's Jail in New Orleans. Botts inquired about their status as free men and then commanded that they be beaten. Dickerson recalled the horror: "We were ordered into the prison yard, stripped, and one after the other tied to a ladder, laying on the ground with our faces down, and each received thirty-five lashes on the bare skin, with what they called a bull whip. He then told us that if we ever mentioned the steamboat New Castle, or the name of Captain Wilson, or New York, that we should have as much more." Botts sold the three men to auctioneer Jonathan Rudesel, who in turn sold them to slaveholders. What began as an opportunity for gainful employment on the waterfront for these African American men turned into the nightmare of kidnapping and enslavement in the South.[95]

Isaac's sensational story of kidnapping captivated antislavery activists who argued that slavery encroached upon the liberties and rights of all Northerners. In 1839 a white abolitionist named Theodore Dwight Weld published the book *American Slavery as It Is*, which contained firsthand accounts of the brutality of slavery. Weld cited the Wright case to make the point that "the slave states afford[ed] no protection to the liberty of colored persons, even after those persons bec[ame] legally free."[96] Hundreds of cases of "man-stealing," a term that abolitionists used to refer to the kidnapping of African American women, men, and children, were recorded in pre–Civil War America. Pure greed motivated kidnappers, and the denial of African American civil rights enabled many kidnappers to avoid prosecution and punishment for their crimes.[97] Abolitionists such as John Russwurm proposed establishing a vigilance committee or "Protecting Society, of Philadelphia for the preventing of kidnapping."[98] Vigilance committees were organized throughout the 1830s to help victims like Isaac Wright win back their freedom.

The work of the African American abolitionist David Ruggles kept Wright's case at the forefront of the African American and antislavery press. Ruggles was secretary of the Committee of Vigilance, a New York–based organization founded in 1835.[99] Part of the charge of the committee was "converting things into men, and providing them an asylum, and paying also for legal advice and counsel."[100] Upon learning of the capture of the three men from Stephen Dickerson's father, who had received a letter from Stephen describing their ordeal, Ruggles began gathering evidence against Wilson, whom Ruggles accused of playing a direct role in the capture and enslavement of Isaac, Stephen, and Robert.[101] Wilson was arrested in New York City for "enveighling [sic] and selling as slaves, free citizens of the United States."[102] After a few months, however, the charges against Wilson were dismissed. Undeterred, Ruggles pursued Thomas Lewis, who was later arrested and jailed for his many crimes, but Isaac, Stephen, and Robert were still enslaved.

The Committee of Vigilance hatched a rescue plan whereby Joshua Coffin would play a crucial role in bringing Isaac back to the North. Coffin, a native of Newbury, Massachusetts, had graduated from Dartmouth College in 1817 and embarked upon a teaching career in Massachusetts, New Hampshire, and later Pennsylvania, where he opened a school for African American children.[103] He risked his life to help self-emancipated slaves. In 1838 he arrived in Memphis, Tennessee, and walked to nearby Raleigh to meet Hinson Gift, who now owned Isaac. Gift had agreed to free Isaac upon the presentation of free papers. But Gift, a gambler, had lost a large sum of money and sold Isaac to Jonathan Simpson to settle the debt. Coffin quickly formulated an alternate rescue plan. He paid another slave, Dudley, to bring Isaac to the woods to meet him. Coffin then instructed Isaac, "As soon as the boat which you now hear coming stops at the landing, go straight on board and take your place among the deck passengers, and I will go to the captain and agree for our passage." The plan worked. Coffin and Isaac traveled back to Philadelphia in late December 1838 on the *Brazils*.[104]

Isaac Wright was no longer subject to the whims of slaveholders, but he still risked recapture and punishment, not to mention possible harm to his family. The *Colored American* ran an article with the headline "Isaac Wright Free!," though the description was not quite accurate.[105] Coffin confessed that he took Isaac "away from Memphis without the consent or knowledge of any human being in Memphis or Raleigh," so Isaac could not claim free status. The free papers that Coffin had allegedly secured on Isaac's behalf were not presented to Jonathan Simpson, nor did Coffin pay to purchase Isaac's freedom. Under North Carolina law, Isaac still belonged to Simpson. But that did not dull this abolitionist victory. Coffin described Isaac as "a fine fellow" and said, "His gratitude and joy on being delivered is unbounded." Stephen Dickerson pursued a legal route to win his freedom, but Robert Garrison likely remained enslaved. Though Isaac felt "unbounded," he was effectively a fugitive slave twice over in the nineteenth-century world of American slavery.[106]

After returning to New York City, Isaac attended antislavery meetings, where he lectured on the terrible violence of slavery and its devastating impact on African American life in the North and South. One listener wrote, "We had never heard a speaker tell his own history with such simplicity and propriety of manner; and as for the narrative itself, the intense interest with which it was heard till after ten o'clock, was the best evidence of its thrilling power."[107] As a member of the Committee of Vigilance, Isaac donated small sums of money to the organization in the 1840s.[108] The *National Anti-Slavery Standard* reported that he was "industriously working for L. H. Parker and Co., furniture dealers, where he makes a good use of his freedom."[109] This furniture company specialized in making closets, card tables, and chairs, among other items, so Isaac may have been engaged in skilled labor.[110]

In the early years of their marriage, Isaac and Rosetta lived somewhere in the state of New York before returning to New York City in 1847.[111] Their first child, a daughter named Mary Emma, was born in November 1843. Rosetta bore six more children: Isaac Jr., Anna, Letitia, Rosetta Jr., Alice, and Grace. In New York City, Isaac worked as a carman transporting goods, an occupation that previously excluded African Americans. The historian Graham Hodges estimates that eight thousand carmen worked in the city by 1855 and that most carmen worked for companies, while African Americans "tended to work as single entrepreneurs."[112]

Even though she gave up teaching, Rosetta may have participated in antislavery activities in New York City alongside Elizabeth Jennings Jr. and Fanny Tompkins. As a student at the Young Ladies' Domestic Seminary, Rosetta and the Turpin sisters, and probably Serena deGrasse too, had attended antislavery meetings. A year after she left the seminary, Serena attended the ninth anniversary of the American Anti-Slavery Society meeting in May 1842 held at Broadway Tabernacle in New York City.[113] In the early 1850s Serena and her sister Maria, Fanny Tompkins, Jane M. Vogelsang Forten, Maria W. Stewart, and Elizabeth Jennings Jr., among others, established the North Star Fair Association to raise money on behalf of Frederick Douglass's newspaper, *North Star*.[114] Their goal was to increase the newspaper's circulation to other regions in the United States as a way to support "their oppressed race . . . and plead for their redress."[115]

African American women's activism in the abolition movement took on renewed importance as northern black communities marshaled a robust response to the passage of the Fugitive Slave Act in 1850.[116] The Compromise of 1850, which aimed to quell tension between the slaveholding South and non-slaveholding North over territory acquired during the Mexican-American War, consisted of five statutes. The most controversial, the Fugitive Slave Act, compelled federal authorities, state officials, and private citizens to assist in returning fugitive slaves to their enslavers.[117] Anyone who failed to comply risked being fined up to $1,000 and imprisoned for six months.[118] The historian Manisha Sinha characterizes the black response to this law as "radical."[119] Leaders promised to resist by practicing self-defense, aiding fugitive slaves, and authoring appeals condemning the law. The North Star Fair Association, for instance, organized a fair in February 1851 to benefit the Committee of Thirteen, which provided legal support to those who were fugitive slaves or were accused of being so. Fanny Tompkins, secretary of the association, reported that the fair received great "public patronage" and raised nearly $300.[120] Such organizing certainly saved some free blacks and fugitive slaves from the grip of southern slavery.

The specter of reenslavement probably never faded from view for Isaac or Rosetta. How could it, with new cases of kidnapping and recapture emerging throughout the North, including the arrest of James Hamlet in New York City in September 1850 and the rendition of Shadrach Minkins in February 1851, among others?[121] Isaac remained fearful that he too might be reenslaved, so he sought help from Nathaniel Gray, a white missionary and a mechanic by trade.[122] Hubert Bancroft, Gray's biographer, noted that Gray helped "several slaves fleeing from bondage," including Isaac.[123] Bancroft reported that in 1850 Isaac fled to California with Gray aboard the *Sarah Sands*, but that is doubtful. First, passenger records did not list Isaac Wright, although an N. Gray was listed. Second, the captain of the *Sarah Sands* was none other than J. Dayton Wilson! An anxious Isaac, burdened with the status of fugitive slave, would surely have been unlikely to board a ship captained by one of the men who may have had a role in kidnapping him the first time. More likely, Isaac fled, at first, with his family in tow just as the Fugitive Slave Act was enacted. For instance, neither Isaac nor Rosetta were listed in the New York City directories for 1850–51 or 1851–52. Sometime in 1852 Isaac returned to New York City and resumed work as a carman. By the mid-1850s he had departed New York City to take up a seafaring life, traveling from California to Hawaii and then Australia and living apart from his wife and children for upwards of three years.[124]

Rosetta and Isaac had to consider the safety and security of their family, especially their children, since the Fugitive Slave Act made it illegal for any person to aid or harbor a fugitive slave. The Wright family thus moved often, usually without Isaac. The birth of daughter Alice in 1855 offers the best estimate of the time of the family's arrival in Maine, and, through burial records we can surmise that Rosetta and her children resided in southern Maine. Isaac Jr. died on April 13, 1856, at age eleven and was buried at Riverside Cemetery in Springvale, York County, Maine. The African American population in the Pine Tree State remained quite small throughout the nineteenth century, but Springvale was about forty miles from Portland, so Rosetta and her children may have lived there. Isaac would soon reunite with his family after Nathaniel Gray gave him money to travel to Maine.

Rosetta cared deeply about her children's education, for she returned to New York City in 1857 so that her children could attend the public schools there.[125] Another daughter, Grace, was born in 1857, which means Isaac lived with the family at least for a few months. Alice and her siblings were part of the 44 percent of African American children between the ages of five and sixteen who attended school, a rate on par with that of white children.[126] In December 1857 Rosetta joined the Broadway Tabernacle Church, which was reorganized as a Congregational church in 1840 by David Hale. When she attended religious services there, she heard Reverend Joseph Parrish Thompson, a white Yale College graduate and abolitionist, preaching about God's love, antislavery principles, and women's suffrage. Isaac's name did not appear on the church membership list, but their children likely attended services and perhaps even the Sunday school linked to the church.

In 1860 the sociopolitical climate of the United States worsened as sectional conflict over slavery intensified. In the U.S. presidential election that year, Republican Abraham Lincoln bested Stephen A. Douglas, John C. Breckenridge, and John Bell. Though Lincoln opposed slavery on moral grounds, he had no plans to abolish it. As a colonizationist, he ran on a platform calling for the containment of the expansion of slavery until it reached extinction. Nor did Lincoln believe in racial equality. During the Douglas-Lincoln debates in 1858, Lincoln stated matter-of-factly, "I will say then that I am not, nor ever have been, in favor of bringing about in any way the social and political equality of the white and black races."[127] A month after his victory in December 1860, South Carolina seceded from the Union, and within two months six more southern states followed suit. These political challenges, coupled with the continuation of American slavery, brought great uncertainty to fugitive slaves, possibly even more than existed before. Right around Lincoln's election and the secession of South Carolina at the end of 1860, Isaac probably fled—again. At that point, all contact between Rosetta and Isaac had apparently ceased.[128]

Despite Rosetta's fantastic education at a prestigious female seminary and her connection to the New York City teaching network, she probably did not return to teaching. *Trow's New York City Directory* for 1860–61 listed Rosetta M. Wright, but not Isaac, as in previous entries.[129] As head of her household, Rosetta relied on help from family and friends. (According to census records, nine-year-old Rosetta Jr., lived with her uncle Abraham in New Milford, Connecticut, in 1860.) With Isaac gone, Rosetta was effectively a widow whose husband left behind no estate. Legally still a married woman, she now took on a new role as the sole breadwinner, working as a laundress. In antebellum New York City, many African American women, whether married or unmarried, had to take over the economic leadership of their family, as Rosetta did, by entering the labor market. African American women in nineteenth-century New York City often worked in low-paying occupations, as servants, laundresses, and cooks.[130] A laundress earned low wages but, according to the historian Julie Winch, "it was work [a woman] could do at home while [she] cared for [her] children."[131] For Rosetta, this line of work enabled her to maintain some degree of autonomy without worrying about upsetting social conventions of womanhood or defying patriarchal versions of a domestic ideal.

More importantly, though, Rosetta's work as a laundress helped her family survive financially. This was not a passing occupation undertaken in the short term due to financial necessity; a resilient and resourceful Rosetta toiled as a laundress for nearly ten years.[132] The 1870 *New York City Directory* lists her as a widow living with her children: twenty-three-year-old Anna, twenty-two-year-old Letitia, nineteen-year-old Rosetta Jr., and fifteen-year-old Alice. In the 1870 U.S. Federal census, Rosetta's occupation was listed as "keeping house." By 1872 the Wright children had accepted their father's apparent death; that year Letitia opened an account at the U.S. Freedman's Bank wherein she noted her father as "Isaac—dead."[133]

Just as Rosetta found her path after leaving the Young Ladies' Domestic Seminary, so too did she make a way for herself and her family by instilling in her children a love for learning. She stressed the value of education despite the fact that the reality of her situation did not lead to socioeconomic mobility. Her own situation, working as a laundress, betrayed the limited employment opportunities available even for educated African American women. By 1868 daughter Letitia D. Wright had been teaching in the primary department at Colored Grammar School No. 3 on West 41st Street until her illness and eventual death in August 1878. Her mother actually received the remainder of her salary, from August 19 to September 1, 1878, which totaled $22.58.[134] The younger Rosetta taught in Brooklyn and was part of a generation of great teachers who worked with Sarah J. Smith Tompkins, the first African American female principal in the New York City public school system.[135] The Wrights' eldest daughter, Anna, taught school too before marrying Henry H. Williams and relocating to Albany; they had three children: Arthur, Gertrude, and Letitia. By 1880 Anna had passed away and Rosetta was raising her grandchildren, along with help from daughter Alice.

Alice would go on to make teaching a lifelong endeavor, devoting thirty-three years to the profession. She received her schooling at Colored Grammar School No. 3, under the guidance and leadership of Charles Reason, an eminent African American educator. Born in 1818, Reason began teaching in New York City in the 1830s, before taking up a position as a professor of mathematics at New York Central College in 1849. Three years later he served as principal of the Institute for Colored Youth in Philadelphia, then returned to New York City, where he taught in black public schools for thirty years. One of his former students, Maritcha Lyons, recalled that Reason taught his students "how to study . . . [and] to those mentally alert, aspiring, and diligent he disclosed vistas of interest."[136] At Colored Grammar School No. 3, Alice was one of two hundred students. In a June 1869 commemoration of the new building that now housed the school, students performed "recitations, dialogues, songs and choruses," and Alice herself gave a speech entitled "Our Savings Bank." As visitors such as Charles B. Ray toured the building, they spied a neat space with student drawings adorning the walls. Passionate educators like Reason fought to ensure that black public schools thrived for the coming generations.[137]

African American women teachers like Mary E. Eato also ensured that black public schools thrived. Born in 1844 in New York City to Timothy and Sarah Jane Eato, Mary was a star student at Colored Grammar School No. 3, to which she returned as an assistant teacher. In addition to her teaching duties, she joined St. Mark's Church, which had been established in 1871, and she taught at the Sabbath school there. Maritcha Lyons remembered that Mary Eato's "exalted model of a cultured, christian woman lies enshrined in the hearts of those privileged to know her; a lasting memorial for imitation, emulation and aspiration."[138] African American women such as Frances Reynolds Keyser and Adena C. E. Minott studied with

Eato and went on to become community leaders themselves. In 1891 Eato earned a master's degree in pedagogy; she taught African American children in New York City public schools for forty-four years before her death in 1915.[139] African American women teachers like Eato espoused purposefulness and modeled Christian womanhood.

Perhaps inspired by her mother, her sisters, and her African American teachers, Alice Wright embarked upon a teaching career in 1874 in the primary department at Colored Grammar School No. 3. A year earlier, ten African American women, including Alice, had passed the competitive entrance exam to earn admission into the Normal College of the City of New York (now called Hunter College).[140] The Colored Normal School, which opened in the 1850s, had closed in 1874 due to low student attendance. The Normal College of the City of New York, a tuition-free public institution, aimed to provide teacher training opportunities for young women, regardless of race or religion. Linda Perkins has argued that the college was "one of the most significant institutions in the higher education of African-American women."[141] Despite her admission into the college, Alice did not enroll in the 1870s. She retook the entrance exam in June 1890, enrolled the following year, and graduated with a Bachelor of Arts degree from the Academic Department in 1895, becoming "one of the first colored graduates of the Normal City College."[142] Though Rosetta likely never returned to formal teaching, she saw the network of African American women teachers thrive through her own daughters' achievements.

Isaac too would have been proud; perhaps he even congratulated Alice on having achieved so much, for the two could have met in 1885. That year, the *San Francisco Post* featured an interview with sixty-eight-year-old Isaac, who had "iron gray hair and side whiskers and mustache, frizzled and curly, and black and gray."[143] He had not died after all. Nathaniel Gray located him and provided him with funds to travel back to New York City after a twenty-five-year absence from his family.[144] Many years earlier, Isaac's friend Stephen Dickerson had recounted that he thought often of his home when he had been kidnapped and enslaved. Isaac too no doubt thought of his home and family, but he did not go back immediately, and not after the Emancipation Proclamation was issued by Lincoln in 1863, not after the end of the Civil War in 1865, not after the passage of the Thirteenth Amendment to the U.S. Constitution that abolished slavery in 1865, not after the Fourteenth Amendment that granted citizenship to African Americans in 1868, and not after the Fifteenth Amendment that granted African American men voting rights in 1870. Underlying this experience of African American familial separation during and after slavery was a near-debilitating fear of recapture, no matter the law of the land. In Isaac's case, fear and anxiety prolonged familial separation, but in other cases these emotions foreclosed any possibility of reunification.[145]

We do not know whether it was by ship or train, but on February 11, 1885, Isaac began his journey from San Francisco to New York City. Whether he actually arrived in New York City is unknown. If he reached Rosetta's home, it is difficult to imagine how she and Alice reacted.[146] Were they shocked, angry, relieved, or some combination of those and other emotions? That is also unknown, but it is perhaps telling that Rosetta's status as a widow never changed in the *New York City Directory*.[147] She continued to live with her daughter Alice until, on May 28, 1896, she died from chronic interstitial nephritis and senile gangrene.[148] She was buried at Woodlawn Cemetery in New York City.

Rosetta's early educational work reveals that a network of educator-activists emerged in early nineteenth-century New York City. These educators believed in the power of the schoolhouse and the efficacy of teaching to win voting rights, stop prejudice, abolish slavery, and achieve civic inclusion. Though African American women lacked access to the same teaching recruitment networks that benefited white women, they still joined the teaching profession. No matter the duration of their career, these educators regarded teaching as purposeful work that strengthened the African American community. Rosetta Morrison Wright retreated from the teaching profession after her marriage, then settled into life as a wife and mother, as did her friend and assistant teacher Ursula James. The impact of slavery, however, devastated the Wright family, even after slavery itself was abolished, and likely interfered with any possibility that Rosetta may have had of a return to teaching.

Still, Rosetta's actions show that she, like other African American women, maintained a lifelong commitment to the notion of purposeful womanhood. Though only briefly involved in this network of educator-activists, Rosetta eventually brought her own daughters into it, especially Alice. Alice's obituary noted that she "was the consistent Christian, a friend to the friendless, a help to the helpless and a mother to the motherless."[149] She too led a purposeful life and exemplified the women described by Hallie Q. Brown who "left their impress upon the important work of public education. These women by restrained, industrious and unselfish living, exerted a marked influence for good over the young who literally sat at their feet."[150]

PART II

God Protect the Right

4 /   Race, Gender, and the American High School

Sarah Parker Remond's greatest wish in life was "to be educated."[1] Numerous challenges made that especially difficult to realize. In 1834 nine-year-old Sarah and two of her sisters, Maritchia Juan and Caroline, qualified for admission to the East School for Girls, a recently established public high school in Salem, Massachusetts. But not long after their admission, school officials unceremoniously kicked them out when the town adopted a policy of racial school segregation. Similar developments unfolded elsewhere. In 1840 seventeen-year-old Eunice Ross applied to attend the recently established coeducational public high school in Nantucket. She met all qualifications, yet school officials denied her admission. Such stories defy categorization as a simple narrative of educational exclusion. A closer look reveals a richer, more complicated history, in which ambitious young African American women turned the public high schools of Massachusetts into a battleground.

At the turn of the century, African Americans and their allies began to view education as a way to resist white supremacy and second-class citizenship while promoting black civil rights. This realization coincided with a noteworthy educational innovation: the public high school. Seaport towns such as Salem and Nantucket responded favorably to the 1827 Massachusetts state law that required large towns to establish a public high school. Young African American women refused to let a policy of racial segregation at the primary school level deter them from entering the public high school, or "democracy's college," as it was called. In fact, the creation of public high schools provided a lever for African American activists to introduce educational reforms, namely equal school rights. When school officials in Salem and Nantucket blocked African American access to the public high school, Eunice and Sarah fought for their rightful place and, by doing so, fueled a larger struggle to abolish racial segregation at all levels of public education in the state. Too often the history of school desegregation overlooks the role of young African American women, but they inspired and energized educational reforms in Massachusetts.[2]

A comparison of Salem and Nantucket shows the importance of distinct local conditions and histories as well as broader shared dynamics. For instance, public schools in both seaport towns eventually arrived at a policy of racial segregation, but they followed a slightly different timeline and were driven by different motivations. Hence I use the term "hyperlocal" to register specific practices within public schools located in the same town. Just because one public primary school in a particular area enrolled African American children did not mean that another primary school a few miles away would follow suit. Amid these local differences, African American activists in both towns developed and enacted similar protest strategies, such as boycotting, writing editorials, and petitioning. These shared strategies bring to light African American women's social reform networks, which sustained the equal school rights campaign and ultimately led to the abolition of racially exclusive schools in both towns in the 1840s.

The Massachusetts Bay Colony cultivated a rich tradition of education dating back to the seventeenth century. Among English colonists, family and church played important roles in catechizing children and teaching them to read and write. In some cases, wealthy English families hired private tutors to provide their children with basic and advanced learning. Two laws codified the colony's educational approach. A 1642 law required parents or guardians to ensure that their dependents achieved basic literacy. A revision of this law in 1648 offered greater specificity and authorized selectmen to punish parents or guardians for neglecting their children's learning.[3] In 1647 another law required towns of fifty families or more to operate a school and employ a teacher to instruct children in reading and writing so that they could read the Holy Bible and avoid falling prey to Satan, who "kept men from the knowledge of the Scriptures."[4] A few decades later the *New England Primer*, published in Boston in the late 1600s, became the preferred textbook in New England schools as it combined religious instruction with literacy. By the eighteenth century, schools were in the business of teaching both literacy and morality.

A push by African Americans for formal schooling followed the development and expansion of African American communities in Massachusetts. As the Bay State transitioned from slavery to freedom, African Americans navigated a tense racial landscape. The Quock Walker case, which involved an enslaved African American man suing for his freedom, gradually led to the abolition of slavery in the state in the late eighteenth century. Yet five years later the General Court of Massachusetts enacted a law to curb black migration. Nevertheless the African American population grew from 5,463 in 1790 to 6,452 in 1800 and 6,737 in 1810.[5] Amid this tension, Prince Hall, an African American abolitionist and founder of the first African Masonic lodge, delivered a petition in October 1787 to the General Court of Massachusetts, pleading that some "provision may be made for the education of" African American children in Boston, since African Americans, like whites, paid taxes to support common schools.[6]

So-called African schools emerged within this context. Many American towns and cities with a sizable free black population operated one, oftentimes initiated by African American activists and sometimes supported by public funds. For instance, Daniel Coker and George Collins, both free African American men from New York, operated an African school in Baltimore.[7] In 1810 an African school in New York City, conducted upon the Lancastrian plan that stressed peer teaching, offered students lessons in reading, writing, and arithmetic.[8] These subjects, in addition to spelling and sometimes geography, were most often taught, providing basic skills and building blocks for advanced study. For African American children who were sometimes barred from other educational opportunities, African schools were a boon.

The African school movement produced at least one unintended consequence, however. It established an early precedent for racially exclusive schools, since its student body consisted of African American children. As public schools grew in size and number, African schools would be compelled to serve all African American children and youth in a given area, no matter their age or educational level. In response, an editorialist in *Freedom's Journal* remarked that "the benevolence of the age ha[d] founded and endowed Seminaries of Learning for all other classes and nations," but the "children of Africa" were excluded.[9] These exclusionary practices, coupled with the transformation of African schools into one-stop school shops, so to speak, angered some activists, who began to strategize about creating independent private schools for boys and girls that offered advanced study.

African schools educated boys and girls together, but gender imbalances existed. In seacoast towns and cities, the maritime industry dominated, so many African American male youth who had attended an African school set sail, surrendering advanced schooling opportunities. To be sure, maritime work was a common occupation among black male New Englanders. In Providence, Rhode Island, for instance, the historian W. Jeffrey Bolster counted "one quarter of African American household heads" as mariners.[10] Seafaring enabled these young men to be brave and strong all the while claiming status as breadwinners. This trend of early school leaving surely existed among young white male youth too, who left school earlier than their female peers.[11] Nonetheless gendered divisions of labor in African American communities along the seacoast meant that young African American women, and not men, found themselves at the forefront of efforts to abolish racially exclusive schools.

Before the establishment of public high schools in Massachusetts, young African American women's options for advanced schooling in the state were extremely limited. Most private seminaries did not welcome young African American women. Sarah Parker Remond recalled that her mother, Nancy, searched far and wide within Salem's much lauded private school system to find a place for her daughters, but no private school would accept them on account of their race. Colleges were not welcoming either, since the vast majority did not admit women. But a new educational development would create a crucial opportunity—however inadvertent—for young African American women. In 1821 Boston established the English Classical School, later renamed the English High School, one of the first of its kind for boys. Five years later public high schools for girls were built in New York and Connecticut. Secondary education received a legislative boost in Massachusetts when the state mandated the creation of public high schools and a specific curriculum to boot. Young, middle-class African American women and their families were intrigued.

Public high schools aimed to educate citizens to an advanced level and prepare them for a career. As the historian Johann Neem argues, the high school was "'democracy's college,' where graduates would be prepared to enter the adult world."[12] Henry Barnard, a white educational reformer and early advocate of secondary education, defined the high school as "a public or common school for the older and more advanced scholars of the community . . . in a course of instruction adapted to their age, and intellectual and moral wants, and . . . to their future pursuits in life."[13] Educational reformers believed that high schools should be open to all social classes. A selective admissions process, anchored by an entrance exam, rewarded merit above all else.[14] Yet too often students' access to a public high school, let alone achievement, depended largely on the socioeconomic status and racial background of their family.[15] Hence these schools had a student body of mostly young, white, middle-class women and men.

African American women's pursuit of a high school education elicited a similar response of exclusion in Salem and Nantucket, but specific local conditions shaped that path. Salem and Nantucket had slight geographic, socioeconomic, and demographic variations. Both towns counted a relatively small number of African American residents: in 1840, 571 African Americans resided in Nantucket, constituting 6 percent of the town's population, and 292 African Americans called Salem home, less than 1 percent of the population. Both towns had separate black neighborhoods, an African school, strong religious and social institutions, and smart and ambitious young African American men and women. These small, close-knit communities shared similar educational histories, marked by discrimination, racial segregation, and inequality.

Both Nantucket and Salem eventually segregated their schools by race, which would have to be undone by African American activists, but they operated on a different timeline, which underscores that public schools were "hyperlocal," deeply rooted in their local context. In Nantucket the school committee decided to uphold a de facto policy of racial school segregation that had been in place for some fourteen years. Most white residents supported that decision. In late eighteenth-century Salem, however, racially mixed schools were, if not common, then at least existent for a few decades. It was not a foregone conclusion, then, that African American and white children would be schooled separately in Salem.

With a thriving maritime industry and a rising finance sector, Salem enjoyed greater wealth in the seventeenth and eighteenth centuries than did Nantucket. Yet, according to the historian Rebecca R. Noel, Salem "always hosted an underclass of transient mariners, odd-jobbers, and servants, white and black."[16] In addition to employment as sailors and domestic servants, African American residents worked as hairdressers, gardeners, chimney sweeps, and caterers. Numbering well over two hundred by 1820, this diverse community occupied an area of Salem known pejoratively as "Roast Meat Hill," but the name did little to dampen residents' organizing or ambitions. In 1805 a group of African Americans, who referred to themselves as "true and faithful citizens of the Commonwealth," had formed the African Society, a mutual aid organization with social, political, and educational aims.[17] Members performed music at community events and funerals, organized the local black vote, and promoted religious and intellectual improvement. African Americans in Salem sometimes partnered with the African Society in Boston to plan social functions and host ministers.

When it came to public schooling in Salem, African American boys studied alongside white boys at public grammar schools, which in the late eighteenth century were sometimes called writing schools.[18] These schools were thought to be the next level after primary schools. In July 1793 William Bentley, a white minister and a member of the school committee, visited one such grammar school, the Centre School, and reported that an African boy named Titus Augustus distinguished himself as he "read, & shew writings equal to any of [his peers]" while "another African [was] as stupid as the worst of them."[19] Variation existed in the scholastic achievements of African American and white boys alike. A year later Bentley visited again, and this time Isaac Augustus was the star pupil.[20] Were Titus and Isaac brothers? Or were they possibly the same person? It is unclear, but Salem's public grammar schools—and probably the three public primary schools that existed in the early 1800s—were not racially exclusive.

During the late eighteenth and early nineteenth centuries, wealthy whites in Salem patronized private schools, believing they represented social refinement and provided cultural capital.[21] Public schools developed slowly, and private schools boasted high-quality teachers and offered more areas of study, such as English grammar and geography, in addition to the core subjects of reading, writing, and arithmetic. The historian Maris Vinovskis finds that Salem's private school system enrolled a higher "percentage of students . . . compared to other [Massachusetts] communities."[22] Not surprisingly, then, when private and public schools competed for white students, the latter almost always lost.

Things changed, however, in the 1810s and 1820s. A national trade embargo in 1807 hurt Salem's economy, triggering a gradual shift in student enrollment from private to public schools. Between 1826 and 1843 the number of private schools fell by almost one-third, from sixty-nine to forty-nine.[23] This decline coincided with the expansion of the public school curriculum as subjects such as geography and elocution were added. Still, mostly poor whites populated public schools. And like their more well-off white counterparts, poor white parents refused to have their children learn alongside African American children. Bentley remarked, "Pride will not suffer them to unite."[24] African American children and youth were barred from attending some, though not all, of Salem's public schools. William Dodge, a well-respected white schoolteacher and abolitionist, taught "a small number of colored scholars with white" at North Fields English School in the early decades of the 1800s.[25] In the 1820s three African American boys attended the West School run by Frederick Emerson. In other words, Salem public schools were not just local, but hyperlocal, ordered by customs in particular areas of this seaport town.

The African School in Salem opened in 1807, about eighteen years before Nantucket's African School. Joshua Spaulding, a white minister who welcomed African Americans to his congregation, actually approached Bentley about establishing such an institution.[26] Spaulding then recruited Chloe Minns, who was semiliterate: she could read but could not write well. Nonetheless she impressed the school committee, including Bentley, who accepted Spaulding's recommendation that she was the "best person to keep such a school."[27] The endorsement likely spoke as much to her strong moral character as any literary qualifications (or lack thereof). She began teaching in 1807 and within three years had learned to write, demonstrating her own educational ambition and devotion as a teacher. On one of his visits to the school, Bentley observed that Chloe had kept the school of thirty-six children in "good order."[28] In 1810 he toured the school again, noting in his diary that thirty children attended, some of whom "repeated their hymns with great ease and propriety."[29] Upwards of forty boys and girls at this school learned reading, writing, and arithmetic.

Born around 1781 in Connecticut, Chloe Putnam was a mixed-race African American woman. She married Daniel Minns, an African American hairdresser, on January 20, 1799, in Boston. They called Boston home before Chloe accepted the teaching position at Salem. They may have occupied separate residences, or perhaps Chloe traveled to Salem while Daniel remained in Boston.[30] They probably had two children. On May 13, 1816, Daniel died of consumption at age forty-five. As the administrator of his estate, Chloe advertised in the *New England Palladium* seeking to settle his debts and receive any outstanding payments.[31] On February 6, 1817, Bentley presided over the marriage ceremony of Chloe Minns and Schuyler Lawrence, an African American caterer and later chimney sweep, who had been widowed with five children. Bentley described Schuyler as a "man of good person & of good manners" and referred to the couple as "the first grade of Africans in all our New England towns."[32] Chloe, or Clarissa Lawrence, as she preferred to be called, had been married twice before, according to Bentley, though records indicate only the marriages to Daniel and then to Schuyler. In any case, the couple resided at 8 High Street, an area at the center of Salem's African American community.[33]

Needlework must have been part of the curriculum at the African School in Salem since a sampler made by Sarrah Ann Pollard, an African American female student, survives. Multicolored flowers, blue birds, a vase, and brown dogs decorate this 20½" x 21" square silk embroidered sampler, along with Sarrah's signature and a verse:

Work Done At Year 1818
Clarrisa [Chloe] Lawrence School
virtue the the [sic] chief beauty of the ornament mind the nob
lest virtue of the female kind beauty without virtue is [no value].[34]

This verse reflected a fairly common discourse, that women who possessed both beauty and virtue improved society. Did Clarissa stress to girls the importance of moral character? It appears likely based on this sampler. Sarrah also gained practical skills in needlework. More than just a domestic task, needlework allowed young women to sew garments for themselves and family members and to earn money. Some women who studied sewing regarded it as important paid craftwork.[35] Moreover samplers held symbolic value, demonstrating a young woman's refinement, artistry, and learning.[36]

By all accounts, Clarissa was a great teacher. Bentley acknowledged as much when he declared that she had "acquitted herself with great honor, as to her manners & as to her instructions."[37] After sixteen years of teaching, she retired in 1823, and soon afterward the African School closed.

Clarissa's retirement brought about a short lull in public school opportunities for African American children, yet the public school system in Salem expanded during this period. Seventeen public schools existed, representing the primary and grammar levels.[38] Some African American children once again went to school with white children. In 1824 six African American children were present at a public primary school taught by Eliza Gray in Salem's Ward 1. Two years later a primary school for African American children, taught by an African American man, regularly welcomed fifty boys and girls, but it closed after only a year.[39] The remaining educational options for African American children included enrolling at a private school, if neither money nor race were barriers; attending one of the public schools, if race were not a barrier in a particular area; hiring a private tutor; home schooling and self-study; or attending Sunday school.

Sunday schools offered African American adults and children a pathway to literacy. In 1818 a group of white women in Salem founded the Clarkson Society, named after a white British abolitionist, Thomas Clarkson, that aimed to provide religious instruction to African Americans. The association and its teachers imparted lessons that emphasized "industry, economy, temperance" to transform African Americans into "useful members of society."[40] To that end, the texts used included the Bible as well as other religious readers published by Cummings, Hilliard, and Company in Boston.[41] At the same time, however, the Clarkson Society reinforced racial myths, asserting, for example, that African Americans could not be expected to abide by the "restraints of well ordered society" since they possessed as a "prevalent characteristic" the "love of amusement." Though meant to explain that learning was a gradual process, the statement reproduced a harmful racial mythology. Still, African American women and children flocked to the Sunday school, with most of the population—hovering around 167 in 1810—attending occasionally, and about 51 attending regularly. This level of participation attested to African Americans' love of *learning*.[42]

African American men attended Sunday school in Salem infrequently because they were at sea or working, and a few were wholly uninterested.[43] Reports and editorials written by or about the Clarkson Society thus highlight the achievements of African American women and their families. One report detailed the efforts of an "infirm grandmother who is waited on to and from school by an affectionate granddaughter, and both receive instruction in the same class." An editorialist praised a woman who had entered the school able to read only two-syllable words but soon read Bible verses.[44] The Clarkson Society also operated an evening school for African American women, which still existed in 1832.[45] In 1818 African American women founded the Colored Female Religious and Moral Reform Society, which acted as a sort of community watchdog association "report[ing] violators of decency and decorum."[46] This association also collected funds in order to help those in need. Through such activities and organizations, a network of literate African American girls and women took shape in Salem.

The educational opportunities for African American women, however, paled in comparison to those available to white women. Prior to 1827, when it came to public education, young white women could receive advanced learning only on a part-time basis and only at public schools for young men. The 1827 state law requiring large towns to establish a high school spurred the Salem school committee to establish separate public high schools for young men and women. For white women, this new educational path became the default teacher education program, outpacing even teaching institutes, or "normal schools," in terms of enrollment.[47] While the white female student population at the secondary level increased, young white men often abandoned their studies. In fact attrition rates soared due to "opt-outs," or other opportunities for young men, such as an apprenticeship. The higher white male youth dropout rate was directly tied to the notion that high school was irrelevant. By the late nineteenth century, the historian David Tyack concludes, young white women "outnumbered boys as both students and graduates of high schools."[48]

Salem soon became an innovator in women's advanced education. Two high schools for young women opened in October 1827: the East School for Girls, supervised by Rufus Putnam, and the West School for Girls, supervised by Henry Hamilton. Demand for women's education in the town was high, with nearly four hundred applicants, all of whom were nine years of age or older. Since each school accommodated only 150 students, the school committee made age a determining factor, accepting older girls, even though many of the "younger applicants" were among the "brightest and most promising Scholars."[49] Each high school was organized into three grade levels, with classes in geography, arithmetic, English grammar, writing, and reading. On August 26, 1828, an examination of these schools prompted the school committee to reflect, "However our sisters are the weaker vessels physically, they are not so much so intellectually as some would have us believe."[50]

A young woman at either of these public female high schools enjoyed a remarkable educational experience. Within a few years the cap on student enrollment increased to 160, though daily attendance hovered around 130. Students displayed their work at annual examinations, including sophisticated maps they had constructed. They also performed recitations and other exercises in an orderly fashion. One observer remarked that these young women had risen to the occasion, "dressed so neat," and "look[ed] so happy." Young women thus demonstrated their hard work, talent, and intelligence, which some observers linked to their appearance.[51] Just as school committee members envisioned, public high schools were "among the richest gifts, which a community can confer upon [the young]."[52]

Apparently one African American girl learned of this rich gift, since the Salem school committee debated the "question of admitting a colored female to the high school for girls."[53] Her name was not recorded in reports, but the school committee decided to admit her to the East School for Girls in 1830. She probably belonged to a respectable family with strong Christian values. Both she and her family may have known multiple members of the school committee who could vouch for her character, intelligence, and readiness for advanced study. Perhaps she knew Rufus Putnam, a highly skilled teacher who shunned popular educational practices such as awarding prizes. He ran the Evening School for Females, which offered courses in arithmetic and bookkeeping.[54] He also acted as secretary of the Anti-Slavery Society of Salem, which was founded in January 1834 and boasted a membership of 420.[55] A majority of the school committee, and probably Putnam too, favored admitting this student.

Was the student Harriet D. Morris? Perhaps. Harriet was the daughter of York and Mercy Thomas Morris. York worked as a bootblack before becoming a waiter in wealthy white Salem homes, while Mercy, a homemaker, actively participated in mutual aid organizations such as the Colored Female Religious and Moral Society of Salem.[56] Harriet's twin brother, William, attended the North Fields English School in the 1820s. One of her younger brothers, Robert, who would go on to become a prominent lawyer leading the school desegregation fight in Boston, worked for John G. King, a white Salem lawyer who once served on the school committee. Given the family's belief in education and their connections to the community, they probably supported the educational ambition of their eldest daughter. If not twelve-year-old Harriet, then someone like her deserved an opportunity to continue her education in 1830, probably after having attended the African School before it closed or possibly the primary school for African American children that lasted for only a year. Whatever the case, this ambitious young woman felt prepared to matriculate at the East School for Girls.

Upon her enrollment, this young woman broke through an educational barrier to become the first African American student to attend a public high school in Salem. Previously, African American boys attended grammar schools alongside white boys, but no African American boy had ever been admitted to the all-white, all-male English High School in Salem. Reaching this new educational height was notable, as it demonstrated this young woman's desire to seek advanced education, despite rumblings from white residents.

As a matter of fact, the presence of this young woman at the East School for Girls perturbed some white residents. On May 7, 1831, the school committee discussed the "sensitive" issue of accepting African American children in public schools. A question even arose challenging the "legality" of such a practice. In response, the committee "designate[d] some of their body to obtain counsel relative to the subject," and it was found that the committee had acted within the law.[57] Some white residents relented, perhaps adopting a politics of tokenism: they remained uneasy but seemingly tolerated one African American woman attending the female public high school. How long did she attend? Did she graduate? It is unknown, but the community apparently left her alone.

Following this anonymous trailblazer, more African American girls in Salem took advantage of this educational opportunity, including Sarah Parker Remond (Figure 4.1). Her abolitionist parents, John and Nancy Lenox Remond, married in 1807 in Boston and settled in Salem, where they ran a successful catering business. John, born in Curacao, came to Salem in the 1790s because of its educational opportunities.[58] Sarah described her mother as a vivacious woman who instilled in her children values such as industry, strength, and discipline, which constituted a "genuine New England woman," according to Sarah.[59] Nancy also taught her daughters knitting, sewing, and cooking. Sarah and her siblings learned to read and write at home, but the Remonds did not have a library, so Sarah hunted down books to read. Sarah's oldest brother, Charles, attended one of the Salem public schools, while she and her two youngest sisters, Maritchia Juan and Caroline, went to the public primary schools, where the "children generally treated us kindly, although we were very frequently made to feel that prejudice had taken root in their hearts."[60]

Wishing to extend their studies, the Remond sisters took and passed the high school entrance exam to enter the East School for Girls probably sometime in late spring 1834. Despite possessing both the drive and the intelligence to more than earn their place at the school, the sisters were ultimately thwarted by racial prejudice. The sight of African American girls "promiscuously seated with the white children" appalled one resident.[61] On June 7, 1834, the day after Sarah's tenth birthday, David Becket and 175 other Salem residents submitted a "remonstrance" to the school committee requesting the expulsion of "the colored girls" from the East School for Girls and the creation of a separate school solely for African American children and youth.[62] The forty-seven-year-old Becket, a descendant from the long line of famous Becket shipbuilders, was a spar

FIGURE 4.1. Sarah Parker Remond (1824–1894) was an African American abolitionist who lectured on the wrongs of slavery and prejudice. She eventually studied in the United Kingdom and then relocated to Italy, where she became a medical doctor. Courtesy of the Peabody Essex Museum, Salem, MA.

maker and wood wharfinger who married Elizabeth Townsend in 1817 and had a few children, including at least one daughter, fourteen-year-old Mary Elizabeth, who likely attended the East School for Girls with the Remond sisters.[63]

Jealousy and fear prevailed when the school committee bowed to the pressure of Becket. The Remond girls excelled at their studies; indeed Putnam characterized them as "among his best pupils, for good lessons, punctuality, &c."[64] Yet the sisters were met with a salvo of hatred, despite their display of achievement—or, actually, because of it. The *Christian Reflector*, a newspaper edited by a white Salem abolitionist named Cyrus

P. Grosvenor, relayed the facts: "A colored girl was admitted to the Female High School in Salem, and in a short time, by her good behavior, and, especially, by 'getting to, or very near the head of her class,' so 'outraged public opinion' that, in order to get her out of the way of the aspirings of their beloved, but degraded children, the city went to the expense of setting up a separate school for colored children."[65] White parents had underestimated the intelligence and ability of Sarah and her sisters, believing that they possessed neither the aptitude nor the inclination to surpass their own daughters. But Sarah did, and the community punished her and the other African American residents for it.

These petitioners used the discourse of harm to cast Sarah's scholastic success as injurious to them, their white daughters, and, quite possibly, the white Salem community. Sarah had maximized her scholastic talent, thus outclassing all of her white female peers. That could not continue, especially since the American racial hierarchy, even in a gendered context, dictated that African Americans were subordinate to whites. Hence Sarah's white female peers' "feelings" were hurt.[66] Becket's petition operated as a tool to reset the racial and gender order. No longer would any white student have to compete with an African American student and lose. Removing the Remond girls from the public high school precipitated a policy to remove all African American children from the Salem public schools and ghettoize them in a single African school.

The Remond sisters were expelled; Putnam delivered the news to them and their parents. While Becket claimed that he and other white Salem residents did not seek to "injure the colored citizens," Sarah recalled feeling hurt by this turn of events.[67] Having to go to a separate school, Sarah argued, would "brand [her and her sisters] with degradation." She wrote, "I longed for some power to help me crush those who thus robbed me of my personal rights." She and her sisters had a right to learn on terms equal to that of whites.[68]

Most members of the school committee fell in line behind Becket and his ilk. A subcommittee of five—Charles A. Andrew, C. F. Putnam, John M. Ives, James W. Thompson, and Charles W. Upham—concluded that a separate school should be established. The larger school committee unanimously agreed. On July 24, 1834, a town meeting was held on a Thursday morning to determine "if the town [would] instruct the school committee to provide a school . . . for the instruction of colored children."[69] The town endorsed the plan and a separate school was built.

Black Salemites protested, but there was no stopping the momentum of racial prejudice, at least in the short run. John Remond shared his disapprobation with members of the school committee, some of whom he must have known. Whatever connections he had, however, did not help in this case. An anonymous editorialist pointed out the wasteful economics of building a separate school—upwards of $1,200. But such a point had no impact.[70]

Members of the Salem school committee along with the public claimed that the African School was a pillar of success, but it certainly was not equal to the white public schools. A Salem resident praised Charles F. Putnam for being "particularly laborious and faithful in serving the town" and claimed, "The present flourishing and gratifying condition of the School for Colored Childeen [sic] is owing in a great degree to his indefatigable and public spirited exertions."[71] Yet most African American children, no matter their sex or aptitude, assembled at one schoolhouse, while seventeen public schools were available to differentiate white children by location, age, sex, and grade. At first this lack of differentiation within the African School did not deter African American children. In 1838, during his visit to Salem, Charles B. Ray, the African American newspaper editor, wrote that he was "extremely pleased with the recitations and appearance of the children."[72] He used his observations as evidence that African American children were not prone to idleness since their parents had encouraged them to grow intellectually, despite educational inequities.

The principal at the African School was now William Dodge, an experienced schoolteacher who had taught African American children before.[73] "Master Dodge," as he was affectionately called, maintained a good rapport with the African American community. In the first few years of his tenure at the African School, about sixty African American children attended.[74] He later recalled "no inferiority of capacity in the colored youth to acquire knowledge of all branches taught in [his] school."[75] In addition to his teaching duties, he served as president of the Essex County Anti-Slavery Society and, alongside Schuyler Lawrence, Cyrus P. Grosvenor, and Rufus Putnam, attended the New England Antislavery Convention in 1834. At some point, he even helped ferry a kidnapped African man back to his home in West Africa. In 1841 he resigned his position at the African School and moved to Illinois. The school committee thanked him for his "long and useful service . . . of 34 years."[76]

Prior to 1835 the practice of racial school segregation in Salem was erratic and haphazard, stopping when a teacher retired and starting up when whites, whether poor or wealthy, demanded. Even then, a few

African American and white children sat together in the same classroom. Concurrently Salem's private schools declined and the public school system gained ground. African American students rarely, if ever, enrolled at any of Salem's private schools, but they did attend the African School and some of the other public schools such as the North Fields Writing School and the East School for Girls. A policy of racial school segregation became systematic in 1834 because of white resentment toward the Remond sisters. Just as African Americans in Salem experienced educational inequality, so too did African Americans in Nantucket. Compared to Salem, though, Nantucket's path to a policy of racial school segregation was more straightforward.

The African American community in Nantucket proudly claimed a mixed-race heritage partly to assert their rootedness. In the mid-seventeenth century, the Wampanoag people inhabited the island before the arrival of Europeans. In the 1660s English families began to occupy the western part of the island, eventually pushing out the Native American inhabitants.[77] English settlers then enslaved Africans, who were regarded as property in legal records. African slave resistance, however, accelerated the gradual abolition of slavery in Nantucket in the 1770s. Seneca Boston, the son of Prince Boston, who had been enslaved but sued for his freedom, worked as a weaver and married Thankful Micah, a Wampanoag woman, and together they settled with their six children at what would become 27 York Street in the southern part of the island.[78] These interracial couplings were not rare. After 1763 thirty-six marriages between African American men and Wampanoag women in Nantucket were recorded.[79] The Boston family sparked black settlement along York and Pleasant streets, an area that soon became known as "New Guinea." Men in this community worked as barbers, mariners, blacksmiths, laborers, and servants, while women tended to the home and sometimes worked as servants in white households.[80] By 1800 the African American population had doubled from the previous decade, totaling 228.

This community remained unified and activist-oriented in the early nineteenth century. Absalom Boston, born in 1785 to Seneca and Thankful, became a community leader. Not much is known about Absalom's childhood, but when he was around thirty-seven he captained the *Industry*, a whaling vessel with an all-black crew. The high seas were no doubt dangerous, but even more so for African American seamen, who were vulnerable to kidnapping and enslavement, not to mention illness and death. Absalom's success made him a preeminent and respectable figure in Nantucket. A property owner, innkeeper, and abolitionist, he cofounded the African Baptist Society as well as the African Meeting-house. By 1820 about 244 African Americans lived in Nantucket. In addition to free blacks born on the island, this community included fugitive slaves and other newcomers. Mary Ellen Pleasant, for instance, arrived on the island as a young female servant in the Hussey house-hold but eventually found success as an entrepreneur.[81] Arthur Cooper, a fugitive slave from Alexandria, Virginia, arrived with his wife Mary and their children in Nantucket around 1820. Camillus Griffith, a white slave catcher, soon hunted them down. White Quaker families in the area such as the Macys and the Gardners hid the Coopers. Even amid threats to their livelihood, not to mention ongoing racial discrimination, Afri-can Americans worked to build a thriving community in Nantucket.[82]

African American women such as Lucy Cooper, Hannah Cook Boston, and Zilpha Elaw strengthened Nantucket's African American institutions. In 1827 Lucy married Arthur Cooper, whose first wife had died. When Lucy passed away at the age of 110 on February 3, 1866, the *Nantucket Inquirer & Mirror* recounted her eventful life: stolen from Africa, enslaved in South Carolina, and then forcibly taken to Newport, Rhode Island, before escaping to Nantucket. With her strong Christian beliefs, Lucy was regarded as a respectable woman who supported her husband as he participated in activities at Zion African Methodist Epis-copal Church.[83] Similarly Hannah Cook Boston helped her husband. Born in Dartmouth, Massachusetts, in 1795, she married Absalom, who had been twice widowed, in 1827. She handled the domestic work while also helping with innkeeping duties and tending to the African Meet-inghouse. Hannah likely crossed paths with Zilpha Elaw, who preached at the Meetinghouse. A free black woman from Pennsylvania, Zilpha moved to New Jersey, where she taught African American schoolchil-dren. After being called to preach, she traversed the east coast, eventu-ally landing in Nantucket in 1832. Illness felled her shortly thereafter, but her daughter Rebecca as well as some white Quaker women nursed her back to health. Nantucket was her home until she traveled to Eng-land, where she wrote her autobiography, *Memoirs of the Life, Religious Experience, Ministerial Travels, and Labours of Mrs. Zilpha Elaw*, which was published in 1846. Her daughter remained in Nantucket. When Rebecca Elaw Crawford died at seventy-one, her obituarist remembered her as "most estimable in her daily life, and truly faithful to all her domestic duties."[84] Whether performing domestic tasks or participating in community activities, African American women sustained self-help organizations, churches, and schools.

As in Salem, African American leaders in Nantucket lobbied for more formal and permanent avenues of schooling. There had been a Sunday school for African American children to obtain religious and moral instruction.[85] And Rhoda Harris ran a school for African American children.[86] But these schools would prove fleeting. In 1822 Essex Boston, Peter Boston, and Jeffrey Summons wished to build a school and requested financial assistance from the Society for the Propagation of the Gospel in Foreign Parts, a British organization dedicated to proselytizing among Native Americans. "There are among the coloured people of this place remains of the Nantucket Indians; and that nearly every family in our village are partly descended from the original inhabitants of this and neighboring places," the three leaders wrote in a letter.[87] Given the mission of the Society for the Propagation of the Gospel in Foreign Parts, these leaders drew attention to Native American ancestry among African Americans as a way to garner support. In 1825 these leaders set their sights on building a school. By March of that year, trustees, which included Absalom Boston and Jeffrey Summons, had been appointed to collect and manage donations.[88] Summons, a black Quaker born in 1756 who worked as a laborer before amassing a modest estate, officially deeded land to the trustees so long as they agreed to establish a permanent school.[89] A month later, in April 1825, the school opened, but with the town providing only a small amount of money it was badly underfunded.[90]

In the early 1820s Nantucket had not yet established any public schools. White children could attend private schools, such as Simeon Balch's English School, which opened in 1822 and cost $3 per quarter, but African American children did not have access to these schools.[91] Other informal learning opportunities existed, such as homeschooling, tutoring, and attending Sunday school. Nantucket citizens, however, wished for a public school, and Samuel Jenks, editor of the *Nantucket Inquirer*, spearheaded that effort. Nantucket established its public schools in 1827, two years after the creation of the African School. Four hundred white children attended the public schools, and the town assumed partial control over the African School, where thirty black children attended.[92] Racially distinct public schools now existed in Nantucket.

Teachers at the African School aimed to produce upstanding and honorable citizens by making moral character a central focus of the curriculum. The first teacher was Frederick Baylies, a white minister and missionary who had been sent to the school by the Society for the Propagation of the Gospel in Foreign Parts. He had established schools in other northeastern towns, spending about one month at each school teaching writing, reading, and spelling. Schools for African American and Native American children, he argued, prepared them for the "prospect of future *usefulness*."[93] One observer noted the "progress" that students made in "literature, morality and civil deportment" under his guidance.[94] During his absences, a Miss Thomson, probably Priscilla Boston Thomas, taught forty to fifty students at the school. She was the daughter of Rhoda Jolly, a Wampanoag woman, and Peter Boston, a free black Revolutionary War veteran, one of the founders of the African School and Absalom Boston's uncle. Jacob Perry then took over the school, probably in 1828, making him the first African American male teacher there. Described in the *Nantucket Inquirer* as "an intelligent and worthy man of color," Perry also served as pastor of the African Baptist Church. Under his tutelage, more than half of the students could read the Bible and write. An observer declared the "various specimens of writing, reading, spelling, &c. [of the students] were very commendable, and the conduct of the pupils unexceptionable."[95] Because of the school's ongoing financial issues, Perry soon vacated his post. Eliza Bailey took over and was succeeded by Anna Gardner. These teachers, the school's trustees, and likely the families who sent their children to this school understood that education, in the words of one Nantucket editorialist, provided "the surest passport to honor and happiness, and the best guarantee of . . . civil and religious liberties."[96]

The African School had turned African American youth into scholars. There was no better example than seventeen-year-old Eunice Ross, who had mastered multiple subjects and gained fluency in French. The youngest member of her family, Eunice had five older siblings, including a brother, James Jr., and four sisters, Martha, Maria, Elizabeth, and Sarah.[97] Her mother, Mary Sampson Ross, was probably a homemaker, while her African-born father, James, worked as a laborer.[98] Like many young African American men, James Jr. embarked upon a career as a mariner before running a boardinghouse for sailors. By 1860 he and his wife, Sarah, had acquired $400 in real restate.[99] Eunice's sister Sarah may have attended the African School before becoming a servant in the family of Benjamin Coffin, where she remained for fifty-seven years. During that time she nurtured a close relationship with the Coffin family, for her obituarist considered her an "esteemed member of the household, and a remarkable friend."[100]

Eunice's teacher at the African School was Anna Gardner, the daughter of white Quaker antislavery activists Oliver and Hannah Macy Gardner.

It was the Gardner and Macy families who helped to hide Arthur Cooper and his brood from a slave catcher back in the 1820s. The antislavery activism of Anna's parents certainly influenced Anna's own decision to take up the cause of black civil rights, but she was also inspired by Absalom Boston, who once worked as a servant in her grandfather's home. Upon Absalom's early recommendation, the Gardner family began reading Garrison's *Liberator*. Anna then subscribed to the newspaper, which shaped her worldview: "I was an enthusiastic Republican before I was an Abolitionist, and this paper served at once to remove the delusion which I had fondly cherished, that we were living in a true republic."[101] She served as secretary of the Nantucket Female Anti-Slavery Society, which had been established in February 1838 and had thirty-three members.[102] A year later that organization merged with the all-male Nantucket Anti-Slavery Society, founded in July 1837, and the Nantucket Colored Anti-Slavery Society, which African American men formed in February 1834.[103] The newly minted County Anti-Slavery Society boasted a membership of over 350 Nantucketers, black and white, men and women. Antislavery sentiment was growing in this area.

Perhaps Anna's inclination toward public service influenced her decision to teach at the African School starting in 1836, a position she held for several years.[104] The school committee, consisting of prominent white men from Nantucket, praised Anna's work, calling her an "able, zealous and faithful teacher . . . eminently qualified to assist in elevating a race hitherto looked down upon, to a rank and station, in which colour shall no longer be considered a mark of ignorance, a cause for legal exception, or an excuse for oppression."[105] In this case, an empathetic teacher taught reading, writing, orthography, arithmetic, and geography and thus prepared African American children to uplift themselves and their community. At the same time, however, the remark demonstrated precisely what African Americans faced: that some white Americans had accepted an a priori assumption that blackness justified their second-class citizenship and oppression. For her part, Anna, like Prudence Crandall and other white teachers before her, knew otherwise and sought to promote black advancement through education. She herself may have briefly attended the coeducational private high school on Orange Street run by Cyrus Peirce in the 1830s.[106] Peirce, a native of Waltham, Massachusetts, who studied theology at Harvard College, eventually left the ministry to devote his life to teaching. In 1838 he relinquished his successful private school to serve as principal of the newly organized public Nantucket High School, which Anna attended while she held her position at the African School.

Educational reformers predicted that high schools like the one at Nantucket would benefit an entire community and compete with private schools. Historians estimate that 321 public high schools were established nationally before 1860, with over half located in Massachusetts, New York, and Ohio.[107] Most high schools were located in cities, sustained by a local tax base, and supervised by local and state authorities. By the mid- to late nineteenth century, a standard course of study included arithmetic, algebra, geometry, grammar, composition, botany, astronomy, geology, chemistry, physiology, and natural philosophy.[108] The *Nantucket Inquirer* called the Nantucket High School "one of the most perfect institutions of its class in New England," as about eighty students of both sexes attended.[109] Still, public high schools themselves remained widely variable.[110] Some select institutional models existed, such as Philadelphia's Central High School for Boys, which was regarded as the "people's college" not only because it offered collegiate degrees but also because educators worked with taxpayers to shape the curriculum to fit the needs of the community.[111] For youth who had no plans to attend college, a high school like Central or Nantucket represented a great opportunity.

Having exhausted the curriculum at the African School, Eunice Ross aspired to continue her studies at Nantucket High School. She found support from her family and her teacher, Anna Gardner, who helped her prepare for the high school entrance exam. In 1839 a prospective student to the Nantucket High School had to exhibit expertise in academic subjects such as reading, writing, arithmetic, and English grammar. Along with this knowledge, applicants had to supply a "certificate of good conduct" and a note on their academic progress from a current teacher.[112] Anna Gardner's aid proved instrumental, but Eunice was ambitious in her own right.

Amid the expansion of Nantucket public schools, Eunice unwittingly forced the community to tackle a tough question: Did the African School meet the needs of youth who sought advanced study? African American children gained the rudiments of literacy and arithmetic, and further individual tutoring was available, but the African School was not a high school; it did not officially provide courses in geometry, history, theology, Latin and Greek, and other "higher branches of English education," and it did not receive funding equal to that of the all-white public schools.[113] Moreover Nantucket, like other towns, took advantage of recent educational reforms to institute a distinct schooling structure, consisting of an infant, primary, grammar, and high school. Educational reformers argued that this structure enabled students to learn better and teachers to teach better.[114] Racial school segregation deprived African American children of these groundbreaking reforms and excluded them from new theories regarding childhood and learning.

Upset by this educational injustice, the trustees of the African Meetinghouse refused to rent its space to the town to operate the African School. Town officials then earmarked funds to construct a new schoolhouse, the York Street School, which opened in 1839.[115] The York Street School enrolled only African American children and youth, seemingly excluding them from the white grammar schools and the high school. The question of public school segregation was hotly debated, and race relations on the island became even more strained. Nantucket newspapers mocked African Americans and cast them as outsiders.[116] In 1838 members of the North Congregational Church blocked African American women from entering the building to attend an antislavery meeting alongside white women. Eliza Barney, wife of Nathaniel Barney, and Harriet Peirce, wife of Cyrus Peirce, defended African American women and argued that "character should be the test of respectability and standing, and not the color of the skin."[117] The Nantucket Atheneum, a meeting place and library, shut its doors to African Americans.

Segregationists then penned missives to the press, branding African Americans inferior and accusing abolitionists of trying to engineer race mixing. What abolitionists were trying to engineer was equal school rights. The abolitionist Samuel J. May noted that Cyrus Peirce "remonstrated and contended, with his wonted earnestness and determination . . . against the decision" to send African American children and youth to separate schools.[118] As president of the Nantucket County Association for the Promotion of Education and Improvement of Common Schools, Peirce certainly had a platform to express his views. Founded in 1837, this education society boasted one hundred members who shared an interest in strengthening public schools. At regular monthly meetings, men and women discussed a variety of topics, from the utility of teaching human physiology to whether young men and women should study the same subjects.[119] At a meeting in March 1839, a provocative question arose: "Should the public provision for popular education be so enlarged as to provide what is called a 'liberal education for *all* qualified applicants'?"[120] Was this question alluding to whether children of color could gain access to the public grammar and high schools? Probably. The prevailing opinion among this group is unknown, but Cyrus's views were clear, and the issue of equal school rights was now front and center.

In August 1839 the *Nantucket Inquirer* ran an ad soliciting "applications from females, for the situation of Teacher" at the African School.[121] Anna Gardner may have left in protest of the school committee's upcoming decision to deny African American youth admission to the public high school. By 1839 school committee members had probably learned that Anna had been tutoring Eunice to take the high school entrance exam. Some members, such as Samuel Jenks, brother-in-law of Cyrus Peirce and a school segregationist, may have told Anna that that was unfavorable. Maybe Anna left her position because of her increasing involvement in the antislavery movement. She later recalled of this period in her life, "I determined to give all I possessed to pro-mote the maligned anti-slavery cause."[122]

Sometime in 1840 seventeen-year-old Eunice arrived at a schoolhouse in Nantucket, on time, with a "slate and pencil" in hand, to take the high school entrance exam.[123] She was one of eighteen young men and women seeking admission, and the only person of color. Eunice passed the exam and met the other qualifications. Nathaniel Barney, a white Quaker abolitionist and member of the school committee, called her "the best qualified to enter of any that did apply." In June 1840 Edward Gardner, another school committee member and a cousin of Anna, made a formal request at a town meeting to allow qualified African American children to attend the high school. John H. Shaw, a white abolitionist, put forth a similar motion. But in the end, both motions were defeated and the school committee rejected Eunice Ross.[124]

Despite the rejection, Eunice represented what was possible, and she inspired another African American girl to seek advanced study. Sometime in 1843 this unnamed girl applied for admission to the high school. The school committee ultimately declared her "not qualified," which might mean that she failed the entrance exam.[125] Educational inequities made it challenging for even the best students. Ostensibly, if African American children had access to infant, primary, and grammar schools, they would be better prepared to take and pass the high school entrance exam and subsequently flourish at the high school. Eunice's intellectual achievements were thus all the more remarkable.

Both Nantucket and Salem grappled with this thorny issue of racial segregation in public education. In Nantucket the African School operated continuously for over a decade and actually preceded the creation of white public schools. It appeared to be successful, so much so that Eunice Ross wished to pursue advanced study by matriculating at Nantucket High School. The Nantucket school committee refused to admit her,

even though she passed their entrance exam. Objectively she was qualified and met all requirements, aside from being white. Likewise Salem's
African School had been defunct for some eight years before the school
committee reconstituted it in 1834 to appease white Salem residents.
Soon African American activists and their allies in both towns rallied
around these young women. They pursued various protest strategies,
from organizing and writing op-eds to petitioning and boycotting to
abolish racially exclusive public high schools. The campaign eventually
evolved with the aim to desegregate the entire system of public education
in each locale.

Nantucket registered a more immediate protest response, rallying as a
community within a year of Eunice's denial. The majority of the African
American population, which hovered around 576 in 1840, appeared to
support equal school rights. On February 23, 1842, community members convened at Zion AME Church, where two key resolutions were put
forth. The first, proposed by William Serrington, an African American
minister once described by Frederick Douglass as a man of "deep piety"
and "high intelligence," cited a Massachusetts law that provided access
to public education for all children regardless of race.[126] Serrington and
other community members argued that they had every right to see "their
youth educated in the same schools which are common to the more
favored members [white inhabitants] of this community."[127] The second
resolution, offered by William W. Morris, an African American innkeeper and abolitionist who had presided over the Nantucket Colored
Anti-Slavery Society in the mid-1830s, thanked white allies at the school
committee meetings who vocally supported equal school rights. Eunice
Ross's educational ambition and later the school committee's rejection
of her application provoked these declarations of educational justice and
full citizenship. African American Nantucketers knew their rights and
were prepared to fight for them.

The response from the African American community in Salem differed partly because the Remond family left town. John and Nancy
moved their family over one hundred miles away, to Newport, Rhode
Island, in order to provide their children with advanced schooling.
Perhaps they had learned about Newport from their son-in-law, James
Shearman, an oyster dealer who had grown up there. The public schools
in Newport, however, were also segregated. Though the Remonds balked
at sending their daughters to a segregated public school in Salem, they
enrolled Sarah—and likely Caroline and Maritchia Juan—at an all-black
private school in Newport. From their perspective, perhaps there was no

contradiction: a racist majority had instituted racially segregated public schools in Salem, but in Newport, sending their daughters to an all-black private school indicated some degree of choice. The Remond girls likely went to a school run by the African Benevolent Society, an organization founded in 1807. They may have taken courses in arithmetic, English grammar and composition, history, and geography. What kept Sarah grounded was her love of reading. She read newspapers daily and also novels, which she said were "resources of which *even* prejudice could not deprive [her]."[128] Her educational purpose was greater than white supremacy.

Salem's early history and Sarah's place in it influenced the Remond family's departure. Some controversy followed the unnamed African American girl who first attended the East School for Girls, but Sarah's scholastic achievement had propelled white residents to move swiftly to segregate public schools. White residents thus tagged her as an unwitting catalyst for the return to a policy of racial segregation. Sarah hinted at this when she confessed that racial prejudice "cast its gigantic shadow over [her] whole life."[129] Fleeing Salem may have had everything to do with shielding Sarah from the weight of such an unjust burden. White racists powered the policy on racial segregation, not Sarah's scholastic achievement. After a six-year respite, the Remond family returned, right before the school in Newport closed in 1842; they then renewed the fight for equal school rights in Salem.[130]

African American activists also publicized the long-standing oppression under which they suffered. In Nantucket, William Serrington, William W. Morris, and William Harris authored an address to the school committee and their fellow Nantucket residents remarking that they felt like "an INJURED PORTION of [that] community" because their rights had been violated. At the same time, they, as citizens of the Commonwealth, staked their claim to the same educational rights as whites.[131] They concluded their address, invoking the Latin phrase "mentem non frontem hominis spectato," which roughly translates to "regard the mind not the face of a man."[132] Demonstrating the erudition of Serrington, Morris, and Harris, and by extension, that of the African American community, the Latin phrase also urged white Nantucketers to reject racial prejudice and uphold the law to extend school privileges to all equally.

Similarly, African American activists in Salem touted their rights as citizens to be part of an inclusive community on equal terms. Activists rejected two key educational initiatives: the school committee had assigned Thomas B. Perkins, from nearby Lynn, Massachusetts, to lead the African School, and it approved plans to construct a new building on Mill Street.[133] The extent of Sarah Parker Remond's direct involvement in this campaign is not clear, but her stance on the issue left no doubt: she argued that segregated schools impeded African American uplift.[134] Her brother Charles Lenox Remond agreed when he denounced segregated schools as "pro-slavery."[135] In March 14, 1844, an editorial in the *Salem Register* summarized the campaign, though it erroneously stated that African Americans had petitioned for a separate school in 1834, when in fact it was racist white residents who had forced that result. In any case, John Remond played an important role in this campaign for educational justice. He approached a school committee member, expressing his deep frustration with racial school segregation and demanding a place for his two grandchildren at an all-white primary school. "I demand, as a citizen," John said, "to put my children to school. I have lived in this city many years, demeaned myself well and paid my taxes." The school committee member denied him, citing regulations. With great fervor, John and Nancy Remond then declared, "[We] never will allow, for a moment, that our children or any colored children, can, with justice, be shut out from participating freely in fair and open competition in all the advantages of the public schools."[136]

The fight for equal school rights demanded African American women's activism, not simply because these particular cases involved young African American women but also because women were valuable organizers. In Nantucket at least four women, Maria B. Cooper, Eunice Ross, Rebecca Pierce, and Charlotte D. Brown, attended a community meeting at AME Zion Church in 1841 to help gather subscriptions for David Ruggles's newspaper, *Mirror of Liberty*.[137] These women probably contributed to the campaign for equal school rights too. Besides Eunice Ross, at least one African American woman participated for sure: Charlotte Dyer Brown. Listed as "C. D. Brown" in the meeting minutes, Charlotte had endorsed the second resolution put forth by William W. Morris.

Charlotte was a proponent of equal school rights. Born in 1800 to mixed-race free parents from Newport, Rhode Island, Sampson Dyer and Patience Allen Dyer, Charlotte was one of five children, including Charles, Trilonia, Harriet, and Sampson Jr. The Dyer family lived on Atlantic Avenue in Nantucket, though the elder Sampson frequently traveled as a mariner and later a ship's steward in the China trade in the 1790s. During his travels, Spoilum, a Chinese artist, painted his portrait. In the early 1800s Sampson embarked on sealing ventures near the Cape of Good Hope, which generated wealth and clout. But in 1810 he left Nantucket for good after learning that Patience had been engaged in an affair with Samuel Harris and was pregnant.[138] Despite this drama, the Dyer family garnered some respect from the broader Nantucket community.

Charlotte acted as a leader among African American women in Nantucket. She was three times widowed; her first husband was Edward Johnson and her second was Jeremiah Brown.[139] As a young married woman, Charlotte presided over the Female Colored Union Society, which raised $9 to donate to the Massachusetts Anti-Slavery Society in 1839.[140] This organization may have been an auxiliary to the larger Colored Female Union Society, founded in Boston in 1831 to aid widows and orphans.[141] On July 22, 1842, Charlotte's husband Jeremiah died from consumption. In his will, which he signed with an "x," he bequeathed the bulk of his estate to his "beloved wife." His donation of $15 to York Street Baptist Church and $20 to AME Zion Church spoke to the Johnsons' ties to both black churches as well as the importance of these churches to the community.[142] In 1846 Charlotte married William W. Morris, with whom she had crossed paths many times in their activist circles. Four years later fifty-year-old William and fifty-year-old Charlotte resided in the Dyer household with Charlotte's mother, Patience; Charlotte's half-brother, Samuel C. Harris, a seaman; and her half-sister, Patience Harris Cooper.[143] William owned real estate totaling $800.[144] Charlotte's sister Trilonia lived nearby with her husband, Stephen Pompey, a seaman who owned property worth $800, while her other sister, Harriet Dyer Rodney, remarried in September 1831 to John N. Frazier, an African American mariner who claimed $500 in real estate. By 1855 William W. Morris had probably passed away, widowing Charlotte.[145] She died on April 16, 1864, in Edgartown, Massachusetts, from "disease of the head."[146] The full extent of Charlotte's activism will probably remain unknown to us, though her peers surely recognized it.

Just as Charlotte Brown contributed to the fight for racial equality in Nantucket, so too did Clarissa Lawrence in Salem. After retiring from her teaching position at the African School in Salem, Clarissa worked in racially mixed spaces, which might suggest that she supported equal school rights. In 1833 she resurrected the Colored Female Religious and Moral Society of Salem, which had been inactive for some time.[147] In addition to leading that organization, she served as vice president of the Salem Female Anti-Slavery Society, which was all black before it accepted white women as members. She was one of two African American women delegates from Massachusetts at the Anti-Slavery Convention of American Women held in Philadelphia in 1839; the other delegate was Julia Ward Williams, an alumna of the Canterbury Female Seminary.[148] At that convention, the white abolitionist Susan Grew put forth a motion to increase black educational opportunities. Clarissa seconded that motion, and then highlighted the complex problem of racial prejudice. "We meet the monster prejudice *every where*. It kills its thousands every day. It follows us every where, even to the grave," she proclaimed.[149] "Faith and prayer" helped her through the suffocating, seemingly inescapable nature of racial prejudice, and she implored her predominantly white audience to invoke their own religious faith as they worked side by side to end slavery and prejudice. Clarissa remained involved in the abolition and moral reform movements until she passed away in Salem at seventy-two years of age.

Editorials about equal school rights were sometimes written to elicit sympathy for the young women at the center of these disputes. One editorialist writing in the *Nantucket Inquirer* questioned why Eunice Ross had been denied admission to the high school: "Did she enjoy an equal privilege with the 17 who were admitted, when she was examined, none of whom was so well qualified as herself? Did she enjoy the benefit of our school law?"[150] The answer was no. This editorialist declared that Eunice's race and her status, or lack thereof, factored into the school committee's decision. "If she had been the daughter of some of our citizens, nay, if she had been the daughter of Fair Play [a segregationist editorialist], he would have known it; but she was the daughter of an obscure colored man, and his oppressors had power and numbers on their side, and those were sufficient to exclude her from a constitutional right." The power of the school committee thus derived from its ability to dismiss a young woman from an "obscure" family. This editorialist concluded that an "injustice . . . was done that girl." Eunice, smart and ambitious, had been victimized, a casualty of a white racist majority.[151]

In the early 1840s African American men, including James Ross and Absalom Boston, campaigned for seats on Nantucket's school committee. Although they lost, a few white Nantucket abolitionists were unexpectedly voted onto the school committee, and they desegregated the public primary and grammar schools, citing religious and legal justifications. An annual report encouraged African American children, "Take your place in the school, you are equally as well entitled to it as any other child; take it and improve it to the utmost and God protect the right."[152] Over fifty African American and white students went to York Street School, and about fifteen African American children attended the grammar schools. Although Nantucket had desegregated its primary and grammar schools, the high school remained segregated. White Nantucket abolitionists were soon unseated and racial school segregation once again became policy.

African American parents in both Nantucket and Salem then pursued another strategy: boycotting. In Nantucket, mothers and fathers withdrew their children from the York Street School in order to sustain the equal school rights battle. This protest strategy meant cutting off one tried-and-true educational avenue with the aim of creating better schooling opportunities in the long run. To make up for this sudden educational loss, African American children attended a makeshift school with volunteer teachers. Put in a bind, the school committee resorted to sending white students to the York Street School to keep it open. Similarly, in Salem, enrollment at the African School slipped from sixty students to twenty-eight, then twenty-two, and eventually seventeen. The school committee declared, "An almost universal disquietude existed amongst the colored people about their school."[153]

Others turned to petitioning, a practice long held to be a legitimate and popular act of political protest among abolitionists in Massachusetts. When abolitionists petitioned to repeal the interracial marriage ban, for instance, they framed their support for the repeal within a narrative of moral reform and the larger struggle for racial equality.[154] The very last line from the 1842 petition on the interracial marriage ban sought to undo "all other laws of this Commonwealth (if any such there be) which make any distinction among the inhabitants on account of Colour, or for any real or supposed differences of races."[155] In February 1843 the interracial marriage ban was repealed.

Three tropes characterized equal school rights petitions: a declaration of citizenship, a denunciation of segregation as injurious and insulting, and an invocation of state law, which could rectify the situation. In December 1843 African American activists in Salem petitioned the school committee. This petition, signed by forty-three African American residents, described "separate schools" as "inexpedient" and harmful to African American children.[156] Two years later, in 1845, 105 African Americans in Nantucket signed their own four-page petition. They complained that upwards of forty children had been "deprived of their right to equal instruction with other children in [the] common schools." When petitioners denounced the "insults and outrages upon their rights, quite equal to being imprisoned in a *South Carolina* jail," they drew a parallel between slavery in the South and racial prejudice in the North, not to mention exposing Massachusetts as anything but a model of republican ideals. At first, activists tried to pursue legal recourse, but there was apparently no avenue for a case. This Nantucket petition to the senate and house of representatives of Massachusetts thus constituted an appeal to the state to "protect all children in their equal rights to the schools" despite the ruling of a local school committee.[157]

African American women's activist network facilitated the circulation of these petitions. On the Nantucket petition, Absalom Boston and thirty-five other African American men signed their names on the left side of the page, while Hannah Cook Boston, Lucy Cooper, Rhoda Boston, Sarah Ross, and sixty-five other African American women signed their names on the right half. The larger number of women signees bespeaks their activity and persistence in procuring signatures. The order of signees coincided with the petition's circulation from person to person and from household to household: Patience Harris signed, then Patience Cooper, then Charlotte D. Brown, and then Harriet Frazier. This handwritten petition, which the African American activist Edward Pompey submitted in January 1845, represented African Americans' right to protest as well as an intellectual and sociopolitical defense of a generation of African American children.[158]

Eunice Ross was one of a contingent of antebellum women reformers who exercised their right to petition. In 1838, around the age of fifteen, she had signed her name to an antidiscrimination petition alongside fifty-two other African Americans, including Absalom Boston and her own sister Sarah. That petition to the state legislature, which listed male signees on the left and female signees on the right, sought to "repeal all laws in the State, which make any distinction among its inhabitants, on account of color."[159] A year later, along with over six hundred other women, including Anna Gardner, she signed a petition calling for the abolition of slavery and the slave trade in the District of Columbia. In 1840 Eunice signed her name to three more state petitions, one opposing the admission of Florida as a slave state, another advocating the repeal of the interracial marriage ban in Massachusetts, and another condemning the gag rule, which prohibited discussions of abolitionist petitions in Congress. Thus Eunice had already been schooled in the power of petitioning before she authored her own petition (Figure 4.2).

Eunice's eighty-three-word petition to the Massachusetts state legislature demonstrated her knowledge of community affairs and her sophistication. Though written in the third person, it likely was authored by Eunice to affix to Edward J. Pompey's petition, or "prayer," as she called it—a term that carried multiple meanings in the antebellum era,

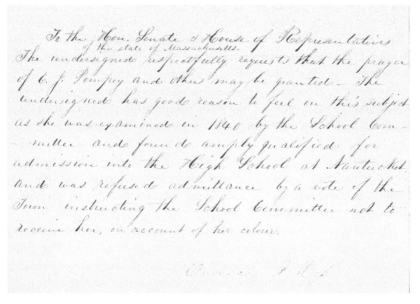

FIGURE 4.2. In this petition, Eunice Ross (1824–1895) described her educational ambitions, particularly her qualifications to attend Nantucket High School, even though the school committee had rejected her on account of her race. SC1/series 229. Passed Acts. Acts of 1855 Chapter 256, An Act in amendment of "An Act concerning public schools," passed March 25, 1845. Petition of Eunice Ross, February 27, 1845. Courtesy of the Massachusetts Archives. Boston.

signifying a request for this particular objective and the earnestness of the appeal and its Christian premise: equal access to public schools for all children regardless of race. In neat penmanship, Eunice established her authority to speak against the policy of racial school segregation. She proclaimed that her examination before the school committee proved her to be "amply qualified" to attend Nantucket High School, yet a town vote had instructed the school committee to deny her admission because of her race.[160] Peter Macy, a white abolitionist, and 235 other white Nantucket residents filed another petition supporting those of Pompey and Eunice.[161] Eunice's petition signaled her own quest for knowledge and that of other young African American women.

These petitions also functioned as solemn declarations of African American women's literacy. Generally, literacy rates were higher in New England compared to other areas in the United States, though exact numbers for free blacks in the region are unavailable. These petitions, however, provide a rough minimum estimate, at least at the local level. The 1840 U.S. census counted 147 African American women in Nantucket. Five years later, this number may have inched up slightly. Since seventy women inscribed their names on these petitions, then at least 45 to 50 percent of African American women in Nantucket were literate, or at least could sign their name. In comparison, the historian Nancy Cott estimates that a majority of white New England women were literate by 1840.[162] After all, white women benefited from the expansion of public schools and private female seminaries. During this struggle for equal school rights, African American women demonstrated that they had taken advantage of their limited schooling opportunities, and some, like Eunice, wanted more.

In March 1845 the state of Massachusetts passed legislation ensuring legal recourse for any child excluded from a public school: "Any child, unlawfully excluded from public school instruction, in this Commonwealth, shall recover damages therefor, in an action on the case, to be brought in the name of said child, by his guardian or next friend, in any court of competent jurisdiction to try the same, against the city or town by which such public school instruction is supported."[163] The idea of the tyranny of the majority prompted some state politicians to support this statute, but its vague wording left some abolitionists questioning its enforceability.[164] This legislation did not immediately desegregate Nantucket public schools. To the contrary, the school committee, populated as it was by segregationists, initially ignored it. What the legislation did provide, however, was a path forward for African American activists.

In June 1845 seventeen-year-old Phebe Ann Boston entered the fight for equal school rights by applying for admission to Nantucket High School. Unlike Eunice, Phebe was not from an obscure family; her father was Absalom Boston. As a prospective applicant, Phebe first had to obtain a letter of recommendation from a teacher confirming her qualifications. Only then could she take the high school entrance exam, which had changed slightly since Eunice had taken it some five years earlier. This time a prospective applicant had to arrive at the high school with "*Colburn's Sequel*, a slate and pencil, and a *National Reader*" in hand.[165] *Colburn's Sequel* was a very popular arithmetic schoolbook written by Warren Colburn, a white mathematician from Massachusetts. *The National Reader*, a highly praised schoolbook compiled by John Pierpont, contained lessons in reading and speaking. Though deemed qualified, ostensibly after meeting all requirements for admission to the high school, Phebe was still rejected by the school committee. Absalom Boston sued under the 1845 Massachusetts law.[166]

Regional newspapers characterized Absalom's lawsuit as "novel" and "interesting," as it directly raised the legal issue of public schooling and racial prejudice in a local municipality in the North. Several newspapers ran the same story, which focused on a proud father fighting for his daughter to have access to schooling beyond the primary school level. The crux of the case centered on whether African American children should be admitted to public schools on an equal footing with white children, particularly if a school already existed exclusively for African American children. One newspaper noted that whatever the courts decided, "the decision [would] be an important one, as a precedent."[167] That was true in the courtroom and the community.

In early September 1845 a town meeting was held to decide how to handle the lawsuit. Despite objections from other school committee members, Caleb Cushman, a lighthouse keeper and later a deputy sheriff, successfully urged the committee to defend the lawsuit. A school committee report in 1846 justified racial school segregation as a guard against race mixing. An editorialist praised the committee for acting within its right to deny admission to Eunice Ross and, by extension, Phebe Boston. "This girl [Eunice Ross] never had a place in the school," the editorialist surmised. Such a remark declared that Eunice did not and would never belong at this high school, for she was neither white nor a scholar. This editorialist then concluded with a rallying cry: "Blacks and whites must forever be distinct races."[168] But this sentiment did not carry over to the school committee.

In 1847, all Nantucket public schools began to admit African American children and youth. What provoked this equal school rights victory? One newspaper attributed it to voters selecting candidates for the school committee who held positions on other issues besides the equal school rights debate.[169] Hence the election of a white integrationist majority officially opened up the public schools. The *Liberator* noted, "One year has wrought an entire revolution," owing to the passage of the 1845 Massachusetts public school law.[170] Yet equal school rights had dominated local politics for years precisely because of unrelenting African American agitation. Arguably the rejection of Phebe Ann Boston converted some indecisive white Nantucket residents who had great respect for the Boston family. But Phebe never attended Nantucket High School, probably because she was too sick. In August 1849 she died of dysentery in New Bedford, Massachusetts, at twenty-one.[171] In all likelihood, Eunice did not attend the local public high school either. For that matter, Sarah Parker Remond did not return to the East School for Girls in Salem.

Continued black activism combined with the history of Salem as a seedbed for educational innovation accelerated the desegregation of Salem's public schools. Boycotting the African School put financial pressure on the school committee, since funds were being used to educate only a small number of students.[172] Moreover activists had convincingly argued that African American children had a right to attend any of Salem's renowned public schools.[173] Indeed this seaport town earned constant praise from educational reformers such as Horace Mann, who regarded the public schools there as "examples of excellence and models of imitation, superior to any to be found in any other part of the country."[174] The issue of racial school segregation was divisive, even explosive; it could derail the great progress that had been made to further public education. In 1843, a big shift, which saw public school students outnumber private school students two to one, required a firm response by the school committee concerning equal school rights. In February 1844 Stephen C. Phillips, a white abolitionist and former mayor of Salem, helped to recruit some new school committee members, who then voted to abolish the African School, effectively desegregating the public schools, making Salem the first municipality to do so.

Legal arguments buffered the Salem school committee's decision. Some white Salem residents held a meeting where they called the committee's vote "ill judged and obnoxious" and nominated two local politicians who vowed to overturn this decision.[175] That would fail. The Salem school committee solicited Richard Fletcher, a white Boston lawyer, to author a brief on the policy of racial school segregation. He provided a history of the public school system in the Bay State and asserted that the school committee had "no lawful power to exclude colored children from the public schools." The committee's subsequent resolutions attested to that. The victory at Nantucket to desegregate grammar schools in 1844 certainly impacted the Salem school committee's decision. The *Salem Register* reprinted an excerpt from the Nantucket resolution that highlighted African Americans' state constitutional rights for protection, their legal rights, and the right of an education for all.[176]

Eunice Ross, Sarah Parker Remond, and four other African American women whose names we do not know were determined to take advantage of recently established public high schools, but some white residents hindered them. In response, African American activists, with young women leading the way, organized a durable and effective campaign against racial exclusion at all levels of public education in Nantucket and Salem. They wrote op-eds, petitioned, boycotted, and sued, all the while arguing for educational justice and equal school rights. The 1845 Massachusetts law opened up a legal route for African American children and their families to address unequal school access.

By fighting to attend "democracy's college," these young women refused to curtail their intellectual ambitions. Neither Eunice nor Sarah, however, attended their local public high school. Such was the fate of forerunners who opened up educational opportunities for other African American girls and boys, even though those same opportunities would never come back around for them. While African American youth did not attend American public high schools in large numbers until the early twentieth century, African American activists and their allies in Salem and Nantucket fought to ensure that race was not the reason. These activists could, for the time being, claim victory after abolishing racially exclusive public schools in these seaport towns.[177] The fight for equal school rights was thus a continuation of early African American educational activism. It also helped to engender subsequent campaigns from Boston to Providence.

5 /   Black Girlhood and Equal School Rights

Nine-year-old Nancy Woodson should have been awarded the prestigious City Medal to honor her academic success. Ever since 1792 the Boston school committee had been distributing Franklin medals, named after its benefactor, Benjamin Franklin, to recognize male student achievement. Nearly thirty years later, girls were awarded the equivalent City Medal. This silver medal, measuring 34mm in diameter, was pierced at the top so it could be worn or hung. Recipients also attended a ceremonial dinner at Faneuil Hall.[1] By all accounts a high-achieving student, Nancy, a Boston native, excelled in reading, writing, and arithmetic. After her examination at the all-black Smith School in Boston in 1829, she and two classmates, William Cooper Nell and Charles A. Battiste, earned high honors. But Nancy did not receive a medal, nor did her two classmates. They were not even invited to the ceremonial dinner.

In the place of a medal, Nancy, William, and Charles each received a simple voucher to purchase a book, *The Life of Benjamin Franklin*. A letter to the editor of the *Boston Courier* noted this galling unfairness, asking, "Why do the School Committee deprive the colored children of [medals]?"[2] Denying a medal to high-achieving African American students was symbolic of the educational inequalities within the nascent Boston public school system. How Nancy felt about this incident is not known, but William recalled that this "heart-sickening" moment spurred him to do all he could to abolish racial discrimination in Boston public schools.[3] It would take him nearly twenty years, beginning in 1836 and concluding in 1855 with the abolition of racially exclusive schools.

The scholarly narrative on the Boston campaign for equal school rights is extensive, as legal scholars have examined the *Roberts v. City of Boston* case of 1850, which set the precedent for the "separate but equal" doctrine, and as historians have studied the African American separatist and integrationist factions.[4] What has been overlooked is the centrality of gender, women, and girlhood in this campaign. Benjamin Roberts Sr., an African American proponent of equal school rights, advocated for the education of all of his children, but he made a very deliberate and calculated decision to build a legal case around his five-year-old daughter, Sarah. Why? Arguably because an African American girl might be able to garner public sympathy by embodying qualities such as love, kindness, innocence, and capability. Sarah was portrayed as a symbol of humanity deserving legal protection and educational justice.

Quite a few Boston-based activists, both men and women, began to support the Roberts family and the fight for equal school rights. Their protest strategies and tactics included advocating for black girls' education, asserting African American rights as citizens of the Commonwealth of Massachusetts, petitioning the city of Boston as well as the state, pushing for equal school rights legislation, boycotting the Smith School, and relocating to nearby towns such as Roxbury and Cambridge that had already abolished racially exclusive schools. Amid this surge of activism, the African American girl became the face of the equal school rights campaign in antebellum Boston.[5]

To many African Americans, the city of Boston was both a place teeming with opportunity and a place of peril. African American men and women had access to only a few vocations; they were crowded into the North End area of the city before eventually migrating to the Beacon Hill area; they experienced racial segregation in houses of worships and all the way to the schoolhouse. Nevertheless an increasing number of African Americans flocked to the city. By 1800 Boston counted a little over 1,100 African American residents; twenty years later the population had reached 1,726, making it one of the largest free black communities in the North.[6] As the historian Jared Hardesty writes, African Americans in turn-of-the-century Boston secured a livelihood within the "continuum of unfreedom" that shaped their everyday experiences.[7]

Various institutions, from mutual aid societies to churches, helped to strengthen the African American community in Boston. The African Society, a mutual aid organization founded in 1796, encouraged members to support each other, monetarily and spiritually.[8] Likewise, the African Meetinghouse on Belknap Street, an institution unto itself, was dedicated in 1805 and served as a church, a school, and a meeting place. Thomas Paul Sr., a black Baptist minister, led religious services at the church for over twenty years.

African Americans in Boston charted their own path to schooling. In 1798 sixty African Americans organized a private school in the home of Primus Hall, who encouraged activists to continue to fight for public schooling. In 1800 George Middleton, an African American veteran of the Revolutionary War, petitioned the city of Boston to support a school for African Americans. Middleton adopted a patriotic tone as he and sixty-six other signees rejected the idea that schooling African Americans would be "impolitic and dangerous," and instead reasoned that knowledge went hand-in-hand with civic virtue and peace. The petitioners set their plea within the rich history of education in the Bay State while highlighting similar educational initiatives in Philadelphia and New York City. The petition was denied; it would be one of many rejected petitions concerning African American education.[9]

In 1808 the school once located at Primus Hall's house moved into the basement room of the African Meetinghouse. For years African Americans exercised community control over this school as they organized fundraisers and hired African American teachers such as Cyrus Vassell, Prince Saunders, and Peter Tracy. Saunders, a Vermont native, was remembered as "one of the best educated colored men ever reared in this country," having studied at Dartmouth College before teaching school in Colchester, Connecticut, and then Boston.[10]

Inequality and racial segregation were built into the Boston public school system from the very beginning. Boston public schools officially opened in 1789. Amid the rise of urbanization and industrialization in the early nineteenth century, Horace Mann and other educational reformers regarded schools as powerful institutions that could transmit to all young Americans a common language and shared values.[11] Common school reform soon took hold. With the goal of ensuring all children access to free primary schooling, Mann overhauled the Massachusetts public school system by financing schools through taxes, lengthening the academic year, and increasing teachers' salaries, among other reforms.

In 1812 the Boston school committee appropriated $200 per year to support the school in the African Meetinghouse, which offered classes at the primary and grammar school levels. City selectmen had accepted a bequest from Abiel Smith, a wealthy white merchant who supported African American education. The African School was then designated a grammar school for African American children ages seven to fourteen. Grammar schools, the second stage in public schooling, offered an English education consisting of subjects such as "Spelling, Reading, English, Grammar, and Geography" as well as "Writing, Arithmetic, and Book-keeping."[12]

In 1818 a town vote authorized the appropriation of funds to support public primary schools for children ages four to seven. These schools offered a basic introduction in spelling and reading to prepare children for admission to the public grammar schools. A year later, twenty-eight primary schools enrolled 1,359 children, but apparently none of the schools welcomed African American children.[13] In July 1820 African School No. 1, the first black public primary school in Boston, opened in a room adjacent to the African Grammar School in the African Meetinghouse, with upwards of fifty children attending. Increasing student enrollment led to the establishment of African School No. 2 on Southac Street in December 1822, which soon enrolled thirty-three students. Another primary school, located in Robinson's Alley and run by Sally Parkman, was African School No. 3 only unofficially, since the school committee had not authorized it. It closed in 1825 due to low enrollment. Public school opportunities, then, existed for both African American and white children, separately and on an unequal basis.

In this nascent public school system, grammar schools employed male teachers, while women composed the teaching force at primary schools. Importantly, at least two black women held teaching positions for years at the public primary schools. Charlotte Williams Foster, an Afro–Native American woman, taught at African School No. 1, where her teaching was described as "satisfactory" by the school committee.[14] In contrast, African School No. 2, under the charge of Naomi Jeffers, was in decline.[15] The primary school committee fired Jeffers, and in July 1824 hired Catharine Paul, an African American schoolteacher and the wife of Thomas Paul Sr. Catharine relocated African School No. 2 from Southac Street to her residence on George Street, where, under her leadership, student enrollment grew from forty to sixty. The school committee noted that the school was now "more orderly and cleanly . . . and in the studies and manners of the children there is much improvement."[16] Both Charlotte Williams Foster and Catharine Paul, and later Paul's children, Susan, Ann, and Thomas Jr., were among the early African American teachers who supported black intellectual achievement.

In 1833 the Boston school committee authorized the construction of a new school building for African American children and youth. On March 3, 1835, the new building, christened the Abiel Smith School, opened on Belknap Street, adjacent to the African Meetinghouse.[17] This new building housed two black primary schools, with the grammar school occupying the upper level. Though new, the building was still inferior to the white public grammar school buildings. Rufus Spaulding, a white clergyman and agent of the American Union for the Relief and Improvement of the Colored Race, remarked as much in his 1837 statistical report on Boston's black population. About 1,757 African Americans resided in Boston, of which 1,310 were in families; 275 were young African American men, and 299 were young African American women. About 169 children overall could read; 272 children attended schools; and 288 children attended Sunday schools. The educational "facilities" for African American children were "by no means ordinary," Spaulding wrote, "though perhaps not fully adequate to their wants."[18]

The Smith School building was deficient: it was overcrowded, lacked a yard and greenery, and did not receive the resources of white schools.[19] In August 1838 Primus Hall and thirty African American male activists, including John T. Hilton, complained to the Boston school committee about the "inconveniences in having but one school to which to send our children."[20] They had agreed to remain in this building, despite knowing that "the law gave us equal rights with other citizens to send our children to any school in the place." Their petition, then, requested the expansion of the Smith School building and use of the lecture room at the English High School. What the Boston school committee and City Council decided is unclear, but the Smith School building was not expanded.[21]

Moreover African American students' academic achievements continued to be overlooked publicly. An observer praised students at the Smith Grammar School exhibition in August 1836 for "distinguish[ing] themselves in the attainment of useful knowledge," but the same observer complained that city newspapers failed to publish the names of five students who had earned academic prizes.[22] The students' names were recorded in the *Liberator*: Arabella Dalton, George Jones, Joseph Putnam, Nestor Freeman, and George Colburn. Not much had changed since Nancy Woodson's own educational success had been disregarded some seven years earlier.

In theory, the Boston school committee could have settled this matter over academic prizes by recognizing the achievements of both African American and white children equally, but deep-rooted educational inequities in the school system would not be overcome so easily. In 1838 city newspaper editors did finally publish the names of high-achieving African American students; three girls were acknowledged (Isannah Hall, Frances Tash, and Rosanna Sewall) and three boys (Frederick Barbadoes, Isaac Snowden, and Benjamin Fowler).[23] At that point Abner Forbes, a white antislavery activist, taught at the Smith Grammar School, and Sarah Forbes, his wife, served as his assistant; 180 students were enrolled, though daily attendance averaged about 115.[24] While all high-achieving white students at Boston public schools received medals, the six African American students were given books, probably the same one Nancy Woodson got, *The Life of Benjamin Franklin*. This slight suggested that neither the Smith Grammar School nor its students measured up to white students and other public schools. Yet another generation of African American girls and boys endured unequal treatment. William Cooper Nell took action: he began conducting research, gathering evidence, and crafting arguments to promote equal school rights (Figure 5.1).[25]

Throughout the 1840s activists continued to criticize the Smith School building for being dilapidated, overcrowded, and underresourced, though they often praised students who, despite these failures, possessed and displayed "superior gifts and ambition" at yearly school exhibitions.[26] In the mid-1840s African American students finished last in the annual examination. Whether this was a clever calculation to underperform is unknown, but the message was clear: the Smith School offered only a mediocre education. Nell and his allies soon organized the School Abolishing Party.[27] Invoking the word "abolition" was no doubt a discursive strategy to call forth the abolition movement and the scourge of American slavery. Just as slavery must be abolished, so too must racial segregation in public schools. Moreover associating as a party implied African American activists' determination to use political and legal strategies to end racial discrimination in schools.

An early casualty in the fight for equal school rights may have been Nancy Woodson. For five years Nancy had worked at her alma mater as an assistant teacher. Then in 1840 the Boston primary school committee concluded that she was an ineffective teacher and replaced her with Mary B. Symmes, who had been an assistant teacher at the all-white Adams School. But just a few months earlier, Nancy had earned praise from the African American community for her excellent teaching.[28] Her firing galvanized activists who argued that the school committee asserted undue control over the Smith School. But Nancy was not able to reclaim her job. By 1850 she had moved to Charlestown and married

FIGURE 5.1. William Cooper Nell (1816–1874), a Boston
native and son of black abolitionists, worked as a journalist, writer, and activist. If Horace Mann is thought to
be the father of American public schools, Nell was the
secretary of African American education in the mid-
nineteenth century, recording African American students'
achievements in Boston public schools. Courtesy of the
Massachusetts Historical Society.

John Quincy Weaver, an African American barber. It appears that her
husband deserted her, for she was granted a divorce in 1861.[29] Nancy
lived with her father, Joseph, a blacking maker (a producer of shoe polish)
who had amassed a valuable estate—about $4,000 in property and $1,000
in personal effects.[30] Joseph died in 1874, and Nancy stayed in Charlestown before moving into St. Monica's Home for Sick Colored Women
and Children on Highland Street in Boston, the former homestead of

William Lloyd Garrison.[31] The teaching position at the Smith School may well have been her last.

In spring of 1844 the campaign for equal school rights hit its stride as African Americans deployed the tried and true tactic of a school boycott, which had proven successful at Salem and Nantucket. On May 21, 1844, African Americans at the First Independent Baptist Church passed seven resolutions, including a commitment to "withdraw their children from the exclusive school established in contravention of the equality of privileges which is the vital principle of the school system of Massachusetts."[32] Attendance at the Smith School dropped from 263 in 1840 to 51 by 1849.[33] Amid this boycott, activists established ad hoc independent schools so children would not be completely deprived of learning. Some African American families, including John T. Hilton's, even relocated to nearby towns such as Charlestown and Chelsea, where schools welcomed all children, regardless of race. Despite the hassle that relocating posed, this "local brain drain" stripped the city of Boston of upstanding African American taxpaying residents. This tactic also reflected the long-standing tradition among many African American parents to move to areas that fully supported their children's schooling.

Relentless criticism of the Smith School put Abner Forbes's job in jeopardy. At one point, African American leaders such as Joel W. Lewis had thanked Forbes for helping to increase educational opportunities by purchasing science equipment and organizing lectures.[34] Yet in 1844 Forbes confronted accusations of indecency, immorality, and abuse. African Americans alleged that he severely beat his students and shirked his teaching duties by reading newspapers and doodling in his journal during school hours. If that were not enough, it was alleged that Forbes believed that African Americans were inferior.[35] The African American community now wanted him to go. What changed in a matter of a few years to push the community to turn on Forbes? Did his skills as a teacher deteriorate? Perhaps. Had African American parents always overlooked his shortcomings in the hopes that their children would have access to an education? One mother admitted as much. The fact remains, however, that proponents of equal school rights wished to abolish the Smith School; Forbes was flotsam, and some of the complaints had been substantiated anyway.

One vocal critic of Forbes was Angelina Brinton Gardner, an African American woman born in Providence, Rhode Island, in 1800, who married Caesar Gardner, a waiter, on August 22, 1824, and relocated to Boston. The Gardners had three children, Edward, James, and Angelina.

A churchgoing woman, the elder Angelina labored as a washerwoman amid her activist work. At an organizational meeting at Belknap Street Church on August 5, 1850, she was one of only a few women to give remarks endorsing equal school rights.[36] Other proponents prepared a detailed report providing evidence of Forbes's misdeeds. Angelina testified that Forbes had detained her son Edward after school, and when she arrived to rescue him, Forbes had yelled, "Out, you vile wretch!" Forbes could neither confirm nor deny her testimony; he claimed that his memory failed him. But Angelina's reputation as an upstanding Christian woman of character convinced many African Americans that Forbes had verbally abused her and her son.[37]

The complaints against Forbes included dramatic testimony from African American girls such as Lucretia Hilton, the daughter of John T. Hilton and Lavinia Ames. Lucretia reported that she had not learned much under Forbes's instruction, but once she attended a grammar school in Cambridge under the direction of an instructor "who saw no distinction in the *natures* of his pupils," she became a high-achieving student.[38] She would soon join her father in the equal school rights struggle. Another girl escaped to the Boston House of Reformation for Juvenile Offenders rather than experience Forbes's abuse. African American girls confirmed that the Smith School was not just intellectually subpar but that Forbes had traumatized the children and crushed their desire to learn.

Despite testimony from Angelina Gardner and other witnesses, the Boston school committee exonerated Forbes, but he did not keep his teaching position for long. Some of the allegations were, in fact, true, which he admitted, but he claimed that "for the last year, there had been no cause of complaint."[39] Nevertheless a city school report found that the Smith School was in an "unsatisfactory [and] deplorable condition."[40] The school committee soon replaced Forbes with Ambrose Wellington, another white teacher, but the staffing change did little to encourage children to return to school. A majority of African Americans demanded abolition or else. In 1846 the Massachusetts Anti-Slavery Society endorsed equal school rights and vowed to help "in securing [for African Americans] the full and equal enjoyment of the public schools."[41]

While some women like Angelina Gardner came to educational activism later in life, others were born into it. Sarah Clarissa Roberts came from a family of educator-activists. Her paternal great-grandfather, James Easton, built a manual labor school for young men of color in Bridgewater, Massachusetts. Her paternal great-uncle, Hosea Easton, was a lecturer, minister, and writer who published a treatise denouncing prejudice and promoting black civil rights. Robert Roberts, Sarah's paternal grandfather, wrote about his experience as a servant in *The House Servant's Directory: or, A Monitor for Private Families, etc.* (1827). He was also part of the planning committee to build a manual labor college for African American youth in New Haven, Connecticut, in the late 1820s. Sarah's maternal grandfather, Samuel Fowler, had been enslaved in New York before escaping at the age of thirty and settling first in Salem and then Charlestown.[42] A laborer, he owned real estate valued at $4,000 in 1850. The Eastons, the Fowlers, and the Robertses had all signed their names to a variety of state-level petitions concerning the annexation of Texas, Boston's interracial marriage ban repeal, the Fugitive Slave Act, and eventually equal school rights.

In 1847 Benjamin and Adeline Roberts decided to enroll their five-year-old daughter Sarah at the all-white, coed Otis School, which was closest to their West End residence and a great school too.[43] Isaac F. Shepard, a white Harvard graduate, was the school's principal, a position he would hold for nearly thirteen years. He decided to admit Sarah.[44] Enrolling Sarah first at the Otis School, and not their nine-year-old son Benjamin Jr., was a deliberate move by the Robertses. African American activists were certainly aware of sentimental culture that had shaped the concept of childhood innocence. As the scholar Robin Bernstein argues, "in the second half of the nineteenth century, white childhood, and especially white girlhood, became laminated to the idea of innocence."[45] Yet African American activists reconfigured this concept of childhood innocence to depict the black girl as good-hearted, pious, and admirable. A child like Sarah might be afforded some regard and her plight might elicit some kind of affective reaction from the white public; she only wanted to go to school nearest her home.

Remarkably Sarah attended the Otis School without facing any problems. At first the family cheered their success. In fact Benjamin Sr. reported that Sarah enjoyed "equal treatment and courtesy." Encouraged, Sarah's parents then applied to enroll Benjamin Jr. in a "higher department" at the Otis School. They notified Isaac F. Shepard and alerted the school committee, which apparently found the prospect of yet another African American student so unpalatable that they reconsidered even Sarah's admission. The school committee refused to admit Benjamin Jr. to the Otis School and barred him from the "next nearest school."[46] Sarah was then expelled from the Otis School, having been there only a few weeks; a police officer escorted her off school property.[47] Benjamin

Sr. then applied to various school subcommittees, but Sarah continued to be denied access. Outraged, he appealed to the Boston school committee. Meanwhile other examples emerged of Boston primary school teachers expelling African American children: William Brown's children attended the Hancock School briefly before being expelled, as did John St. Pierre's children.[48] But it was Sarah C. Roberts who would be the legal test case.

Benjamin Sr.'s decision to sue on Sarah's behalf, and not on his son's, was strategic. Benjamin Jr. had been outright denied entry to the Otis School. Benjamin Sr. could have sued the city of Boston under the 1845 Massachusetts law that granted legal protection to a child who had been excluded from a public school, but he apparently declined to do so. Instead it seems that Benjamin Sr. relied on social assumptions tied to Sarah's gender and age: a five-year-old girl might produce a more positive outcome compared to a nine-year-old African American boy. Such was the case when Sarah attended the Otis School for a few weeks. The decision to sue on Sarah's behalf would transform her into an icon for educational justice.

In front of an audience that included white school committee members, Benjamin Roberts Sr. and his allies put forth a gendered argument to back their case to abolish the Smith School. In addition to broader claims about equality and citizenship, Robert Morris, one of the first African American lawyers in the United States and a native of nearby Salem, asserted that it was not only wasteful, tiring, and "inconvenient" for African American children to travel great distances from their home to reach the Smith School, but it also "expose[d] the health of [African American] females." Calling attention to girls' health might have reminded some residents of earlier complaints against former teacher Abner Forbes, who had created an unhealthy and abusive environment for African American children at the Smith School. This campaign for equal school rights thus concerned African American girls' well-being.

Arguably Benjamin Sr. and Morris were aware of the gender dynamics at play in earlier equal school rights cases in Salem and Nantucket. Both men had ties to Salem; they probably knew the Remonds, if not Sarah Parker Remond. Morris even cited Fletcher's opinion in the Salem case in his remarks on equal school rights.[49] In a speech delivered before the Daughters of Samaria, an African American self-help organization, Morris recognized that "great responsibilities rest upon us all and in the performance of these important duties we must marshall all our highest and best intellectual powers and forces. In the elevation of our race,

I know of no power or element so great as the influence of woman."[50] Morris was not only an advocate of women's educational rights, but he also sought to help African American girls and women reach these intellectual heights.

Benjamin Sr. hired Robert Morris to represent his daughter Sarah in the lawsuit against the City of Boston. In the Suffolk County Court of Common Pleas in March 1848, Morris filed a writ and asked for $600 in damages.[51] More than the money, both Morris and Benjamin Sr. wanted African American children to have access to all public schools. Furthermore, they wanted to claim another victory in the long struggle for black civil rights, which saw the abolition of the interracial marriage ban in 1843 and the end of racial segregation in railroad cars soon thereafter. Defending Sarah in a court of law also represented a potential reckoning for Benjamin Sr., who had wrestled with his own feelings of inferiority as a school-age child attending a racially segregated school.

When the Suffolk County Court of Common Pleas ruled in favor of the City of Boston, Robert Morris filed an appeal to the Massachusetts Judicial Supreme Court in October 1848. He recruited Charles Sumner, the Harvard-trained attorney, abolitionist, and future U.S. senator, to represent Sarah. Peleg Chandler defended the city of Boston, with Chief Justice Lemuel Shaw presiding. In his lengthy remarks, Sumner celebrated the common school as a distinctly New England institution, with all of its tradition and success. Massachusetts was certainly a forerunner in public education. School committees had been empowered to make decisions regarding the age, sex, character, and preparedness of potential students. But could race be a qualification to exclude some children from certain public schools? The Roberts case provoked this question. The primary school committee wished to use race as one criterion for organizing schools, but another rule stated that students "go to school nearest their residence."[52] How could these two provisions be reconciled for an African American child such as Sarah, who lived closest to an all-white school?

To Sumner, the answer was clear: any racial distinction in the public school system was "not equality before the law," an argument he repeated throughout his remarks. This case amplified the campaign for equal rights that African Americans had waged years earlier, and Sumner riffed on that to affirm African American equality. Sarah had to pass five different primary schools on her way to the Smith School. This long walk was more than an "inconvenience"; it was oppressive—the very definition of inequality. Sumner became a sort of educator in the courtroom:

he discussed the meaning of "equality" in ancient philosophy, gave a brief history of the French Revolution, and cited the Declaration of Independence as well as the Massachusetts state constitution. What Sarah and what many African Americans desired was centuries old: equality before the law.[53]

Sumner depicted Sarah as a smart and determined five-year-old. He referred to her as a "little child" three times, heightening the need for the court to protect her and her opportunity for schooling. "Before the Court," he claimed, "we are all children." He captured Sarah's pleading voice when he said "[Sarah] asks at your hands" and "calls upon you" to defend her personal rights. Perhaps the vulnerability of an African American girl would sway the judge and result in African American children's equal access to Boston public schools.[54]

Sarah might have been "little" in stature, but Sumner characterized her as "strong" and pious, a child of God. Just as young African American women in the Prudence Crandall controversy had invoked an ethic of Christian love decades earlier, so too did Sumner now in court. He accused the Boston school committee of dealing in "caste," quoting various clergymen who stated that caste relegated African Americans to "perpetual debasement" and weakened the bonds of humanity.[55]

Sumner's legal argument avowed the rights of black girls, even though his language at times followed patriarchal assumptions. He invoked masculine gender norms, though this case involved a five-year-old African American girl. For instance, he described African Americans as "legal voter[s]," but only African American men could vote, and even then, only in a few states. Why, then, use masculine gender norms to frame the argument against racial discrimination? In the early nineteenth century, masculine gender norms predominated. A five-year-old African American girl's proximity to these practices of citizenship actually sanctioned her argument for protection and equality. This line of reasoning thus upheld black girls' educational rights.[56]

For the most part many whites opposed the campaign for equal school rights. Some, who might be called "preservers," wanted the Boston public school system to operate as it always had. *Flag of Our Union*, a newspaper with a high circulation, called the equal school rights campaign an "amalgamation campaign," and its editor, Maturin Ballou, urged whites to "withdraw their children from the schools" if the school committee welcomed African American children.[57] Other white Boston residents were wary of a boycott but did express concern at the prospect of racially desegregated schools; they were pragmatists. A Boston school committee member summarized that viewpoint when he argued that God intended to separate the races since African Americans were "incapable of receiving the same amount of instruction in a given time and at the same age [as white children]."[58] Benjamin Roberts Sr. and William Cooper Nell sought to defeat these viewpoints.

In March 1850 the court ruled in favor of the Boston school committee. Chief Justice Shaw protected the power of the school committee to regulate "the system of distribution and classification" in public schools.[59] The ruling was a dispiriting setback that put African American activists at a crossroads: Go forward with the campaign or desist? Activists decided to push on.[60] Not all African Americans in Boston endorsed the equal school rights campaign, but apparently the majority did. At a meeting at the Belknap Street Church in August 1849, ninety-two African Americans vowed to boycott the Smith School, while five did not.[61] One of the nay votes had to have come from Thomas Paul Smith. Born around 1827, Smith was a member of the prominent Paul family. His mother, Ann, married a musician named Elijah W. Smith. After his mother's sudden death at the age of twenty-seven, Thomas was raised by his aunt Susan Paul and his grandmother Catharine Paul.[62] Both Catharine and Susan no doubt shared their love of learning and teaching with Ann's children. Pauline Hopkins, an African American writer and distant relative, remembered that Ann's children "passed much of their younger days . . . under the instruction of their accomplished Aunt."[63] Thomas Paul Smith and his siblings attended the Smith School. He was denied admissions to a Boston public high school but later matriculated at Phillips Academy, a well-respected private school in Andover, Massachusetts, for at least a year. He later returned to Boston, where he ran a used clothing shop, joined the Young Men's Literary Society, and participated in the abolition movement, working alongside Hilton, Nell, and Bethsheba Fowler, Sarah Roberts's maternal grandmother and an early supporter of Garrison's *Liberator*. He also married into the Roberts family when he wed Elizabeth Augusta Roberts.

At a school committee meeting, Thomas Paul Smith rejected the closing of the Smith School. An observer described him as a young man of "unassuming manners and modest deportment." First, Thomas claimed that African American children at white public schools would face constant "jeers and sneers."[64] He was right. At some public primary schools in New Bedford, teachers ostracized African American children, segregated them in the classroom, and forced misbehaving white students to sit in the "nigger seat" as punishment.[65] Elizabeth Garrison and her siblings, for example, went to the public primary schools in Concord, Massachusetts. At Concord's bicentennial celebration in 1835, Abba Prescott, a nine-year-old white girl, held hands with Elizabeth Garrison during the procession—a daring sight since Elizabeth had been "ill-treated" previously.[66] Thomas Paul Smith warned that African American children would suffer intellectually, psychologically, and socially if schools were racially desegregated.

Smith suggested that an all-black educational environment, however, offered a refuge from white supremacy and the cruelty of white racists; there, impressionable African American children could avoid being victimized.[67] He reasoned that children benefited from having African American teachers. His support for the Smith School may have been based on his personal experience, since he himself had studied there. No doubt he wished to preserve a notable, if somewhat flawed, institution. Following Smith's remarks, the Boston school committee decided in August 1849 to keep the Smith School open and to exclude African American children from all other public schools.

Smith found an ally in his uncle, Thomas Paul Jr., whom he recruited as headmaster at the Smith School.[68] Paul Jr., the son of Thomas and Catharine Paul, had attended the Smith School for seven years before matriculating at the ill-fated Noyes Academy in New Hampshire.[69] He apprenticed as a printer under William Lloyd Garrison and sought to follow in his family's footsteps as an educator. He believed wholeheartedly in educating African Americans to be useful members of society. Becoming the headmaster at his alma mater would enable him to share what he had learned with the next generation. In 1835 he had proposed opening a school, but he had trouble drumming up interest. He tried again six years later; this school would teach African American children subjects such as English, math, Latin, and foreign languages, unlike any school in the Boston area at that point.[70] His school failed, but his desire to educate African American children did not wane. He took a teaching position at the Free Colored School in Albany, New York, and his nephew Thomas Paul Smith accompanied him.[71] Paul Jr. then moved to Providence, where he successfully ran the Meeting Street Grammar School for African American children.[72] But now in Boston was his chance to realize his dream of educational leadership, despite the looming equal rights campaign. Talented, educated, and driven, he possessed the qualifications to take over the Smith School. The Boston school committee appointed him headmaster in September 1849.[73]

Shortly thereafter, Chloe Lee joined Thomas Paul Jr. as an assistant teacher. Lee, a Providence native, volunteered at church activities for the First Independent Baptist Church of the People of Color and embraced reform causes such as the interracial marriage ban repeal.[74] She relocated to Boston, where she had taught at the Smith School in the primary department for six years. The Boston school committee judged that she possessed "remarkable propriety" and discharged her "duties with conscientious fidelity." So Lee was stunned when Ambrose Wellington sought her resignation in 1847, claiming that he wanted to hire a better teacher. She wrote a letter expressing her dismay and asking for her position to be reinstated, but apparently her request was denied. She then enrolled at the State Normal School at Framingham.[75] At first, nobody in town offered to board her on account of her race, but Horace Mann and his wife took her in. She resumed her position as assistant teacher at the Smith School in Boston under Thomas Paul Jr.'s leadership, but did not remain for very long. In September 1850 she petitioned the school committee for partial salary owed to her, but her petition was denied.[76] After a short illness, Lee died of consumption in 1856 at forty-one years old. Her death notice recognized her labor as an "instructress" at the Smith School.[77]

Contentious disputes over racial school segregation turned violent in May 1851. A group of African American men, including William J. Watkins and Julian McCrea, beat up Thomas Paul Smith. Two years earlier Watkins and Smith had debated equal school rights, with Smith arguing that "colored schools [were] institutions . . . of great advantage to the colored people."[78] Watkins accused Smith of obstructing the equal school rights campaign, thus paving the way for the Massachusetts Supreme Court ruling in *Roberts v. Boston*. Watkins and others wanted to punish Smith and probably pummel other separatists into silence. As the historian Hilary Moss argues, this attack sought to mark Smith and those like him as "hostile to freedom."[79] Six men were charged with assault, including Benjamin Roberts Sr., who confessed to knowing about the attack against the "obnoxious" Smith. Watkins defended himself, and the jury ruled in his favor. McCrea and Roberts were both found guilty and fined.

Since the *Roberts* case brought no recourse, Benjamin Roberts Sr. led a petition drive throughout Massachusetts. William Lloyd Garrison wished Roberts "success in his laudable undertaking" and announced this petition drive in the *Liberator*.[80] Roberts gathered nearly five hundred signatures by 1851; he separated African American and white petitions, likely because he thought African American signees ought to present a collective message. White allies later submitted four separate petitions: three from white men with a total of 305 signees, including Wendell Phillips and Charles Sumner, and one with eight signatures from white women, including Thankful Southwick and Ann G. Phillips, the wife of Wendell Phillips. The petition written and signed by African American activists stated their "grievances," asserted their rights as "natives of the state" (no doubt a veiled reference to the wave of Irish immigration), and explained their opposition to the Smith School. Jonas W. Clark, Lewis Hayden, and forty other African American men signed for themselves and their families, totaling 186 persons.

In exercising his fundamental right to petition on behalf of his daughter, his son, and his other children, Benjamin Sr. cited his deep ties to Massachusetts, particularly his birthright status as "a Bostonian" and his grandfather's service in the American Revolution. He framed his complaint against the school committee as "impos[ing] upon the *weak*," just as the British had done to the colonists during the Revolutionary era. In 1851 he submitted another petition, once again asserting his citizenship while presenting a serious educational grievance. He claimed that he and others had "been deprived of certain rights and privileges that every citizen of this Commonwealth is entitled to under the Constitution and the Laws." In this instance, he invoked three types of citizenship: local, as a taxpaying resident of Massachusetts; national, as a legal subject of the United States; and ancestral, as, in his words, the "son of a respectable citizen of Massachusetts." His desire to enroll Sarah at a public school, he wrote, actually was a manifestation of his good citizenship. He wanted to pass on to his children the values of good citizenship, but Sarah and Benjamin Jr. had been deprived after their rejection from the Otis School.[81]

Benjamin Sr.'s second petition demanded educational justice, which explains why he requested recompense. Advocating for African American equality in antebellum New England was a laborious undertaking. Writing in the third person, he described his loss of time, the expense in prosecuting for his rights, the amount he paid for private instruction for his children while they remained in Boston and for damages sustained by his children "on account of the unjust dealings of the public servants of the City of Boston." He believed redress was an obligation of the state. Moreover his words served as a reminder of the painstaking labor of African American activists who had to fight for civil rights that should have been theirs by virtue of their humanity and citizenship. In some ways, the petition was a sociopolitical rejoinder to Chief Justice Shaw's ruling in the *Roberts* case. It anticipated the demand from

African American leaders at the national emigration convention in 1854 for "redress of our grievances . . . which we suffered at the hands of this American people."[82] African Americans, whether enslaved, free, or self-emancipated, deserved recompense.

As the petition campaign was pending, the Roberts family crisscrossed the greater Boston area, probably searching for good public schools for their children. Initially Benjamin and Adeline Roberts remained in Boston and paid for their children to be tutored. Then they moved to Cambridge, where they resided close to Lunsford Lane, an African American writer and former slave, and his wife Martha. Cambridge public schools were highly regarded and not racially exclusive.[83] The Cambridge school committee even celebrated the Broadway Primary School for its racially diverse student body, consisting of "the Anglo-Saxon, Teutonic, Celtic and African."[84] Perhaps Sarah and her siblings attended this primary school.[85] By 1855 the Roberts family had relocated to Somerville, where the children attended public schools, and their mother added to the family income by cleaning classrooms in the town's schools.[86] In 1860 the family had moved to Chelsea, Massachusetts, but curiously seventeen-year-old Sarah boarded with her eighty-four-year-old grandfather Samuel Fowler in Charlestown.[87] Did Sarah act as a caregiver to Samuel, who passed away in 1863? Did she prefer Charlestown to Somerville? Whatever the case, Sarah had likely concluded her schooling by that point.

Despite Benjamin Roberts Sr.'s efforts, momentum for the equal school rights campaign waned temporarily amid the rise of fugitive slave cases in Boston. During the 1840s some states throughout the North, including Massachusetts, passed personal liberty laws, which denied authorities use of jails to detain fugitive slaves, but the issue of fugitive slave captures only escalated.[88] Abolitionists organized vigilance committees to protect and shelter self-emancipated slaves. In Massachusetts, two organizations were especially prominent: the Boston Vigilance Committee and the Anti-Man-Hunting League.[89] Members of these organizations, such as Henry I. Bowditch, William Cooper Nell, and Robert Morris, took immediate action when the fugitive slave cases of Shadrach Minkins, Thomas Sims, and Anthony Burns gripped the city of Boston. Chief Justice Shaw ruled in the Sims and Burns cases to uphold the Fugitive Slave Law. A mob aided Minkins in a daring escape to Canada from a Boston courthouse in 1851. That same year, Sims was rendered back to slavery in Georgia, the first Boston casualty of the Fugitive Slave Law. Burns would have suffered the same fate had it not been for abolitionists who purchased his freedom.

These shocking spectacles of fugitive slave renditions certainly tormented black Bostonians, but it did not stop their fight for the abolition of slavery. Benjamin Roberts Sr. made and circulated broadsides warning free blacks about talking to police officers. He also started his own newspaper, the *Self- Elevator*, and began touring New England with Henry Box Brown, a slave from Virginia who had escaped by mailing himself in a box. Nell, Morris, and Thomas Paul Smith put their lives on the line as they facilitated fugitive slave escapes. But the equal school rights campaign soon rebounded.

In 1853 a five-year-old child named Edward Pindall applied to attend a white public primary school closer to his home. The Pindalls were white, legally speaking, since a legal precedent in Massachusetts stated that any person with at least 50 percent "white blood" was indeed white.[90] Nevertheless the fair-skinned Pindalls allied themselves with the African American community in Boston. For instance, William, Edward's father, petitioned the state legislature to charter a black military company, the Boston Massasoit Guards, led by Robert Morris. In this instance, the Pindalls strategically, and perhaps in cooperation with equal school rights proponents, used their near-whiteness to trick the school committee into admitting Edward. It worked. In August 1853 Andrew Cushing, a school committee chairman, permitted Edward to attend an all-white public school. Two weeks later, Edward was expelled when his racial background came to light. His father then hired Robert Morris to sue the City of Boston. The case offered Morris a legal do-over, although in practice this case focused more on the racial status of a five-year-old child rather than the issue of equal school rights. During the trial, two doctors even examined Edward and concluded that he was "one-sixth or one-eighth African blood."[91] The jury sided with the city. Morris wished to appeal, but apparently no such appeal was ever filed.[92] A legal route to educational equality had once again been denied.[93] Even though this case did not involve an African American girl, it demonstrates that African American activists were still thinking strategically. The equal school rights campaign had been revived.

William Cooper Nell then embarked upon a petition drive of his own throughout the eastern part of the state, from Nantucket to Charlestown. The same short statement accompanied each petition: "The undersigned inhabitants of———, respectfully request the Legislature to provide, some efficient means to prevent the colored children of Boston from being deprived of the equal privileges of the Common Schools of that city." On the left side were signatures from men, or "legal voters," and on the right were signatures from women. Absalom F. Boston, Sarah Ross (Eunice Ross's sister), and fifty-three others signed the Nantucket petition. Sarah Roberts's maternal grandfather and grandmother, Samuel Fowler and Bethsheba Fowler, signed the Charlestown petition, along with fifty-three others.

Nell relied on an activist network powered by African American women who gathered nearly 1,600 signatures. For example, Charlotte Forten, an African American woman writer and poet, collected signatures while she resided in Salem with the Remond family.[94] Maritchia Juan, Nancy, Susan, and, perhaps most notably, Sarah all signed the Salem petition. One of Forten's activist comrades was Amy Matilda Williams Cassey Remond, wife of Charles Lenox Remond. Prior to marrying her second husband, Charles, and settling with him in Salem, Amy, the daughter of Peter H. Williams of New York City, had married Joseph Cassey, a black Philadelphia barber and abolitionist. Upon her death in August 1856 at the age of forty-eight, the Salem community remembered her as an "estimable lady" in her activist work.[95]

African American mothers embodied political strength, doing much of the campaign legwork. Nell remembered the "vigilant" mothers who "accompanied [him] to the various school-houses, to residences of teachers and committee-men."[96] One was Joanna Turpin Howard. In 1844 she had married Edwin F. Howard, an African American barber and caterer, and together they resided in New York before moving to his hometown of Boston (Figure 5.2). There they settled in the West End area, where Edwin owned his own business and Joanna raised their three children: Adeline, born in 1845; Edwin Clarence, born in 1846; and J. Imogen, born in 1848. Joanna was regarded as "cultured, refined and intellectual," an excellent guide for her children.[97] In 1855 Edwin's sister Cordelia and her husband John V. deGrasse lived at the Howard home for a while. Joanna had gone to school with Serena deGrasse, John's sister. Active in the abolition movement, the Howards worked alongside luminaries such as Frederick Douglass and Wendell Phillips. They employed Irish servants, owned real estate valued at $3,000, and had a personal estate totaling $1,000. Perhaps it was in this home where Joanna and other African American mothers strategized with Nell.

Joanna herself had attended a racially integrated female seminary, the Young Ladies' Domestic Seminary in upstate New York, where she received first-rate schooling, and with her sister Lucretia attended social functions alongside their white female peers.[98] Joanna's school experience foreshadowed her advocacy for equal school rights some fifteen

FIGURE 5.2. Edwin F. Howard and his wife Joanna Turpin
Howard were prominent African American activists in
antebellum Boston. They had three children, all of whom
became well-educated. Courtesy of Yale Collection of
American Literature, Beinecke Rare Book and Manuscript Library, Yale University.

years later. Perhaps she, like other proponents, believed that racial integration would lessen racial prejudice and foster more sociability among
the races, or maybe she just wanted her three children to have the same
kind of educational opportunities as white children. Whatever the case,
Joanna signed the Boston petition in 1855 requesting that the legislature

"prevent the colored children of Boston from being deprived of the equal privileges of the Common Schools."[99]

The difference between Roberts's 1851 petition drive and Nell's in 1855 was contextual: for one, the political climate had changed in a matter of just four years, and the political will to pass educational reform had increased. Roberts's petitions for "forbidding . . . the exclusion of children from any Public School of this Commonwealth merely on account of Color" had received considerable support.[100] William Schouler, a Scottish immigrant and journalist who served in the Massachusetts legislature, received the petitions, which were referred to the joint committee on education. A bill was drafted stating, "No applicant for admission to any of the public schools in this Commonwealth shall be excluded therefrom on account of color or race."[101] The grammar school committee declared that the bill would ruin Boston public schools.[102] The senate passed the bill, but the house rejected it, and a close vote of 122 to 120 denied a motion to reconsider.[103]

Four years later the political tide had turned as Know-Nothing Party victories swept the Massachusetts legislature in 1854. The historian Carleton Mabee argues that the party, with its anti-immigration, anti-Catholic, and, in Massachusetts, antislavery stance, could "tolerate the small, Protestant Negro minority . . . rather than the rapidly growing Catholic Irish" in Boston.[104] Some African American activists rode this wave of anti-immigrant sentiment to get equal school rights legislation passed.[105] By 1854 some whites had been converted to the equal school rights cause anyway: the *Boston Telegraph* endorsed the abolition of racially exclusive schools, and so did the Boston City Council. One of the new state legislators was Charles W. Slack, who was sympathetic to equal school rights and chairman of the committee on education. In February 1855 Nell submitted to Slack the twelve separate petitions from approximately 1,600 residents in ten different cities and towns.[106] Slack then authored a bill and a detailed report, citing Charles Sumner's arguments in the *Roberts* case and Richard Fletcher's remarks. He also tried to tackle the bugbear among white Americans that the presence of African American children in public schools would harm white children. White teachers testified that no evidence of harm or chaos existed in public schools in towns such as Nantucket and Salem where African American children attended with white children. Slack concluded his report by emphasizing the greatness of public education: "[It] suits our institutions, promotes the feeling of brotherhood, and the habits of republican equality."[107] Denying African Americans equal access to schools, he insisted, was a wrong that had to be rectified. The bill wound its way through the leg-islative process, passing all of its stages, before arriving on the desk of Governor Henry Gardner, a Know-Nothing Party member who on April 28, 1855, signed the bill into law.

Most African American parents had by then abandoned the Smith School, leaving it to its fate, and in early September 1855 the Boston school committee officially closed it.[108] Racially exclusive schools had now been destroyed, which Nell and his proponents viewed as a vic-tory, but it meant tearing down an African American educational insti-tution that had existed for sixty years. A severance package from the Boston school committee did little to boost Thomas Paul Jr.'s spirit; he was dejected, lacking "zeal," Nell observed.[109] Some anxious whites may have shared Paul's emotions, though their reasons differed. Doomsday predictions poured in from some white observers who prayed for God to "save the Commonwealth of Massachusetts" from this calamity.[110] Nell ignored such fears, focusing instead on preparing African American stu-dents to enter Boston public schools, issuing suggestions for parents to ensure that their children were punctual and well-dressed. Boston pub-lic schools, he wrote, were "temples of learning" that African American children had to respect.[111]

African American mothers celebrated this civil rights milestone alongside other activists. On September 3, 1855, the first day of the school year, African American children entered various public schools throughout the city and sat beside white children. African American mothers trooped from school to school to ensure that their children had been welcomed. On December 17, after some anxiety about school integration had cleared, the African American community honored Nell with a stupendous celebration at the Twelfth Baptist Church. William Lloyd Garrison, Wendell Phillips, and Charles Lenox Remond attended, as did Joanna Turpin Howard and her children. In his remarks, Nell stressed the important role of African American women and children in the long struggle for educational justice. "Truth enjoins upon me the pleasing duty," he intoned, "of acknowledging that to the *women,* and the *children* also, is the cause especially indebted for success."[112] He men-tioned the *Roberts* case, but since he did not mention the Roberts family, Sarah Roberts, who would have been around thirteen at the time, prob-ably did not attend the celebration.

The immediate beneficiaries of this new order were African American youth and their parents. In July 1856 twelve-year-old Adeline T. Howard was one of the many young women at the exhibition of the Wells School for Girls. She completed exercises in history, arithmetic, bookkeeping, and declamation; probably sang songs; and drew artwork that may have been featured in the exhibition hall.[113] That month, she earned her diploma, along with another young African American woman, Elizabeth Norton Smith, who had also attended Nell's victory celebration.[114] Three other African American students graduated from Boston public grammar schools that year. Nell acted as a pseudo-compiler of the African American student experience in Boston public schools, publishing the educational achievements of youth in the *Liberator* to broadcast their aptitude and capability.

The Boston case energized the equal school rights campaign in Rhode Island, which followed a similar path, particularly concerning protest strategies and rhetoric. African American activists in Rhode Island had signed and submitted petitions years earlier pleading for voting rights, which they eventually won. Petitions seeking equal school rights soon followed. George T. Downing placed editorials in Rhode Island newspapers citing white proponents of the Boston campaign, who testified to the benefits of racial school integration. For example, I. A. Page, a white teacher at the Dwight School in Boston, affirmed that three African American children attended his school and "not the least objection ha[d] ever been made by either parent or scholar."[115] African American activists borrowed rhetorical terms and practices by referring to their campaign as a campaign for equal school rights and by deeming it their duty, as property owners and taxpaying citizens, to fight for the "abolition of caste schools."[116] Unlike black Bostonians, African Americans in Rhode Island could also frame their claim to equality through black military service during the Dorr Rebellion, an 1842 uprising against the state government concerning universal suffrage.

An African American girl even took center stage at a Rhode Island state legislative committee hearing in 1859. Sallie Holley, a white abolitionist, lecturer, and educator from Connecticut, had written a letter supporting equal school rights in the Ocean State, and eighteen-year-old Clementina Parker read aloud Holley's remarks at this hearing. Clementina was the daughter of African American activists Ransom Parker and Amy F. Parker, a Canterbury Female Seminary alumna. Clementina had been denied admission to the Girls' Department of Providence High School, despite her qualifications. The written remarks on educational equality were Holley's, but Clementina's voice added weight and immediacy to the matter.[117] Holley argued that education was a fundamental right for every child. She highlighted the African American female experience, asking, "Why cannot white and black young ladies recite their lessons as amicably to the same teachers in Providence as in London?" She mentioned Oberlin College, her alma mater, and Antioch College, two racially integrated institutions of higher education.[118]

The Lyons family entered the equal school rights fight some years later. They had survived a harrowing escape from New York City during the Draft Riots of 1863, when mobs targeted government buildings before directing their ire at African Americans. These violent mobs destroyed private homes, including that of the Lyonses, and set fire to the Colored Orphans' Asylum and other institutions. Hundreds of people perished, and eleven African American men were lynched.[119] Wielding his pistol, Albro Lyons, the family's patriarch, shielded his wife and children from direct physical harm.[120] His wife, Mary Marshall Lyons, and their children, Therese, Maritcha, Mary Elizabeth Pauline, and Albro Jr., escaped first to New London, Connecticut, where they stayed with the Anderson family.[121] Then Mary and the children boarded with the Remond family in Salem, before continuing on to Providence, a city that Mary (and probably Albro too) chose because of "its reputation for good schools."[122]

After settling in Providence, Mary Marshall Lyons planned to enroll her three youngest children at the public schools closest to their residence at 18 A Street, but the school committee equivocated. In the spring of 1864 Maritcha graduated from Colored School No. 3, under the tutelage of Charles Reason and his assistants, Helen Appo and Mary Anderson, fully prepared for advanced study. However, she was ineligible to attend Providence High School because the school committee refused to accept her diploma, according to Maritcha, for it had been "issued by a caste school."[123] The school committee told her to enroll at a grammar school in Rhode Island. For five weeks, Maritcha attended the all-white Bridgham Public Grammar School in Providence led by F. B. Snow; she then took and passed the examination to enter Providence High School. But still she could not matriculate.

Mary then secured a meeting with Daniel Leach, superintendent of the Providence public school system. The meeting turned into an impromptu interview of Mary and Maritcha, who had accompanied her. Leach sought to ascertain exactly what the Lyons family was up to; a rumor accused them of moving to Providence solely to test the question of racial school segregation.[124] That was not *exactly* true; the family chose Providence because of its high-quality public schools. Leach asked Maritcha what studies she wished to pursue at the high school and why. Maritcha apparently answered clearly and confidently, for she had always been studious. Nonetheless Leach ruled that the Lyons children were only eligible to attend the Pond and Meeting Street schools, which had been designated for African American children, about three miles from their home.

The Lyons family found allies in J. Erastus Lester, a white lawyer, and in Elizabeth H. Smith, a well-respected African American teacher. Smith, an alumna of the Canterbury Female Seminary, taught at the all-black coeducational Meeting Street School, served as principal there, and, at one point, led an Evening School for African American adults.[125] She even presented curricular demonstrations on spelling to her fellow educators at the Rhode Island Institute of Instruction.[126] In fact a school segregationist tried to use Smith's achievements as a teacher to argue that the all-black school offered a fine education, since it outperformed some of the all-white schools in Providence: "Mrs. Smith, herself a colored person of refinement and education, has attained the proud position of being the *first school in America* in the department of spelling accurately the most difficult, as well as the simple words of our language, and that in mental arithmetic it stands second to none in New England."[127] By all accounts, Smith was an accomplished teacher. As a proponent of equal school rights, she risked her teaching position, but according to Maritcha, Smith "did not hesitate to speak and to write against drawing a color line in civil affairs."[128]

Mary Marshall Lyons defended her family as well as their values and aspirations. She knew all about standing up for one's rights since her sister Gloriana Catherine Marshall had attended the Canterbury Female Seminary. Maritcha wrote that her maternal grandmother, Elizabeth Hewlett Marshall, was a "poor white of English descent" and a pious woman who learned to read the Bible later in life.[129] Elizabeth had taken Mary with her to travel to Connecticut to give testimony during Frederick Olney's arson trial in 1834. And Mary probably heard about her friend Sarah Parker Remond's school experience, since a young Mary worked as a saleswoman in John and Nancy Remond's confectionary shop in Newport. Conversations about the struggle for African American women's education likely influenced Mary some thirty years later when she wrote to the city newspaper, *Providence Evening Press*, and to James Y. Smith, Rhode Island's governor. She dismissed the rumor of a calculated plot to desegregate public schools and instead shared that she, a hairdresser, and her husband, a merchant, only "strived to bring up [their] children so that they may be good and intelligent citizens."[130] African American parents like the Lyonses linked education with citizenship, and they wanted to instill in their children positive traits, a goal that might have resonated with white Providence families if racial prejudice had not been a factor.[131]

In an editorial, Mary Marshall Lyons offered two compelling reasons for white community leaders to endorse equal school rights: African American military service in the Civil War and Rhode Island's supposed wish to stand "shoulder to shoulder" with "her elder sister," Massachusetts. She exploited the familiar narrative of male military service, which Prudence Crandall's defense attorneys raised in the *Crandall v. Connecticut* trial in the 1830s, to draw attention to a long tradition of black patriotism and to legitimize her claim for racial equality. She imagined that African American soldiers would be most disappointed that their "little ones" faced this "foul stain" of discrimination. She admitted that her family had one recourse: to orchestrate a costly move to the "glorious Bay State," where "equal school privileges" had been won.[132] George T. Downing had done just that, relocating to Boston with his wife, Serena deGrasse Downing, and their children in the early 1860s. Thus Lyons's editorial worked in conjunction with the petitions filed by Downing, Ransom Parker, and other activists who had inaugurated the legal fight for equal school rights in Rhode Island in 1855.

Initially both Mary Marshall Lyons and George T. Downing failed to persuade the school committees in Providence, Newport, and Bristol—the only cities in the state operating segregated public schools—to enact equal school rights legislation. In 1864 the Rhode Island state legislature weighed the merits of the petitions signed by African Americans favoring equal school rights. A majority of the education committee members in the state house reasoned that since most Rhode Island residents rejected racially mixed schools, the policy should not be adopted. Besides, the state's public school system, they argued, relied upon the patronage of wealthy residents who, if disgruntled by a school desegregation order, would return to the private school system, crippling public schools.[133] Asa Messer Gammell, a white school proprietor representing Warren, Rhode Island, in the legislature, countered these arguments by reading letters from teachers and school officials in Boston and Salem who reported no real problems in racially mixed schools.[134] The bill was nevertheless filibustered.[135] In 1865 the Providence school committee intended to resolve the quandary of educational access for African American children by building more schools solely for African Americans. But Mary Marshall Lyons did not request a new school building for her children; she wished for them to "be admitted in the schools already built."[136]

Though young African American women before her, like Clementina Parker, had been denied admission to the Girls' Department of Providence High School, Maritcha enrolled in 1865, a few months prior to the passage of an equal school rights law.[137] The dire predictions of a public school system crippled by racial integration did not come to pass. Yet all was not perfect in that moment. Maritcha stated that her "classmates were more or less friendly," but much could be inferred by "more or less." She had a friend in Lucia Tappan, whose paternal grandfather was John Tappan, the brother of abolitionists Arthur and Lewis Tappan. During her first few years at Providence High School, Maritcha noticed that either her desk was oddly placed in the classroom, or she was assigned a single desk rather than a double desk. In her senior year, she finally occupied "a sunny window seat." Despite these racist incidents, she continued to produce stellar work. Her compositions on the Draft Riots of 1863 and the Underground Railroad even surprised her teacher, Sarah E. Doyle, who asked, "Is what you wrote really true, or have you been letting loose your imagination?" Maritcha replied, "The half has never been told."[138]

In her last year of study, in May 1869, Maritcha attended the high school exhibition held at Providence City Hall, where she was one of five students selected to read her essay before a large receptive audience.[139] An observer noted that her essay on art, mythology, and Christianity "ranked equally well with those of any of her associates."[140] The original handwritten essay was still in her private collection at her death on January 28, 1929. After graduating, she thanked her teacher Sarah E. Doyle, a Providence High School graduate herself and later a renowned educator, for being her "guiding star during the last school year when I was fretting to be free to try my way over the unchartered sea of life."[141] Like many before her, Maritcha initially stumbled as she tried to find her purpose but ultimately found her calling as a teacher. Doyle provided Maritcha a letter of recommendation for teaching positions, which praised her "high standing . . . for excellent scholarship and deportment."[142] Maritcha's achievements as an educator at Brooklyn public schools and an activist were even reported in Providence newspapers.[143]

Continued activism among African American leaders, students, and their allies, coupled with the shifting trajectory of the Civil War, finally convinced Rhode Island state legislators to pass an equal school rights bill. Maritcha later remembered delivering her "maiden speech," at the age of sixteen, before the state legislature, "plead[ing] . . . in a trembling voice . . . for the opening of the door of opportunity."[144] Figuratively speaking, Eunice Ross's petition to the Commonwealth of Massachusetts to attend Nantucket High School in the 1840s had become Maritcha's testimony in front of Rhode Island state legislators in the 1860s. Others launched into action, writing terse editorials on the merits of equal school rights; accusing opponents of being proslavery, then a damning insult given the new objective of the Civil War to emancipate slaves; submitting more petitions to the state legislature and governor; and calculating the potential power of the black male vote.[145] In 1865 Thomas Wentworth Higginson, a white abolitionist and colonel in a black regiment during the Civil War, moved to Newport, where he became chairman of the school committee and outlawed racially exclusive public schools.[146] Cumulative victories paved the way for the enactment of the equal school rights bill in March 1866. The bill provided, "No distinction shall be made on account of race or color of the applicant in any publicly-funded school in the state."[147] An eleven-year battle resulted in yet another victory for equal school rights.

For William Cooper Nell, the equal school rights campaign was a manifestation of the "theory of an *equal* common school system," which had not yet occurred throughout the North.[148] Nell claimed the growing public school system should uphold, not frustrate, racial equality. The Massachusetts and Rhode Island campaigns for equal school rights thus gradually advanced Nell's theory. In 1858 a correspondent of the *Anti-Slavery Bugle* stated, "New York must soon follow."[149] African American activists and their allies successfully waged an equal school rights campaign in Buffalo and Rochester, and some racially mixed public schools existed in Brooklyn and New York City. But as the historian Carleton Mabee concludes, the equal school rights campaign in New York "remained weak" in the mid- to late nineteenth century.[150] New York would not enact legislation to desegregate its public school system until the twentieth century. Its neighboring state, New Jersey, followed a similar timeline, though the public schools in the northern counties there had previously outlawed racially exclusive public schools. Massachusetts and Rhode Island thus stood out as symbols of the theory and practice of equal school rights.[151]

Some thirty years after Nancy Woodson's City Medal had been denied her, high-achieving African American female youth could now be awarded that honor. In 1860 nineteen-year-old Mary Louisa Lockley at the Bowdoin School in Boston received the City Medal. Nell noted that "her composition [on Conversation], penmanship, diagrams, and other exercises, were highly meritorious."[152] Mary Louisa worked as a bookkeeper before she married St. John Appo, an African American journalist,

FIGURE 5.3. J. Imogen Howard was the daughter of Joanna Turpin and Edwin F. Howard. She graduated from Girls' High and Normal School in Boston before embarking upon a successful career as a schoolteacher in New York City's public schools. Courtesy of Yale Collection of American Literature, Beinecke Rare Book and Manuscript Library, Yale University.

in 1872.[153] J. Imogen Howard (Figure 5.3), the younger sister of Adeline T. Howard, graduated in 1863 from the Wells School for Girls as a City Medal Scholar.[154] The City Medal was eventually discontinued, but youth attending Boston public grammar and high schools could qualify for the Franklin Medal. In 1864 Elizabeth Norton Smith at the Wells School received the Franklin Medal, a remarkable achievement praised by Nell.

The success of the equal school rights campaign in Massachusetts prepared the way for advanced schooling opportunities for young African American women at the well-renowned Girls' High and Normal School in Boston. The school had a storied history. A high school for girls had opened in Boston in January 1826, with many interested applicants. A worried Josiah Quincy III, the penny-pinching mayor of Boston, discontinued the school in 1828 for it was too popular and too costly. Educational reformers looking to train young women as teachers for primary and grammar schools spearheaded the establishment of the Normal School in 1852, with about one hundred young women enrolling in the inaugural class.[155] The school flourished, and the course of study expanded from two years to three. In 1854 the school became the Girls' High and Normal School, offering coursework in "Latin, French, and German" as well as drawing and music.[156]

In 1863 J. Imogen Howard became the first African American student to matriculate at Girls' High and Normal School. Admission was competitive yet straightforward. A prospective applicant had to be "over fifteen and under twenty," with strong teacher recommendations, and successfully pass a difficult entrance exam that tested reading, English grammar, arithmetic, and geography. According to Pauline Hopkins, there was some "apprehension" about J. Imogen's admission because of her race, even after she passed the examination, but William Henry Seavey, the school's principal, and another teacher, Emma Temple, apparently welcomed her.[157] J. Imogen graduated in 1866, making her the first African American graduate from this institution.[158] She probably participated in the well-attended annual exhibition, which required selected students to read aloud their compositions, complete other exercises, sing, and sometimes perform teaching demonstrations.[159] By 1867 approximately four hundred graduates had been placed in teaching positions.[160]

J. Imogen later earned high praise for her intelligence, character, and talent as a teacher in New York City public schools, part of her life's mission to uplift the race.[161] She worked at Colored Grammar School No. 4 in New York City along with Sarah J. Smith Tompkins Garnet, then

FIGURE 5.4. Adeline T. Howard, an African American schoolteacher in Washington, D.C., was the daughter of Joanna Turpin Howard and Edwin F. Howard and the sister of J. Imogen Howard and Edwin Clarence Howard. Courtesy of Yale Collection of American Literature, Beinecke Rare Book and Manuscript Library, Yale University.

principal and a well-respected teacher herself. J. Imogen thought highly of her students, particularly their enthusiasm and curiosity for learning, despite the fact that their parents were, in her assessment, often "very ignorant."[162] Educating African American girls was impactful, but she sought to educate boys and girls equally. Her community ties deepened over the years as she pursued further study, earning a master's degree from the College of the City of New York, then acting as principal of the

Colored Evening School in the city. These were precisely the kinds of opportunities that Joanna Turpin Howard hoped for her children. She did not get to see her children's many achievements, since she died in 1872 in Shreveport, Louisiana, but her activism lived on.[163]

J. Imogen's sister, Adeline, also became a teacher (Figure 5.4). After graduating from the Wells School for Girls, Adeline traveled to Richmond, Virginia, with her friend, the Afro–Native artist Edmonia Lewis, to teach freed people. After a short period of time, Adeline settled in Washington, D.C., where she continued her teaching career.[164] A profile of her in the *Washington Bee* described her as "dignity personified, with an intellectual look."[165] A strict disciplinarian, she maintained high standards in her classroom. She often sought out opportunities to learn more about the latest innovations in pedagogy. She eventually rose to principal of the Wormley School for African American children in Washington, D.C.

Academic success also followed Edwin Clarence Howard (Figure 5.5). He probably attended Boston public schools before traveling to Monrovia, Liberia, in 1861 to attend Liberia College. There he studied for four years with the notable African American scholars Alexander Crummell and Edward Blyden. He returned to the United States and, in 1866, entered Harvard University Medical School, graduating in 1869, making him one of the first black graduates of that institution. He worked as a physician in Philadelphia and participated in voluntary associations. His sisters, Adeline and J. Imogen, moved to the City of Brotherly Love after retiring from the teaching profession.[166] In 1910 Edwin and J. Imogen, who was working as a bookkeeper in a hospital, shared the same residence as their maternal aunt Lucretia Turpin Bowers.

Even in the 1870s and 1880s the *Roberts* case lived on in public memory, though the details of the battle had faded in some people's minds. The *Christian Era* published a twentieth-anniversary retrospective in 1869 on the case, noting that Sarah Roberts was but a "little colored girl" in 1849.[167] Sarah had meanwhile matured into a woman in her midtwenties. Though she was the subject of a court case, education did not appear to be her life's devotion. In 1865 twenty-two-year-old Sarah moved back to the Roberts family homestead in Boston, while her eighteen-year-old sister, Caroline, attended racially integrated schools, as did her siblings, William, Samuel, Charles, and Martha. On February 13, 1867, Sarah wed John Casneau, the son of West Indian immigrants and a Civil War veteran. In 1870 John worked as a janitor in Boston while Sarah was a homemaker.[168] Sarah and John later moved to New Haven, Connecticut.

FIGURE 5.5. Edwin Clarence Howard, an African
American medical doctor, was the son of Joanna Turpin Howard and Edwin F. Howard and the brother
of J. Imogen and Adeline T. Howard. Courtesy of
the James Weldon Johnson Collection, Yale College
of American Literature, Beinecke Rare Book and
Manuscript Library, Yale University.

Curiously the 1879 *New Haven City Directory* listed Sarah as a widow
of John Casneau, but John had not died; rather, he had moved to Providence, Rhode Island, where he married Hattie, an African American
woman, in 1878 and adopted her two daughters.[169] In October 1879 he
filed for divorce in New Haven Superior Court, accusing Sarah of having an affair with Charles Caesar, an African American porter.[170] The
divorce was granted.

Sarah stayed in the New Haven area. Her sister Caroline A. Roberts Wilson Price and her brother-in-law Eugene B. Price, an African American printer, lived in New Haven too. In December 1880, Sarah married Charles Dyer, an African American butcher, but their relationship soon ended, probably after Charles was arrested in July 1882 for "assaulting his wife and kicking her out of doors" at their residence at 115 Frank Street.[171] On December 15, 1887, Sarah married twenty-seven-year-old Mahlon G. Laws, an African American laborer who worked at D. T. Welch & Company in New Haven.[172] Sarah apparently led a quiet life with Mahlon. While the equal school rights campaign had dominated her childhood, perhaps she purposefully decided that this history, as effectual as it was, would not define her womanhood. When her mother, Adeline, died in 1887, newspapers from Ohio to Alabama reprinted the death notice, which mentioned that the *Roberts* lawsuit paved the way for "throwing open the doors of the city schools to the colored children of Boston."[173] Benjamin Sr.'s death six years earlier at the age of sixty-six went comparatively unnoticed.[174] In any case, Adeline bequeathed her property and other effects to her seven living children, including Sarah. On April 27, 1896, Sarah C. Roberts Casneau Dyer Laws died of cancer in the town of Orange, New Haven County, Connecticut.[175]

In the eighteenth and nineteenth centuries, African American education was a grassroots effort in Boston. Parents sought to expand schooling opportunities for their children and, in doing so, built an activist network that became increasingly focused on reforming the Boston public school system. As educational reform was under way in Salem and Nantucket, Boston activists such as William Cooper Nell, Benjamin Roberts Sr., and Angelina Gardner rallied for equal school rights and were joined by white abolitionists who sought educational justice for African American children and youth.

Though the *Roberts* case did not immediately prompt the abolition of racially exclusive schools, it heralded the 1855 Massachusetts law that did so. Many African Americans in the Boston area—and really, throughout the state—celebrated this civil rights milestone. For activists like Nell, this victory also meant that the Boston school committee would finally recognize and reward the achievements of all smart children. African American children had been scholars before—Nancy Woodson could attest to that—but now they had some recognition. Increased opportunities for advanced schooling had enabled young African American women to grow intellectually, morally, and spiritually and to share their learning with the community as mothers, activists, and teachers.

6 / Character Education and the Antebellum Classroom

Twenty-seven-year-old Susan Paul entered her classroom in Boston's Smith School building as fifty excited boys and girls greeted her. These well-behaved children listened attentively to Susan's every direction as she read the Bible and reviewed spelling exercises. Susan and her students alike were exemplars of intelligence, character, and kindness. These, at least, were the impressions of a visitor to the school, who remarked, "Such discipline, such undeviating obedience and docility, I have never witnessed in a white school."[1] Other visitors, including white observers, shared warm and enthusiastic comments about Susan's school. Even the white British phrenologist Johann Gaspar Spurzheim made a special effort to visit her school and observe her students.[2]

Was there something distinguishing about Susan Paul's pedagogy or Susan Paul herself? Or was the everyday act of African American children learning in a classroom a sufficiently curious sight? While archival records do not answer these questions precisely, classroom observations featured in newspapers coupled with Susan's own writings provide a peek into an antebellum classroom and its curriculum. Susan stressed the concept of character in her pedagogy, and she was not the only African American woman teacher to do so. The public letters, short stories, and narratives written by African American women teachers "stood as examples of educational progress and activism," the historian Erica Armstrong Dunbar argues. These documents also demonstrated the importance of character building for life and leadership.[3] Shared bonds of faith, commitment to activism, and belief in character education to shape the next generation thus united these teachers.

With its roots in ancient civilization, character education concerned both moral and intellectual development, envisioned as a sort of positive feedback loop. Supported by a vast majority of Americans during the nineteenth century, character education was grounded in Christian values such as empathy, charity, love, obedience, and self-discipline.[4] The popular schoolbooks of the day were the Bible and, later, *McGuffey Readers*, edited by William McGuffey, a white educator. *McGuffey Readers* wove biblical principles into memorable stories, poems, and speeches that taught reading, spelling, and oratory.[5] The historian Carl Kaestle concludes that character education became a distinct part of public school instruction throughout the nineteenth century, with "far more emphasis . . . placed on character . . . than on literacy, arithmetic skills, analytical ability, or knowledge of the world."[6]

Women teachers taught character education in the primary school classroom, and they viewed this work as a divine mission. Emma Willard, a white educator and reformer from Connecticut, ran Troy Female Seminary in New York. In 1819 she published her *Plan for Improving Female Education*, a vigorous endorsement of women's education. Her plan included teaching young women the "system of morality, enforced by the sanctions of religion," which would, in turn, enable them to fulfill specific moral duties that benefited the family and the nation.[7] Willard's seminary became a model for other women's teacher training institutions. Likewise Catherine Beecher, sister of the famed novelist Harriet Beecher Stowe, argued in *An Essay on the Education of Female Teachers* (1835) that education ought to form character, so a focus on moral and religious instruction was paramount.

In their commentary on female education and women teachers, both Willard and Beecher wrote in reference to white women, not women of color, but conversations about female education and morality circulated in African American women's networks too. The full extent of these conversations remains unknown to us, but Garrison's *Liberator* sheds some light. In 1832 an editorialist identified as "a young lady of color" described attending weekly meetings at the Female Literary Association of Philadelphia. She affirmed that "the cultivation of a woman's mind is all important," and she emboldened women to continue to seek knowledge and "enrich [their minds]." Her concluding words were a piercing proclamation: "Let nothing prevent you in this laudable pursuit in which you are engaged; and be assured you have *my* warmest wishes for your continued success."⁸ The pursuit of knowledge required collective support and encouragement; this proclamation reminded young African American women that they were not, in fact, working in isolation.

African American women teachers—Susan Paul in Boston, Sarah Mapps Douglass in Philadelphia, Ann Plato in Hartford, Charlotte Forten in Salem, and others—made character and morality an essential part of their pedagogy. Teaching character education to African American children in particular was significant for two reasons. First, African American children (and other children of color) would surely confront racial prejudice in the United States, and character education would prepare them to cope and navigate that reality. Second, the values associated with character education motivated children and taught them how to behave as good, purposeful citizens. White children, then, could learn to be allies, fighting against racial prejudice.

While the place of character education in public schools continues to be debated today, few scholars have linked such discussions to the early efforts of African American women teachers. Recognizing this history is crucial to understanding the long roots and provenance of these debates and also to acknowledging the pioneering work performed by African American women teachers. Though legitimately problematized today for its later imbrication with respectability politics within the African American community, the concept of character in the nineteenth century was nothing short of revolutionary insofar as it explicitly sought to enable African American children to take their rightful position as morally upright, educated, Christian citizens, fully worthy of equality and justice. The stories that follow capture some of the thoughts and experiences of African American women who saw teaching as a calling, not simply to educate their students but also to emancipate their communities and their race.

Born in 1809, Susan Paul had an older sister, Ann Catharine, and a younger brother, Thomas Jr. They grew up in a Baptist household with their parents, Thomas Sr., from Exeter, New Hampshire, who served as pastor of the First African Baptist Church in Boston for over twenty years, and Catharine, a well-respected teacher. An eloquent man, Thomas Sr. was celebrated for his "dignified, urbane, and attractive [manners];—his colloquial powers . . . his intellect . . . and his influence."⁹ Susan and her siblings were probably homeschooled by their mother and then privately tutored. By 1837 twenty-five-year-old Thomas Jr. had qualified for admission to Dartmouth College. Neither

Ann nor Susan attended college, but they were tutored by Claudius Bradford, a white abolitionist, clergyman, and later professor at Antioch College in Ohio. In 1821 Bradford offered classes in French to male and female students, so the Paul sisters likely learned French along with other common subjects such as English grammar, literature, geography, and history.[10] Years later Bradford remembered Susan as "one of the best, both in scholarship and lady-like behavior, [he] ever had."[11] Her obituary highlighted her intelligence and her "excellent education; her talents and address were of a high order."[12]

As abolitionists, Susan and her siblings were committed to black emancipation and civil rights. An opponent of the American Colonization Society, Ann regarded herself and other African Americans as full American citizens. As officeholders in the Garrison & Knapp Society, a literary and education association for African American women established in 1833, Ann and Susan fundraised and convened monthly meetings "devoted to studying history, reading useful and interesting books, writing, [and] conversing upon the sufferings of [their] enslaved sisters."[13]

This association even contributed $15 to make William Lloyd Garrison a life member of the New England Anti-Slavery Society. The Paul siblings continued to grow intellectually by participating in other literary associations and activist organizations.

All of the Paul children became well-respected educators.[14] Thomas Jr. taught in Albany, Providence, and Boston, notably at the Smith Grammar School. Ann taught a Sunday school in Boston.[15] She married Elijah W. Smith Sr., and they had four children. At twenty-seven she died of lung fever, and Elijah moved to New Orleans, leaving Susan and her mother to raise his children. In addition to her role as a guardian to her niece and nephews, Susan taught at a public primary school.[16]

Written observations, newspaper advertisements, and her own writings document Susan's work. These sources open a window into an antebellum classroom led by an African American woman. By stressing the importance of character in her lessons, Susan prepared the next generation of African American children to act as purposeful members of their community. She also urged parents to nurture and direct their children to follow God and to always do what was right and good.

Sarah Mapps Douglass, another key figure in this story, was a well-educated African American woman from a prominent free black abolitionist family in the Northeast. Born on September 9, 1806, in Philadelphia to

Grace Bustill Douglass, a milliner, and Robert Douglass Sr., a hairdresser, Sarah—and probably her five siblings—received their early education at a Quaker school and at a school operated by their mother and James Forten, a wealthy African American sailmaker. When Grace died in 1842, her obituary mentioned her "self-devotedness to the cause of education."[17] Sarah inherited this same devotedness, composing essays, poems, and stories on subjects like teaching, the abolition of slavery and racial prejudice, and the necessity and power of Christian faith. The Bible was her foundation for intellectual and moral growth. She sympathized with enslaved African American women who had "no Bible" and "had never been taught to read: No ray of light penetrates the darkness of their mental vision."[18] For her, the advancement of her race and the abolition of slavery were bound together.

Sarah Mapps Douglass and Susan Paul were both forerunners in the development of African American literary associations in the 1830s. Sarah joined the Female Literary Association of Philadelphia, which aimed to support the "mental improvement of females."[19] She wrote to Garrison asking him to publish the association's constitution in the *Liberator* in order to inspire other African American women to organize and be active in their communities. Garrison agreed, and went even further, publishing the writings of some of the association's members.[20] The Afric-American Female Intelligence Society in Boston had a similar objective, focusing on African American women's intellectual and moral improvement. This association welcomed African American male and female orators such as Hosea Easton and later Maria W. Stewart.[21] Literary associations were thus important educational spaces that enabled women to discuss pressing issues from law and politics to slavery.[22]

Participating in literary societies prepared African American women to contribute to and influence interracial antislavery societies. In November 1833 a group of young men raised money to provide twenty-four-year-old Susan Paul with a life membership in the New England Anti-Slavery Society.[23] A few months prior to her membership, Susan and her Boston Juvenile Choir, an ensemble of her primary school students, gave a rousing musical performance at one of the meetings. A year later she joined the Boston Female Anti-Slavery Society. Similarly, in Philadelphia, Sarah's mother, Grace, along with Lucretia Mott, a white Quaker abolitionist, among others, organized the Philadelphia Female Anti-Slavery Society (PFASS) in December 1833. Over the decades Sarah took several leadership positions in the organization, including secretary and member of the Board of Managers.

Unsurprisingly, the paths of these two women soon crossed. The first national Women's Antislavery Convention took place in New York City in May 1837. Sarah Grimké contacted the female antislavery societies in Boston and Philadelphia specifically to invite African American women to serve as delegates. That first year over one hundred women attended, including at least ten African American women, though Susan Paul was not there, possibly due to financial difficulty. It is almost certain, however, that she and Sarah Mapps Douglass met the following year at the second Women's Antislavery Convention, held at Pennsylvania Hall in Philadelphia. Over two hundred women assembled, and Sarah and Susan occupied leadership roles at the convention: Sarah as treasurer and Susan as one of nine vice presidents.[24]

The site of this women's antislavery convention in Philadelphia was significant. In 1838 the City of Brotherly Love was a large, bustling urban area with growing immigrant and African American populations. Free black migration rose at the turn of the century, as the number of African American residents increased from 1,381 in 1800 to 14,500 in 1830, nearly 10 percent of the total population. African Americans worked as entrepreneurs and teachers as well as laborers, mariners, and servants. Middle-class black households existed, but most African American residents struggled to support their families while also fighting for basic civil rights like education. In 1818 public schools opened under the leadership of controllers who excluded African American children from these schools. After continued agitation from African American residents and their allies, coupled with changing social conditions, the controllers established a public school for African American children in September 1822.[25] A year later 237 children had registered, but this segregated public school lacked resources, occupied a dilapidated building, and had a higher student-to-teacher ratio compared to the white public schools. In many ways, Philadelphia's public school system resembled that in Boston and other cities in the Northeast. African Americans denounced such blatant inequality, and soon the school was relocated to a building on Lombard Street. Two white teachers used the Lancastrian system of peer instruction. A decade later the presence of African American children at segregated public schools began to decline as racial abuse and white violence seized Philadelphia and left African Americans reeling. A mob actually burned down Pennsylvania Hall during the second Women's Antislavery Convention in 1838.

Some African American parents with financial means abandoned public schools as an option for their children and retreated to the private school system, which had a long tradition in Philadelphia. This system included charity schools too. In the eighteenth century, African Americans and their white allies had established a few different schools: abolitionists such as Anthony Benezet, a Quaker, opened a school that educated soon-to-be leaders such as Absalom Jones and James Forten; Quakers founded organizations like the Association for the Free Instruction of Adult Colored Persons; and abolitionist organizations such as the Pennsylvania Abolition Society subsidized African American schools. In 1804 the African Methodist Episcopal Church established a school for African American girls and boys, where Absalom Jones taught for a while.[26] While private schools had disadvantages, namely limited capacity, cost, and the possibility of closure, they still offered more continuity and sometimes were of a higher quality compared to the public schools. Benjamin C. Bacon noted as much in his 1856 statistical report on African American education, stating, "The condition of the Colored Public Schools generally, was formerly not as good as that of the Charity Schools."[27] In 1854, 1,031 black students enrolled in the public schools and 331 in the private schools, and a little under 1,000 students attended benevolent and charity schools. There was no high school for African American youth.

Of the thirteen private schools in operation in 1854, the school led by Sarah Mapps Douglass was the oldest, having been established in 1835. This school, initially run by Rebecca Buffum, the daughter of the white abolitionist Arnold Buffum, was intended to be racially integrated; young African American women attended, but it remains unclear whether young white women did too. Buffum's school cost $5 per quarter, with the PFASS offsetting some of the costs.[28] After her marriage to Marcus Spring in 1836, Buffum relinquished her teaching duties.[29] At the same time, Sarah Mapps Douglass had just returned to Philadelphia after teaching at an African American public primary school in New York City for three years. She took over Buffum's school at a salary of $300.[30] In 1839 PFASS reported that Sarah's school was in a "flourishing condition, numbering thirty pupils."[31] Appreciative of the support, Sarah nevertheless disagreed with the Board of Managers about the day-to-day operations and management of the school. By 1840 she had decided to operate her school independently, with the PFASS paying rent for the school building. A year later she announced in the *Public Ledger* that she "ha[d] resumed the duties of her SCHOOL in SEVENTH, below Arch."[32] In 1853 she united her school with the Institute for Colored Youth, a Quaker secondary school founded in Pennsylvania in 1837 for African

American children. She then supervised the Girls' Preparatory Department within the Institute, a position she held for decades.

While in Philadelphia at the antislavery convention, Sarah and Susan could have found time to trade stories about teaching, both its joys and its woes. If her published short story "A True Tale for Children" was any indication, Sarah faced some trying times in the classroom, confessing, "There have been times when my spirit has been bowed, as it were to the earth by the unkind behaviour of children."[33] The very first paragraph of this didactic story asked young readers to respect their teachers by being kind and obedient. Susan probably would have echoed those sentiments. But even the toughest school day did not induce these women to abandon the profession. Sarah once wrote to her friend Rebecca White, a white reformer and daughter of the wealthy inventor Josiah White, "God called me to the responsible and honorable office of Teacher . . . to be a faithful shepherdess to the lambs committed by Him to my keeping."[34] African American women teachers took their work to heart and to God.

Records about Sarah's school are scant, but the *Colored American* briefly profiled it. The curriculum revolved around science, literature, and religion, three fields that the newspaper's editors claimed would "expand the youthful mind, refine the taste, and assist in purifying the heart."[35] Of the thirty or so young women studying there, some came from prominent free black families in the North and South, including the Dickerson sisters, Martina and Mary Anne, from Philadelphia; the Webb sisters, Edith and Genie, also from Philadelphia; and Mary Wormley from Virginia. Sarah continued to influence her students even after they left her school. For instance, she painted stunning flowers in the friendship albums of the Dickerson sisters. Friendship albums documented some of the semiprivate reflections of young middle-class schoolgirls on subjects such as womanhood and marriage; in this particular case, they also demonstrated the importance of kindness in student-teacher relationships. Sarah once wrote, "Flowers have ever been to me earnest, solemn holy teachers," so when she carefully painted a fuchsia (Figure 6.1) from James Andrew's *Lessons in Flower Painting* in Mary Anne's friendship album, she was folding floriculture into the sacred, science into religion.[36]

Just as Sarah modeled responsibility, honor, and faithfulness as a teacher, so too did she ingrain those same values in the children she taught. She recalled a moment when an African American orphan boy, who had been "mischievous and disobedient" in the past, brought her some violets. This kind gesture "repaid [her] for months of anxiety which

FIGURE 6.1. The friendship album of Mary Anne Dickerson, a student at Sarah Mapps Douglass's school in Philadelphia, included various poems, letters, and illustrations, like this one. Douglass painted this fuchsia. Courtesy of the Library Company of Philadelphia.

[she] had suffered on his account."[37] More than simply making amends, it demonstrated Sarah's talent as a teacher who could transform disobedient students into dutiful scholars. African American children thus learned to respect their teacher, each other, and the sacred space of the classroom.

In addition to instilling values such as respect and self-discipline in boys and girls, Sarah also affirmed a reciprocal model of care in her pedagogy. When her brother was sick, her young students sympathized with her. One student, Frances Robinson, wrote her a letter, citing the Book of John, chapter 1, to remind her to rely on God's strength. Touched by this display of care and piety, Sarah copied Frances's letter in a private letter to Rebecca White.[38] Frances cared about her teacher and wished to brighten her day. Such actions reveal Sarah's influence and appreciation as well as Frances's own sense of solicitude.

Even among the most committed educators, teaching at times brought forth moments of sheer disillusionment and even doubt in one's abilities. Sarah expressed deep frustration with her "lazy" students: "I feel so poor and ignorant, so barren and empty, that I tremble when the hour for school arrives."[39] This remark stood in stark contrast to earlier reflections, when she described how much her students inspired her. She once wrote that she actually missed her smart students: "[They] would greet me with bright faces and loving words, and when they go away a shadow seems to fall upon me."[40] Both of these real, honest, though seemingly conflicting comments lay bare the difficulty of a teacher's labors. Sarah no doubt appreciated her work in the classroom; it was her calling, but it induced stress, particularly when the number of students increased or administrative issues surfaced. But Sarah *never* quit, for the stakes were too high.

If doubts about teaching were not enough, African American women teachers throughout the Northeast routinely experienced incidents of racial prejudice in their daily lives. Susan's and Sarah's roles in the abolition movement made them targets of racist vitriol. For example, in March 1834 Susan reserved three coaches for transportation from Boston to Salem to take her students to an antislavery meeting. The drivers, upon seeing Susan and her students, refused to transport them and yelled, "We would sooner have [our] throats cut from ear to ear."[41] Susan later relayed the incident in the *Liberator*: "This is but a faint picture of that spirit which persecutes us on account of our color—that cruel prejudice which deprives us of every privilege whereby we might elevate ourselves—and then absurdly condemns us because we are not more refined and intelligent." This phenomenon, the "paradox of racial prejudice," vexed African Americans and their allies. Susan shared her disgust, and then pivoted to thanking Salem residents, including John Remond and Cyrus P. Grosvenor, who had welcomed her and her students. This public admonition of the white racist drivers juxtaposed with the display of gratitude toward abolitionists was one way to challenge racial prejudice.[42]

Like Susan, Sarah also described a particularly stinging encounter with racial prejudice. Sarah's grandfather Cyrus Bustill, who had been enslaved, converted to Quakerism because of his last owner, Thomas Prior, who eventually manumitted Cyrus. Cyrus, his wife, Elizabeth, and their eight children, including his daughter, Grace, attended religious services, though they were not members. Years later, when Grace and her children attended Arch Street Meeting, they had to abide by segregated seating patterns.[43] These racist policies within a house of worship wounded Sarah, who remembered weeping and feeling "indignant," as she questioned, "Are these people Christian?"[44] Her feelings resembled those of other free black women who confronted racial prejudice. Sarah Forten, an African American poet whose parents were James and Charlotte Vandine Forten, wrote to a friend that racial prejudice "often engendered feelings of discontent and mortification in [her] breast."[45] To cope and protect herself, she avoided racist people. Sarah Mapps Douglass could probably relate, as she wished her mother "would not persist in going among [Quakers]."[46] In 1843 she publicized her protest against the Society of Friends in the pages of the *National Anti-Slavery Standard*. Rebuking a white Quaker correspondent who doubted that African Americans had any desire to become Quakers, Sarah honored her mother's Quaker faith but denounced racial prejudice within the Society of Friends as "unchristian conduct."[47]

African American women teachers turned to didactic children's literature about race and slavery in order to reach white children, whom they would probably never teach in a public school classroom in places such as Philadelphia and Boston. Teachers like Sarah Mapps Douglass were well suited for that task, given their writing talent, religious faith, and success in the classroom. For instance, Sarah wrote a short biography of her sister, Elizabeth, born in 1806 in Philadelphia, who suffered from "Diseased Hip Joint."[48] Sarah's parents enrolled ten-year-old Elizabeth at a school near their home; Elizabeth worked hard and eventually became the best student in her class. Her achievement, however, unnerved her classmates, who teased her, scorned her, and "complained so frequently to their parents, that a negro stood above them." As the conflict brewed, the teacher confronted neither the students nor the parents about their actions; instead Elizabeth was expelled. Sarah denounced the teasing and scorn as a "sin" and urged her "little readers" to reject such behavior in favor of practicing empathy and love. "Could you feel for one moment the anguish of being despised merely for your complexion?" Sarah taught her readers to act by "throw[ing] this unholy prejudice from [them]." Sharing Elizabeth's story opened up an opportunity for Sarah to memorialize her sister.[49]

Sarah's story also contained a message for African American children, namely that African Americans coped with mounting incidents of racism by clinging to their faith and by persevering. "Perseverance" was a watchword of sorts, oftentimes invoked during moments of distress and crisis. For instance, Sarah had counseled young African American women to persevere by enrolling at the Canterbury Female Seminary in

Connecticut in 1833 despite growing controversy there. She reiterated this sentiment in the story about her sister. Being expelled from school saddened Elizabeth, but it did not change her character; it deepened her values. "Obedience, gentleness, patience, and perseverance, shone with peculiar lustre in her character," Sarah recalled. Their mother home-schooled Elizabeth, who memorized verses from the Bible, helped tend to the home, and looked after her younger siblings. Sarah concluded her story by asking her readers and listeners "if the character of Elizabeth appear[ed] the less lovely to them, because her complexion differed from theirs?" Her own reply to the question was "I am sure every *good* child will answer 'No!'" She hoped that white children reading or listening to this story in the *Liberator* would learn to love freely without prejudice and that African American children would learn never to let racial prejudice compromise their character.[50]

Other African American women teachers, with no known affiliation with the abolition movement, also taught character education. Ann Plato, for example, regarded Christian piety as a defining virtue of a life well lived. Born in the early 1820s in New York, Ann, an Afro-Native woman, was a bibliophile who read the work of great poets and scientists, from Felicia Hemans to John L. Comstock. Her biographer Ron Welburn speculates that she must have received advanced schooling, either in her hometown of Long Island or in Connecticut, because of her impressive "elocutionary and rhetorical skills," not to mention her scientific knowledge.[51] In 1841 she joined the Talcott Street Congregational Church in Hartford, Connecticut, and published her *Essays; Including Biographies and Miscellaneous Pieces, in Prose and Poetry.* A year later she began teaching at the Elm Street School.[52] In 1845 she taught forty-seven students, ranging in age from four to sixteen, who piled into a 24-by-20-foot room with three windows. The accommodations, according to a school committee report, were terrible. The assigned textbooks included the Bible as well as Webster's *Spelling Book*, Smith's *Geography*, and even Comstock's *Natural Philosophy*, which distinguished Ann as a well-read teacher, since very few public schoolteachers in Hartford taught Comstock's book.[53] Little else is known about Ann's school, but her essays and poems on education offer some insights into her pedagogy.

In her essay "Two School Girls," Ann described her model learner as curious, industrious, and self-disciplined. Her story featured a conversation between two schoolgirls. One girl, who appreciated learning for learning's sake and visited a natural history exhibition, led a more fulfilling life compared to the girl who showed only superficial interests in her schoolwork. In presenting this contrast, Ann linked intensive learning with character formation. She asserted that the first schoolgirl, hungry for knowledge, knew "that strength of intellect is acquired by conquering hard studies, and strength of character by overcoming obstacles."[54] This essay offered a clear message: study well, study hard, and study fully to sharpen the mind and forge one's character. African American women writers like Ann Plato did not, according to the literary scholar Katherine Clay Bassard, "assume a large, literate audience of black women as readers," though they could imagine a "*potential* community" in the near future.[55] Nevertheless African American schoolgirls and women of color who did read Ann's essay could follow this advice to be curious, to self-teach, and to pursue knowledge. No known records about her exist after 1847, but Ann's work as a writer and teacher demonstrate her belief in character education.

Boston-area teachers taught character education too, though the city's public primary schools for African American children were only open occasionally.[56] In 1829 Boston had two official public primary schools for African American children: Susan Paul's school on George Street and Charlotte Williams Foster's school on Belknap Street. Susan's mother had run African School No. 2 on George Street from her own home for three or four years before Susan took over. In the 1830s this school, renamed Boston Primary School No. 6, was the only continuously operating public primary school for African American children in Boston; upwards of sixty students attended each year, among them Susan's niece and nephews. Foster was an Afro-Native woman born in Stoughton, Massachusetts, around 1796 to Isaac Williams, who had been enslaved and later fought in the American Revolution, and Elizabeth Will, a Ponkapoag Indian.[57] In 1814 Charlotte married Samuel F. Foster and they had one child, Horatio W. Foster. In 1822 she began teaching at what would become Primary School No. 5, a position that she held for at least eight years and probably longer. Her first husband must have died, for she married Nicholas Myers in August 1836. She then retired from the teaching profession and became a homemaker.

Private schools for African American children existed in Boston, but they were sometimes makeshift and temporary. Nathaniel Southard, a white abolitionist and printer, opened a school at West Center Street Chapel for African American boys and girls in February 1834, but the school closed shortly thereafter.[58] Nancy Jasper, an African American teacher, had a bit more luck. Her school for African American children opened in May 1833 and soon morphed into the Garrison Juvenile

Society, a literary and religious association for children and youth named after William Lloyd Garrison. Nancy taught reading, spelling, music, and needlework.[59] The Belknap Street Church, where Nancy's husband, Samuel, served as a deacon, hosted annual exhibitions for the Society. The first exhibition included African American community leaders such as John T. Hilton and Samuel Snowden and white abolitionists like William Collier. Collier praised Nancy for her hard work in expanding the number of young scholars in this literary society from four to ninety-four. She charged a small fee and depended on fundraising and donations to cover expenses. The literary society folded in 1836.[60]

Given the fleeting nature of Boston's private school system, most African American children attended racially segregated public schools.[61] Sometime in the 1830s Boston Primary School No. 6 moved from its location at the Paul family home on George Street to the Smith school building on Belknap Street, which the city built and opened in 1835.[62] Catharine Paul told Edward Abdy, an English writer and antislavery activist who visited the family, that she and Susan had been eager to move because the family home was in a rough neighborhood. It was also the case that their home had fallen into disrepair, making it, in a friend's words, "uninhabitable in storms."[63] In 1837 the Pauls moved to Grove Street in the Beacon Hill area. Catharine also told Edward Abdy about two recent incidents of racial discrimination. First, Susan was not permitted to travel by stagecoach from Boston to Exeter, New Hampshire, due to racial segregation in travel, but instead had to procure a gig, at great expense, just to visit friends. Second, Susan had planned to move to another area in Boston and relocate her school but had been "informed, that the inhabitants of the street, in which she was about to settle, had resolved to eject her or pull the building down, if she persisted in her determination."[64] The Smith school building thus housed, quite literally, African American public education: two primary schools and one grammar school.[65]

As a primary school teacher, Susan Paul taught standard subjects such as reading and arithmetic, but she also imparted to her students a heavy dose of Christian piety. To be sure, all public primary school teachers in Boston were instructed to open and close the day with prayer.[66] In 1828 Susan had a class of about seventy-two African American boys and girls, ages five to ten. Some visitors to the school noted that she successfully governed her classroom with kindness as students followed her directions.[67] These visitors concluded, "[Susan Paul is] well qualified for the arduous service in which she is engaged, possessing an accurate knowledge of the branches in which she teaches, and a readiness and facility of communication." Students apparently displayed "respectful manners" and demonstrated their expertise in spelling, arithmetic, and English grammar. [68] Five years later not much had changed. Observers noted that her students "appeared very cheerful, and were remarkably orderly" and "in no way appeared at all inferior to white children."[69] By all accounts, Susan was a masterful teacher with sharp-minded students.

Susan schooled her students in the power of civic activism by immersing them in the abolitionist cause. She and her students attended the quarterly meetings of the New England Anti-Slavery Society, where they listened to abolitionist lecturers such as Samuel J. May and David L. Child.[70] On August 1, 1834, she took her students to South Reading, Massachusetts, to commemorate the one-year anniversary of the abolition of slavery in the British colonies, an event celebrated by African Americans across the North and in Canada.[71] That Susan took her students to this event demonstrates the importance of social activism and diasporic commemoration.[72]

Susan's students sang in the Boston Juvenile Choir, which performed concerts that advanced the abolitionist cause, denounced racial prejudice, and celebrated black intellectual achievement. The choir, made up of fifty students at one point, sang patriotic and anticolonization songs at antislavery events throughout New England. Their patriotic, antislavery, and anticolonization songs became part of the struggle for African American emancipation. One song, "The Garden," sung by a twelve-year-old boy named Hoyt, described the classroom as a beautiful "fragrant garden" where students soaked up knowledge passed on to them by their teacher.[73] At one concert, an attendee noted that Susan and her students possessed "practical knowledge of the science of music," another that the children's "countenances beamed with intelligence."[74]

Cultivating moral habits in young African American children was the cornerstone of Susan's pedagogy. She modeled great care in her interactions with students and taught values such as respect and kindness in her daily lessons. Certainly visitors to her classroom and attendees at her students' concerts noticed this part of her teaching, but it also emerged in her own writings, including a biography of a six-year-old student named James Jackson Jr.

James was born into a large family of modest means in Boston on December 5, 1826. He had at least two sisters, Sarah and Ann Jennette, and probably two brothers.[75] His father, James Sr., worked as a laborer, while his mother, Elizabeth, was a homemaker and later a nurse. The Paul family knew the Jackson family; Thomas Paul Sr. united twenty-six-year-old James Sr. and twenty-one-year-old Elizabeth Cook in holy matrimony on September 23, 1813. The Jackson family moved around the Boston area quite a bit but lived on Southac Street for a while. When James Sr. died in April 1829, he was remembered as a "respectable man of color."[76] Given the family's financial instability, James Sr. was buried at the South Burial Ground in Boston, a cemetery owned by the city.

Just a few months after James Sr.'s passing, Elizabeth married William Riley, an African American clothes dealer from Boston. Together the Rileys reared their children and became prominent members in abolitionist and religious organizations. Elizabeth, along with other African American activists, raised money to support Garrison's *Liberator* in its early years. Voluntary associations were important to the Jackson-Riley family: at least one of Elizabeth's children, Ann Jennette, participated in Nancy Jasper's Garrison Juvenile Society.[77] Elizabeth served as president of two voluntary associations: the Colored Female Union Society and the Afric-American Female Intelligence Society. While leading these organizations, Elizabeth worked as a nurse in wealthy white homes.[78] Neither she nor William could write, so they relied on their children to pen letters for them.[79] By 1840 the Rileys had amassed $1,800, but they fell on hard times and lost almost all of it. Still, they maintained ownership of their home and William ran his clothing shop at 22 Brattle Street. The Rileys attended Leonard Grimes's Twelfth Street Baptist Church, and prior to that, Elizabeth hosted parties for African American children attending the Belknap Street Church's Sunday school.[80] William's untimely death in July 1849 widowed Elizabeth once again.[81]

Memoir of James Jackson offers glimpses of this free black family in the early 1830s, but first and foremost it tells the story of pious and industrious six-year-old James Jackson Jr. Divided into seven chapters, it traces James's educational and spiritual maturation. What he studied at school was reinforced by what his mother taught him at home. His life was cut short when he fell ill with tuberculosis and died on October 31, 1833.[82] In her preface to *Memoir of James Jackson*, Susan Paul made it clear that she aimed for James's story to evince the "moral and intellectual powers" of a black child and to "[break] down that unholy prejudice which exists against color."[83] James Loring, a white printer who knew the Paul family, published *Memoir of James Jackson* in 1835, and Garrison advertised it in the *Liberator*. It sold eighteen copies at one antislavery meeting. The text is significant beyond its story of a young boy, because it shows how

an African American female teacher in the antebellum era organized her school and taught her students.[84]

Susan did not shy away from classroom discussions about American slavery. She explained that cruel slaveholders bought and sold African American children, women, and men; she lamented the fact that African Americans were often barred from reading the Bible; and she mentioned the terrible physical and psychological violence that they endured. Enslaved children, for instance, did not, and in some states could not, attend school, Susan asserted, "or [were] taught by kind Sabbath school teachers." These revelations affected James, who told his mother that he would pray for the enslaved every day; Susan transcribed the prayer: "O Lord, pity the poor slaves, and let them be free, that they may have their liberty, and be happy as I am,—and may they have good teachers to learn them to read, as I have, and make them all very good. Amen." A free black child, James grappled with the reality of slavery and, through prayer, figuratively baptized himself an abolitionist. Susan's young readers could then recite a prayer that reminded them of the importance of African American emancipation and the universal human quest for knowledge. She asked her young readers, "Will you remember and offer the same prayer for slaves and all in distress?"[85] Such abolitionist sentiment explained why the Baptist Sabbath School Society and the Orthodox Congregational Sabbath School Society refused to publish the biography.[86]

If the plight of enslaved African Americans failed to elicit empathy in children, Susan could point to the mistreatment of the nation's poor and disabled. She narrated a terrible moment when James witnessed mean and unruly boys throwing dirt, stones, and callous words at a poor, old, disabled woman on the street. With tears in his eyes, James ran home and asked his mother, "Does not the great God see those wicked boys?" An empathetic James imagined, "If I was poor, I should want some one, who had plenty of all these things, to give me some of them." His behavior exemplified the importance of charity, especially toward the oppressed. After sharing this moment in *Memoir of James Jackson*, Susan stepped back into her role as teacher and reminded her readers, "If every one would obey this precept [of goodness] as they ought, no person would be despised or abused because they are poor, or because they had dark skin, nor for any other reason but because they are bad, and even then, we should pity and not despise them." She concluded that all discrimination would cease once children, and adults too, acted compassionately and with sincere concern for each other.[87]

James's enthusiasm for learning refuted racist claims that African American children had little desire for educational advancement and lacked intellectual faculties worth cultivating. He learned the alphabet quickly, and, from then on, "whatever lesson his teacher directed his class to learn," he "immediately commenced, and cheerfully continued to study, until he had entirely learned it." As one of Susan's best scholars, he followed the word of God, listened carefully to his teacher, obeyed his mother, and with all of the goodness in his heart he helped his class-mates by tutoring them and sharing his toys and fruit with them. Not only was James teachable, but he also taught others. Susan wrote that he possessed "excellent traits of character" that others should model. By writing this biography, she intended for her young white and African American readers to embody these traits.[88]

The portrayal of an African American child exhibiting good conduct allowed Susan to expose the folly of racial prejudice. "It is the *conduct*," she insisted, "that makes the boys or men or women bad." She provided the following anecdote, as told to her by a friend, to illustrate this point. While walking down the street, Susan's friend heard a white woman threaten to "carry [a young white boy] down to Belknap-street, and give [him] to the *old black man*." "The old black man" represented danger and isolation, a potential punishment that may have stopped the white child from misbehaving but that also engendered prejudice. When Susan's friend, an African American man, walked past the woman and boy, the boy grew frightened. The point was clear: racial prejudice resulted from unchristian pedagogy.[89]

Susan guided the students directly under her care and also those beyond her classroom. On July 4, 1836, Mr. Morrill, the superintendent of the Union Evangelical Sabbath School of Amesbury and Salisbury, Massachusetts, wrote a letter to Susan and her students. Apparently Morrill and his students had "heard about" Primary School No. 6, which suggests that they read *Memoir of James Jackson*. Morrill's students decided to donate their 4th of July pocket money to her school: "[It is a] show [of] our respect for you and your teacher, and the interest we feel in your welfare." Two weeks later Susan, along with her students, responded to this gift, calling it an "act of love" that enabled them to purchase books and to provide aid to poor students. These kinds of charitable acts sowed the bonds of friendship across the color line, and it was on display for all to read in the *Liberator* as well as in the local North Shore newspaper, the *Essex North Register and Family Monitor*.[90]

Both the classroom and *Memoir of James Jackson* became sites for Susan to help children develop a moral identity. Like many other teachers, Susan used the Bible, focusing on the Ten Commandments and hymns, to impart lessons on empathy, honesty, and selflessness. She stressed children's moral agency by reading to them biblical passages such as Matthew 19:13–15, wherein children receive Christ's blessing. Likewise James emerged in his biography as a caring, inquisitive, morally fit, and well-liked boy, worthy of emulation by all. His strong moral character christened him a purposeful member of society; moral character was thus linked to good citizenship and the prosperity of the nation.

Elizabeth Jackson Riley also constructed a home where she reinforced what Susan taught, especially in religious matters. Susan admitted that James received very little academic teaching at home since his mother worked outside of the home and her "cares were so numerous as to prevent giving that attention to James which she desired to give him."[91] For working-class women like Elizabeth, working outside of the home was an economic necessity.[92] Moreover her limited facility in reading and writing made it a challenge for her to instruct her son. But she did offer him a definition of faith and goodness. When James Sr. died, she explained to her children that his new home was now in heaven. "All good people . . . go to heaven," she affirmed. The memory of their father, then, was of a good man. James Jr. formed a strong bond with his mother, confiding in her, obeying her, listening to her, and praying with her. When confronted with any kind of doubt, he modeled his conduct upon that of his mother. Two African American women—Susan and Elizabeth—thus guided James's maturation, a realization that cast African American women as moral, pious, and respectable.

But what of William Riley, James's stepfather? His obituary described his life as "distinguished by his Christian virtues," yet Susan completely ignored his role in James's life.[93] James's siblings were likewise only briefly mentioned. James Sr.'s death certainly shattered the Jackson family; forming the American stepfamily offered a mode of repair. "Remarriage," according to the historian Lisa Wilson, "almost always led to the creation of the stepfamily."[94] Free black families thus appreciated the social constructs surrounding ideal family life. When William died in 1849, he bequeathed $25 to his wife's children by her first husband, referred to as such in his will. To his own three biological children with Elizabeth, he left the total sum in a bank account to be split equally among them. The demarcation between the Jackson children and the Riley children may have extended far beyond William's will. In any case,

William influenced the Jackson children too, but *Memoir of James Jackson* highlighted the intellectual and moral character of African Americans through the depiction of the black woman and child.

Susan concluded *Memoir of James Jackson* by reviewing its key elements. She queried her readers, "What do you remember particularly that you have read about [James] in this book?" To all of her readers, children and adults, men and women, African Americans and whites, rich and poor alike, she exhorted, "Love your enemies" and "Do to others as you wish others to do to you."[95] She wished for all to follow a sort of Christian law of love, as other African American girls and women activists had articulated years earlier.[96]

While Susan engaged in educational and reform work, her labors at home never lessened. On the contrary, she cared for her aging mother, three young nephews, and a niece. She confided in her friend, the white abolitionist and writer Lydia Maria Child, about her mounting financial problems. She struggled to pay the $200 monthly rent at 3 Grove Street, and she had accrued personal debts. In what little spare time she had, she worked as a seamstress, but her earnings did not allow her to discharge her debts. Child found that Susan's mind "appeared to be in a state of pitiable anxiety and perplexity."[97] Susan asked to borrow $100 from her abolitionist friends, and they sent her around $40, for which she expressed her sincere gratitude. Tragedy struck once again when her fiancé, whose name we do not know, died in 1840. A racist incident set in motion Susan's eventual demise a year later. She traveled to New York on a steamboat during inclement weather and was barred from taking cover in the women's cabin because of her race. She fell ill and died from consumption on April 19, 1841, thirty-two years old.

Abolitionists lamented Susan's death, as did her students. Her death notice appeared in at least five Massachusetts newspapers, from the *New Bedford Register* to the *Christian Reflector*. The white abolitionist Benjamin C. Bacon eulogized her, remarking that she joined the abolition movement because of "the simple fact that oppression existed."[98] To his mind, Susan embodied the spirit of a genuine reformer, a freedom fighter. This central objective—to fight oppression—shaped her pedagogical approach and partly explains why she stressed character education. As the historian Lois Brown argues, in *Memoir of James Jackson*, Susan left behind "practical pedagogical models for white [and black] teachers to implement in their classrooms, homes, and communities."[99]

The Paul and Riley families remained close. Susan's brother, Thomas Paul Jr., returned home to Boston in 1841, where he, his mother, and

sister Ann's four children lived together in a brick house on Fruit Street. Seven years later, on October 29, 1848, Catharine died at the age of seventy-three. A mere two weeks earlier, Thomas Paul Smith—Anne's eldest son—had married Elizabeth Augusta Roberts, the daughter of Sarah Easton and Robert Roberts. He still cared for his younger siblings while operating a clothing and dry-cleaning business at 38 Brattle Street.[100] In 1855 twenty-eight-year-old Ann Jennette Jackson and her three half-siblings—William Jr., George, and Eliza—lived together with two of the Paul-Smiths, Elijah W. Smith Jr. and Susan P. Smith. Six years later thirty-year-old Elijah Jr. and twenty-five-year-old Eliza Riley were married by Leonard Grimes. The bride and groom were likely members of the Twelfth Street Baptist Church, just as their parents had been.[101]

African American women teachers like Susan Paul were remembered fondly long after their deaths. In 1846 African American community members at Belknap Street Church saluted her and other deceased comrades for their boundless activism. After the Civil War, Sarah H. Southwick, a white abolitionist from New England, published *Reminiscences of Early Anti-Slavery Days*, wherein she briefly memorialized Susan as "warmly loved and respected by those who knew her." Southwick mentioned Susan's work as a teacher, though she mistakenly described her school as private, when it was certainly public. Southwick remembered Susan as "educated and intelligent, and [that] abolitionists associated with her and invited her to their houses as a friend and guest." Among abolitionists and African American residents of Boston, Susan Paul was not forgotten.[102]

Such recognition and memorialization, however, rarely equated to financial security for teachers who lived to old age. In the mid- to late nineteenth century, many single, middle-class teachers retired from the profession only to face severe financial hardship. Both African American and white women teachers earned low salaries. In Massachusetts the ratio of female to male teachers' salaries "remained around 40 percent throughout the period," even though the number of female teachers steadily increased in the pre–Civil War era.[103] Many women teachers depended on their salaries for basic survival and were thus unable to save money.[104] Charlotte Williams Foster Myers, for example, had taught for at least eight years at Primary School No. 5 in Boston. Widowed by the 1860s, she claimed Ponkapoag Indian heritage and filed a petition with Massachusetts for financial assistance in the amount of $52 per year, which the state granted. A few years later she petitioned for an increase to $104, given her "feeble health and . . . indigent and destitute circumstances."[105] This request was also approved. Her repeated submission of similar petitions over subsequent years revealed her ongoing need for financial support.

Myers appears to have embraced her mixed-race heritage. First, her teaching career suggests that she, like Ann Plato of Hartford, was committed to purposeful work through the education of African American children. Second, in 1879 she applied for admission to the Home for Aged Colored Women, a Boston-area residence for poor, elderly African American women established in 1860. At first she did not wish to move there because she found the rules to be "too strict," but circumstances compelled her to reconsider. Admissions records mentioned her career as a Boston schoolteacher as well as her near-white complexion. She used the resources available to her and sought out the social assistance that she needed and for which she qualified. She lived at the Home for Aged Colored Women for a while, but was later declared "insane" and dismissed. She died at age eighty-seven from apoplexy on February 9, 1885, in Taunton, Massachusetts.[106]

Sarah Mapps Douglass enjoyed a slightly different fate after she retired from teaching. In 1855 she married William Douglass, an African American pastor at St. Thomas Protestant Episcopal Church in Philadelphia and a widower with nine children. Six years later he died. Sarah never stopped teaching and, after taking courses at the Female Medical College of Pennsylvania and the Pennsylvania Medical University, began giving lectures on physiology and hygiene from Philadelphia to Washington, D.C. At the age of seventy she retired from a teaching career that spanned fifty years. She reminisced, "Doing the *work* I *love*; doing it with all my heart and soul and mind and strength!! Finding my rich reward in knowing my record is on high."[107] On February 6, 1880, a group of African Americans, including some of her former students, hosted a celebration for seventy-three-year-old Sarah at her home on 508 Powell Street in Philadelphia, where they praised her work, thanked her for her commitment to children and the larger community, and raised money for her subsistence.[108] She died on September 8, 1882.

African American communities as far away as Washington, D.C. remembered Sarah Mapps Douglass for her untiring commitment as an educator.[109] A dynamic, hardworking teacher, she had dedicated her life to her God-given calling, which her mother encouraged. Even when Sarah herself questioned her purpose, those around her never did. In 1880 the *People's Advocate* published a tribute to her, which may well have been written by John W. Cromwell, an African American teacher and

FIGURE 6.2. Charlotte Forten (1837–1914) was a well-educated African American writer, abolitionist, and lecturer from Philadelphia who taught at public and private schools from Salem, Massachusetts, to the Sea Islands of South Carolina during the Civil War era. Courtesy of the Peabody Essex Museum, Salem, MA.

later civil servant who graduated from the Institute for Colored Youth in 1864 and knew Sarah well. "Her life has been a *useful* one; directly, to the people among whom she has labored; indirectly, to the whole nation, for she has added to the sum of its intelligence and morality."[110] To Cromwell, Sarah was a model of purposeful womanhood.

This earlier generation of African American women teachers paved the way for the next, which included Charlotte Forten (Figure 6.2) and the Smith sisters, Elizabeth and Florence. Born on August 17, 1837, to Robert Forten and Mary Virginia Wood, Charlotte grew up in Philadelphia as a member of the prominent Forten-Purvis family. Mary died when Charlotte was only three years old; her maternal grandmother, Edy, and her father raised her. As a child, she received private tutoring since her father boycotted Philadelphia's segregated schools. When he learned that Salem's public schools admitted African American children, he sent sixteen-year-old Charlotte there in 1854. She boarded with the Remond family while attending the Higginson School.

Attending this school in Salem would enable Charlotte to fulfill her calling as a teacher, a path etched out for her by her father and other family members. The Higginson School, formerly the West School for Girls, had a solid reputation for preparing young women to lead a purposeful life.[111] Believing that everyone had a calling, Charlotte wrote a hymn:

> Not the great and gifted only
> He appoints to do his will,
> But each one, however lowly,
> a mission to fulfil.[112]

With her father's backing, she vowed, "[I shall] spare no effort to become what he desires that I should be . . . to prepare myself well for the responsible duties of a teacher, and to live for the good that I can do my oppressed and suffering fellow-creatures."[113] For Charlotte, self-education and formal schooling went hand-in-hand, so she studied diligently and read widely.

Racial prejudice, though, never faded in Salem, and Charlotte felt it. Twenty years before she arrived, Sarah Parker Remond had been expelled from one of the public high schools for girls simply because of her race, a story Sarah may have told Charlotte. Though Charlotte could now attend a public high school for girls, her classmates were unabashedly racist, and that reality wore her down; if only her classmates could accept the notion that "it is character alone which makes the true man or woman!"[114] Charlotte counted a few friends, though, including Mary Shepard, the white principal of the Higginson School. She and Charlotte enjoyed frank conversations about slavery and racism, but Mary, a believer in character education, counseled Charlotte to "cultivate a Christian spirit in thinking of [her] enemies," an invocation of scripture.[115] Charlotte could not help but feel that "no other injury could be so hard to bear, so very hard to forgive, as that inflicted by cruel oppression and prejudice."[116]

Like young African American women activists before her, Charlotte constantly sought self-improvement, but moments of self-doubt sometimes crept in. She devoured books by Charles Dickens, Nathaniel Hawthorne, and Hannah More. She learned French and German as well as European history. She also read the Bible, citing passages such as Hebrews 13:3, which reminded her of the suffering that enslaved African Americans experienced in the South. Her learning shaped her activism, as she published poetry in antislavery newspapers, helped to gain signatures for the Boston school desegregation petition campaign, attended antislavery meetings throughout Essex County, and joined the Salem Female Anti-Slavery Society. Yet Charlotte doubted her own intellectual and activist abilities. She wrote in her diary, "Have realized more deeply and bitterly than ever in my life my own ignorance and folly. Not only am I without the gifts of Nature, wit, beauty and talent; without the accomplishments which nearly every one of my age, whom I know, possesses; but I am not even *intelligent*."[117] Her insecurities were directly tied to her desire to lead a purposeful life, as the women who came before her had done. Indeed she found inspiration in African American foremothers like Phillis Wheatley, whom she regarded as a "wonderful gifted woman [whose] character and genius" disputed the myth of African American inferiority.[118]

Following her calling as a teacher, Charlotte decided to study at the female-only Salem Normal School, which had opened in 1854 with Richard Edwards, a Welsh native, as principal. This was one of a handful of public normal schools established in nineteenth-century Massachusetts, where teaching was regarded as a "consecrated mission."[119] The first Massachusetts state public normal school was founded in 1839 at Lexington, with a goal of providing more rigorous and robust training to prospective primary school teachers through a one-year certificate program. In 1843 Lexington Normal School graduated its first African American student, Mary E. Miles, who had previously studied at the Canterbury Female Seminary in Connecticut and the Young Ladies' Domestic Seminary in New York. In 1852 Annie E. Wood, Charlotte's aunt, attended the normal school at West Newton.[120] Normal schools enrolled a fairly diverse group of students, including women and people of color. Certainly teachers taught in public and private schools without a normal school certificate, but normal schools offered free or low-cost tuition, valuable training, and a pipeline to teaching positions. The scholars Mary-Lou Breitborde and Kelly Kolodny report that, by 1870, "eighteen states had at least one normal school."[121]

To gain admission, a prospective student had to provide proof of high moral character in addition to passing an exam and providing letters of recommendation. In March 1855 Charlotte passed the entrance exam and earned admission. She would soon learn much more about the teaching profession and deepen her knowledge in common academic subjects such as astronomy, geography, and geometry. But just as she prepared to enter Salem Normal School, her father summoned her to return home; he doubted that Charlotte, or any African American person, for that matter, could secure a teaching position at a school in Massachusetts. At that point, the petition campaign in Boston to abolish racially exclusive public schools was working its way through the state legislature, though Salem had desegregated its schools eleven years earlier. But who knew whether the teaching force would be racially desegregated too? After Richard Edwards told Charlotte that, upon her graduation, she would indeed be able to find a teaching position in Salem, her father relented. A relieved Charlotte commenced her studies in this intellectually stimulating environment. "More and more pleasant becomes my Normal School life," she wrote.[122]

Normal schools emphasized character education as part of their teacher preparation curriculum. The typical normal school classroom opened with students reading scripture, and the curriculum included "principles of piety and morality common to all sects of Christians."[123] Charlotte had already been exposed to character education at the Higginson School and in her earlier studies in Philadelphia. She revealed her familiarity with character education in a hymn that she composed:

> But, with hope of aiding others,
> Gladly we perform our part;
> Nor forget, the mind, while storing,
> We must educate the heart.[124]

She entered the teaching profession with her eyes wide open, seeking to educate a child's mind *and* heart.

In her various teaching experiences, Charlotte encouraged her young students to be purposeful. Upon graduation in 1856, she accepted a position at Epes Grammar School, making her one of the first African American women teachers in Salem's racially integrated public schools. A few years later she resigned due to ill health—probably consumption. She returned to Philadelphia, where she privately tutored her cousins, the children of Robert Purvis and Harriet Forten. Robert was still boycotting Philadelphia's public schools and refusing to pay taxes until these schools accepted African American children.[125] It was in June 1858 that

Charlotte recorded in her diary a visit to Sarah Mapps Douglass's school, which "seem[ed] to be well-conducted."[126] A few years later Charlotte taught at the Lombard Street School run by her aunt, Margaretta Forten, before moving to the South Carolina Sea Islands to teach recently emancipated African American children. In one classroom lesson, she told the story of Toussaint L'Ouverture, whom she described as a "noble" hero, in order to "inspire [her students] with courage and ambition (of a noble sort), and high purposes."[127]

Beyond the teaching profession, Charlotte remained active, engaged, and mindful—"to have done something for *others* as well as for [her] self."[128] The New England branch of the Freedmen's Union Commission hired her, and she also had other teaching stints in the South. In December 1878 she retired from the teaching profession after her marriage to Francis J. Grimké, pastor at the Fifteenth Street Presbyterian Church and nephew of the Grimké sisters, the well-known white abolitionists and women's rights advocates. She continued her writing, participated in her husband's church, and helped to establish and support the National Association of Colored Women.

Like Charlotte Forten, the Smith sisters of Boston were also part of the next generation of African American women teachers. Born on October 23, 1846, in Boston, Elizabeth Norton Smith was raised by her father, John, a free black man from Virginia, and her mother, Georgianna, a mixed-race woman from Nova Scotia. Elizabeth, better known as "Lizzie," had five younger siblings, including Florence, born in 1856, and Harriet, born in 1864. The Smith children grew up in an abolitionist household in the West End and attended schools there. Lizzie earned high honors at the Bowdoin School and later studied at the Girls' Normal and High School. After her graduation, she worked as a teacher in the South before returning to the Bay State, where she taught at Joy Street Primary School, making her the first African American teacher in a racially integrated Boston public school.[129] All of Lizzie's sisters became teachers too; Florence, also a graduate of the Girls' High and Normal School, taught in Washington, D.C., and Harriet in Boston. In 1890 Lizzie and Harriet counted only two other African American women teachers in Boston: Mollie Lewis and Alice Miller.[130] These four women constituted less than one half of 1 percent of the total number of Boston-area public schoolteachers.[131] When Lizzie died in December 1899, her obituary celebrated her as a pioneer in Boston public school education, praised her as a devoted teacher and "great friend" to her students, and revered her as a "woman of rare intellectual attainments."[132] She had followed in the footsteps of educators before her, and other African American women would follow after her.

As contemporaries, Sarah Mapps Douglass and Susan Paul both grew up in the Northeast in vibrant African American communities that stressed Christian purposefulness. Inspired by their own mothers to pursue a teaching career, they regarded teaching as God's calling and vowed to do all they could to educate the rising generation of African American children. The knowledge, skills, and values necessary for good citizenship thus included studying English grammar, arithmetic, geography, and history, to name a few subjects; strong skills in writing and rhetoric; and upholding values such as respect, hard work, integrity, and self-discipline. Such learning guided each child and served as a foundation for good character. The efforts of these teachers directly challenged the racist ideologies of their time and were often undertaken in the face of public opposition, with little to no financial support.

Outside of the classroom, Sarah and Susan wrote poetry, short stories, and didactic literature that celebrated black intellectual achievement, good moral character, and the eradication of oppression. They confronted and condemned racial prejudice while encouraging civic activism among children and adults. Their writings were multifaceted, as pedagogical lessons, as testaments to African American character, and as reminders of the great influence of teachers. Though working in different cities in the Northeast, Sarah in Philadelphia and Susan in Boston, these women laid the foundation for the next generation of educators, such as Charlotte Forten and the Smith sisters. Well aware of the path that African Americans trod in pursuit of knowledge, these teachers held steadfast to their belief in teaching as purposeful work.

Conclusion: Going Forward

The fight for African American education was at times cruel and frustrating, replete with loss, the victories slow and unsteady. Yet African American girls and women went forward anyway, seeking learning to help themselves, their families, and their communities. Education was of vital importance to African Americans—a personal goal for many, an individual quest for self-definition, and a key to collective racial uplift. The very act of a young woman applying for admission to a female seminary or a public high school constituted a step toward reform, and if successful, her attendance was a radical act of bravery. When racist white leaders erected arbitrary spatial boundaries to contest African American education, young women moved to new and unfamiliar places in pursuit of knowledge. A rural village in Connecticut might be just as inhospitable as a public high school in a small seaport town. Nevertheless these girls and women steeled themselves to handle what awaited them. They did not emerge unscathed, however. On the contrary, deep wounds lingered, but these young women did not lose faith as they fought for their right to learn, and thus for all African American children to learn.

Certainly the proliferation of female literary societies in the Northeast in the early nineteenth century demonstrated that African American women cared deeply about intellectual culture. In fact, African American girls and women used these informal educational spaces to network and support more formal educational spaces. Hence the controversy surrounding the Canterbury Female Seminary was a watershed moment in African American girls' and women's education precisely because it spurred young women and their allies to articulate what was at stake in the struggle for advanced schooling. Sarah Mapps Douglass and other activists conveyed the urgency of expanding educational opportunities for young women. African American male leaders, in particular, began to forge common ground with their female counterparts to combat racial and, to a lesser extent, gender prejudice, especially as coeducational institutions sprang up in African American communities. White abolitionists contributed to the cause by building racially diverse schools and welcoming African American girls and women at all-white institutions. Race and gender thus shaped the struggle for educational inclusion and equal school rights from Canterbury, Connecticut, and Clinton, New York, to Boston, Massachusetts.

Believing that education was a fundamental right, young African American women pushed their way into schoolhouses across the Northeast. These women promoted new ideas about African American womanhood, as they deployed a variety of protest strategies to challenge racial prejudice at female seminaries and public high schools. White opponents to African American education, however, sought to reset both the racial and the gender order, as seen in the Canterbury case as well as the Salem controversy. While some white colonizationists like Andrew T. Judson maligned the character of young African American women, whipping up opposition among Canterbury's white residents, African American women students and activists espoused an ethic of Christian love as they fought for inclusion and belonging. At public high schools in Massachusetts, Eunice Ross and others mobilized by organizing protests for equal school rights. In doing so, they ignited a shift from caste schools to democratic schools.

In newspaper editorials and public speeches, activists touted the benefits of racial diversity in public and private schools. The Young Ladies' Domestic Seminary in Clinton, New York, was proof of concept. White women who had been schooled alongside African American women learned the realities of racial prejudice, and some even began to fight for racial equality and freedom. As this book reveals, eradicating racial prejudice in public and private schools was an uphill battle. Prejudice was, and arguably still is, multidimensional, complex, and unstable, shifting across geographic space and historical periods. Arguments for the benefits of racial diversity in schools and the necessity of equal school rights would have to be stated, louder and more vigorously, again and again.

Hence racial segregation, and efforts to abolish it, in public education in Massachusetts were hyperlocal, moving in fits and starts. Sarah Parker

Remond's fight in Salem is exemplary. During a fifty-year period, city officials and the majority of white residents in Salem oscillated between a policy of racial school segregation and racially mixed schools. Thanks to Sarah, her sisters, her parents, and their allies, a successful equal school rights campaign would be mounted and would abolish racially exclusive public schools in 1844. The Salem campaign in turn encouraged activists in Nantucket to keep fighting, which then stirred up Boston activists who pursued statewide public school desegregation legislation, that then stimulated a statewide equal school rights campaign in Rhode Island, all of which changed the American educational landscape.

Even among African American girls and women who confronted prejudice in pursuit of advanced schooling and teaching careers, there was a diversity of experiences. For instance, Hiram Huntington Kellogg stressed Christian piety and social reform at the Young Ladies' Domestic Seminary, but some young women, like Serena deGrasse, grappled with their religious identity, while others, like Margaret Morrison, embraced it. Likewise some young women excelled at certain academic subjects, while others struggled. What these women shared was a realization that advanced schooling charted new intellectual pathways on the road to becoming purposeful women.

Young African American women understood themselves to be—and, importantly, explicitly referred to themselves as—purposeful women. To be sure, the power of the domestic circle and a mother's influence on her family was part of this ideology, but many African American women worked outside of the home. In whatever circle a woman occupied, she had to be purposeful, that is, active, resilient, and forward thinking. African American teachers reminded the public that character and equality were American values. They also taught character education in their classroom, emphasizing Christian faith, goodness, and morality. African American women, whether mothers, wives, reformers, teachers, activists, or a combination thereof, encouraged future generations to work for educational reform in order to bring about an egalitarian system of education, black civil rights, and freedom in the United States.

Championing schooling and teaching did not imply that education was a panacea, however. Rosetta Morrison's story made that clear. During a childhood marked by domestic labor, Rosetta—who could not even retain her given name Maria—worked, learned, and qualified for admission to the Young Ladies' Domestic Seminary. She studied there for a few years before establishing her own school in Brooklyn. It was slavery—its economic and political power—that disrupted her life and that of her husband and children. No amount of schooling could have stopped the impending tragedy of familial separation and loss. Education, however, did allow Rosetta to instill in her children a passion for learning and teaching. No doubt she hoped for a better future, as many African Americans did.

The network of African American teacher-activists continued to expand into the late nineteenth century. It welcomed more women who found their purpose through teaching. African American women in Ohio, for instance, participated in teacher organizations such as the Ohio Colored Teachers' Association, where they debated pedagogy.[1] In literary and debate societies, women continued to shape the narrative on black intellectual achievement. By publicizing moments of educational success and defeat in the black press, teachers, especially those who had moved to the South to school freed people, strategized and fundraised. J. Imogen Howard and Adeline T. Howard were career teachers, as were the daughters of Rosetta Morrison, to name only a few. Having witnessed their mothers' struggle, this younger generation understood that they too would have to carry on the fight for equal school rights well into the twentieth century.

Acknowledgments

I realize now that I pursued a version of this research project as early as high school. My mother Rose gently reminded me every now and then to learn well and to study hard. She even modeled it for me when she went back to college to earn her undergraduate and graduate degrees when I was a teenager. On a few evenings I sat in the back of a college classroom, watching and waiting for her. I am grateful that I witnessed her pursuit of knowledge, and I am thankful that she advocated for me and my education at every turn. With her support, I was able to earn a scholarship to attend a small private high school where teachers encouraged my intellectual growth and curiosity.

Later, when my aging grandfather—a key figure in my life whose faith kept me going—needed my help and my mom lost her job, I worried about how I would pay for college. I am grateful to have received a Gates Millennium Scholarship, which funded my undergraduate education at the University of California, Los Angeles. There I had amazing teachers, like G. Jennifer Wilson and Jenny Sharpe, who deepened my knowledge of African diasporic literature and culture while helping me find my way.

My research on African American education began in earnest in graduate school at the University of Massachusetts, Amherst, where I trained with esteemed historians and literary scholars like John Bracey Jr., Amilcar Shabazz, Ernie Allen, Esther Terry, Michael Thelwell, James Smethurst, and Steve Tracy in the Department of Afro-American Studies. In Bill Strickland's graduate seminar, I read about Prudence Crandall's seminary, which I had never heard of; I wanted to learn more about the young African American women who had flocked to that school only to have to flee a year later. Bill's positive feedback and scholarly suggestions led me to my larger project. In Manisha Sinha I found a perfect mentor and brilliant scholar to guide me on this research journey into early nineteenth-century America. The debt I owe her is enormous. She provided me with excellent training in historical research methods and writing, read an early draft of this book, and encouraged me when doubts crept in. And as if that were not enough, she was a beacon of incredible generosity and kindness. I still benefit from her advice.

I extend my heartfelt thanks to scholars Erica Armstrong Dunbar, Maggie Nash, and Bill Harris for reading the entire book manuscript. Erica championed my work years ago, and her sustained feedback in conversations as well as at conferences and workshops helped me clarify my argument and sharpen my claims. She also introduced me to an exciting scholarly community during my residency at the Library Company of Philadelphia, for which I will always be indebted. Her impeccable research, mentorship, and leadership continue to inspire me. I feel lucky to have met Maggie Nash when I was a wide-eyed graduate student. Maggie has also mentored me and supported my scholarship. Her fantastic work on women's education in nineteenth-century America informed my own. Moreover her careful reading of the manuscript reminded me to ground my historiographical claims in a solid engagement with the secondary literature. Bill Harris read a nearly completed draft of the manuscript at the eleventh hour and brought to my attention some sources I had overlooked. His sage advice has markedly improved the manuscript.

In 2011 extraordinary colleagues welcomed me into the History Department at the College of Wooster in Ohio. I appreciate the support that I received, which kept my research moving along. I am fortunate to have learned from Greg Shaya, Madonna Hettinger, and Jeff Roche, among others, that high-quality teaching and rigorous research are complementary. I participated in thrilling conversations about pedagogical innovation with faculty such as Katie Holt, Ibra Sene, Margaret Ng, Leslie Wingard, and others as well as with students, whose questions prompted me to delve deeper into the history of African American women's education.

Like the girls and women whose stories I trace in this book, I have benefited from educational networks in which I soaked up the brilliant work of scholars while also sharing my own research. Sitting in Hilary

Moss's office, I learned as much as I could about the history of education. She offered excellent feedback on drafts of my work, suggested that I present my work at the History of Education Society, and told me about the Spencer Foundation. For that, I am so grateful. Linda Perkins is a phenomenal scholar whose book on Fanny Jackson Coppin inspired me; I appreciate her scholarship and her mentorship. I broke bread with Tiffany Gill as she helped me navigate the mysteries of journal article publication. My dear friend Shannon King read drafts of this book and reminded me that the magic is in revising. Carol Lasser gave me numerous insights that vastly improved my historical thinking. Lucy Knight deserves special recognition for sharing with me her exciting research discoveries on Sarah Mapps Douglass and Philadelphia abolitionists. I also thank the following scholars who, in one way or another, provided me with great support: Gabrielle Foreman, Leslie Harris, Cathy Kelly, James Anderson, Joycelyn Moody, Sharla Fett, Rosetta Marantz Cohen, Aston Gonzales, Jessica Linker, James T. Campbell, Laura Lovett, Britt Rusert, Natalie Dykstra, Yveline Alexis, Vanessa Fabien, Elizabeth DuClos-Orsello, and Emily Murphy. For fruitful research leads, I thank Beth Salerno, Ezra Greenspan, Jennifer Rycenga, Lisa Baskin, Anne Boylan, Barbara Beeching, and Mike Jirik. I am also indebted to the work of discussants at conferences and workshops; Mary Kelley, Christopher Span, and Laura Muñoz, among others, engaged my work and asked thought-provoking questions.

I received assistance from librarians and archivists across the country. I thank Kaz Kozlowski at the Prudence Crandall Museum; Jurretta Heckscher at the Library of Congress; Joellen ElBashir at the Moorland-Spingarn Research Center of Howard University; staff at the University of Rhode Island Archives; Krystal Appiah, who is now at the University of Virginia Library; Connie King and Jim Green at the Library Company of Philadelphia; F. Keith Bingham at Cheyney University; Megan L. Goins-Diouf at Bowling Green State University; Abby Houston at Syracuse University Libraries; Sierra Dixon at the Connecticut Historical Society; Lauren Stark at the Schomburg Center for Research in Black Culture; Marta Crilly at the Boston City Archives; the staff at Oberlin College; Maryjo McAndrew at Knox College; and George Comeau at Canton Historical Society. I also thank the volunteers at the Clinton Historical Society as well as Mary Elliot and Katie Knowles at the Smithsonian National Museum of African American History and Culture for giving me a tour of the museum and pointing out Amelia Lyons's school book.

Generous research fellowships gave me the time and space to write this book. The National Academy of Education and the Spencer Foundation supported my scholarship and invited me into an amazing intellectual community of established scholars such as Carl Kaestle, Jonathan Zimmerman, Charles Payne, and Deborah Loewenberg Ball. I also met the emerging scholars Katy Schumaker, Shirin Vossoughi, Michael Hevel, and others. A short-term research fellowship from the American Antiquarian Society came at just the right time. I thank Paul Erickson, Caroline Sloat, and Elizabeth Pope, who put me in touch with Richard Morgan. I also met whip-smart fellows and new collaborators, among them Tara Bynum, whose enthusiasm for eighteenth-century African American literature is contagious. A short-term fellowship from the Massachusetts Historical Society allowed me to do genealogical research on free black families and complete my fifth chapter. I thank Conrad E. Wright and Anna Clutterbuck-Cook. The Malamy Fellowship at the Phillips Library enabled me to improve parts of this manuscript that focused on Massachusetts. I thank Jennifer Hornsby and Meaghan Wright for directing me to important collections. I am grateful to have received a Program in African American History postdoctoral fellowship from the Library Company of Philadelphia, where I made significant progress on the book manuscript.

A version of chapter 1 appeared in the *Journal of Social History*. Portions of that chapter were also published in two edited volumes, Margaret Nash's *Women's Higher Education in the United States* (New York: Palgrave Macmillan, 2018) and Leslie Harris's *Slavery and the University: Histories and Legacies* (Athens: University of Georgia, 2019). I acknowledge Oxford University Press, Palgrave Macmillan, and the University of Georgia Press for granting me permission to reprint this material.

At the University of New Hampshire I work with generous colleagues, many of whom deserve special mention for going above and beyond the call of duty: Rachel Trubowitz, Aria Halliday, Julia Rodriguez, Reggie Wilburn, Sean Moore, Dennis Britton, Delia Konzett, Siobhan Senier, Monica Chiu, Robin Hackett, Samantha Seal, and Ellen Fitzpatrick. I benefited from a one-semester leave to complete this book. The Center for the Humanities provided funding to finish the index, while Kathrine Aydelott got me access to key databases. And in just a few years Julie Williams has shown me what it means to lead with integrity.

It has been an absolute delight to work with Clara Platter at New York University Press. Clara responded positively to the manuscript almost immediately and walked me through the book production process. I thank her for answering my many questions promptly and patiently, for advising me on how to respond to revisions, and, most of all, for believing in my ability to tell this story. My editor extraordinaire Kim Greenwell read the entire manuscript multiple times with a keen eye, providing constructive criticism that made this book so much better. My smart and savvy research assistant, Sherard Harrington, shared citations with me, helped secure permissions and images, and corrected errors.

I would be remiss not to mention the good cheer of friends near and far, especially Raymond Gunn, Leah Mirakhor, and Barbara Thelamour.

My family cheered me on when I shared new research findings and lifted me up when I hit roadblocks. I remember my eldest daughter, Ella, asking me if I needed help finding Elizabeth H. Smith's name in a document. Ella's good energy propelled me, even as my research took me away from her for long stretches at a time. I hope she and her sister Maya see themselves as part of the legacy of African American girls' activism. I also thank the Baumgartners of Rheinfelden, Germany. Ever the adventurer, my husband, Stefan, moved with me to Massachusetts over a decade ago and has remained with me every step of the way. I am grateful for his unbounded love and devotion, for his optimism and companionship. I am also thankful that he reminded me, at a crucial point in this process, why I should write and share this history.

Appendix A: List of Black Students at the Canterbury Female Seminary in Connecticut

Student Names	*Birthplace*
Sarah Harris (Fayerweather)	Connecticut
Mary Harris (Williams)	Connecticut
Harriet Rosetta Lanson	Connecticut
Eliza Glasko (Peterson)	Connecticut
Miranda Glasko (Overbaugh)	Connecticut
Jerusha Congdon (West)	Connecticut
Elizabeth H. Smith	Rhode Island
Ann Eliza Hammond	Rhode Island
Sarah Lloyd Hammond	Rhode Island
Mary Elizabeth Miles (Bibb Cary)	Rhode Island
Amy Fenner (Parker)	Rhode Island
Julia Williams (Garnet)	South Carolina or Massachusetts
Elizabeth Douglass Bustill	Pennsylvania
Elizabeth Henley (Stewartt)	Pennsylvania
Henrietta Bolt (Vidal)	New York
Theodosia deGrasse (Vogelsang)	New York
Gloriana Catherine Marshall	New York

Appendix B: List of Black Students at the Young Ladies' Domestic Seminary in New York

Student Names	*Birthplace*
Mary Elizabeth Miles (Bibb Cary)	Rhode Island
Rosetta (Maria) Morrison (Wright)	Connecticut
Margaret Morrison	Connecticut
Lucretia Turpin (Bowers)	New York
Joanna Turpin (Howard)	New York
Serena deGrasse (Downing)	New York
Ursula James (Johnson)	New York

Appendix C: List of Black Families in the Northeast

The Morrison Family of Hartford, CT, and New York City
James Morrison (father)
Rosetta Morrison (mother)
   Abraham J. Morrison (1810–1869)[1] m. Emeline Cassey
   Elizabeth Morrison Foster
   Margaret Morrison (1816–1839)
   Rosetta Morrison (1817–1896) m. Isaac Wright (1817?–?)
      Mary Emma Wright (1843–1847)
      Isaac Wright Jr. (1845–1856)
      Anna Wright (1847–?) m. Arthur Williams
      Letitia Wright (1848–1878)
      Rosetta Wright (1851–?)
      Alice C. Wright (1855–1921)

The deGrasse Family of New York City
George deGrasse (father)
Maria Van Salee deGrasse (mother)
   Maria M. deGrasse (1809) m. Peter Vogelsang[2] (1815–1887)
   Isaiah deGrasse (1813–1841)
   Emma C. deGrasse (1814–?)
   Theodosia deGrasse (1817–1854) m. Peter Vogelsang (1815–1887)
   Serena deGrasse (1823–1893) m. George T. Downing (1819–1903)
   John V. deGrasse (1825–1868) m. Cordelia L. Howard (1823–1899)
   Georgenia deGrasse (1832–1849)

The Turpin Family of New York

Joseph Thomas Turpin (father)
Adaline Leggett Turpin (mother) m. Theodore S. Wright (1797–1847)
    Joanna Turpin[3] (1825–1872) m. Edwin F. Howard (1813–1893)
        Adeline T. Howard (1845–1922)
        Edwin Clarence Howard (1846–1912)
        J. Imogen Howard (1848–1937)
    Lucretia Turpin (1826–1911) m. Thomas J. Bowers (1820–1885)
        Alice C. Bowers (1854–1880)
    Eliza Turpin (1827–?) m. Benjamin Gregory
        Milton Gregory (1853–?)
    Joseph H. Turpin (1829–1897) m. Carolina Ellis

The Remond Family of Salem, MA

John Remond (father)
Nancy Lenox Remond (mother)
    Nancy Remond (1809–1878) m. James L. Shearman
    Charles Lenox Remond (1810–1873) m. Amy Matilda Casey
        (1808–1856)
    Susan Remond (1812–1879)
    Maritchia Juan Remond (1816–1899)
    Cecilia Remond (1816–1912) m. James Babcock Jr.
    Cornelius Remond (1817–1821)
    Mary Remond (1819–1820)
    Sarah Parker Remond (1824–1894) m. Lazzaro Pintor
    Caroline Remond (1827–1908) m. Joseph Putnam

The Paul Family of Boston, MA

Thomas Paul (father)
Catharine Waterhouse Paul (mother)
    Ann Catharine Paul (1808–1835) m. Elijah W. Smith Sr. (1831–1885)
        Thomas Paul Smith (1827–1889?) m. Elizabeth Augusta Roberts[4]
        (1828–?)
        Elijah W. Smith Jr. (1830–1895) m. Eliza D. Riley
        Susan P. Smith Vashon (1835–1912)
    Susan Paul (1809–1841)
    Thomas Paul Jr. (1812–1885) m. Eusebia Louella Moss

The Riley Family of Boston, MA
William Riley (father)
Elizabeth Cook Jackson Riley (mother)
    James Jackson Jr. (1826–1831)
    Sarah Jackson
    Ann Jennette Jackson
    William Riley Jr.
    George Riley
    Eliza Riley (1836–?) m. Elijah W. Smith Jr. (1830–1895)

The Roberts Family of Boston, MA
Benjamin F. Roberts (father)
Adeline Fowler Roberts (mother)
    Benjamin Franklin Roberts Jr. (1838–1897) m. Adelaide Hull
    Thomas Clarkson Roberts (1840–?)
    Sarah Clarissa Roberts (1843–1896) m. John Casneau
    Robert Roberts (1844–1857)
    Caroline Roberts (1847–1928) m. Eugene Beamon Price Sr.
    Adeline Fowler Roberts (1849–1852)
    William Fowler Roberts (1852–1931) m. (Mary) Louisa Lenox
    Samuel Roberts (1854–1895) m. Bertha Courtney
    Charles Sumner Roberts (1857–1891) m. Helen Lenox
    Martha Roberts (1862–1905) m. William H. Nutter
    Henry Roberts (1866–?)

The Lyons Family of New York and Providence, RI[5]
Albro Lyons (father)
Mary Marshall Lyons[6]
    Therese Lyons (1846–1924) m. Charles Burrill
    Maritcha Lyons (1848–1929)
    Max Lyons (1849–?)
    Mary Lyons (1850–?)
    Albro Lyons Jr. (1854–1906)

The Forten Family of Philadelphia
James Forten
Charlotte Vandine Forten
    Margaretta Forten (1806–1875)
    Charlotta Forten (1808–1814)

Harriet Forten (1810–1875)

Robert Forten (1813–1864) m. Mary Virginia Woods Forten (1817–1840)

    Charlotte Louise Forten (1837–1914) m. Francis J. Grimké

Sarah Forten (1814–1883?)

James Forten Jr. (1817–?) m. Jane M. Vogelsang[7] (1819–1852)

    James Vogelsang Forten

Thomas Forten (1820–1897)

William Forten (1823–1900)

Mary Forten (1827–?)

Appendix D: Physical Attacks on Black Schools in the Northeast, 1830–1845

Incident	Location	Source
Prudence Crandall's school	Canterbury, Connecticut	*Liberator*, September 20, 1834
Noyes Academy	Canaan, New Hampshire	*New Hampshire Patriot and Gazette*, August 17, 1835
Mrs. Giles Buckingham's Academy for the Instruction of Negroes	Norwich, Connecticut	*Gloucester (MA) Telegraph*, September 9, 1835
Miss Ward's School	Zanesville, Ohio	*Liberator*, July 16, 1836
Red Oak Seminary	Brown County, Ohio	*Philanthropist*, September 25, 1838
Orphan School for Colored Boys	Philadelphia, Pennsylvania	*Philadelphia Inquirer*, May, 19, 1838
Colored School	(15 miles from) Chillicothe, Ohio	*Philanthropist*, December 24, 1839
Colored School	Pee Pee Creek, Pike County, Ohio	*Philanthropist*, June 22, 1842
Mary Cheney's School	Big Bottoms, Pike County, Ohio	*Philanthropist*, May 10, 1843
Colored School	Logan County, Ohio	*Philanthropist*, October 13, 1841

NOTES

Notes to Introduction

1. Sarah Mapps Douglass, "Sympathy for Miss Crandall," *Emancipator*, July 20, 1833.

2. In this book, I discuss African American women's networks of learning such as literary clubs, antislavery organizations, charitable groups, and church and religious organizations insofar as they relate to the creation of public and private schools. These learning networks would soon include schools and, later, teacher organizations. Needless to say, informal learning networks existed, but such archival records are not extant.

3. A term like "middle class" was an unstable category in the antebellum era, especially for African Americans, but I agree with historians who nevertheless trace an emerging black middle class in the nineteenth century. For scholarship on class formation and early African American communities, see, for instance, Gary B. Nash, *Forging Freedom: The Formation of Philadelphia's Black Community, 1720–1840* (Cambridge, MA: Harvard University Press, 1998); Leslie Harris, *In the Shadow of Slavery: African Americans in New York City, 1626–1863* (Chicago: University of Chicago Press, 2003).

4. Here I take a cue from Emma Jones Lapsansky, who points out that African American girls and women "shared a cultural unity and some common goals," which I trace throughout my book. See Emma Jones Lapsansky, "Feminism, Freedom, and Community: Charlotte Forten and Women Activists in Nineteenth-Century Philadelphia," *Pennsylvania Magazine of History and Biography* 113, no. 1 (January 1989): 7.

5. Ronald E. Butchart, *Schooling the Freed People: Teaching, Learning, and the Struggle for Black Freedom, 1861–1876* (Chapel Hill: University of North Carolina Press, 2010), xix. African American sites, from the church to the beauty shop, have operated as political and social spaces, particularly during the nineteenth and twentieth centuries. See, for instance, Tiffany M. Gill, *Beauty Shop Politics: African American Women's Activism in the Beauty Industry* (Urbana: University of Illinois Press, 2010).

6. Hilary J. Moss, *Schooling Citizens: The Struggle for African American Education in Antebellum America* (Chicago: University of Chicago Press, 2009), 103.

7. Mary Kelley refers to this intersection of education and women's civic preparedness as gendered republicanism. This term, however, lies within, not outside of, the racial apparatus at work in the antebellum era, which privileged whiteness. Mary Kelley, *Learning to Stand and Speak: Women, Education, and Public Life in America's Republic* (Chapel Hill: University of North Carolina Press, 2006), 113.

8. Erica Armstrong Dunbar, *A Fragile Freedom: African American Women and Emancipation in the Antebellum City* (New Haven, CT: Yale University Press, 2008), 6–7.

9. Dunbar, *A Fragile Freedom*, 131; Martha S. Jones, *All Bound Up Together: The Woman Question in African American Public Culture, 1830–1900* (Chapel Hill: University of North Carolina Press, 2007), 3; Patrick Rael, *Black Identity and Black Protest in the Antebellum North* (Chapel Hill: University of North Carolina Press, 2002), 120. Jane E. Dabel demonstrates in her work that working-class African American women "chose their own forms of leisure," regardless of whether those activities were considered respectable. See Jane E. Dabel, *A Respectable Woman: The Public Roles of African American Women in 19th-Century New York* (New York: New York University Press, 2008), 107; Leslie M. Harris, *In the Shadow of Slavery: African Americans in New York City, 1626–1863* (Chicago: University of Chicago Press, 2003), 122–23. The historian Evelyn Brooks Higginbotham argues that in the late nineteenth century "black Baptist women's opposition to the social structures . . . of white supremacy may be characterized by the concept of the 'politics of respectability.'" Higginbotham's analysis of the politics of respectability has generated considerable discussion and many interpretations that have shaped the field of African American women's history. See Evelyn Brooks Higginbotham, *Righteous Discontent: The Women's Movement in the Black Baptist Church, 1880–1920* (Cambridge, MA: Harvard University Press), 186. For a recent critique of the ideology of respectability, see Brittney C. Cooper, *Beyond Respectability: The Intellectual Thought of Race Women* (Champaign: University of Illinois Press, 2017).

10. Linda Perkins, "The Impact of the 'Cult of True Womanhood' on the Education of Black Women," *Journal of Social Issues* 39, no. 3 (Fall 1983): 18.

11. Here I am appreciative of the work of Lois Brown, especially her call for scholars to "read what we have, behold the intimate, value the private that is exhibited in public buildings and public spheres, and make *history hers* in as many ways as we can." Lois Brown, "Death-Defying Testimony: Women's Private Lives and the Politics of Public Documents," *Legacy* 27, no. 1 (2010): 138.

12. Lucia McMahon, "'She Pursued Her Life-Work': The Life Lessons of American Women Educators, 1800–1860," in *Women's Higher Education in the United States: New Historical Perspectives,* edited by Margaret Nash (New York: Palgrave Macmillan, 2018), 29.

13. Thomas Woody, *A History of Women's Education in the United States* (New York: Science Press, 1929), 1: 397. See, also, Martha MacLear, *The History of the Education of Girls in New York and in New England 1800–1870* (Washington, DC: Howard University Press, 1926). The scholarship on the female seminary movement in the United States has expanded since the 1980s. See, for instance, Leonard I. Sweet, "The Female Seminary Movement and Woman's Mission in Antebellum America," *Church*

History 54, no. 1 (March 1985): 41–55. Recent studies have challenged many of Sweet's conclusions, particularly Margaret Nash, *Women's Education in the United States 1780–1840* (New York: Palgrave Macmillan, 2005); Mary Kelley, *Learning to Stand and Speak: Women, Education, and Public Life in America's Republic* (Chapel Hill: University of North Carolina Press, 2006); and Lucia McMahon, *Mere Equals: The Paradox of Educated Women in the Early American Republic* (Ithaca, NY: Cornell University Press, 2012). For a general overview of female seminaries, see Kristen Welch and Abraham Ruelas, *The Role of Female Seminaries on the Road to Social Justice for Women* (Eugene, OR: Wipf and Stock, 2015).

14. "Third Anniversary of the Ladies Literary Society of the City of New York," *Colored American,* September 23, 1837.

15. For an overview of the African American experience in the antebellum North, see Leon F. Litwack, *North of Slavery: The Negro in the Free States, 1790–1860* (Chicago: University of Chicago Press, 1961); Leonard P. Curry, *The Free Black in Urban America, 1800–1850: The Shadow of the Dream* (Chicago: University of Chicago Press, 1981); R. J. Young, *Antebellum Black Activists: Race, Gender, and Self* (New York: Garland, 1996); James Oliver Horton and Lois E. Horton, *In Hope of Liberty: Culture, Community and Protest among Northern Free Blacks, 1700–1860* (New York: Oxford University Press, 1997); Gayle T. Tate, *Unknown Tongues: Black Women's Political Activism in the Antebellum Era, 1830–1860* (East Lansing: Michigan State University Press, 2003); Kathy L. Glass, *Courting Communities: Black Female Nationalism and "Syncre-Nationalism" in the Nineteenth-Century North* (New York: Routledge, 2006).

16. Some historians speculate that Blanche V. Harris was denied admission to the Young Ladies' Seminary in Monroe, Michigan, on account of her race. Such speculation certainly fits what we know about the female seminary movement in nineteenth-century America, but more information is needed to corroborate this claim.

17. Carol Lasser, "Enacting Emancipation: African American Women Abolitionists at Oberlin College and the Quest for Empowerment, Equality, and Respectability," in *Women's Rights and Transatlantic Antislavery in the Era of Emancipation,* edited by Kathryn Kish Sklar and James Brewer Stewart (New Haven, CT: Yale University Press, 2007), 321. Lasser's essay recovers biographical information on some of the African American women students at Oberlin College. Further research is still needed. I suspect that one student, Eliza Weldon from New York, attended the Canterbury Female Seminary and then the preparatory department at Oberlin College during the 1837–38 school year. See *General Catalogue of Oberlin College, 1833[–]1908* (Oberlin, OH: Published by the College in Connection with the Celebration of its Seventy-Fifth Anniversary, 1909), 1035.

18. W. E. Bigglestone, "Oberlin College and the Negro Student, 1865–1940," *Journal of Negro History* 56, no. 3 (July 1971): 198.

19. This research insight from Carol Lasser invites historians to think about education beyond Oberlin College.

20. Maritcha Remond Lyons, "Memories of Yesterdays: All of Which I Saw and Part of Which I Was: An Autobiography," unpublished manuscript, ca. 1924, 16, box 2, folder 2, Harry A. Williamson Papers, Schomburg Center for Research in Black Culture, New York Public Library.

21. Studies on African American education in the nineteenth-century North include Carter G. Woodson, *The Education of the Negro Prior to 1861: A History of*

the Education of the Colored People of the United States from the Beginning of Slavery to the Civil War, 2nd ed. (Washington, DC: Associated Publishers, 1919); Carleton Mabee, Black Education in New York State from Colonial to Modern Times (Syracuse, NY: Syracuse University Press, 1979); Jacqueline Jones Royster, Traces of a Stream: Literacy and Social Change among African American Women (Pittsburgh, PA: University of Pittsburgh Press, 2000); Elizabeth McHenry, Forgotten Readers: Recovering the Lost History of African American Literary Societies (Durham, NC: Duke University Press, 2002); Davison M. Douglas, Jim Crow Moves North: The Battle over Northern School Desegregation, 1865–1954 (New York: Cambridge University Press, 2005); Shirley Wilson Logan, Liberating Language: Sites of Rhetorical Education in Nineteenth-Century Black America (Carbondale: Southern Illinois University Press, 2008); and, more recently, Moss, Schooling Citizens. Scholarship on African American women's education in the nineteenth century includes Ellen N. Lawson and Marlene D. Merrill, The Three Sarahs: Documents of Antebellum Black College Women (New York: Edwin Mellen Press, 1984), which focuses on Oberlin College; Linda M. Perkins, Fanny Jackson Coppin and the Institute for Colored Youth, 1865–1902 (New York: Garland, 1987), which examines Coppin's education and her teaching career in Philadelphia. My book is the first full-length study to explore African American women's education in the early nineteenth-century Northeast.

22. See, for instance, Jones, All Bound Up Together; Dunbar, A Fragile Freedom; Dabel, A Respectable Woman; Teresa Zackodnik, Press, Platform, Pulpit: Black Feminist Publics in the Era of Reform (Knoxville: University of Tennessee Press, 2011); Amrita Chakrabarti Myers, Forging Freedom: Black Women and the Pursuit of Liberty in Antebellum Charleston (Chapel Hill: University of North Carolina Press, 2011).

23. Douglass, "Sympathy for Miss Crandall."

24. David Walker, Walker's Appeal, in Four Articles, Together With, a Preamble, to the Colored Citizens of the World, But in Particular, and Very Expressly to Those of the United States of America, 2nd ed. (Boston: David Walker, 1830), 36–37; Peter P. Hinks, To Awaken My Afflicted Brethren: David Walker and the Problem of Antebellum Slave Resistance (University Park: Pennsylvania State University Press, 1997), 107.

25. For studies on African American literacy and education in the slaveholding South, see Thomas Webber, Deep Like the Rivers: Education in the Slave Quarter Community (New York: Norton, 1978); Robert C. Morris, Reading, 'Riting, and Reconstruction: The Education of Freedmen in the South, 1861–1870 (Chicago: University of Chicago Press, 1981); James D. Anderson, The Education of Blacks in the South, 1860–1935 (Chapel Hill: University of North Carolina Press, 1988); Janet Duitsman Cornelius, "When I Can Read My Title Clear": Literacy, Slavery, and Religion in the Antebellum South (Columbia: University of South Carolina Press, 1991); Heather A. Williams, Self-Taught: African American Education in Slavery and Freedom (Chapel Hill: University of North Carolina Press, 2005); Christopher M. Span, From the Cotton Field to the Schoolhouse: African American Education in Mississippi, 1862–1875 (Chapel Hill: University of North Carolina Press, 2009); Ronald E. Butchart, Schooling the Freed People: Teaching, Learning, and the Struggle for Black Freedom, 1861–1876 (Chapel Hill: University of North Carolina Press, 2010).

26. Johann Neem, Democracy's Schools: The Rise of Public Education in America (Baltimore, MD: Johns Hopkins University Press, 2017), 27.

27. Alexander James Inglis, *The Rise of the High School in Massachusetts* (New York: Teachers College, Columbia University, 1991), iv.

28. See, for instance, the work of Deborah Gray White, "Mining the Forgotten: Manuscript Sources for Black Women's History," *Journal of American History* 75, no. 1 (June 1987): 237–42; Ula Taylor, "Women in the Documents: Thoughts on Uncovering the Personal, Political, and Professional," *Journal of Women's History* 20, no. 1 (Spring 2008): 187–96; Marisa J. Fuentes, *Dispossessed Lives: Enslaved Women, Violence, and the Archive* (Philadelphia: University of Pennsylvania Press, 2016).

29. For archival collections, I found letters exchanged between African American students and their teacher in the Butler-Everett Family Collection at Bowling Green State University Libraries in Ohio. For digital collections, I relied upon the Yale Indian Papers Project to identify Charlotte E. Williams Foster Myers as a mixed-race woman of Ponkapoag Indian heritage; the Antislavery Petitions Massachusetts Dataverse from Harvard University contains digitized copies of the original petitions submitted by Benjamin Roberts Sr. and William Cooper Nell; and the New York Wills and Probate Records 1659–1999 database helped me learn more about the Morrison family of Hartford, Connecticut.

30. While I appreciate Britt Rusert's reflections on the idea that disappointment might be "productive of new ways of reading and analyzing the archive," I think that we, as scholars, should be, not so much disappointed in our affective relation to the archive, but, as the scholar Tara Bynum writes, much more "willing to engage with [the mundane]." See Britt Rusert, "Disappointment in the Archives of Black Freedom," *Social Text* 33, no. 4 (December 2015): 19–33; Tara Bynum, "Cesar Lyndon's Lists, Letters, and a Pig Roast: *A Sundry Account Book*," *Early American Literature* 53, no. 3 (2018): 841.

31. Bettina Aptheker, *Tapestries of Life: Women's Work, Women's Consciousness, and the Meaning of Daily Experience* (Amherst: University of Massachusetts Press, 1989), 12; Elsa Barkley Brown, "African-American Women's Quilting," *Signs* 14, no. 4 (Summer 1989): 923.

32. I refer to many of the historical actors in this study by first name for a few reasons. First, I wish to allay confusion since there are generational designations for both women (and men) in this story. Second, some of the women studied herein have shared surnames, so I distinguish them by first name. Third, I recognize that we will never *know* these historical actors, but I sincerely wish to allow for some level of familiarity by sometimes using the first name after initially introducing the full name.

33. This book is certainly part of the long history of school desegregation, yet African American activists in the early nineteenth century did not use the terms "school desegregation" or "racial school integration." Instead, equal school rights, that is, the right of all to a quality education, defined their efforts. As much as I can, I use the term "equal school rights," not only because the activists studied herein invoked it but also because it more aptly fits how both *race and gender* shaped the struggle for educational equality. Occasionally and where applicable, I use the term "school desegregation" to describe the process of abolishing racially exclusive policies and practices in public and private schools. I also use the term "racial school integration" to highlight democratic and racially inclusive practices that take into account educational opportunity, access, and equity.

34. In many ways, the African American girls and women whom I study in this book were forerunners to the African American girls and women who led the school desegregation fight during the twentieth-century Black Freedom movement. See Rachel Devlin, *A Girl Stands at the Door: The Generation of Young Women Who Desegregated America's Schools* (New York: Basic Books, 2018).

Notes to Chapter 1

1. Carl R. Woodward, "A Profile in Dedication: Sarah Harris and the Fayerweather Family," *New England Galaxy* 15, no. 1 (Summer 1973): 5.

2. Susan Strane, *A Whole-Souled Woman: Prudence Crandall and the Education of Black Women* (New York: Norton, 1990), 22. According to Harris family lore, Sarah Harris and her family attended the Westminster Congregational Church in Canterbury, Connecticut.

3. "Canterbury Female Boarding School," *Norwich (CT) Courier*, March 21, 1832.

4. Mary Clark to Amy Baldwin, undated, Baldwin Family Papers, box 2, folder 6, Connecticut Historical Society, Hartford.

5. Woodward, "A Profile in Dedication," 5. Woodward is the only source for the contention that Sarah worked as a servant. It is plausible, though, since free black girls and women often had to support themselves and their families as domestic servants. In September 1857 Sarah's mother, Sally, relayed that Sarah's sister, Mary, had "gone to housekeeping in Norwich in that brick house by the side of the New Congregational Church." Letter from Sally Prentice Harris to Sarah Harris Fayerweather, September 20, 1857, Fayerweather Family Papers (hereafter FFP), 1836–1962, University of Rhode Island Library Special Collections.

6. Prudence Crandall, "Letter from Miss Crandall [May 7, 1833]," *Liberator*, May 25, 1833.

7. Maria W. Stewart, "Lecture. Delivered at the Franklin Hall, Boston, September 21st, 1832," *Liberator*, November 17, 1832.

8. Letter from Sarah Harris Fayerweather to William Lloyd Garrison, February 8, 1866, Anti-Slavery Collection, Boston Public Library.

9. Donald E. Williams Jr. posits that Sarah made an initial request and then followed up once again before receiving a reply from Prudence Crandall: *Prudence Crandall's Legacy: The Fight for Equality in the 1830s, Dred Scott, and Brown v. Board of Education* (Middletown, CT: Wesleyan University Press, 2014), 135.

10. Crandall, "Letter [May 7, 1833]."

11. Samuel J. May, *Some Recollections of Our Antislavery Conflict* (Boston: Fields, Osgood, 1869), 41–42.

12. Though sometimes called a high school, this all-black school was a seminary, as demonstrated by its curriculum.

13. In *Schooling Citizens*, Hilary Moss provides a fascinating exploration of white opposition to African American education. In my book, I subordinate the discussion of white opposition in favor of amplifying African American women's educational activism.

14. Garrisonian abolitionists relied on moral suasion, which required impassioned yet reasoned intellectual arguments to abolish slavery and promote racial equality.

African American women students at Prudence Crandall's seminary, I argue, used this tactic to frame their ethic of Christian love.

15. The scholarship on Prudence Crandall is sizable. For instance, Edmund Fuller, *Prudence Crandall: An Incident of Racism in Nineteenth-Century Connecticut* (Middletown, CT: Wesleyan University Press, 1971), recounts this episode in history with an eye toward understanding racism in the United States, while Marvis O. Welch, *Prudence Crandall: A Biography* (Manchester, CT: Jason, 1983), gives a biographical account of Prudence's life, with Canterbury occupying a rather large part. Philip S. Foner and Josephine F. Pacheco, *Three Who Dared: Prudence Crandall, Margaret Douglass, Myrtilla Miner: Champions of Antebellum Black Education* (Westport, CT: Greenwood Press, 1985), place Prudence alongside other white women educators who embodied a distinct sense of duty and courage. In any case, this scholarship largely overlooks the activism of young African American women students.

16. Crandall, "Letter [May 7, 1833]."

17. Benjamin Rush, *Thoughts upon Female Education, Accommodated to the Present State of Society, Manners, and Government, in the United States of America . . .* (Philadelphia: Printed by Prichard & Hall, 1787), 25.

18. For an interesting essay on Benjamin Rush and the Young Ladies' Academy, see Margaret A. Nash, "Rethinking Republican Motherhood: Benjamin Rush and the Young Ladies' Academy of Philadelphia," *Journal of the Early Republic* 17, no. 2 (Summer 1997): 171–91.

19. Mary Kelley, *Learning to Stand and Speak: Women, Education, and Public Life in America's Republic* (Chapel Hill: University of North Carolina Press, 2006), 67. For an overview of the early history of academies and seminaries in the United States, see Nancy Beadie and Kim Tolley, eds., *Chartered Schools: Two Hundred Years of Independent Academies in the United States, 1727–1925* (New York: Routledge/Falmer, 2002).

20. Almira H. Lincoln Phelps, *Essay on Female Education and Prospectus of the Rahway Institute* (Rahway, NJ: Guest, 1839), 4.

21. While most young women who attended female seminaries fell within this age range, it was not unusual to see young women in their early twenties enrolled at female seminaries too.

22. Nash, *Women's Education in the United States, 1780–1840*, 101–2.

23. For an intriguing book on social status and education in early America, see Nancy Beadie, *Education and the Creation of Capital in the Early American Republic* (Cambridge, UK: Cambridge University Press, 2010).

24. Linda Kerber, *Women of the Republic: Intellect and Ideology in Revolutionary America* (Chapel Hill: University of North Carolina Press, 1980), 11. For more on the concept of republican womanhood in early America, see Barbara Welter, "The Cult of True Womanhood: 1820–1860," *American Quarterly* 18, no. 2, part 1 (Summer 1966): 151–74; Nancy F. Cott, *The Bonds of Womanhood: "Woman's Sphere" in New England 1780–1835* (New Haven, CT: Yale University Press, 1977); Mary Beth Norton, *Liberty's Daughters: The Revolutionary Experience of American Women, 1750–1800* (Boston: Little, Brown, 1980); Kelley, *Learning to Stand and Speak*; Catherine Kerrison, *Claiming the Pen: Women and Intellectual Life in the Early American South* (Ithaca, NY: Cornell University Press, 2006).

25. Sweet, "The Female Seminary Movement and Woman's Mission in Antebellum America," 43.

26. U.S. Federal Census 1830.

27. "For the Freedom's Journal," *Freedom's Journal*, August 10, 1827.

28. Scientific racism exploded in the nineteenth and early twentieth centuries, as philosophers and scientists such as Georges Cuvier, Franz Pruner, and Samuel George Morton published numerous studies on race. For an exploration of scientific racism and African American culture, see Britt Rusert, *Fugitive Science: Empiricism and Freedom in Early African American Culture* (New York: New York University Press, 2017).

29. Kelley, *Learning to Stand and Speak*, 97.

30. "Albany Female Seminary," *Albany (NY) Argus*, July 19, 1844; "Albany Female Seminary in Division Street," *American Masonic Register*, August 5, 1843. I thank Jessica Linker for this insight and source.

31. Beadie, *Education and the Creation of Capital in the Early American Republic*, 111; Margaret A. Nash, "'A Triumph of Reason': Female Education in Academies in the New Republic," in *Chartered Schools: Two Hundred Years of Independent Academies in the United States, 1727–1925*, edited by Nancy Beadie and Kim Tolley (New York: Routledge/Falmer, 2002), 67.

32. *Catalogue of the Officers and Students of Bradford Academy, Bradford, Massachusetts, October 1839* (Haverhill, MA: E. H. Safford, 1839), 9.

33. I call these spaces *predominantly* white and female because I have found catalogues indicating that a few female seminaries enrolled nonwhite students or white male students. For instance, a female student by the name of Dee-wau-dau-a-gek-heh from Buffalo Creek Reservation appears among the list of students in the 1852 Sharon Female Seminary circular. See *Circular of the School, and a Description of Apparatus & Astronomical Instruments, with a Catalogue of Pupils* (Philadelphia: T. E. Chapman, 1852).

34. Lucia McMahon, "A More Accurate and Extensive Education than Is Customary: Educational Opportunities for Women in Early Nineteenth-Century New Jersey," *New Jersey History* 124, no. 1 (2009): 13. Sometimes the term "boarding school" was used interchangeably with "seminary" and "high school." The historian Lucia McMahon points out that some proprietors deliberately used the term "seminary" to ensure permanency for their institutions and to achieve further parity between women's and men's education. McMahon's assertion makes sense: the move toward the use of the term "seminary" appears to have been deliberate. Yet more research needs to be done in this area because some teachers, such as William Russell at Abbott Female Academy, argued that "academy" was the superior term as it conveyed the high level of instruction offered at such an institution.

35. William Russell, *The Education of Females, An Address, Held at the Close of the Autumn Term of Abbott Female Academy* . . . (Andover, MA: Allen, Morrill & Wardwell, 1843), 22–23.

36. Mary Eckert to Solomon Eckert, December 19, 1837, box 1, folder 10, Eckert-Black Family Collection 1792–1866, William L. Clements Library, University of Michigan.

37. Kelley, *Learning to Stand and Speak*, 54.

38. Letter from William Lloyd Garrison to Simeon Jocelyn, May 30, 1831, African American Resources Collection (hereafter AARC), Connecticut Historical Society, Hartford.

39. Letter from Prudence Crandall to W. L. Garrison, February 12, 1833, in Wendell Phillips Garrison and Francis Jackson Garrison, eds., *William Lloyd Garrison, 1805–1879: The Story of His Life* (New York: Century, 1889), 317. Elizabeth Hall married Thomas Hammond, described in the January 19, 1828, issue of the *Juvenile Gazette* as a "respectable man of colour," who died at the age of forty-two on January 13, 1828. The Hammonds had another daughter, Margaret, who died the same year as her father, at the age of sixteen.

40. Letter from Esther Baldwin to Amy and Hannah Baldwin, May 4, 1833, Baldwin Family Papers, box 1, folder 7, Connecticut Historical Society, Hartford.

41. "Gen. Tallmadge," *Columbian Register* (New Haven, CT), August 31, 1833.

42. Philip F. Gura, *The Life of William Apess, Pequot* (Chapel Hill: University of North Carolina Press, 2015), 7.

43. "High School for Young Colored Ladies and Misses," *Liberator*, March 2, 1833. I suspect the fact that rhetoric as a course did not appear in the advertisement was an oversight by Prudence. There is also the possibility that she continued to teach it but removed it from the advertisement because of increasing uneasiness regarding women's public speaking in antebellum America. For more on public speaking and women's education, see Kelley, *Learning to Stand and Speak*.

44. *First Annual Report of the American Anti-Slavery Society . . . Sixth of May, 1834 . . .* (New York: Dorr & Butterfield, 1834), 47.

45. Letter from Prudence Crandall to Simeon Jocelyn, April 17, 1833, AARC. Probably only the Harris sisters were day scholars. Since the vast majority of students were not from the town of Canterbury, they most likely boarded at the school. Olive Harris, a sister of Sarah and Mary, may have enrolled at the Canterbury Female Seminary later that year. She would have been about eleven. In 1844 she married Frederick Olney, worked as a teacher, and raised her children.

46. "Scenes in Canterbury," *Liberator*, June 22, 1833.

47. "Selected: Benefits of a Good Trade and Good Habits," *Colored American*, March 11, 1837.

48. "In Memoriam," *People's Advocate (Washington, DC)*, October 29, 1881.

49. Carla L. Peterson, *Black Gotham: A Family History of African Americans in Nineteenth-Century New York* (New Haven, CT: Yale University Press, 2011), 40.

50. Simeon Jocelyn, "Obituary Notice," *Liberator*, April 2, 1836.

51. "Miss Crandall's School," *Liberator*, April 5, 1834.

52. "From the Canterbury School," *Liberator*, July 6, 1833.

53. Zillah, "Sympathy for Miss Crandall," *Emancipator*, July 10, 1833, emphasis in original.

54. Here I have relied on the records of Kazimiera Kozlowski, former curator at the Prudence Crandall Museum, to identify the African American female students at the Canterbury Female Seminary. Kozlowski contends that Sarah Mapps Douglass's cousin Elizabeth Douglass Bustill, a Philadelphia native, also attended the seminary. Bustill was the daughter of Elizabeth (Mary) Hicks Bustill and David Bustill, who operated a school for African Americans in Harrisburg, Pennsylvania.

55. Zillah, "Sympathy for Miss Crandall."

56. Christopher Cameron, *To Plead Our Own Cause: African Americans in Massachusetts and the Making of the Antislavery Movement* (Kent, OH: Kent State University Press, 2014), 99.

57. May, *Some Recollections of Our Antislavery Conflict*, 48.

58. "Slavery," *Liberator*, April 6, 1833. Given the essay's publication date, it was likely authored by either Sarah Harris, Ann Eliza Hammond, or Sarah Lloyd Hammond, Crandall's first African American students.

59. Joseph Lancaster, *The British System of Education* (London: J. Lancaster and Longman, 1810), 42.

60. *A Statement of Facts, Respecting the School for Colored Females, in Canterbury, Ct. Together with a Report of the Late Trial of Miss Prudence Crandall* (Brooklyn, CT: Advertiser Press, 1833), 16.

61. Jocelyn, "Obituary Notice." Harriet Rosetta Lanson may have been related to Grace Lanson.

62. "From the Canterbury School," *Liberator*.

63. Letter from William Lloyd Garrison to Simeon Jocelyn, May 30, 1831, AARC. The other boosters were Arthur Tappan of New York, Benjamin Lundy of Washington, DC, and Thomas Shipley and Charles Pierce of Philadelphia. For excellent analyses of the proposed manual labor college in antebellum New Haven, Connecticut, see James Brewer Stewart, *Abolitionist Politics and the Coming of the Civil War* (Amherst: University of Massachusetts Press, 2008); Moss, *Schooling Citizens*.

64. Leonard Worcester, *An Address on Female Education* (Newark, NJ: n.p., 1832), 2–3.

65. Samuel Young, *Suggestions on the Best Mode of Promoting Civilization and Improvement* (Albany, NY: Hoffman and White, 1837), 32. Young may have been quoting the French writer Louis-Aimé Martin.

66. Kelley, *Learning to Stand and Speak*, 32, 15, emphasis in original.

67. Letter from William Lloyd Garrison to George W. Benson, [March 8, 1833], reprinted in Walter M. Merrill, ed., *The Letters of William Lloyd Garrison* (Cambridge, MA: Belknap Press, 1971), 1:212.

68. May, *Some Recollections of Our Antislavery Conflict*, 45.

69. May, *Some Recollections of Our Antislavery Conflict*, 49, 47, emphasis mine.

70. Rufus Adams and Andrew T. Judson, "Miss Crandall's Negro School," *Boston Post*, July 31, 1833.

71. Andrew T. Judson, "Appeal to the American Colonization Society," *Fruits of Colonization*, March 22, 1833.

72. Hazel Carby's work has greatly enriched my understanding of the construction of black womanhood in antebellum America. See, in particular, *Reconstructing Womanhood: The Emergence of the Black Female Novelist* (New York: Oxford University Press, 1987); Perkins, "The Impact of the 'Cult of True Womanhood' on the Education of Black Women," 18.

73. Crandall, "Letter [May 7, 1833]."

74. "The Canterbury Controversy," *Commercial Advertiser (CT)*, August 21, 1833.

75. "Negro School in Canterbury," *Norwich (CT) Republican*, March 27, 1833.

76. Crandall, "Letter from Miss Crandall [May 7, 1833]."

77. *Catalogue of the Officers and Members of the Seminary for Female Teachers at Ipswich, Massachusetts for the Year Ending April 1839* (Salem, MA: Register Press, 1839), 19, Education Collection, box 27, folder 11, Sophia Smith Collection and Smith College Archives, Northampton, MA.

78. "Negro School in Canterbury."

79. "The Canterbury Farce," *United States Telegraph*, August 1, 1833.

80. "Look Here!," *Liberator*, July 20, 1833.

81. *The Public Statute Laws of the State of Connecticut, Book 1* (Hartford, CT: John B. Eldredge, 1835), 392. The full name of the act is An Act for the Admission of Inhabitants in Towns and for preventing charge on account of such as are not admitted therein.

82. May, *Some Recollections of Our Antislavery Conflict*, 45–46, 51.

83. Letter from Prudence Crandall to Simeon Jocelyn, AARC.

84. "More Barbarism," *Liberator*, May 18, 1833.

85. Jocelyn, "Obituary Notice."

86. "Address, Written by One of Miss Crandall's Scholars," *Liberator*, August 3, 1833.

87. "Address, Written by One of Miss Crandall's Scholars," emphasis mine.

88. "George Benson to William Lloyd Garrison, [March 5, 1833]," *Liberator*, March 9, 1833.

89. "From the Canterbury School," *Liberator*.

90. Paul Goodman, *Of One Blood: Abolitionism and the Origins of Racial Equality* (Berkeley: University of California Press, 1998), 246.

91. "Address, Written by One of Miss Crandall's Scholars."

92. Sarah C. O'Dowd, *A Rhode Island Original: Frances Harriet Whipple Green McDougall* (Hanover, NH: University Press of New England, 2004), 46.

93. "Ladies Department, Appeal," *Liberator*, August 17, 1833.

94. *Statute Laws of Connecticut*, 321–32.

95. *Supplement to the Revised Code of the Laws of Virginia* (Richmond, VA: Samuel Shepherd, 1833), 244–45.

96. "Virginia Legislature. House of Delegates," *Richmond (VA) Enquirer*, December 8, 1831.

97. Strane, *Whole-Souled Woman*, 80.

98. May, *Some Recollections of Our Antislavery Conflict*, 55–56.

99. "Persecuted Children's Complaint," *Liberator*, January 11, 1834.

100. "More Barbarism," *Liberator*; "Savage Barbarity," *Genius of Universal Emancipation*, July 1833.

101. "Colonization Meeting," *Liberator*, July 20, 1833.

102. May, *Some Recollections of Our Antislavery Conflict*, 61–62. The first issue of the *Unionist* appeared on July 2, 1833. Samuel J. May wrote and edited much of the content in the first few issues, and then Charles Burleigh took over.

103. "Miss Prudence Crandall," *New Bedford (MA) Mercury*, April 19, 1833.

104. "Miss Crandall," *Rhode-Island Republican*, July 24, 1833.

105. *New Hampshire Gazette* as quoted in "Miss Crandall," *Rhode-Island Republican*, July 24, 1833.

106. May, *Some Recollections of Our Antislavery Conflict*, 58–59. Ellsworth came from a prominent New England family: his father, Oliver Ellsworth, was a senator from Connecticut and third chief justice of the U.S. Supreme Court. Ellsworth married Emily Webster, daughter of Noah Webster. The younger Ellsworth later served as governor of Connecticut and justice of the state supreme court.

107. Williams, *Prudence Crandall's Legacy*, 115.

108. Andrew T. Judson, *Remarks, To the Jury, on the trial of the Case, State v. P. Crandall* (Hartford, CT: John Russell, Printer, 1833), 5.

109. *A Statement of Facts*, 15.

110. Williams, *Prudence Crandall's Legacy*, 122–23.

111. *A Statement of Facts*,16.

112. A Passer-by, "Miss Crandall's School," *Liberator*, July 6, 1833.

113. No title, *Connecticut Courant*, August 26, 1833.

114. Williams, *Prudence Crandall's Legacy*, 134–36.

115. "Miss Crandall's Second Trial," in *The Abolitionist: Or Record of the New England Anti-Slavery Society* (Boston: Garrison & Knapp, 1833), 163.

116. "Trial of Miss Prudence Crandall (continued)," *Connecticut Courant*, September 9, 1833.

117. *Report of the Arguments of Counsel, in the Case of Prudence Crandall, plff. in error, vs. State of Connecticut* (Boston: Garrison & Knapp, 1834), 6.

118. James Kent, *Commentaries on American Law*, 10th ed. (Boston: Little, Brown, 1860), 2:258.

119. *Report of the Arguments of Counsel*, 22.

120. *Report of the Arguments of Counsel*, 6.

121. Corinne T. Field, *The Struggle for Equal Adulthood: Gender, Race, Age, and the Fight for Citizenship in the Antebellum United States* (Chapel Hill: University of North Carolina Press, 2014), 63.

122. This defense rested on white male normativities of citizenship to make a case for African American women's pursuit of learning. The social, political, and legal systems did not quite allow for much else, though African American women activists often defined citizenship as civic activism, or what I call *civicship,* in their own writings.

123. Stephen Kantrowitz, *More Than Freedom: Fighting for Black Citizenship in a White Republic, 1829–1889* (New York: Penguin Press, 2012), 6.

124. Zillah, "For the Liberator," *Liberator*, 21 July 1832.

125. Maria W. Stewart, "Farewell Address to Her Friends in the City of Boston [delivered September 21, 1833]," *Meditations from the Pen of Mrs. Maria W. Stewart* (Washington, DC, 1879), 80.

126. *Report of the Arguments of Counsel*, 31.

127. Kent, *Commentaries on American Law* 2:258.

128. "Letter from Charles Stuart [June 24, 1834]," *New York Evangelist*, July 5, 1834.

129. "Canterbury," *Liberator*, June 14, 1834; "Weighty Argument!," *Liberator*, June 28, 1834.

130. "Suspicious Occurrence," *Liberator*, February 8, 1834.

131. Letter from Prudence Crandall to Simeon Jocelyn, AARC.

132. Letter from William Lloyd Garrison to Helen E. Benson, [August 18, 1833], reprinted in Merrill, *The Letters of William Lloyd Garrison*, 399.

133. Letter from Lucretia Mott to Phebe Post Willis, [September 13, 1834], in Beverly Wilson Palmer, ed., *Selected Letters of Lucretia Coffin Mott* (Urbana: University of Illinois Press, 2002), 29. Joseph Parrish, a white Quaker activist and president of the Pennsylvania Abolition Society, apparently balked at the idea, citing concerns about the city's problems with racial violence.

134. For an overview of the Philadelphia race riot in 1834, see John Runcie, "'Hunting the Nigs' in Philadelphia: The Race Riot of August 1834," *Pennsylvania History* 39 (1972): 187–218.

135. *Proceedings of the New-England Anti-Slavery Convention . . .* (Boston: Garrison & Knapp, 1834), 24.

136. "Miss Crandall's Case," *Vermont Chronicle*, August 8, 1834, emphasis in original.

137. "The Separation," *Liberator*, November 22, 1834.

138. May, *Some Recollections of Our Antislavery Conflict*, 71.

139. "The Separation," *Liberator*.

140. "Colored Temperance Convention," *Liberator*, July 30, 1836.

141. Jocelyn, "Obituary Notice."

142. In the 1840s Prudence Crandall Philleo had relocated with her husband to Providence, Rhode Island, where she reportedly ran a "select Academy," which included some African American children. Less is known about other African American women students who attended the Canterbury Female Seminary. Based on my research, Elizabeth Henly, a Philadelphia native, served as a delegate to an antislavery convention in 1838. Amy Fenner, sometimes styled Emma Fenno, married Ransom Parker in 1837, and they resided in Providence. The Parkers' daughter would later play a role in the desegregation of Providence public schools. Jerusha Congdon, born in October 1816 in New London, Connecticut, married William West in 1842 and settled in Windham County, Connecticut. Eliza Weldon, from New York, was listed as a student at Oberlin College in 1837. Henrietta Bolt, born in 1817 in New York, married Theodore Vidal. Her mother, Margaret, was born in the West Indies sometime around 1792 and resided with the Vidals. See Henry Highland Garnet, "Notes by a Traveller No. 1," *Emancipator and Republican*, November 19, 1845; "Requited Labor Convention," *Pennsylvania Freeman*, March 15, 1838; "Married," *Liberator*, June 9, 1837; *General Catalogue of Oberlin College 1833–1908* (Published by the College, 1909), 1035.

143. Davis Day, "Instruction of Colored People," *Philanthropist*, October 13, 1841.

144. *Proceedings of the Anti-Slavery Convention, Assembled at Philadelphia . . .* (New York: Dorr & Butterfield, 1833), 18–19.

145. "Letter from Theodore Weld to Lewis Tappan [March 18, 1834]," *Genius of Universal Emancipation*, May 1834. It remains unclear how long Weld's proposed school was in operation, or if it ever opened. Charlotte Huntington Lathrop married Reverend Henry Cherry on August 3, 1836, in Plainfield, Massachusetts, and was a missionary in India starting in November 1836. She died a year later in Sri Lanka. Incidentally, at least two of Lathrop's sisters also did missionary work.

146. "New School for Colored Females," *Liberator*, April 26, 1834.

147. N, "Honor to Whom Honor Is Due," *Liberator*, August 14, 1840.

148. "A School for the Instruction of Colored Females . . . ," *Liberator*, April 19, 1834.

149. Rebecca Buffum Jr., "School," *Liberator*, November 1, 1834.

150. "Notice," *Liberator*, July 30, 1836.

151. Hallie Quinn Brown, *Homespun Heroines and Other Women of Distinction* (Xenia, OH: Aldine, 1926), 18.

152. "From Rev. Jehiel C. Beman," *Friend of Man*, November 29, 1837.

153. "Died," *Christian Recorder*, January 22, 1870. In this obituary, Julia Ward Williams Garnet was described as having "wore herself out in the service of her God and her people."

154. Letter from Sarah Harris Fayerweather to Isabella Fayerweather Mitchell, March 2, 1855, box 1, folder 4, FFP.

155. Letter from Helen Benson Garrison to Sarah Harris Fayerweather, June 5, 1863, box 1, folder 2, FFP.

156. Letter from Sally Prentice Harris to Sarah Harris Fayerweather, September 20, 1857, box 1, folder 3, FFP; James Oliver Horton and Lois E. Horton, *In Hope of Liberty: Culture, Community, and Protest Among Northern Free Blacks, 1700–1860* (New York: Oxford University Press, 1997), 114.

157. Welch, *Prudence Crandall*, 195.

158. Letter from Emma Philleo Goodwin Whipple to her sister-in-law, June 1, 1862, AARC.

159. Old Fernwood Cemetery, South Kingston, Washington County, RI.

160. "Colored Schools Broken Up, in the Free States," *American Anti-Slavery Almanac* 1, no. 4 (1839): 15.

Notes to Chapter 2

1. I provide the approximate ages of these students (in 1838) based on biographical records.

2. After careful and lengthy research, I positively identified these seven African American women students based on an analysis of school catalogues, newspaper articles, letters, and other materials. Rosetta Morrison's letter revealed her to be a student at the Young Ladies' Domestic Seminary. Likewise Serena deGrasse exchanged letters with her former teacher Elizabeth Everett. Margaret Morrison's obituary placed her at the seminary. Letters from Hiram Kellogg confirmed the identity of Ursula James and the Turpin sisters. Mary E. Miles's name appeared on the master list of students in the 1841 Young Ladies' Domestic Seminary catalogue, and Serena mentioned Mary in her letters to Everett.

3. Enobong Hannah Branch and Melissa E. Wooten, "Suited for Service: Racialized Rationalizations for the Ideal Domestic Servant from the Nineteenth to the Early Twentieth Century," *Social Science History* 36, no. 2 (Summer 2012): 180.

4. Shirley J. Yee, *Black Women Abolitionists: A Study in Activism* (Knoxville: University of Tennessee Press, 1992), 41; Perkins, "The Impact of the 'Cult of True Womanhood' on the Education of Black Women," 18; Nancy A. Hewitt, "Beyond the Search for Sisterhood: American Women's History in the 1980s," *Social History* 10, no. 3 (October 1985): 300–302. Historians have introduced various concepts of American womanhood that decenter the cult of Christian domesticity. For instance, Frances Cogan explores the notion of Real Womanhood in *All American Girl: The Ideal of Real Womanhood in Mid-Nineteenth-Century America* (Athens: University of Georgia Press, 1989), and Natasha Kraus examines the formation of the New Woman in *A New Type of Womanhood: Discursive Politics and Social Change in Antebellum America* (Durham, NC: Duke University Press, 2008). Scholars of African American women's history have theorized various models of womanhood, especially in the study of twentieth-century African American history and culture. See, for instance, Treva Lindsey's conceptualization of New Negro Womanhood in *Colored No More: Reinventing Black Womanhood in Washington, D.C.* (Urbana: University of Illinois Press, 2017), and Ashley D. Farmer's discussion of a plurality of womanhood(s) in *Remaking*

Black Power: How Black Women Transformed an Era (Chapel Hill: University of North Carolina Press, 2017).

5. "In Memoriam," *People's Advocate (Washington, DC)*, October 29, 1881. For more on the African Union Meeting and School House, see *A Short History of the African Union Meeting and School-House, Erected in Providence (R.I.) in the Years 1819, '20, '21; With Rules for its Future Government* (Providence, RI: Brown & Danforth, 1821).

6. I reached this educated guess based on a process of elimination. Letters from Hiram Kellogg reveal Margaret's arrival date at the seminary as well as the Turpin sisters' and Ursula James's. It was Mary, Rosetta, or Serena who first arrived at the seminary. Serena likely would not require reduced tuition since her family appeared to be part of the emerging black middle-class in New York City. Based on that, Rosetta or Mary must have been the first to arrive, but given Margaret's arrival date (and that she may have arrived with her sister Rosetta), I figured that it was Mary who arrived first.

7. Letter from Lucy B. Williams and Samuel J. May to Lucretia Motte [*sic*], June 25, 1834, reel 31, Philadelphia Female Anti-Slavery Society Correspondence, Pennsylvania Abolition Society Papers, Historical Society of Pennsylvania. Lucy B. Williams of Brooklyn, Connecticut, was likely related to Herbert Williams, a white lawyer and member of the Brooklyn Congregational Church, where Samuel J. May served as minister.

8. "Condition and Prospects of the Fugitives in Canada," *Liberator*, October 10, 1851.

9. Letter from Peter Williams to Gerrit Smith, September 4, 1834, box 39, General Correspondence, Gerrit Smith Papers (hereafter GSP), Special Collections Research Center, Syracuse University Libraries.

10. In the early 1830s Mary Lyon visited the Young Ladies' Domestic Seminary and later adopted features from that institution when she established Mount Holyoke Seminary in South Hadley, Massachusetts, in 1837.

11. "Manual Labor School for Young Ladies," *Western Luminary (KY)*, September 4, 1833.

12. "Domestic Seminary for Young Ladies," *American Annals of Education* (November 1834): 499.

13. *Catalogue of Officers, Teachers and Pupils, of the Ontario Female Seminary, Canandaigua, April, 1834* (Canandaigua, NY: Morse & Harvey, 1834), 8.

14. Nash, *Women's Education in the United States, 1780–1840*, 101. The nursing course was eliminated at the seminary in the late 1830s.

15. Research shows that the Burned-Over District extended beyond the boundaries of upstate New York. See, for instance, David L. Rowe, "A New Perspective on the Burned-Over District: The Millerites of Upstate New York," *Church History* 47, no. 4 (December 1978): 408–20.

16. Mary P. Ryan, *Cradle of the Middle Class: The Family in Oneida County, New York, 1780–1865* (Cambridge, UK: Cambridge University Press, 1981), chapter 1.

17. Charles Grandison Finney described this area as "a wilderness . . . [where] no religious privileges were enjoyed by the people." Though Finney had studied law, he experienced a religious conversion in 1821 that inspired him to live his life as an evangelist. Under the tutelage of a white Presbyterian minister George Washington Gale, Finney deepened his knowledge of theology and proselytized in New York and other states. His belief in personal salvation and moral reform attracted thousands of men

and women from various denominations, resulting in a spate of Finneyite revivals. During the second decade of the nineteenth century these revivals called young men like Hiram Kellogg to the ministry. Ada Marie Peck, *A History of Hanover Society: Together with a Genealogical Mention of Many Prominent Families* (Waterville, NY, 1901), 110.

18. "Death of Mrs. Mary G. Kellogg," *New York Evangelist*, April 27, 1879.

19. Glenna Matthews, *"Just a Housewife": The Rise and Fall of Domesticity in America* (New York: Oxford University Press, 1987), 10.

20. Lucia McMahon, *Mere Equals: The Paradox of Educated Women in the Early American Republic* (Ithaca, NY: Cornell University Press, 2012), 5–6.

21. "Domestic Seminary for Young Ladies," 499.

22. *Catalogue of the Young Ladies' Domestic Seminary. Clinton—August, 1834* (Utica, NY: Bennet & Bright, Printers, 1834), 11.

23. Proverbs 31:10–12.

24. Augustine (Lewis Woodson), "The West.—No. VI.," *Colored American*, July 13, 1839.

25. Charles B. Ray, "Female Education," *Colored American*, March 18, 1837.

26. Charles B. Ray, "Female Education," *Colored American*, November 23, 1839.

27. "Female Influence," *Palladium of Liberty*, April 3, 1844.

28. Beatrice, "Female Education," *Liberator*, July 7, 1832.

29. Mary Still, *An Appeal to the Females of the African Methodist Episcopal Church* (Philadelphia: Peter McKenna and Son, 1857), 6.

30. *Minutes and Proceedings of the First Annual Meeting of the American Moral Reform Society Held at Philadelphia . . . 14th to the 19th of August, 1837* (Philadelphia: Merrihew and Gunn, 1837), 40.

31. Letter from Mary E. Miles to Gerrit Smith, September 18, 1846, box 27, General Correspondence, GSP. This letter had been wrongly attributed to Mary Mills, but I have confirmed that Mary Miles wrote it. In the letter she identifies her residence as No. 9 Plain Street in Albany, New York, and that was where she had been teaching in the late 1840s.

32. Jan DeAmicis, "Slavery in Oneida County, New York," *Afro-Americans in New York Life and History* 27, no. 2 (July 2003): 69–76.

33. Daniel E. Wager, ed., *Our Country and Its People: A Descriptive Work on Oneida County, New York* (Boston: Boston History Company, 1896), 192.

34. Judith Wellman, *Grass Roots Reform in the Burned-Over District of Upstate New York: Religion, Abolitionism, and Democracy* (New York: Routledge, 2011), 131–33. Born in Utica in March 7, 1797, Gerrit Smith moved to Peterboro, a town that had been named for his father, Peter. Smith attended Clinton Academy and then Hamilton College, graduating with honors in 1818. He led the New York State Anti-Slavery Society for three years after Alvan Stewart's inaugural year.

35. *Proceedings of the New York Anti-Slavery Convention, Held at Utica, October 21, and New York Anti-Slavery State Society, Held at Peterboro', October 22, 1835* (Utica, NY: Standard & Democratic Office, 1835), 46.

36. *First Utica Directory for the Year 1817* (Utica, NY: Williams and Williams, 1817), 17.

37. "Seminary for Colored Persons," *Vermont Chronicle*, July 23, 1835.

38. Smith, like Beriah Green, was an educational pioneer. Incidentally, *Friend of Man* published articles and editorials supporting black intellectual achievement. See, "Talents of the Colored Race," *Friend of Man,* January 26, 1841.

39. "Colored School in Utica," *Friend of Man,* February 1, 1837, emphasis mine.

40. Jermain Wesley Loguen, *The Rev. J. W. Loguen, as a Slave and as a Freeman: A Narrative of Real Life* (Syracuse, NY: JGK Truair, 1859), 352.

41. Loguen, *The Rev. J. W. Loguen, as a Slave and as a Freeman,* 351.

42. Beriah Green, *Address, Delivered at Whitesborough, N.Y., September 5, 1833* (Utica, NY: William Williams, 1833), 6.

43. Beriah Green, *The Miscellaneous Writings of Beriah Green* (Whitesboro, NY: Oneida Institute, 1841), 235.

44. Beriah Green, *Sermons and Other Discourses with Brief Biographical Hints* (New York: S. W. Green, 1860), 170, 190–91.

45. Milton C. Sernett, *Abolition's Axe: Beriah Green, Oneida Institute, and the Black Freedom Struggle,* rev. ed. (1986; Syracuse, NY: Syracuse University Press, 2004), xx.

46. Hermann Richard Muelder, *Fighters for Freedom: The History of Anti-Slavery Activities of Men and Women Associated with Knox College* (New York: Columbia University Press, 1959), 41.

47. Sernett, *Abolition's Axe,* 46–7.

48. "Oneida Institute," *Friend of Man,* November 15, 1837.

49. Letter from Theodore S. Wright to Gerrit Smith, September 23, 1834, box 40, General Correspondence, GSP.

50. "School for Young Ladies of Color," *New Bedford (MA) Register,* March 16, 1842.

51. Letter from Daniel Alexander Payne to Samuel S. Schmucker, March 20, 1841, Samuel S. Schmucker Collection, Seminary Archives, Lutheran Theological Seminary, Gettysburg, Pennsylvania.

52. "Notice—Randalian Seminary," *Kalamazoo (MI) Gazette,* February 24, 1838.

53. "Editorial Summary," *Friend of Man,* October 6, 1836.

54. Thomas Miller Jr., who died in 1827 at thirty-five years old, owned the property at 87 Cross Street in New York City. Jane Miller was his widow. The editors of the *Colored American* may have mistakenly used the title "Miss" instead of "Mrs." for Jane. Thomas's brother-in-law, Peter Vogelsang Sr., lived at this property too and remained there while an African American female seminary was in operation. Peter Vogelsang Jr., son of Peter Vogelsang Sr. and Maria Miller Vogelsang, would marry Theodosia deGrasse in 1841 in New York City. Theodosia, an alumna of the Canterbury Female Seminary, was the sister of Serena deGrasse. It is possible that after Crandall's seminary closed, Theodosia attended or perhaps even taught at Miss Miller's seminary at 87 Cross Street, where she met Peter. On April 27, 1852, Thomas, the youngest son of Peter Jr. and Theodosia, died at three years old. He was probably named after Peter's uncle, Thomas Miller Jr., and Peter's grandfather, Thomas Miller Sr. ("Died," *Weekly Herald* (NY), May 1, 1852).

55. Enrollment figures for the academic years 1837–38, 1838–39, and 1839–40 are unavailable, thus making it difficult to assess enrollment figures for those years. The 1840–41 catalogue provides only a master list of students.

56. *Catalogue of the Young Ladies' Domestic Seminary Clinton, Oneida Co., N.Y., August, 1837* (Whitesboro, NY: Press of the Friend of Man, 1837), 8.

57. "From Our New-England Correspondent," *New York Evangelist*, July 8, 1837.

58. Leonard Richards, *"Gentlemen of Property and Standing": Anti-Abolition Mobs in Jacksonian America* (New York: Oxford University Press, 1970), 156.

59. Letter from H. H. Kellogg to Gerrit Smith, April 30, 1839, box 24, General Correspondence, GSP.

60. Letter from H. H. Kellogg to Gerrit Smith, April 30, 1839. Thanks to Jessica Linker for helping me read Kellogg's handwriting.

61. Anticolonization was part of antebellum black politics. See Ousmane K. Power-Greene, *Against Wind and Tide: The African American Struggle against the Colonization Movement* (New York: New York University Press, 2014), 14, 18.

62. Letter from H. H. Kellogg to Gerrit Smith, April 30, 1839.

63. Barbara Beeching, *Hopes and Expectations: The Origins of the Black Middle Class in Hartford* (Albany: State University of New York Press, 2017), xviii.

64. Christopher Collier, "In Search of an Education, Seventeenth to Nineteenth Centuries," in *African American Connecticut Explored*, edited by Elizabeth J. Normen (Middletown, CT: Wesleyan University Press, 2013), 140.

65. Charles Henry Bell, *History of the Town of Exeter, New Hampshire* (Boston: J. E. Farwell, 1888), 190.

66. Letter from Mary Elizabeth Rowland to Frances B. Rowland, November 1827, Rowland Family Correspondence, 1764–1860, Connecticut Historical Society, emphasis in original.

67. For more on the lives of household servants in the United States, see, for instance, Faye Dudden, *Serving Women: Household Service in Nineteenth Century America* (Middletown, CT: Wesleyan University Press, 1985).

68. David T. Dixon, "Freedom Earned, Equality Denied: Evolving Race Relations in Exeter and Vicinity, 1776–1876," *Historical New Hampshire* 61 (Spring 2007): 23–24.

69. For a fascinating analysis of the importance of Miss Marsh's school in Wilson's novel, see Eve Allegra Raimon, "Miss Marsh's Uncommon School Reform," in *Harriet Wilson's New England: Race, Writing, and Region*, edited by JerriAnne Boggis, Eve Allegra Raimon, and Barbara A. White (Hanover: University of New Hampshire Press, 2007), 167–81. P. Gabrielle Foreman and Reginald Pitts have uncovered important information about Wilson that shapes how scholars read and understand her novel. See Harriet E. Wilson, *Our Nig; or, Sketches from the Life of a Free Black*, edited by P. Gabrielle Foreman and Reginald H. Pitts (New York: Penguin Books, 2005).

70. There is no evidence that Eliza ever attended the Young Ladies' Domestic Seminary. Born in 1831, she was about four years younger than her sisters.

71. "To Thomas Jefferson from William Turpin, 29 March 1825," *Founders Online*, National Archives, last modified October 5, 2016, http://founders.archives.gov/documents/Jefferson/98-01-02-5090.

72. "Editors," *Cincinnati Daily Gazette*, February 7, 1835.

73. "Will of William Turpin," *Evening Post (New York, NY)*, January 24, 1835.

74. Joseph Thomas Turpin, November 24, 1835, A-0141(25)L, folder 15, file 1835–79, Estate Records, 1775, 1782–1921, series 16, Surrogate's Court, Westchester County Archives and Records Center, Elmsford, NY.

75. "Died," *Freedom's Journal*, March 28, 1829.

76. Bella Gross, "Life and Times of Theodore S. Wright, 1797–1847," *New History Bulletin* 3, no. 9 (June 1940): 133.

77. Manisha Sinha, *The Slave's Cause: A History of Abolition* (New Haven, CT: Yale University Press, 2016), 195.

78. Theodore Wright, "Extract," *Colored American*, November 11, 1837.

79. "Great Anti-Slavery Convention," *Friend of Man*, September 27, 1837.

80. "Letter from Hiram Kellogg to William Goodell, December 23, 1839," *Friend of Man*, January 1, 1840. This letter was reprinted in the *Emancipator* and the *Union Herald*.

81. "Obituary," *Colored American*, May 11, 1839.

82. Letter from H. H. Kellogg to Gerrit Smith, April 30, 1839.

83. "Obituary," *Colored American*, May 11, 1839.

84. A death notice published in July 1849 notes the passing of Georgenia T. deGrasse, the youngest daughter of George T. deGrasse. She was seventeen, which means she was born around 1832. "Died," *Evening Post (New York, NY)*, July 18, 1849.

85. "Family of George DeGrasse and Maria Van Surley Degrasse," box 1, folder 7, Degrasse-Howard Papers, 1776–1976, Massachusetts Historical Society, Boston. Georgenia deGrasse is not listed in this document.

86. Letter from Peter Williams to Gerrit Smith, September 4, 1834; Craig D. Townsend, *Faith in Their Own Color: Black Episcopalians in Antebellum New York City* (New York: Columbia University Press, 2005), 65.

87. Townsend, *Faith in Their Own Color*, 65.

88. "African Celebration," *Long Island (NY) Star* , July 19, 1827.

89. "Dorcas Association," *Freedom's Journal*, February 7, 1829; "Dorcas Association," *Freedom's Journal*, November 21, 1828.

90. For more on nineteenth-century African American communities and the usage of the term "African," see, for instance, James Sidbury, *Becoming African in America: Race and Nation in the Early Black Atlantic* (New York: Oxford University Press, 2007).

91. "Colored Physicians," *Liberator*, June 15, 1849.

92. "Female Education," *Colored American*, November 23, 1839.

93. "Letter from Hiram Kellogg to William Goodell, December 23, 1839," *Friend of Man*, January 1, 1840.

94. "Letter from Hiram Kellogg," *Friend of Man*.

95. Letter from Catharine J. Clarke to Henry A. Clarke, June 25, 1839, Hamilton College Archives, Clinton, New York.

96. Letter from Catharine J. Clarke to Henry A. Clarke, June 25, 1839.

97. Letter from Myrtilla Miner to her family, Clinton, November 8, 1839, Family Correspondence, box 1, Myrtilla Miner Papers, Manuscript Division, Library of Congress, Washington, DC.

98. Letter from Elizabeth to Delia Caroline Fuller, Clinton, October 18, 1836, author's collection. I suspect that this letter is not from Elizabeth Everett but rather a student named Elizabeth. Perhaps it was written by Elizabeth Smith, the daughter of Gerrit Smith. According to Serena's daughter, Serena spent some of her school vacations at Elizabeth Smith's house in Peterboro. See Serena A. M. Washington, *Biography of George Thomas Downing: Sketch of His Life and Times* (Newport, RI: Milne Printery, 1910), 7.

99. Letter from Elizabeth Everett to Her Mother, Clinton, May 20, 1840, box 2, folder 7, Butler-Everett Family Collection (BEFC), Center for Archival Collections, Bowling Green State University Libraries.

100. Kelley, *Learning to Stand and Speak*, 75.

101. Letter from Elizabeth Everett to Her Parents, Clinton, November 22, 1839, box 2, folder 15, BEFC.

102. "Died," *Emancipator*, February 20, 1840.

103. "Married," *Emancipator*, June 24, 1834.

104. "Letter from Hiram Kellogg," *Friend of Man*.

105. "Death of Mrs. Mary G. Kellogg," *New York Evangelist*, April 27, 1879.

106. Letter from Rosetta Morrison to Frances B. Rowland, October 23, 1840, Rowland Family Correspondence, 1764–1860, Connecticut Historical Society.

107. "Letter from Hiram Kellogg," *Friend of Man*.

108. Letter from Mrs. George S. Butler [Elizabeth Gridley], June 1900, Clinton Historical Society, Clinton, NY.

109. Letter from Rosetta Morrison, October 23, 1840.

110. "Letter from Hiram Kellogg," *Friend of Man*.

111. Letter from John Everett to Elizabeth Everett, Steuben, March 17, 1840, box 6, folder 3, BEFC.

112. Letter from Elizabeth Everett to Her Parents, Clinton, November 22, 1839, box 2, folder 15, BEFC.

113. Letter from Rosetta Morrison, October 23, 1840.

114. Charles C. Chapman and Co., *History of Knox County, Illinois* (Chicago: Blakely, Brown & Marsh, 1878), 554.

115. J. W. Bailey, *Knox College, By Whom Founded and Endowed . . .* (Chicago: Press & Tribune Book, 1860), 8–9.

116. In 1843 Kellogg delivered a speech at the World Anti-Slavery Convention where he stated that he had welcomed African American students at his seminary.

117. "Valuable Property for Sale," *New York Evangelist*, May 4, 1839.

118. This census information accords with Rosetta's letter, dated October 23, 1840, when she noted that she traveled with the Turpin sisters from New York City to the seminary.

119. D, "The Clinton Female Institute," *Emancipator*, December 19, 1839.

120. Letter from Harriet Tenney to Mary Ingall, Clinton, February 27, 1840, Knox College Archives, Galesburg, IL.

121. "For the Christian Reflect. Letter: Clinton Seminary [sic]," *Christian Reflector (MA)*, August 4, 1841.

122. Similar remarks can be found in the editorial "Female Education," published in the *Colored American* on November 23, 1839.

123. Letter from Elizabeth Everett to Her Parents, Clinton, October 29, 1840, box 2, folder 7, BEFC.

124. "For the Christian Reflector. Letter: Clinton Seminary," *Christian Reflector (MA)*, August 4, 1841. The Butler-Everett Family Collection contains records about Clinton Seminary after 1841, when the Free Will Baptists ran the institution. It would certainly be worth further study.

125. A.B.O., "Clinton Seminary," *National Anti-Slavery Standard*, October 20, 1842. In December 1841 it was reported that a Native man and seven African American students attended Clinton Seminary. "The Friends of the Oppressed," *National Anti-Slavery Standard*, December 30, 1841.

126. "A Colored Physician," *Frederick Douglass' Paper*, September 22, 1854.

127. *Catalogue of the Young Ladies' Domestic Seminary*, 19–36.

128. *Catalogue of the Young Ladies' Domestic Seminary*, 23.

129. *Catalogue of the Young Ladies' Domestic Seminary*, 27.

130. Letter to Elizabeth Everett from Harriet Gates, April 7, 1841, box 6, folder 4, BEFC.

131. Letter to Elizabeth Everett from anonymous student, Plainfield, June 11, no year, box 6, folder 8, various 1862–1868, BEFC.

132. Letter from Eliza D. Thomas to Elizabeth Everett, Amherst, June 22, 1841, box 6, folder 4, BEFC.

133. Letter from Clarissa M. Palmer to Elizabeth Everett, Parish, New York, June 28, 1841, box 6, folder 4, BEFC.

134. Letter from Jennett Perkins Dickenson to Elizabeth Everett, Syracuse, November 6, 1840, box 6, folder 4, BEFC.

135. "Obituaries," *Colored American*, April 10, 1841.

136. Letter from Serena deGrasse to Elizabeth Everett, September 7, 1841, New York, box 6, folder 4, BEFC.

137. Letter from Serena deGrasse Downing to Elizabeth Everett, May 18, 1842, New York, box 6, folder 5, BEFC, strikethrough in original.

138. For more on the fight to desegregate Albany public schools, see Marian I. Hughes, *Refusing Ignorance: The Struggle to Educate Black Children in Albany, New York, 1816–1873* (Albany, NY: Mount Ida Press, 1998).

139. "Married," *Liberator*, June 16, 1848.

140. "Condition and Prospects of the Fugitives in Canada," *Liberator*, October 10, 1851.

141. "Boarding and Day School," *Liberator*, February 9, 1855.

142. "In Memoriam," *People's Advocate (Washington, DC)*, October 29, 1881.

143. Letter from Serena deGrasse Downing to Elizabeth Everett, box 6, folder 5.

144. "Married," *National Anti-Slavery Standard*, March 7, 1844.

145. "Mr. & Mrs. Geo. T. Downing . . . ," Correspondence—Response to Invitations, box 152-1, folder 41, George Downing Papers, Moorland Spingarn Research Center, Howard University.

146. "Married," *Brooklyn (NY) Evening Star*, October 8, 1845; "Local Intelligence," *Philadelphia Inquirer*, May 7. 1881.

147. "In Memory," *State Journal (PA)*, November 15, 1884.

148. Letter from Serena deGrasse Downing to Elizabeth Everett, May 18, 1842, New York, box 6, folder 5, BEFC.

149. Letter from Eliza D. Thomas to Elizabeth Everett, Amherst, June 22, 1841, box 6, folder 4, BEFC.

150. After his tenure at Knox College, Hiram Kellogg reopened the Young Ladies' Domestic Seminary in 1848 and once again welcomed African American women students, including Louisa Jacobs, the daughter of Harriet Jacobs. The seminary closed for good in 1850. See Harriet A. Jacobs, *Incidents in the Life of a Slave Girl*, edited by Jean Fagan Yellin (Cambridge, MA: Harvard University Press, 1987), 289n1.

Notes to Chapter 3

1. Letter from Rosetta Morrison to Frances B. Rowland, Clinton, October 23, 1840, Rowland Family Correspondence, 1764–1860, Connecticut Historical Society.

2. "Notice," *Colored American*, April 24, 1841.

3. Alexander Crummell, "I have been requested by Mrs. Maria W. Stewart . . . ," in *Meditations from the Pen of Mrs. Maria W. Stewart* (Washington, DC, 1879), 10, emphasis in original.

4. Linda Perkins, "Heed Life's Demands: The Educational Philosophy of Fanny Jackson Coppin," *Journal of Negro Education* 51, no. 3 (1982): 181.

5. I wish to acknowledge here that *all* humans are born free, and African Americans were forced into the institution of slavery by white slaveholders.

6. Graham Hodges, *Root and Branch: African Americans in New York and East Jersey, 1613–1863* (Chapel Hill: University of North Carolina Press, 1999), 164.

7. Craig Steven Wilder, *In the Company of Black Men: The African Influence on African American Culture in New York City* (New York: New York University Press, 2002), 201; Leslie Harris, *In the Shadow of Slavery: African Americans in New York City, 1626–1863* (Chicago: University of Chicago Press, 2003), 88.

8. The historians Carter G. Woodson, Carleton Mabee, Hilary Moss, and Jane E. Dabel, among others, have made similar claims in their work.

9. Editors, "To Our Patrons," *Freedom's Journal*, March 16, 1827.

10. Carl Kaestle, *The Evolution of an Urban School System: New York City, 1750–1850* (Cambridge, MA: Harvard University Press, 1973), 86.

11. Robert L. Church and Michael W. Sedlak, *Education in the United States: An Interpretive History* (New York: Free Press, 1976), 157, 88.

12. Charles C. Andrews, *The History of the New-York African Free-Schools* (New York: Mahlon Day, 1830), 47.

13. Andrews, *The History of the New-York African Free-Schools*, 54.

14. Jane E. Dabel, "Education's Unfulfilled Promise: The Politics of Schooling for African American Children in Nineteenth-Century New York City," *Journal of the History of Childhood and Youth* 5, no. 2 (Spring 2012): 198.

15. Anna Mae Duane, "'Like a Motherless Child': Racial Education at the New York African Free School and in *My Bondage and My Freedom*," *American Literature* 82, no. 3 (2010): 464.

16. "Valedictory Address of Andrew R. Smith," New York African Free School Collection, https://www.nyhistory.org/web/africanfreeschool/archive/78742-21v.html, emphasis mine.

17. "African Free School," *Freedom's Journal*, January 11, 1828.

18. Phyllis F. Field, *The Politics of Race in New York: The Struggle for Black Suffrage in the Civil War Era* (Ithaca, NY: Cornell University Press, 1982), 28.

19. Charles Z. Lincoln, *The Constitutional History of New York: From the Beginning of the Colonial Period to the Year 1905* . . . (Rochester, NY: Lawyers Cooperative Publishing Co., 1906), 2:123.

20. Incidentally, all of these men were associated with Masonic lodges.

21. Wilder, *In the Company of Black Men*, 124.

22. "Married," *Colored American*, May 22, 1841. John Peterson's sister-in-law, Miranda Glasko Overbaugh, actually resided with the Petersons in the mid-1870s and 1880s. John Peterson died on July 14, 1885, at eighty.

23. "First Negro Teacher of New Yory Eulogied [sic]," *New York Age*, June 11, 1914. John Peterson along with Ransom F. Wake and five other African American men founded the Philomathean Literary Society in 1830. Wake, whom the New York Public School Society hired to lead Colored School No. 2 in 1836, taught James McCune Smith, who earned his medical degree in Scotland and practiced medicine in New York City, and William H. Day, a newspaper editor, Oberlin College graduate, and teacher. Wake died from pneumonia on May 18, 1883. See, "Died," *Brooklyn (NY) Daily Eagle*, May 19, 1883.

24. "Public Schools," *Colored American*, January 30, 1841; *Longworth's American Almanac, New-York Register, and City Directory, for the Sixty-Fourth Year of American Independence* . . . (New York: Thomas Longworth, 1839), 416. Prince Loveridge died in October 1867. See "Died," *Church Journal*, October 16, 1867. This claim that schools could make citizens also appeared in the writings of Thomas Jefferson and later in the work of Horace Mann, who spearheaded the common school movement in Massachusetts.

25. Carla Peterson, *Black Gotham: A Family History of African Americans in Nineteenth-Century New York* (New Haven, CT: Yale University Press, 2011), 138.

26. "To The Senior Editor, No. III New Haven," *Freedom's Journal*, August 17, 1827.

27. "Celebration," *Freedom's Journal*, March 28, 1829.

28. William Oland Bourne, *History of the Public School Society of the City of New York* (New York: William Wood, 1870), 674.

29. Bourne, *History of the Public School Society of the City of New York*, 676.

30. "Mrs. Tompkins' School [sic]," *Colored American*, October 9, 1841.

31. These schools used to be under the management of the New York Manumission Society but were taken over by the Public School Society in 1834. In 1842 the New York City Board of Education started to distribute money to private organizations before eventually managing the public schools. See A. Emerson Palmer, *The New York Public School: Being a History of Free Education in the City of New York* (New York: Macmillan, 1905), 25–26.

32. "The Colored Evening Schools," *New York Tribune*, December 27, 1856.

33. "Grand Oratorio," box 152-2, folder 45, George Downing Papers, Moorland-Spingarn Research Center, Howard University.

34. "Grand Entertainment by Colored School No. 2," *New York Tribune*, March 23, 1864.

35. Kathleen Weiler, *Country Schoolwomen: Teaching in Rural California, 1850–1950* (Stanford, CA: Stanford University Press, 1998), 14.

36. Julie Roy Jeffrey, *Frontier Women: "Civilizing" the West? 1840–1880* (New York: Hill and Wang, 1998), 20, 46.

37. Letter from Rosetta Morrison to Frances B. Rowland, Clinton, October 23, 1840, Rowland Family Correspondence, 1764–1860, Connecticut Historical Society.

38. "Teacher," *Colored American*, March 28, 1840.

39. Judith Wellman, *Brooklyn's Promised Land: The Free Black Community of Weeksville, New York* (New York: New York University Press, 2014), 1, 13.

40. Wellman, *Brooklyn's Promised Land*, 252n11.

41. "Temperance Meeting Association," *Colored American*, July 24, 1841.

42. "African School," *Long Island (NY) Star*, January 18, 1815.

43. "Exhibition," *Long Island (NY) Star*, December 19, 1839.

44. "Colored School Exhibition," *Long Island (NY) Star*, April 28, 1836.

45. "Letters to Rev. T[heodore] S. Wright, of New York.—No. II," Amos Beman Scrapbook I, pp. 60–62, Beinecke Library, Yale University.

46. "Colored School," *Brooklyn (NY) Evening Star*, August 13, 1841. This article was reprinted in the *Colored American*, September 4, 1841.

47. Washington took preparatory courses at Kimball Union Academy in New Hampshire for two years and gained admission to Dartmouth College in 1843. For more on education and Washington's work, see Ron Welburn, *Hartford's Ann Plato and the Native Borders of Identity* (Albany: State University of New York Press, 2015), chapter 6.

48. "A Competent Colored Male Teacher . . . ," *Brooklyn (NY) Evening Star*, August 6, 1841.

49. *Acts Relating to the City of Brooklyn and the Ordinances Thereof* . . . (Brooklyn, NY: John Douglas, 1836), 66.

50. Henry R. Stiles, *A History of the City of Brooklyn*, vol. 3, *1867–70* (reprint; Westminster, MD: Heritage Books, 2007), 872.

51. Just as the Primary Select School began to flourish, so too did the Colored School of Brooklyn. William J. Wilson directed the Colored School of Brooklyn after Augustus Washington left. At first Wilson, whom the trustees hired in September 1841, taught only thirty-five students, but then enrollment grew to around one hundred. This increase propelled community members to petition the city for funding equal to that given to white public schools. Colored School No. 1, as Wilson's school came to be known, moved to a new building, and more teachers were hired in the 1840s and 1850s, almost all of whom were women, to staff the grammar and primary departments. Wilson's wife, Mary, even worked as principal of the Primary Department in December 1862. In addition to his work in education, Wilson contributed articles and editorials to *Frederick Douglass' Paper* under the penname "Ethiop." For more, see "Exhibition," *Brooklyn (NY) Evening Star*, November 14, 1842; "We Visited Few Days Since . . . ," *National Anti-Slavery Standard*, November 18, 1841; William J. Wilson, "Public Schools for Colored Children," box 1, folder 4, Henry Reed Stiles Papers, Brooklyn Historical Society.

52. Wellman, *Brooklyn's Promised Land*, 6–7.

53. "School Exhibition," *Colored American*, November 13, 1841.

54. Wellman, *Brooklyn's Promised Land*, 238–39.

55. "School Exhibition," *Colored American*.

56. "Select English School," *Colored American*, September 18, 1841.

57. "Notice," *Colored American*, April 24, 1841.

58. "Death of a Colored Clergyman," *New York Times*, February 9, 1877.

59. "Episcopal School," *Colored American*, July 20, 1839.

60. Dabel, "Education's Unfulfilled Promise," 203.

61. "Notice," *Colored American*, October 31, 1840.

62. "Notice," *Colored American*.

63. "Preparatory School," *Genius of Temperance, Philanthropist and People's Advocate*, October 16, 1833.

64. "Notice," *Philanthropist*, March 16, 1842.

65. "School Exhibition," *Colored American*.

66. "School Exhibition," *Colored American*, emphasis mine.

67. "We visited a few days since . . . ," *National Anti-Slavery Standard*, November 18, 1841.

68. Letter from Eliza D. Thomas to Elizabeth Everett, Amherst, June 22, 1841, box 6, folder 4, BEFC.

69. Letter from Serena deGrasse to Elizabeth Everett, New York, September 7, 1841, box 6, folder 4, BEFC.

70. Letter from Maryette Barker to Elizabeth Everett, December 2, 1841, box 6, folder 4, BEFC.

71. Letter from Maryette Barker to Elizabeth Everett.

72. The ideology of racial uplift continues to be debated among historians. Some, like Frederick Cooper, have regarded racial uplift ideology as elitist, classist, and imitative insofar as African Americans uncritically adopted the values of an emerging white middle class in the early nineteenth century, even though those values undercut their interests. Other historians have challenged this interpretation, arguing instead that the ideology of racial uplift was flexible, radical, and empowering for African Americans. My study accords with the latter interpretation. For more on the ideology of racial uplift in early nineteenth-century America, see Frederick Cooper, "Elevating the Race: The Social Thought of Black Leaders, 1827–1850," *American Quarterly* 24 (December 1972): 604–25; Patrick Rael, *Black Identity and Black Protest* (Chapel Hill: University of North Carolina Press, 2002); Elizabeth Rauh Bethel, *The Roots of African-American Identity: Memory and History in Antebellum Free Communities* (New York: St. Martin's Press, 1997); Jacqueline Bacon, *Freedom's Journal: The First African American Newspaper* (Lanham, MD: Lexington Books, 2007); Sinha, *The Slave's Cause.*

73. Erica Ball, *To Live an Antislavery Life: Personal Politics and the Antebellum Black Middle Class* (Athens: University of Georgia Press, 2012), 30.

74. David Tyack and Elisabeth Hansot, *Learning Together: A History of Coeducation in American Public Schools* (New Haven, CT: Yale University Press, 1990), 64; Carl Kaestle, *Pillars of the Republic: Common Schools and American Society, 1780–1860* (New York: Hill and Wang, 1983), 126.

75. Kim Tolley, *Heading South to Teach: The World of Susan Nye Hutchinson, 1815–1845* (Chapel Hill: University of North Carolina Press, 2015), 94. According to the historian Geraldine J. Clifford, quite a few married women teachers in Buffalo, New York, held onto their positions in the pre–Civil War era: *Those Good Gertrudes: A Social History of Women Teachers in America* (Baltimore, MD: Johns Hopkins University Press, 2014), 128.

76. Serena deGrasse Downing to Elizabeth Everett, May 18, 1842, box 6, folder 5, BEFC.

77. "Married," *National Anti-Slavery Standard*, June 1, 1843.

78. U.S. Census, 1850.

79. Among career teachers such as Eliza D. Richards, Sarah Ennalls, Mary E. Eato, and Fanny Tompkins, none married. Maria W. Stewart was widowed and did not remarry. Another notable exception was William J. Wilson's wife, Mary. In 1858 she taught at the Colored Evening School. During and after the Civil War, more African American women teachers such as Sarah Tompkins Garnet married and continued teaching.

80. Julia Winch, *A Gentleman of Color: The Life of James Forten* (New York: Oxford University Press, 2002), 277. Maria, who was the daughter of Thomas Miller Sr., likely

had a brother, Thomas Miller Jr., who lived with his wife, Jane Miller, at 87 Cross Street, near the Vogelsangs. The Vogelsangs lived at 85 Cross Street in the late 1830s. Winch postulates that Maria Miller Vogelsang may have been related to William Miller, an African American clergyman born in 1775 in Maryland, who helped to establish the African Methodist Episcopal Zion Church. By trade, he was a cabinetmaker who split his time between New York City and Philadelphia. William Miller married Harriet Judah Purvis Miller of Philadelphia, who had been widowed after the death of her first husband, William Purvis. After some research, I found no direct links between Thomas Miller Jr. and William Miller, except that Thomas Miller Jr.'s funeral in 1827 was held at 36 Mulberry Street, William Miller's address. It is possible that Maria and her siblings received their early education at Reverend William Miller's School at 36 Mulberry Street. For more on the Purvis family, see Margaret Hope Bacon, *But One Race: The Life of Robert Purvis* (Albany: State University of New York Press, 2007).

81. "Married," *Colored American*, August 1, 1840; "Miss C. Vogelsang's Demise," *Colored American*, February 11, 1899; William L. Calderhead, "Anne Arundel Blacks: Three Centuries of Change," in *Anne Arundel County Maryland: A Bicentennial History, 1649–1977*, edited by James C. Bradford (Annapolis, MD: Anne Arundel County and Annapolis Bicentennial Committee, 1977), 18; "Married," *Brooklyn (NY) Evening Star*, October 1, 1842. For an interesting history of the Bishop family, see *Finding Charity's Folks: Enslaved and Free Black Women in Maryland* (Athens: University of Georgia Press, 2016). For more on Peter Vogelsang Jr. and his military service during the Civil War as part of the 54th Massachusetts Volunteer Infantry, see Douglas R. Egerton, *Thunder at the Gates: The Black Civil War Regiments That Redeemed America* (New York: Basic Books, 2016). Peter was born around 1815, Jane around 1819, and Eliza around 1820. I suspect that Thomas was born between 1815 and 1819.

82. "Matrimony Notice," *Commercial Advertiser*, January 14, 1839.

83. I believe that Jane and James had a daughter, Maria C. Forten, who passed away at the age of four on June 28, 1847. She was buried in William H. Topp's family plot in Albany, New York.

84. "Laws of 1846, Chap. 425. An Act to Incorporate the New York Society for the Promotion of Education among Colored Children," in *Documents of the Assembly of the State of New York* (Albany, NY: Weed, Parsons, 1880), 1795.

85. "New York Colored School, No. 2," *North Star*, May 4, 1849.

86. Winch, *A Gentleman of Color*, 437n25.

87. *Manual of the Board of Education of the City and County of New York* (New York: William C. Bryant, 1852), 128; "Died," *Commercial Advertiser (NY)*, January 15, 1839; "Mortuary Notice," *Public Ledger (PA)*, July 21, 1852.

88. Albany Rural Cemetery, Menands, NY, accessed March 14, 2017, http://albanyruralcemetery.org/search-arc/.

89. "Another Circumlocation Office," *Liberator*, August 21, 1857.

90. "Died," *Douglass' Monthly*, March 1859.

91. *Journal of the Board of Education of the City of New York* (New York: Wynkoop & Hallenbeck, 1884), 837.

92. Elizabeth Jennings Graham, along with other African American women teachers such as J. Imogen Howard, established the New York Kindergarten and Sewing School for Colored Children in 1895. See "The Day's Gossip," *New York Tribune*, February 23, 1897. Graham was also chairperson of the Colored Teachers' Association

in New York. She died on June 5, 1901. See "Death of a Famous Woman Who Won a Famous Suit," *Appeal (MN)*, June 15, 1901.

93. "The Vigilance Committee," *National Anti-Slavery Standard*, August 27, 1840; "Black and White: An Ex-Slave Restored to His Family after Thirty Years' Absence," *Sacramento (CA) Daily Union*, February 14, 1885.

94. "Isaac Wright Free!," *Colored American*, February 9, 1839. This was the advertisement used after his second escape.

95. "Narrative of Stephen Dickenson, Jr. [sic]," *Colored American*, December 5, 1840. Incidentally, Botts later had a relationship with an enslaved woman, Ann Maria Barclay, and had a child with her. See Walter Johnson, *Soul by Soul: Life inside the Antebellum Slave Market* (Cambridge, MA: Harvard University Press, 1999), 114.

96. *American Slavery as It Is: Testimony of A Thousand Witnesses* (New York: American Anti-Slavery Society, 1839), 163.

97. David Fiske, *Solomon Northup's Kindred: The Kidnapping of Free Citizens before the Civil War* (Santa Barbara, CA: Praeger, 2016), vi.

98. "Land of Liberty," *Freedom's Journal*, December 5, 1828.

99. Graham Russell Hodges, *David Ruggles: A Radical Black Abolitionist and the Underground Railroad in New York City* (Chapel Hill: University of North Carolina Press, 2010), 88.

100. "The Vigilance Committee," *Colored American*, April 11, 1840.

101. It is unclear whether Wilson was indeed blameless in the whole affair, but charges against him were eventually dropped. Ruggles then pursued Lewis as the culprit. For more on the case, see Hodges, *David Ruggles*, chapter 4.

102. David Ruggles, "Kidnapping and Arrest," *Colored American*, June 23, 1838.

103. "Joshua Coffin," in *Memorial Biographies of the New England Historic Genealogical Society*, vol. 6, *1864–1871* (Boston: American Anti-Slavery Society, 1905), 2.

104. "Letter from Joshua Coffin, Dec. 23d, 1838," in *Memorial Biographies of the New England Historic Genealogical Society*, 6:5.

105. "Isaac Wright Free!," *Colored American*.

106. "Letter from Joshua Coffin, Dec. 23d, 1838," 6:4.

107. "New Year's Present," *Colored American*, January 2, 1841.

108. "The Treasurer of the New York Committee of Vigilance," *Emancipator*, August 19, 1841.

109. "The Vigilance Committee," *National Anti-Slavery Standard*, August 27, 1840.

110. "Wholesale and Retail Furniture Warehouse," *Colored American*, November 24, 1838.

111. I date their return based on the birth records of their children as well as their entry in the New York City directory. Mary Emma died in New York City in 1847. "Deaths," *New York Evangelist*, November 11, 1847.

112. Graham Russell Hodges, *New York City Cartmen, 1667–1850*, revised ed. (New York: New York University Press, 2012), 171.

113. Letter from Serena deGrasse Downing to Elizabeth Everett, May 18, 1842, box 6, folder 5, BEFC.

114. "To the Friends of Freedom and the Press," *Frederick Douglass' Paper*, April 26, 1850.

115. Fanny Tompkins, "North Star Fair in New York," *North Star*, March 15, 1850.

116. Yee, *Black Women Abolitionists*, 67.

117. The other statutes included organizing the territories of Utah and New Mexico, California entering the Union as a free state, banning the slave trade in the District of Columbia, and the federal government settling Texas border claims and assuming some debt.

118. The 1850 law was meant to strengthen the Fugitive Slave Act of 1793, a federal act intended to provide the legal means to enforce Article 4, Section 3 of the U.S. Constitution mandating the return of fugitive slaves. For more on the fugitive slave law and the abolition movement, see Samuel May Jr., *The Fugitive Slave Law and Its Victims* (New York: American Anti-Slavery Society, 1861); Stanley W. Campbell, *The Slave Catchers: Enforcement of the Fugitive Slave Law, 1850–1860* (Chapel Hill: University of North Carolina Press, 1968); Steven Lubet, *Fugitive Justice: Runaways, Rescuers, and Slavery on Trial* (Cambridge, MA: Belknap Press of Harvard University Press, 2010); Earl M. Maltz, *Fugitive Slave on Trial: The Anthony Burns Case and Abolitionist Outrage* (Lawrence: University Press of Kansas, 2010).

119. Sinha, *The Slave's Cause*, 502.

120. "Report of the New York Ladies' Fair in Aid of the Committee of Thirteen," *North Star*, April 3, 1851.

121. For more on the enforcement of the Fugitive Slave Act, see Campbell, *The Slave Catchers.*

122. "Black and White: An Ex-Slave Restored to His Family after Thirty Years' Absence," *Sacramento (CA) Daily Union*, February 14, 1885; "Death of Nathaniel Gray," *Daily Alta California*, April 25, 1889.

123. "Life of Nathaniel Gray," in *Chronicles of the Builders of the Commonwealth: Historical Character Study*, edited by Hubert Howe Bancroft (San Francisco: History Company, 1892), 7:348.

124. "Black and White," *Sacramento (CA) Daily Union.*

125. "Miss Alice C. Wright Dies in Jefferson County," *New York Age*, March 19, 1921.

126. Dabel, "Education's Unfulfilled Promise," 198.

127. "Mr. Lincoln and Negro Equality," *New York Times*, December 28, 1860.

128. In the 1860 U.S. census taken in June, the census taker recorded Isaac's profession as a carman. But Isaac may not have been living in the household. As the historian Eric Gardner surmises, census takers sometimes registered inaccuracies on rolls, and some African Americans themselves embellished their responses.

129. "Wright, Rosetta," *Trow's New York City Directory Vol. LXXIV, For the Year Ending May 1, 1861* (New York: John F. Trow, 1860), 939.

130. Dabel, *A Respectable Woman*, 67–68. Dabel's chapter "I Washed for My Living: Black Women's Occupations" provides a wealth of information on black working-class women in New York City.

131. Julie Winch, "Introduction: Joseph Willson's Philadelphia," in *The Elite of Our People: Joseph Willson's Sketches of Black Upper-Class Life in Antebellum Philadelphia*, edited by Julie Winch (University Park: Pennsylvania State University Press, 2000), 11–12.

132. "Wright, Rosetta M.," *Trow's New York City Directory, 1867–1868* (New York: J. F. Trow, 1867), 1132. In this directory, Rosetta's occupation is listed as "washing."

133. "Letitia Douglas Wright," Account No. 5183, November 18, 1872, New York Branch of the Freedman's Savings and Trust Company, Registers of Signatures of

Depositors, 1865–1874, RG 101, Records of the Comptroller of the Currency, National Archives and Records Administration.

134. "Warrant No. 14275, [October 28, 1878]," in *Documents of the Board of Aldermen of the City of New York, 1879* (New York: Martin B. Brown, 1880), 154.

135. Hallie Q. Brown, *Homespun Heroines and Other Women of Distinction* (Xenia, OH: Aldine, 1926), 110. Sarah Tompkins was the daughter of Sylvanus Smith and Ann Springstead Smith. Her sister, Susan Smith, earned a medical degree at New York Medical College for Women in the late 1860s and was one of a few African American women physicians in the nation.

136. Lyons, "Memories of Yesterdays, 49."

137. "Opening Exercises of Colored School No. 3," *New York Herald*, June 11, 1869.

138. Lyons, "Memories of Yesterdays," 51.

139. "Eato," *Brooklyn (NY) Daily Eagle*, February 10, 1915.

140. *Annual Report of the President of the Normal College, for the Year Ending December 31, 1873* . . . (New York: Cushing & Bardua, 1874), 41–45. The names of the other women who passed the entrance exam were Ella Emery, Eveline H. Williams, Maria Despenville, Charlotte Thomas, Mary Lewis, Anne L. Dias, Hannah Cathells, Emeline Magnine, and Laura Adair. Both Adair and Dias later recounted some of the challenges they faced as they tried to matriculate at Hunter. "Mrs. Dias-Thomas Honored on 50th Anniversary as a Teacher in N.Y. Schools," *New York Age*, February 5, 1927.

141. Linda Perkins, "African-American Women and Hunter College: 1873–1945," *Echo: Journal of the Hunter College Archives* (1995): 25.

142. "Normal College Girls," *New York Tribune*, June 21, 1890; "Miss Alice C. Wright Dies in Jefferson County," *New York Age*, March 19, 1921.

143. "Black and White," *Sacramento (CA) Daily Union*.

144. "Black and White," *Sacramento (CA) Daily Union*.

145. Heather Andrea Williams, *Help Me to Find My People: The African American Search for Family Lost in Slavery* (Chapel Hill: University of North Carolina Press, 2012), 30.

146. Rosetta was not listed in the New York City directory for 1882–83 or 1883–84. It is possible that she did not reside in New York City proper at that time, so perhaps Isaac and Rosetta never reunited.

147. "Wright, Rosetta M.," *Trow's New York City Directory. Vol. CI. For the Year Ending May 1, 1888* (New York: Trow's Printing & Bookbinding, 1887), 2156.

148. Death Certificate for Rosetta Wright, May 28, 1896, file no. 18211, State of New York Certificate and Record of Death.

149. "Miss Alice C. Wright," *New York Age*, March 19, 1921.

150. Brown, *Homespun Heroines and Other Women of Distinction*, 139.

Notes to Chapter 4

1. Sarah P. Remond, "Sarah P. Remond," in *Our Exemplars, Poor and Rich; or Biographical Sketches of Men and Women*, edited by Matthew Davenport Hill (London: Cassell, Petter, and Galpin, 1861), 277.

2. The recent publication of Rachel Devlin's *A Girl Stands at the Door: The Generation of Young Women Who Desegregated America's Schools* (New York: Basic Books,

2018) promises to change the trajectory of research on gender and school desegregation in twentieth century America.

3. Marcus W. Jernegan, "Compulsory Education in the American Colonies: I. New England," *School Review* 26, no. 10 (December 1918): 741.

4. "Schools," in *The Book of the General Lauues and Libertyes concerning the Inhabitants of the Massachusets, Collected out of the Records of the General Court for the Several Years Wherin They Were Made and Established, and now Revised by the Same Court, and Disposed into an Alphabetical Order and Published by the same Authoritie in the General Court held at Boston the Fourteenth of the First Month Anno 1647* (Cambridge, MA: Printed by Matthew Day according to the order of the General Court, 1648), 47.

5. Jesse Chickering, *A Statistical View of the Population of Massachusetts, from 1765 to 1840* (Boston: Charles C. Little and James Brown, 1846), 122–23.

6. Herbert Aptheker, ed., *A Documentary History of the Negro People in the United States: From Colonial Times through the Civil War* (New York: Citadel Press, 1951), 1:20.

7. "African School," *Federal Gazette (MD)*, October 2, 1809.

8. "African School on the Lancaster plan," *Evening Post (NY)*, January 4, 1810.

9. "African Free Schools in the United States," *Freedom's Journal*, May 18, 1827.

10. W. Jeffrey Bolster, *Black Jacks: African American Seamen in the Age of Sail* (Cambridge, MA: Harvard University Press, 1997), 159.

11. Johann Neem, *Democracy's Schools: The Rise of Public Education in America* (Baltimore, MD: Johns Hopkins University Press, 2017), 25.

12. Neem, *Democracy's Schools*, 27.

13. Henry Barnard, *Report and Documents relating to the Public Schools of Rhode Island, for 1848* (Providence, RI, 1849), 253.

14. David Tyack and Elizabeth Hansot, *Learning Together: A History of Coeducation in American Public Schools* (New Haven, CT: Yale University Press, 1990), 126.

15. Neem, *Democracy's Schools*, 29.

16. Rebecca R. Noel, "Salem as the Nation's Schoolhouse," in *Salem: Place, Myth, and Memory*, edited by Dane Anthony Morrison and Nancy Lusignan Schultz (Boston: Northeastern University Press, 2004), 130.

17. "African Society," *Salem (MA) Gazette*, March 18, 1806; "African Society," *Salem (MA) Gazette*, March 21, 1806.

18. Cyrus Mason Tracy remarked that grammar schools were "anciently called writing schools." See *Standard History of Essex County, Massachusetts: Embracing a History of the County from Its First Settlement to the Present, With a History and Description of Its Towns and Cities* (Boston: C. F. Jewett, 1878), 379.

19. William Bentley, *The Diary of William Bentley, D.D. Pastor of the East Church Salem, Massachusetts*, vol. 2, *January, 1793–December, 1802* (Salem, MA: Essex Institute, 1907), 31.

20. Bentley, *The Diary of William Bentley*, 2:96.

21. Dane Anthony Morrison and Nancy Lusignan Schultz, "Salem Enshrined: Myth, Memory, and the Power of Place," in Morrison and Schultz, *Salem*, 9.

22. Maris A. Vinovskis, *The Origins of the Public High Schools: A Reexamination of the Beverly High School Controversy* (Madison: University of Wisconsin Press, 1985), 32.

23. Duane Hamilton Hurd, compiler, *History of Essex County, Massachusetts, with Biographical Sketches of Many of its Pioneers and Prominent Men* (Philadelphia, J. W. Lewis, 1888), 1:134.

24. William Bentley, *The Diary of William Bentley, D.D. Pastor of the East Church Salem, Massachusetts*, vol. 3, *January, 1803–December, 1810* (Salem, MA: Essex Institute, 1911), 273.

25. "Letter from Father Dodge: The Capacity of the Colored Person to Receive Education," *Waukegan (IL) Gazette*, January 13, 1866.

26. Noel, "Salem as the Nation's Schoolhouse," 145.

27. Bentley, *The Diary of William Bentley*, 3:296.

28. Bentley, *The Diary of William Bentley*, 3:382, 528.

29. Bentley, *The Diary of William Bentley*, 3:500.

30. "Daniel Minns," in *The Boston Directory; Containing Names of the Inhabitants, Their Occupations, Places of Business and Dwelling-Houses. With Lists of the Streets, Lanes, and Wharves; the Town Officers, Public Offices and Banks. And Other Useful Information* (Boston: E. Cotton, 1813), 187.

31. "Notice . . . ," *New-England Palladium*, January 10, 1817.

32. William Bentley, *The Diary of William Bentley, D.D. Pastor of the East Church Salem, Massachusetts*, vol. 4, *January, 1811–December, 1819* (Salem, MA: Essex Institute, 1914), 435.

33. In 1831 Clarissa Lawrence legally changed her name under Massachusetts state law. She held her teaching position as a married woman, which suggests that objections from community leaders about married black women teachers were few and far between, if not nonexistent, in early nineteenth-century Salem. In a matter of decades, married women in some areas throughout the North would be compelled to vacate their teaching positions.

34. "Framed Sampler by Sarrah [*sic*] Ann Pollard," Colonial Williamsburg Online Collections, accessed August 5, 2017, https://artsandculture.google.com/asset/framed-sampler/yQFxzZ6_olqSBw.

35. Marla R. Miller, *The Needle's Eye: Women and Work in the Age of Revolution* (Amherst: University of Massachusetts Press, 2006), 71.

36. Betty Ring, *Girlhood Embroidery: American Samplers and Pictorial Needlework, 1650–1850* (New York: Alfred A. Knopf, 1993), 3.

37. Bentley, *The Diary of William Bentley*, 4:435.

38. Joan M. Maloney, "Mary Toppan Pickman: The Education of a Salem Gentlewoman, 1820–1850," *Essex Institute Historical Collections* 123, no. 1 (1987): 8.

39. Joseph B. Felt, *Annals of Salem*, 2nd ed. (Salem, MA: W. & S. B. Ives, 1845), 1:473–74. The historian Rebecca Noel notes that there may have been as many as seventy students, ages four to twenty-two, in attendance at this school ("Salem as the Nation's Schoolhouse," 14).

40. "Improvement of the Blacks," *Essex (MA) Register*, July 11, 1818. This institution aided African Americans as well as other nonwhite, foreign-born people.

41. "Clarkson Society," *Salem (MA) Gazette*, November 6, 1821.

42. "First Report of the Clarkson Society," *Salem (MA) Gazette*, July 20, 1819.

43. "Education of Africans," *Boston Recorder*, February 9, 1822.

44. "Clarkson Society," *Salem (MA) Gazette*.

45. "Colored People of Salem," *Liberator*, January 7, 1832.

46. "Clarkson Society," *Salem (MA) Gazette.*

47. Neem, *Democracy's Schools*, 110; William Reese, *Origins of the American High School* (New Haven, CT: Yale University Press, 1995), 95.

48. Tyack and Hansot, *Learning Together*, 125, 114–15.

49. "Female Schools," *Essex (MA) Register*, October 29, 1827, capitalization in original.

50. Felt, *Annals of Salem*, 1:475.

51. "To the School Committee of the City of Salem," *Salem (MA) Gazette*, March 9, 1838.

52. Felt, *Annals of Salem*, 1:474.

53. Felt, *Annals of Salem*, 1:476.

54. "Evening School for Females," *Salem (MA) Observer*, October 9, 1830.

55. "Anti-Slavery Society of Salem and Vicinity," *Salem (MA) Gazette*, March 21, 1834.

56. "Boots and Shoes Cleaned," *Salem (MA) Gazette*, May 5, 1815.

57. Felt, *Annals of Salem*, 1:477.

58. "Death of John Remond," *Salem (MA) Register*, March 9, 1874.

59. "Died, at Salem, Mass, Monday, March 18th, 1867, Mrs. Nancy Lenox, Wife of John Remond, 79 Years," *National Anti-Slavery Standard*, May 11, 1867; Remond, "Sarah P. Remond," 276.

60. Remond, "Sarah P. Remond," 278.

61. Letter to the Editor, *Salem (MA) Observer*, July 12, 1834.

62. Felt, *Annals of Salem*, 1:478.

63. David Becket had petitioned the city before, on a variety of issues. See "Town Meeting," *Salem (MA) Gazette*, June 17, 1823. He was a member of the Salem Charitable Mechanic Association, and the Becket family lived on Becket Street in Salem. He committed suicide in June 1836. See "Deaths," *Salem (MA) Gazette*, June 21, 1836; "Items," *Gloucester (MA) Telegraph*, June 25, 1836; Sidney Perley, *A History of Salem Massachusetts*, vol. 2, *1638–1670* (Salem, MA: Sidney Perley, 1926), 225.

64. Remond, "Sarah P. Remond," 279–80.

65. "Negro Post-Masters," *Christian Reflector*, April 5, 1839.

66. "Petition of David Becket," Fam. Mss. 71, Phillips Library, Peabody Essex Museum, Salem, MA.

67. "Petition of David Becket."

68. Remond, "Sarah P. Remond," 279.

69. "Notice," *Salem (MA) Gazette*, July 22, 1834.

70. "Costly Prejudice," *Liberator*, August 23, 1834.

71. "Mr. Editor," *Salem (MA) Gazette*, March 13, 1835.

72. Charles B. Ray, "Dear Brother . . . ," *Colored American*, July 28, 1838.

73. "William B. Dodge," *Salem (MA) Register*, May 7, 1804; "William B. Dodge," *Salem (MA) Observer*, June 16, 1860.

74. "The Colored School," *Salem (MA) Register*, March 14, 1844.

75. "Letter from Father Dodge," *Waukegan (IL) Gazette*, January 13, 1866.

76. Felt, *Annals of Salem*, 1:481.

77. Daniel R. Mandell, *Behind the Frontier: Indians in Eighteenth-Century Eastern Massachusetts* (Lincoln: University of Nebraska Press, 1996), 19.

78. William Swain, a white merchant, enslaved an African couple, Maria and Boston, and their eight children. He agreed to gradually manumit them, but not before

extracting as much of their labor as he could. One son, Prince, born in 1750, would remain enslaved until the age of twenty-eight. Prince was sent to sea on a whaling ship; upon his return, the ship's captain Elisha Folger paid him his wages, completely bypassing John Swain, who now owned Prince after his father William had died. John sued for Prince's wages, but a jury found that Prince could retain his earnings. Prince then successfully sued for his freedom. More legal cases brought by enslaved Africans worked their way through the courts, demonstrating one path to freedom.

79. Frances Ruley Karttunen, *The Other Islanders: People Who Pulled Nantucket's Oars* (New Bedford, MA: Spinner, 2005), 92.

80. Karttunen, *The Other Islanders*, 71.

81. For an interesting biography of Mary Ellen Pleasant, see Lynn M. Hudson, *The Making of "Mammy Pleasant": A Black Entrepreneur in Nineteenth-Century San Francisco* (Urbana: University of Illinois Press, 2003).

82. Cooper was an elder in the African Methodist Episcopal Zion Church on West York Street.

83. "Death of an Aged Colored Woman," *Nantucket (MA) Inquirer & Mirror*, February 10, 1866. The *Nantucket Inquirer & Mirror* was published under different titles in the nineteenth and twentieth centuries. I follow the title indicated by the publication date.

84. "In Memory," *Nantucket (MA) Inquirer & Mirror*, October 27, 1883.

85. "Miscellany," *National (MA) Inquirer*, April 25, 1822.

86. Karttunen, *The Other Islanders*, 80.

87. Thaddeus Mason Harris, *A Discourse Delivered before the Society for Propagating the Gospel among the Indians and Others in North America, 6th November, 1823* (Cambridge, MA: From the University Press by Hilliard and Metcalf, 1823), 44.

88. There were five trustees. In addition to Jeffrey Summons and Absalom Boston, there was Peter Boston, Mikel Deluce, and Charles Godfrey. "Notice," *Nantucket (MA) Inquirer*, October 4, 1828.

89. Karttunen, *The Other Islanders*, 80; "Died," *Nantucket (MA) Inquirer*, December 17, 1831.

90. "African School," *Nantucket (MA) Inquirer*, April 4, 1825.

91. "New School," *Nantucket (MA) Inquirer*, October 15, 1822.

92. "Report of the School Committee," *Nantucket (MA) Inquirer*, March 29, 1828.

93. "Society for Propagating the Gospel among the Indians and Others in North America," *Missionary Herald* 29, no. 2 (February 1833): 69, emphasis mine.

94. "Communications: To the Editor of the Inquirer," *Nantucket (MA) Inquirer*, May 2, 1829.

95. "Communications," *Nantucket (MA) Inquirer*, May 2, 1829.

96. "African School," *Nantucket (MA) Inquirer*, April 18, 1829.

97. Based on newspaper and biographical records, James Jr. was born in 1807, Martha in 1812, Maria in 1815, Elizabeth in 1816, and Sarah in 1819. Martha died in 1833. See "Mortuary Notice," *Nantucket (MA) Inquirer*, August 28, 1833. Maria Ross Shippey Nye was twice married (and twice widowed). Elizabeth married William Miller, a seaman, and they had two children, Martha A. and William. Elizabeth died on January 3, 1855. In 1870 Maria worked as a stewardess; she died on September 17, 1902.

98. Some records list Mary's maiden name as Pompey; in other records, her maiden name was Sampson.

99. U.S. census, 1860.

100. "A Faithful Servant," *Nantucket (MA) Inquirer & Mirror*, August 8, 1896.

101. Anna Gardner, *Harvest Gleanings: In Prose and Verse* (New York: Fowler & Wells, 1881), 17.

102. *Fifth Annual Report of the Executive Committee of the American Anti-Slavery Society, With the Minutes of the Meetings of the Society for Business, and the Speeches Delivered at the Antislavery Meeting on the 8th May, 1838* (New York: William S. Door, 1838), 135.

103. "Nantucket Colored Anti-Slavery Society," *Liberator*, March 7, 1834. The first president of the African American antislavery society was William Harris. Other officeholders were Edward J. Pompey and Absalom Boston.

104. "Public Schools," *Nantucket (MA) Inquirer*, May 11, 1836.

105. William Coffin, et al., "In Town Meeting," *Inquirer and Mirror* (Nantucket, MA), January 13, 1838.

106. "High School," *Nantucket (MA) Inquirer*, April 28, 1832.

107. Tyack and Hansot, *Learning Together*, 122.

108. Neem, *Democracy's Schools*, 54.

109. "The Public High School," *Nantucket (MA) Inquirer*, June 26, 1839.

110. Reese, *Origins of the American High School*, 80.

111. Jurgen Herbst, *The Once and Future School: Three Hundred and Fifty Years of American Secondary Education* (New York: Routledge, 1996), 47.

112. "High School," *Nantucket (MA) Inquirer*, May 25, 1839.

113. "We are enabled to state . . . ," *Salem (MA) Gazette*, March 9, 1838.

114. Neem, *Democracy's Schools*, 121.

115. Barbara Ann White, *A Line in the Sand: The Battle to Integrate Nantucket Public Schools, 1825–1847* (New Bedford, MA: Spinner, 2009), 24.

116. John Saillant, "Before Douglass: Racism and Nationalism in Nantucket's Newspapers in the Early Republic," in *Nantucket's People of Color: Essays on History, Politics, and Community*, edited by Robert Johnson Jr. (Lanham, MD: University Press of America, 2006), 50.

117. "It is often asked how far . . . ," *Nantucket (MA) Islander*, January 30, 1841.

118. Samuel J. May, "Memoir of Cyrus Peirce," *American Journal of Education*, no. 11 (December 1857): 287.

119. "Education Meeting," *Nantucket (MA) Inquirer*, January 27, 1839.

120. "Education Meeting," *Nantucket (MA) Inquirer*, March 23, 1839, emphasis mine.

121. "African School," *Nantucket (MA) Inquirer*, August 14, 1839.

122. "Letter from Anna Gardner to Mrs. C. H. Dall. Nantucket [September 4, 1888]," Caroline Wells Healey Dall Papers, reel 16, box 10, folder 12, Massachusetts Historical Society, Boston.

123. "High School," *Nantucket (MA) Inquirer*, May 25, 1839. Some sources state that Eunice Ross took the high school entrance exam in 1839, but 1840 was the date that Eunice herself provided in her petition.

124. White, *A Line in the Sand*, 45.

125. Nathaniel Barney, "Letter from Nantucket [4th mo. 7th, 1843.]," *National Anti-Slavery Standard*, March 4, 1843.

126. James Walker Hood, *One Hundred Years of the African Methodist Episcopal Zion Church; Or, The Centennial of African Methodism* (New York City, 1895), 541. Serrington, a New York native, served as minister at a few churches, including one at Newburgh, one at Boston, and one at Providence.

127. "At a public meeting . . . ," *Nantucket (MA) Inquirer*, March 5, 1842.

128. Remond, "Sarah P. Remond," 282, emphasis in original.

129. Remond, "Sarah P. Remond," 277.

130. Myra Beth Young Armstead, *Lord, Please Don't Take Me in August: African Americans in Newport and Saratoga Springs* (Urbana: University of Illinois Press, 1999), 30.

131. "At a public meeting . . . ," *Nantucket (MA) Inquirer*, March 5, 1842.

132. S. C. Walker, "Key to the New Latin Reader," in *The New Latin Reader: Containing the Latin Text for the Purpose of Recitation; Accompanied with a Key, Containing the Text, a Literal and Free Translation, Arranged in Such a Manner as to Point out the Difference Between the Latin and the English Idioms* (Boston: Richardson and Lord, 1829), 12.

133. Felt, *Annals of Salem*, 1:481.

134. Remond, "Sarah P. Remond," 281.

135. "Speech of Charles Lenox Remond," *Liberator*, December 28, 1855. Curiously, Remond seemed to acknowledge that African American mothers, eager to educate their children, sometimes had to make tough decisions to send their children to "proslavery schools." That he singled out African American mothers demonstrated that they often made educational decisions concerning their children. He envisioned a day when the abolition of "pro-slavery colored churches" and "pro-slavery colored schools" would beget the "overthrow of slavery" in the United States.

136. "The Colored School," *Salem (MA) Register*, March 14, 1844.

137. "The Mirror of Liberty," *Liberator*, July 30, 1841.

138. Elizabeth Oldham, "Sampson Dyer: Portrait of a Nantucket Mariner," *Historic Nantucket* 63, no. 2 (Fall 2013): 19.

139. *Vital Records of Nantucket, Massachusetts to the Year 1850*, vol. 4, *Marriages (H–Z)* (Boston: New England Historic Genealogical Society, 1927), 99. Charlotte and Edward married on June 18, 1815.

140. "Receipts into the Treasury of the Massachusetts Anti-Slavery Soc. from June 6th to July 1st Inclusive," *Liberator*, July 5, 1839. Charlotte's participation in this auxiliary organization shows the complex organizational networks that African American created and maintained in the early nineteenth century. For more on women's organizational activities in antebellum Boston, see Anne M. Boylan, *The Origins of Women's Activism: New York and Boston, 1797–1840* (Chapel Hill: University of North Carolina Press, 2002).

141. In 1835 the Boston group, led by forty-three-year-old Elizabeth Riley, a well-respected nurse, celebrated its fourth anniversary. Riley was the mother of James Jackson Jr., the subject of Susan Paul's *Memoir of James Jackson*. See chapter 6 in this book.

142. "Jeremiah Brown," Nantucket, Probate Records, 1841–1849, Massachusetts, Wills and Probate Records, 1635–1991, *Ancestry.com*. Brown's will was executed in front of Charles Godfrey and Edward J. Pompey, which indicates Charlotte's (and Jeremiah's) position within the African American community.

143. Patience Harris Cooper was at the center of a murder investigation. For more, see Frances Ruley Karttunen, *Law and Disorder in Old Nantucket* (Nantucket, MA: Nantucket Press, 2007), especially chapter 11, "Murder Most Foul: The Saga of Patience Cooper, Part 3."

144. U.S. census, 1850.

145. In 1851 the *Inquirer* reported the death of a William W. Morris, who had been in Sacramento city. He died at age fifty-one. This death notice probably refers to Charlotte Brown's third husband. See "Died," *Inquirer* (Nantucket, MA), September 29, 1851.

146. "Charlotte Morris," Massachusetts Town and Vital Records, 1620–1988, Edgartown, Births, Marriages and Death, *Ancestry.com.*

147. "Ladies' Department," *Liberator*, February 16, 1833.

148. Catherine Adams and Elizabeth H. Pleck, *Love of Freedom: Black Women in Colonial and Revolutionary New England* (New York: Oxford University Press, 2010), 191.

149. *Proceedings of the Third Anti-Slavery Convention of American Women, Held in Philadelphia, May 1st. 2nd. and 3d. 1839* (Philadelphia: Merrihew and Thompson, 1839), 8, emphasis in original.

150. "Schools and Scholars," *Nantucket (MA) Inquirer*, April 22, 1843.

151. "Schools and Scholars," *Nantucket (MA) Inquirer*, June 3, 1843.

152. "Colored Children in the Public Schools," *Salem (MA) Register*, March 7, 1844.

153. "The Colored School," *Salem (MA) Register*, March 14, 1844.

154. Amber D. Moulton, *The Fight for Interracial Marriage Rights in Antebellum Massachusetts* (Cambridge, MA: Harvard University Press, 2015), 114–15.

155. "Petition of Edward W. Gardner," House Unpassed Legislation 1842, Docket 1153, SC1/series 230, Digital Archive of Massachusetts Anti-Slavery and Anti-Segregation Petitions, Massachusetts Archives, Boston, Harvard Dataverse.

156. "To the School Committee of the City of Salem [Petition]," EC 35—Salem, MA, Report on Blacks in Schools, 1819–1844, Phillips Library, Peabody Essex Museum, Salem, MA.

157. "Petition of Edward Pompey," Passed Acts; St. 1845, c.214, SC1/series 229, Digital Archive of Massachusetts Anti-Slavery and Anti-Segregation Petitions, Massachusetts Archives, Boston, Harvard Dataverse, emphasis in original.

158. Born around 1800 to William and Priscilla Pompey, Edward may have acquired his early education either through homeschooling or private tutoring. As a young man, he led seafaring ventures before returning home to Nantucket, where he operated a store in the New Guinea neighborhood. In addition to his occupation as a businessman, he held key positions in black organizations. He and other African American activists from Nantucket, including Arthur Cooper, organized a convention where they denounced the objectives of the American Colonization Society and declared their freedom, equality, and humanity as citizens of the United States. In 1831 he acted as a subscription agent for the *Liberator* and later the *Colored American*. In February 1834 he helped to establish the Nantucket Colored Anti-Slavery Society, for which he served as secretary. That same year he represented Nantucket at the New England Anti-Slavery Convention. In addition to his antislavery work, Edward presided over the Nantucket Colored Temperance Society. He died from consumption on October 6, 1848. He had a great impact on the community by spearheading these activist initiatives.

159. "Petition 1," Passed Resolves; Resolves 1838, c.34, SC1/series 228, Digital Archive of Massachusetts Anti-Slavery and Anti-Segregation Petitions, Massachusetts Archives, Boston, Harvard Dataverse.

160. "Petition of Eunice F. Ross," Passed Acts; St. 1845, c.214, SC1/series 229, Digital Archive of Massachusetts Anti-Slavery and Anti-Segregation Petitions, Massachusetts Archives, Boston, Harvard Dataverse.

161. John M. Earle, a white Quaker antislavery activist and newspaper editor who served in the Massachusetts House of Representatives from 1844 to 1852, delivered the petition. Incidentally, John's wife, Sarah, was from Nantucket.

162. Nancy F. Cott, *The Bonds of Womanhood: "Woman's Sphere" in New England, 1780–1835* (New Haven, CT: Yale University Press, 1977), 101.

163. "An Act concerning Public Schools, Approved by the Governor, March 25, 1845, Chapter 214," in *Acts and Resolves by the General Court of Massachusetts, in the years 1843, 1844, 1845* (Boston: Dutton and Wentworth, 1845), 70. A summary of the house and senate proceedings was published in the *Liberator* on March 7, 1845.

164. Kyle Volk, *Moral Minorities and the Making of American Democracy* (New York: Oxford University Press, 2014), 124.

165. "High School," *Nantucket (MA) Inquirer*, May 29, 1844.

166. "Novel Suit," *Commercial Advertiser*, September 13, 1845. Other newspapers picked up the story, including the *Public Ledger, New Hampshire Sentinel, Newark (NJ) Daily Advertiser, Salem (MA) Register*, and *Boston Daily Bee*.

167. "Novel Suit," *Niles' National Register* 19, no. 3 (September 20, 1845): 40.

168. "Schools and Colors," *Nantucket (MA) Inquirer*, May 20, 1843.

169. "The Schools," *Warder (MA)*, February 14, 1846.

170. "Triumph of the Right," *Liberator*, February 20, 1846.

171. "Deaths," *Nantucket (MA) Inquirer*, August 23, 1849.

172. "Resolutions of the Salem School Committee," *Common School Journal* 6, no. 20 (October 1844): 326.

173. Letter to the Editor, *Salem (MA) Register*, March 21, 1844.

174. "Salem Schools—Again," *Common School Journal* 4, no. 19 (October 1842): 299.

175. "Ward Two," *Salem (MA) Register*, March 7, 1844.

176. "Colored Children in the Public Schools," *Salem (MA) Register*, March 7, 1844.

177. For more on educational access and the American public high school, see Reese, *The Origins of the American High School*.

Notes to Chapter 5

1. *Documents of the City of Boston, for the Year 1858* (Boston: Rand & Avery, 1859), 1:151.

2. R.M., "Colored Schools," *Boston Courier*, August 21, 1845.

3. William C. Nell, "Equal School Rights," *Liberator*, April 7, 1854.

4. Roderick T. Baltimore and Robert F. Williams, "The State Constitutional Roots of the 'Separate but Equal' Doctrine: *Roberts v. City of Boston*," *Rutgers Law Journal* 17 (1986): 537–52; Morgan J. Kousser, "The Supremacy of Equal Rights: The Struggle against Racial Discrimination in Antebellum Massachusetts and the Foundations of the Fourteenth Amendment," *Northwestern University Law Review* 82 (1988): 941–1010; Douglas J. Ficker, "From *Roberts* to *Plessy*: Educational Segregation and the "Separate but Equal Doctrine," *Journal of Negro History* 84, no. 4 (Autumn 1999): 301–14; James Oliver Horton and Lois E. Horton, *Black Bostonians: Family Life and*

Community Struggle in the Antebellum North (New York: Holmes & Meier, 1979), chapter 6; George Levesque, *Black Boston: African American Life and Culture in Urban America, 1750–1860* (New York: Garland, 1994), chapters 5–7; Scott Hancock, "'The Law Will Make You Smart': Legal Consciousness, Rights Rhetoric, and African American Identity Formation in Massachusetts, 1641–1855," PhD dissertation, University of New Hampshire, 1999; Moss, *Schooling Citizens*, chapter 6; Kantrowitz, *More Than Freedom*, chapter 4.

5. Just as nineteenth-century American fiction writers explored issues of femininity through the literary figure of the African American girl, so too did African American activists make the African American girl the face for educational justice. In her illuminating study, *Black Girlhood in the Nineteenth Century* (Urbana: University of Illinois Press, 2016), Nazera Wright analyzes how nineteenth-century American writers broached issues of femininity through the archetype of the black girl.

6. James Oliver Horton and Lois E. Horton, *In Hope of Liberty: Culture, Community and Protest among Northern Free Blacks, 1700–1860* (New York: Oxford University Press, 1997), 83.

7. Jared Hardesty, *Unfreedom: Slavery and Dependence in Eighteenth-Century Boston* (New York: New York University Press, 2016), 2.

8. George Levesque, *Black Boston: African American Life and Culture in Urban America, 1750–1860* (New York: Garland, 1994), 267–68.

9. Arthur O. White, "Blacks and Education in Antebellum Massachusetts: Strategies for Social Mobility," EdD dissertation, State University of New York at Buffalo, 1971, 96.

10. "Death of Prince Saunders," *Vermont Union Whig*, June 29, 1839.

11. Kaestle, *Pillars of the Republic*, 70.

12. *Public Schools of the City of Boston. September, 1838* (Boston: J. H. Eastburn, City Printer, 1838), 8.

13. "Some Account of the Free Schools in Boston," in *The Prize Book No. IV of the Publick Latin School in Boston*, no. 4 (Boston: Cummings, Hilliard,1823), 3. It is possible that a few public primary schools in Boston in the 1810s operated hyperlocally, whereby a few African American children might have attended those schools, until the establishment of African School No. 1.

14. Joseph M. Wightman, *Annals of the Boston Primary School Committee from its First Establishment in 1818, to its Dissolution in 1855* (Boston: Geo. C. Rand & Avery, 1860), 69. The 1827 Boston Directory listed Charlotte Foster as a "school mistress" at the school in the African Meeting-house on Belknap Street.

15. Naomi Jeffers ran African School No. 2, but the primary school committee fired her and hired Catharine Paul.

16. Wightman, *Annals*, 94.

17. "In School Committee," *Saturday Morning Transcript*, February 14, 1835.

18. "Colored People of Boston," *Boston Recorder*, February 24, 1837.

19. "The Smith School," *Liberator*, August 27, 1836.

20. "Petition of Primus Hall and others," August 6, 1838, City Council Records Series 1.4, Docket 1838-0069-H4. Boston City Archives. Interestingly, the name William Riley, Elizabeth Riley's husband, appeared on this petition. For more on the Riley family, see chapter 6 in this book.

21. The Smith School building housed the Smith Grammar School as well as two primary schools. What is frustrating in these records is that it is often unclear when there is a reference to the Smith Grammar School specifically or one of the primary schools. The "Smith School" seems to have been regarded as one entity, which is yet another example of the educational inequality that African Americans endured. For the sake of clarity, I too refer to the Smith School this way, and where I can, I denote grammar school or primary school.

22. "Smith School," *Liberator*, September 3, 1836.

23. "Award of Medals," *Columbian Centinel (MA)*, August 15, 1838; "Award of Medals," *Weekly Messenger*, August 22, 1838.

24. *The Boston Almanac, for the Year 1838* (Boston: S. N. Dickinson, 1838), 78.

25. "Death of William. C. Nell," *Elevator*, June 27, 1874.

26. "Justice," "Smith School, Belknap-street," *Liberator*, September 2, 1842.

27. Thomas P. Smith, "Vindication," *Liberator*, October 5, 1849; Stephen Kendrick and Paul Kendrick, *Sarah's Long Walk: The Free Blacks of Boston and How Their Struggle for Equality Changed America* (Boston: Beacon Press, 2004), 79–80. William Cooper Nell submitted a petition to the Boston school committee pleading for equal school rights in Boston, but the Boston school committee apparently did not respond.

28. N, "Honors to Whom Honor Is Due," *Liberator*, August 14, 1840.

29. "Divorces in Middlesex," *Boston Evening Transcript*, October 17, 1861.

30. U.S. census, 1860.

31. "Died," *Springfield (MA) Republican*, August 31, 1874.

32. "The Smith School," *Liberator*, June 28, 1844.

33. Horton and Horton, *Black Bostonians*, 78.

34. "Vote of Thanks," *Liberator*, May 11, 1838.

35. "Report," *Liberator*, August 2, 1844.

36. "Equal School Rights Meeting," *Liberator*, August 16, 1850.

37. "Report," *Liberator*. For a while, Gardner ran a boardinghouse. She died on December 11, 1877.

38. "Report," *Liberator*. Lucretia Hilton was born in 1829 in Cambridge, Massachusetts. She worked alongside her parents and her aunt Eunice Russ Ames Davis in the fight for equal school rights in the 1840s. In 1851, she married John Miner Lenox Jr. (1824–1911), whose father was John Lenox Sr., the brother of Nancy Lenox Remond of Salem. Lucretia Hilton Lenox died in 1894. See "Reminiscences," *Woman's Era*, July 1894. Incidentally, two of the Lenoxes' daughters married into the Roberts family of Boston: Helen wed Charles Sumner Roberts, Sarah C. Roberts's brother, in 1880, and (Mary) Louisa wed William F. Roberts, also Sarah C. Roberts's brother, in 1900.

39. "Report," *Liberator*.

40. "Smith School," in *Rules of the School Committee, and Regulations of the Public Schools of the City of Boston* (Boston: John H. Eastburn, 1841), 22.

41. *Fourteenth Annual Report Presented to the Massachusetts Anti-Slavery Society, By Its Board of Managers, January 28, 1846, With An Appendix* (Boston: Scarlett and Laing, 1846), 92.

42. "Death of an Old Colored Citizen," *Liberator*, November 27, 1863.

43. Arthur Wellington Brayley, *Schools and Schoolboys of Old Boston* (Boston: Louis P. Hager, 1894), 114.

44. Shepard later embarked upon a military career, wherein he commanded an African American regiment during the Civil War. "Gen. Isaac Fitzgerald Shepard," *Cambridge (MA) Press*, August 31, 1889.

45. Robin Bernstein, *Racial Innocence: Performing American Childhood from Slavery to Civil Rights* (New York: New York University Press, 2011), 63. Nazera Sadiq Wright discusses how African American writers conceptualize innocence and suffering in their depictions of black girls in her book, *Black Girlhood in the Nineteenth Century.*

46. There are slight variations in this story, especially when it comes to the role of the different subcommittees to which Benjamin Roberts Sr. applied. I privilege the version of the story relayed by Benjamin Sr. in his petition to Massachusetts in 1851.

47. Kendrick and Kendrick, *Sarah's Long Walk*, 99.

48. Benjamin F. Roberts [Sr.], "Equal School Privileges," *Liberator*, April 4, 1851. John St. Pierre, a Boston-born clothing dealer, married a white English woman, Eliza, and they together had nine children. Their daughter Josephine St. Pierre attended the Franklin School in Boston for a while. She married George Lewis Ruffin, a free black man from Virginia who had moved to Boston with his family.

49. "The Smith School," *Boston Semi-Weekly Atlas*, August 15, 1849.

50. Speech of Robert Morris to the Daughters of Samaria Lodge, Boston, undated, Robert Morris Papers, Canton Historical Society, Canton, MA.

51. Kendrick and Kendrick, *Sarah's Long Walk*, 111.

52. Stanley K. Schultz, *The Culture Factory: Boston Public Schools, 1789–1860* (New York: Oxford University Press, 1973), 190.

53. Charles Sumner, *Argument of Charles Sumner, Esq. against the Constitutionality of Separated Colored Schools, in the case of Sarah C. Roberts vs. The City of Boston* (Boston: B. F. Roberts, 1849), 14.

54. Sumner, *Argument of Charles Sumner*, 3–4, 14.

55. Sumner, *Argument of Charles Sumner*, 3, 17–18.

56. Sumner, *Argument of Charles Sumner*, 23.

57. "Amalgamation," *Flag of Our Union*, August 18, 1849.

58. "Rights of Colored Citizens," *Christian Watchman*, September 13, 1849.

59. Luther S. Cushing, *Reports of Cases Argued and Determined in the Supreme Judicial Court of Massachusetts*, vol. 8 (Boston: Little, Brown, 1866), 209.

60. For more on the *Roberts* case, see Gerald Nelson Davis, "Massachusetts Blacks and the Quest for Education: 1638–1860," EdD dissertation, University of Massachusetts, 1977, 183–84; George Dargo, "The Sarah Roberts Case in Historical Perspective," *Massachusetts Legal History* 3 (1997): 37–51. The ruling in the *Roberts* case was often cited as a defense of racial segregation.

61. "Colored Schools—Exclusive Schools," *Congregationalist (MA)*, August 10, 1849.

62. "Died," *Liberator*, June 27, 1835.

63. Lois Brown, *Pauline Elizabeth Hopkins: Black Daughter of the Revolution* (Chapel Hill: University of North Carolina Press, 2008), 83.

64. Thomas Paul Smith, "The Smith School," *Liberator*, February 15, 1850.

65. Schultz, *The Culture Factory*, 160.

66. "Obituary [Abba M. Brooks]," *Christian Register (MA)*, July 5, 1851. Edward Jarvis, a white physician and local historian, remembered the Garrison children as "good

scholars" who "associated on equal terms with the other boys and girls." Jarvis painted an idyllic Concord based more in myth than fact. Edward Jarvis, "Houses and People of Concord, 1810–1820," unpublished manuscript, 1882, 189, Special Collections, Concord Free Public Library, Concord, MA. Elizabeth Garrison (Jackson) would later move to Boston, join the African American activist community there, and then travel down to the South to teach freed people after the Civil War. She, like Elizabeth Jennings Jr. before her, protested racial discrimination in Baltimore public transportation in 1866. See "Civil Rights in Baltimore," *Evening Star (Washington, DC)*, May 16, 1866.

67. "The Smith School," *Boston Semi-weekly Atlas*, August 15, 1849.

68. John H. Roberts, Benjamin Roberts's brother and Sarah's uncle, apparently supported the Smith School as well.

69. Moss, *Schooling Citizens*, 175.

70. Thomas Paul, "To the Public," *Liberator*, October 15, 1841.

71. "Summary," *Boston Recorder*, May 4, 1843.

72. "Colored School," *Liberator*, May 12, 1843; Leonard Williams Levy and Douglas Lamar Jones, *Jim Crow in Boston: The Origin of the Separate but Equal Doctrine* (New York: Da Capo Press), 142.

73. Thomas Paul eventually moved back to Rhode Island, where he worked as a schoolteacher. His daughter, Catherine, continued the legacy of African American teachers in the Paul family by becoming a music teacher.

74. "Fair," *Emancipator and Republican*, May 14, 1845.

75. *General Catalogue of the State Normal School, at Framingham, Mass. 1854. Established at Lexington, 1839. Removed to West Newton 1844. Removed to Framingham, 1853* (Boston: C. C. P. Moody, 1854), 16.

76. "Affairs in and around the City," *Daily Atlas*, September 4, 1850.

77. "Deaths," *Boston Evening Transcript*, June 24, 1856.

78. Thomas Paul Smith, "The Smith School," *Liberator*, February 15, 1850.

79. Moss, *Schooling Citizens*, 221. See also Scott Hancock, "The Elusive Boundaries of Blackness: Identity Formation in Antebellum Boston," *Journal of Negro History* 84, no. 2 (Spring 1999): 115–29.

80. B. F. Roberts, "Equal School Rights," *Liberator*, June 21, 1850.

81. "Petition of Benjamin F. Roberts," House Unpassed Legislation 1850, Docket 2556, SC1/series 230, Digital Archive of Massachusetts Anti-Slavery and Anti-Segregation Petitions, Massachusetts Archives, Boston, Harvard Dataverse, emphasis in original.

82. *Proceedings of the National Emigration Convention of Colored People; Held at Cleveland, Ohio . . .* (Pittsburgh, PA: A. A. Anderson, 1854), 68.

83. "Public Schools in Cambridge," *Cambridge (MA) Chronicle*, March 1, 1851.

84. William Cooper Nell, "The Colored Citizens of Boston," *Liberator*, December 10, 1852.

85. "Deaths," *Boston Evening Transcript*, November 10, 1852. Benjamin Roberts Sr. and his family were either visiting Charlestown or living there since their three-year-old daughter, Adeline, died in Charlestown in 1852.

86. "Died," *Liberator*, March 13, 1857. In 1857 their twelve-year-old son, Robert Roberts, died from brain inflammation; *Reports of the School Committee. Selectmen and Treasurer of the Town of Somerville, Together with a List of Taxes Assessed, for the Year 1857-8* (Boston: William White, 1858), 35.

87. U.S. census, 1860.

88. The Latimer Law, Massachusetts's personal liberty law enacted in 1843, was named after the fugitive slave George Latimer. See Kantrowitz, *More Than Freedom*, 70–83.

89. Sinha, *The Slave's Cause*, 539.

90. Richard Archer, *Jim Crow North: The Struggle for Equal Rights in Antebellum New England* (New York: Oxford University Press, 2017), 134. The case, *Inhabitants of Medway v. Inhabitants of Natick* (1810), established this legal precedent.

91. William Cooper Nell, "Equal School Rights in Boston," *Anti-Slavery Bugle*, November 25, 1854.

92. The Pindall case probably would not have overturned the ruling in the *Roberts* case, nor would it advance the argument that *all* children, irrespective of race, should have access to the same schools.

93. The elder Pindall would sign his name to the 1855 equal school rights petition.

94. I analyze Sarah's experiences in chapter 4.

95. "Died," *Salem (MA) Register*, August 18, 1856.

96. *Triumph of Equal School Rights in Boston. Proceedings of the Presentation Meeting Held in Boston. December 17, 1855* (Boston: R. F. Wallcut, 1856), 8–9.

97. L. A. Scruggs, *Women of Distinction: Remarkable in Works and Invincible in Character* (Raleigh, NC: L. A. Scruggs, 1893), 157.

98. In 1852 twenty-one-year-old Eliza Turpin married twenty-five-year-old Benjamin C. Gregory, an African American waiter. In 1860 Eliza, Benjamin, and their seven-year-old son, Milton, lived with her sister Joanna's family in Boston. Five years later the Gregory family lived in a separate residence in Boston. Benjamin worked as a porter. The family appeared to be on solid economic footing since they employed a servant named Mary Dailey. Milton Turpin Gregory began attending the elite Boston Latin School in 1869, but it appears that he did not graduate.

99. Petition 11, Digital Archive of Massachusetts Anti-Slavery and Anti-Segregation Petitions, Passed Acts; St. 1855, c.256, SC1/series 229, Massachusetts Archives, Boston, Collection Development Department, Widener Library, HCL, Harvard University.

100. "Petition of Benjamin Roberts," Digital Archive of Massachusetts Anti-Slavery and Anti-Segregation Petitions, House Unpassed Legislation 1851, Docket 3139, SC1/series 230, Massachusetts Archives, Boston, Collection Development Department, Widener Library, HCL, Harvard University

101. "Massachusetts Legislature," *Salem (MA) Register*, May 8, 1851.

102. "The Public Schools and Colored Children," *Boston Herald*, May 15, 1851.

103. George Adams, *The Massachusetts Register: State Record for the Year 1852, containing a Business Directory of the State with a Variety of Useful Information* (Boston, 1852), 40.

104. Carleton Mabee, "A Negro Boycott to Integrate Boston Schools," *New England Quarterly* 41, no. 4 (September 1968): 354–55.

105. Kantrowitz, *More Than Freedom*, 167. For a short overview of the Know-Nothing Party's rise in Massachusetts, see Dale Baum, "Know-Nothingism and the Republican Majority in Massachusetts: The Political Realignment of the 1850s," *Journal of American History* 64, no. 4 (1978): 959–86.

106. Some signatures appear twice on certain petitions, but, by my count, the whole number is 1,621. Nell reported 1,496 signatures. See *Triumph of Equal School Rights*

in Boston. Proceedings of the Presentation Meeting Held in Boston. December 17, 1855 (Boston: R. F. Wallcut, 1856), 6.

107. Charles W. Slack, "Commonwealth of Massachusetts," *Liberator*, March 30, 1855.

108. "Grammar School Committee," *Boston Herald*, September 12, 1855.

109. W.C.N., "Equal School Rights in Boston," *Liberator*, August 17, 1855.

110. "Black Laws in Massachusetts," *Liberator*, May 4, 1855.

111. W.C.N., "Colored Scholars in the Boston Schools," *Liberator*, August 3, 1860.

112. *Triumph of Equal School Rights in Boston*, 8, emphasis in original.

113. "Wells School," *Boston Traveler*, July 22, 1856.

114. "An Interesting Record," *Liberator*, August 1, 1856.

115. "[E]qual School Rights in R. Island," *Liberator*, April 17, 1857.

116. "Rhode Island A.S. Convention," *Liberator*, May 6, 1859; Robert J. Cottrol, *The Afro-Yankees: Providence's Black Community in the Antebellum Era* (Westport, CT: Greenwood Press, 1982), 99.

117. Clementina Parker married Peter William Downing, the brother of George T. Downing, in 1860. They set sail for Liberia, and Clementina died just upon arrival in 1861. See "Died," *Christian Recorder*, March 8, 1862.

118. Sallie Holley, "Address to the Legislative Committee on Caste Schools in Rhode Island," *Liberator*, June 10, 1859. In 1858 John T. Waugh of Providence filed a lawsuit on behalf of his son, who had been denied readmission to the Arnold Street School. His son had attended the school for a month, but then had been directed to enroll at the all-black Meeting Street School, where Elizabeth H. Smith, a Canterbury Female Seminary alumna, taught. Apparently some primary and grammar schools in Providence allowed a few African American children to matriculate. Such a policy resembles exactly what happened in Salem, where schools were not just local but hyperlocal. See "Equal School Rights for Colored Children," *Liberator*, February 20, 1857.

119. Leslie Harris, *In the Shadow of Slavery: African Americans in New York City, 1626–1863* (Chicago: University of Chicago Press, 2003), 279–88.

120. "Celebrating Their Golden Wedding," *Brooklyn (NY) Daily Eagle*, November 7, 1890.

121. Perhaps the Lyonses stayed with Jacob Anderson, an African American carman, his wife, Eliza Anderson, and their children.

122. Lyons, "Memories of Yesterdays," 11.

123. Lyons, "Memories of Yesterdays," 7.

124. Leach's line of questioning foreshadowed how school superintendents questioned African American students during the civil rights era school desegregation fight. See Devlin, *A Girl Stands at the Door*, chapter 7.

125. "Report of the Special Committee on Evening Schools in the City of Providence," *Rhode Island Schoolmaster* 13, no. 1 (January 1867): 106.

126. Edwin Martin Stone, *Manual of Education: A Brief History of the Rhode Island Institute of Instruction, including a Synopsis of Annual and Other Meetings, List of Officers and Members, Together with the Constitution and Charter* (Providence, RI: Providence Press Company, 1874), 69.

127. W.M.R., "Hail our White Children be driven from Our Public Schools, or remain in them as Caste or Pauper Schools, to please the Enemies of our Common

Schools?," *Manufacturers' and Farmers' Journal* (Providence, RI), March 2, 1865, emphasis in original.

128. Lyons, "Memories of Yesterdays," 12.

129. Lyons, "Memories of Yesterdays," 2.

130. Mary J. Lyons, "Mr. Editors," *Providence (RI) Evening Press*, October 3, 1864. Advertisements for Mary's hairdressing business appeared in the Providence-based periodical *Manufacturers' and Farmers' Journal* in October 1864. See "Mrs. Mary J. Lyons," *Manufacturers' and Farmers' Journal*, October 27, 1864.

131. Moss, *Schooling Citizens*, 9–10.

132. Lyons, "Mr. Editors." This point about African American military service would be made again just prior to the *Brown v. Board* legal fight. See James T. Patterson, *Brown v. Board of Education: A Civil Rights Milestone and Its Troubled Legacy* (New York: Oxford University Press, 2001).

133. "State of Rhode Island and Providence Plantations," *Providence (RI) Evening Press*, January 17, 1865.

134. "General Assembly," *Providence (RI) Evening Press*, February 23, 1865; "Asa Messer Gammell," in *Proceedings of the Rhode Island Historical Society 1900–1901* (Providence, RI: Printed for the Society, 1902), 51–52.

135. Lawrence Grossman, "George T. Downing and Desegregation of Rhode Island Public Schools, 1855–1866," *Rhode Island History* 36, no. 4 (November 1977): 104.

136. Lyons, "Mr. Editors."

137. *Brief Sketch of the Establishment of the High School, Providence: Together with the Dedicatory Exercises of the New Building* (Providence, RI: J. A. & R. A. Reid, 1878), 103.

138. Lyons, "Memories of Yesterdays," 15.

139. The *Providence Evening Press* reported on the exhibition, but made no mention of Maritcha Lyons aside from providing the title of her essay and listing her as a graduate. See "High School Exhibition," *Providence (RI) Evening Press*, May 5, 1869.

140. "The High School Exhibition," *Manufacturers' and Farmers' Journal* (Providence, RI), May 6, 1869.

141. Lyons, "Memories of Yesterdays," 15–16.

142. S. E. Doyle to Martha Chace, box 2, folder 1, Harry A. Williamson Papers, Schomburg Center for Research in Black Culture, The New York Public Library.

143. "Local News Briefs," *Providence (RI) Evening Press*, April 14, 1870. For an examination of Lyons's activism at the turn of the century, see Val Marie Johnson, "'The Half Has Never Been Told': Maritcha Lyons' Community, Black Women Educators, the Woman's Loyal Union, and 'the Color Line' in Progressive Era Brooklyn and New York," *Journal of Urban History* 44, no. 5 (2018): 835–61.

144. Lyons, "Memories of Yesterdays," 15–16.

145. For more on Downing's role, see Lawrence Grossman, "George T. Downing and Desegregation of Rhode Island Public Schools, 1855–1866," *Rhode Island History* 36, no. 4 (November 1977): 99–105.

146. "The Public Schools of Rhode Island," *Salem (MA) Register*, February 9, 1865.

147. "General Assembly," *Manufacturers' and Farmers' Journal* (Providence, RI), March 1, 1866; "Laws of Rhode Island—An Act in addition to Title XIII. of the Revised Statutes, "Of Public Instruction," *Newport (RI) Mercury*, August 4, 1866.

148. "Equal School Rights for Colored Children," *Liberator*, February 20, 1857, emphasis mine.

149. "Advancement," *Anti-Slavery Bugle*, May 15, 1858.

150. Mabee, *Black Education in New York State from Colonial to Modern Times*, 192.

151. For more on racial policies in New Jersey public schools in the nineteenth century, see Marion Thompson Wright, "Racial Integration in the Public Schools in New Jersey," *Journal of Negro Education* 23, no. 3 (Summer 1954): 282–89.

152. W.C.N., "Colored Scholars in the Boston Schools," *Liberator*, August 3, 1860.

153. St. John Appo, born in 1849, married Mary Louisa Lockley, who was identified as African American. Apparently St. John Appo later decided to pass, and, in all likelihood, his wife, Mary, did too. See Allyson Hobbs, *A Chosen Exile: A History of Racial Passing in American Life* (Cambridge, MA: Harvard University Press), 62.

154. "City Medal Scholars," *Annual Report of the School Committee of the City of Boston, 1863* (Boston: J. E. Farwell, 1863), 205.

155. Lucy Rae Woods, *A History of the Girls' High School of Boston, 1852–1902* (Boston: Riverside Press, 1904), 6.

156. William T. Adams, "The Boston Schools," *Congregationalist*, February 22, 1867.

157. Pauline E. Hopkins, "Famous Women of the Negro Race, VIII: Educators," *Colored American Magazine*, July 1902, 207.

158. "The Girls' High and Normal School," *Boston Herald*, June 29, 1867.

159. "Public Examination of the Girls' High and Normal School," *Boston Traveler*, June 28, 1867.

160. Adams, "The Boston Schools."

161. "Personal," *Congregationalist*, November 13, 1866.

162. Monroe Alpheus Majors, *Noted Negro Women: Their Triumphs and Activities* (Chicago: Donohue & Henneberry, 1893), 291–92.

163. "Obituary," *Elevator*, August 31, 1872. In 1892 J. Imogen Howard was the only African American woman appointed to serve on the New York State Board of Women Managers at the World's Fair.

164. "We regret to learn . . . ," *Liberator*, August 25, 1865; Kirsten Pai Buick, "Lifting as She Climbed: Mary Edmonia Lewis, Representing and Representative," in *Women Artists of the Harlem Renaissance*, edited by Amy Helene Kirschke (Jackson: University Press of Mississippi, 2014), 44. The literary scholar Scott Trafton, *Egypt Land: Race and Nineteenth Century American Egyptomania* (Durham, NC: Duke University Press, 2004), 212, hints that there may have been a romantic relationship between Edmonia and Adeline. I have yet to find any evidence of this in the historical record. For an exploration of Lewis's early education, see Marilyn Richardson, "Edmonia Lewis at McGrawville: The Early Education of a Nineteenth-Century Black Woman Artist," *Nineteenth Century Contexts* 22 (2000): 239–56.

165. "Our Public Schools," *Washington (DC) Bee*, October 18, 1884.

166. Edwin Clarence Howard died in 1912; Adeline died in 1922; J. Imogen died in 1937.

167. "Twenty-Five Years Ago in Boston," *Christian Era*, February 4, 1869.

168. *The Boston Directory embracing the City Record, A General Directory of the Citizens and a Business Directory*, no. 67 (Boston: Sampson, Davenport, 1871), 147. John Casneau, incorrectly spelled Casnean in the directory, lived at 2 Pemberton Square.

169. In 1897 he married Mary E. Smith in Boston and then was wanted in court for bigamy.

170. Divorce Petition of John Casneau, October 1879, New Haven County Superior Court Divorce Files, 1712-1899, box 681, Connecticut State Library.

171. "Police Notes," *Morning Journal and Courier,* July 8, 1882. Charles Dyer had been fined in April 1882 for "breach of peace" against Sarah. See "City Court—Criminal Side—Judge Studley," *Morning Journal and Courier,* April 13, 1882.

172. Marriage record of Sarah Casno (*sic*) and Mahlon G. Laws, December 15, 1887, New Haven, Connecticut, Registrar of Vital Statistics, Marriages in the Town of New Haven 31: 171, Town Clerk, Connecticut.

173. "Obituary Notice," *Boston Daily Advertiser,* February 15, 1887. An unintended result of this legal case was its later use in the 1896 *Plessy v. Ferguson* decision, which codified "separate but equal."

174. Two death notices appeared in Boston area newspapers: "Death Notice," *Boston Daily Globe*, September 8, 1881, and "Died," *Boston Herald*, September 8, 1881.

175. Death record of Sarah C. Laws, April 27, 1896, Orange, New Haven County, Connecticut, Registrar of Vital Statistics, Record of Deaths in the Town of Orange 1: 550, Town Clerk, Connecticut. Sarah's death record listed her as forty years old at the time of death, but of course that was incorrect since it would mean she was born in 1856, when we know that she had been born some ten to thirteen years before that. Interestingly, her marriage record to Mahlon G. Laws also lists the 1856 birth year. Perhaps Sarah had intended to change her age. Incidentally, Mahlon died in New Haven on September 25, 1906.

Notes to Chapter 6

1. "A Visit to Miss Paul's School," *Emancipator,* July 7, 1836.

2. Johann Gaspar Spurzheim allegedly said, "[African American children] will receive their first education as quick, if not quicker than white; they can read and speak as well, but they will be deficient in the English High School." Nahum Capen, *Reminiscences of Dr. Spurzheim and George Combe* (New York: Fowler & Wells, 1881), 24.

3. Dunbar, *A Fragile Freedom*, 105.

4. Neem, *Democracy's Schools*, 48.

5. Thomas Lickona, *Educating for Character: How Our Schools Can Teach Respect and Responsibility* (New York: Bantam Books, 1991), 7.

6. Kaestle, *Pillars of the Republic*, 100.

7. Emma Willard, *A Plan for Improving Female Education* 2nd edition (Middlebury, VT, 1918), 32.

8. Beatrice, "Female Education," *Liberator,* July 7, 1832, emphasis mine. To my knowledge, Beatrice was not one of Sarah Mapps Douglass's known aliases, but the writing in this editorial is similar to Douglass's.

9. "Deaths," *Liberator,* April 16, 1831. Some articles recorded Thomas Sr.'s age as fifty-one, while others said he was fifty-five.

10. "The French Language," *Repertory (MA)*, September 18, 1821.

11. Claudius Bradford, "Character of the African," *Liberator,* August 17, 1838.

12. "Died," *Liberator,* April 23, 1841.

13. "Garrison Society," *Liberator,* February 16, 1833.

14. For more on the Paul family, see Lois Brown, *Pauline Elizabeth Hopkins: Black Daughter of the Revolution* (Chapel Hill: University of North Carolina Press, 2008).

15. "Died," *Liberator*, June 27, 1835.

16. Her nephews were Thomas Paul Smith, born in 1827; Elijah W. Smith Jr., born in 1831; and John Boyer Smith, born around 1835. Her niece was Susan P. Smith, born around 1833. Some secondary sources indicate that, after attending the Smith School, Susan P. Smith enrolled at and graduated from a female seminary at Somerville, Massachusetts. After further research, I have not been able to corroborate this claim.

17. "Tribute to the Memory of Grace Douglass," *Liberator*, April 15, 1842.

18. Sophanisba, "Ella: A Sketch," *Liberator*, August 4, 1832.

19. "Female Literary Association," *Liberator*, December 3, 1831.

20. Letter from Sarah Mapps Douglass to William Lloyd Garrison, February 29, 1832, Anti-Slavery Manuscripts, Boston Public Library, Rare Books Department.

21. "Notice," *Liberator*, March 12, 1831. I suspect that the "Female Benevolent and Intelligence Society" referred to in this advertisement morphed into the Afric-American Female Intelligence Society.

22. Elizabeth McHenry, *Forgotten Readers: Recovering the Lost History of African American Literary Societies* (Durham, NC: Duke University Press, 2002), 68.

23. "The Treasurer of the New-England Anti-Slavery Society acknowledges the receipt of . . . ," *Abolitionist*, November 1, 1833.

24. Ira V. Brown, "'Am I Not a Woman and a Sister?' The Anti-Slavery Convention of American Women, 1837–1839," *Pennsylvania History: A Journal of Mid-Atlantic Studies* 50, no. 1 (January 1983): 10.

25. Harry C. Silcox, "Delay and Neglect: Negro Public Education in Antebellum Philadelphia, 1800–1860," *Pennsylvania Magazine of History and Biography* 97 (October 1973): 445–49.

26. "Education," *Philadelphia Gazette*, September 4, 1804.

27. *Statistics of the Colored People of Philadelphia. Taken by Benjamin C. Bacon, and Published by Order of the Board of Education of "The Pennsylvania Society for Promoting the Abolition of Slavery,"* etc. (Philadelphia: T. Ellwood Chapman, 1856), 5.

28. Advertisement, *Liberator*, January 31, 1835. Earlier advertisements appeared in November 1834. See "School," *Liberator*, November 29, 1834.

29. "Married," *Liberator*, November 12, 1836.

30. Jean R. Soderlund, "Priorities and Power: The Philadelphia Female Anti-Slavery Society," in *The Abolitionist Sisterhood: Women's Political Culture in Antebellum America*, edited by Jean Yellin and John C. Van Horne (Ithaca, NY: Cornell University Press, 1994), 76.

31. "Fifth Annual Report of the Philadelphia Female A.S. Society [January 10, 1839]," *Pennsylvania Freeman*, February 14, 1839.

32. "Sarah M. Douglass," *Public Ledger (PA)*, September 7, 1841, emphasis in original. Sarah's school, at one point located at her residence at 54 Mulberry (Arch), remained under her full control.

33. Zillah, "A True Tale for Children," *Liberator*, July 7, 1832.

34. Letter from Sarah Mapps Douglass to Rebecca White, March 27, 1876, Josiah White Papers, Haverford College Library.

35. "Editorial Correspondence," *Colored American*, December 2, 1837.

36. Letter from Sarah M. Douglass to Rebecca White, May 30, 1855, Josiah White Papers, Haverford College Library; Rusert, *Fugitive Science*, 206.

37. Zillah, "A True Tale for Children."

38. Letter from Sarah Mapps Douglass to Rebecca White, December 16, 1861, Josiah White Papers, Haverford College Library.

39. Letter from Sarah Mapps Douglass to Rebecca White, September 19, 1860, Josiah White Papers, Haverford College Library.

40. Letter from Sarah Mapps Douglass to Rebecca White, n.d. [1855–58], Josiah White Papers, Haverford College Library.

41. "Anti-Slavery Meeting in Salem," *Liberator*, March 29, 1834.

42. Susan Paul, "Letter to the Editor," *Liberator*, April 5, 1834.

43. Margaret Hope Bacon, "New Light on Sarah Mapps Douglass and Her Reconciliation with Friends," *Quaker History* 90, no. 1 (Spring 2001): 31.

44. *Society of Friends in the United States: Their Views of the Anti-Slavery Question, and Treatment of the People of Colour* (Darlington, PA: John Wilson, 1840), 22.

45. Letter from Sarah Forten to Angelina Grimké, April 15, 1837, in *Black Abolitionist Papers*, vol. 3: *The United States, 1830–1846*, edited by C. Peter Ripley (Chapel Hill: University of North Carolina Press, 1999), 221.

46. Sarah M. Douglass to "Esteemed Friend," April 2, 1844, Grimké-Weld Papers, Clements Library, University of Michigan. In her book *Evangelicalism and the Politics of Reform in Northern Black Thought, 1776–1863* (Baton Rouge: Louisiana State University Press, 2010), chapter 5, the historian Rita Roberts argues that Sarah Mapps Douglass's encounter shows how and why some free blacks in the North were wedded to this idea of "Christian republican faith."

47. Sarah Mapps Douglass, "Communications: The Friend," *National Anti-Slavery Standard*, December 14, 1843.

48. Marie Lindhorst concluded that this story was actually based on Sarah Mapps Douglass's sister. See Marie Lindhorst, "Politics in a Box: Sarah Mapps Douglass and the Female Literary Association, 1831–1833," *Pennsylvania History* 65, no. 3 (1998): 272; Julie Winch, ed., *The Elite of Our People: Joseph Wilson's Sketches of Black Upper-Class Life in Antebellum Philadelphia* (University Park: Pennsylvania State University Press, 2000).

49. Zillah, "For the Children Who Read the Liberator," *Liberator*, August 18, 1832.

50. Zillah, no title, *Liberator*, August 18, 1832, emphasis mine.

51. Ron Welburn, *Hartford's Ann Plato and the Native Borders of Identity* (Albany: State University of New York Press, 2015), 114. Welburn's fascinating biography of Ann Plato offers a nuanced discussion of African American and Native American identities. It should spark ongoing discussions about race and racial formation in nineteenth-century New England. More comparative work exploring Afro-Native women in New England is long overdue. At least two teachers identified in this chapter could be part of that discussion: Ann Plato and Charlotte E. Williams Foster Myers.

52. David O. White, "Hartford's African Schools, 1830–1868," *Connecticut Historical Society Bulletin* 39, no. 2 (1974): 49. The city of Hartford operated fourteen public schools, two of which were designated for African American children: the Elm Street School and the Talcott Street School. Incidentally, Augustus Washington, a well-educated African American man who had taught at a school in Brooklyn, New York, relocated to Hartford, where he taught at the Talcott Street School.

53. Robert R. Raymond, "Common School Report," *Supplement to the Courant* (Hartford, CT), March 8, 1845.

54. Ann Plato, *Essays; Including Biographies and Miscellaneous Pieces, in Prose and Poetry* (New York: Oxford University Press, 1988), 40.

55. Katherine Clay Bassard, *Spiritual Interrogations: Culture, Gender, and Community in Early African Women's Writing* (Princeton, NJ: Princeton University Press, 1999), 25.

56. George Levesque, "Before Integration: The Forgotten Years of Jim Crow in Boston," *Journal of Negro Education* 48, no. 2 (Spring 1979): 119.

57. Charlotte had a few siblings, of which I have identified three: Rebecca Williams, born in 1785; Isaac Williams Jr., born in 1792; and Amasa Williams, born in 1793.

58. "Nath'L Southard," *Liberator*, February 15, 1834.

59. "Garrison Juvenile Society," *Liberator*, May 17, 1834.

60. "Garrison Juvenile Society," *Liberator*, May 6, 1836.

61. "Colored People of Boston: From the Report of the Rev. R. Spaulding, to the Boston Auxiliary of the American Union for the Relief and Improvement of the Colored Race," *Boston Recorder*, February 24, 1837.

62. I suspect that Susan Paul's primary school moved into the Smith school building shortly after that building had been constructed in 1835. It was always the intention of the Boston primary school committee to locate the "African Grammar School [and] two African primary schools" within the Smith school building. See "Report on Primary Schools," December 1834, City Council Records Series 1.4, Docket 1834-0086-A, Boston City Archives.

63. "Lydia Maria Child to Jonathan Phillips Esq., [January 23, 1838]," in *We Are Your Sisters: Black Women in the Nineteenth Century*, edited by Dorothy Sterling (New York: Norton, 1984), 185.

64. E. S. Abdy, *Journal of a Residence and Tour in the United States of North America, from April, 1833, to October, 1834* (London: John Murray, 1835), 1:169.

65. "Colored People of Boston," *Boston Recorder*, February 24, 1837.

66. "Boston Schools," *Boston Traveler*, October 31, 2018.

67. "School for Colored Children," *Abolitionist*, August 1, 1833.

68. "African Primary School," *Christian Watchman (MA)*, August 15, 1828.

69. "School for Colored Children," *Abolitionist*.

70. "Anti-Slavery Discourse," *Liberator*, October 5, 1833.

71. "A Colored Jubilee," *Connecticut Herald*, July 19, 1834; "The Great Jubilee," *Liberator*, August 9, 1834; "Slavery," *Newburyport (MA) Herald*, August 5, 1834.

72. "Anti-Slavery Discourse," *Liberator*, October 5, 1833.

73. "Juvenile Concert," *Liberator*, May 12, 1837.

74. "Miss Paul's Juvenile Concert," *Colored American*, March 4, 1837.

75. Anne M. Boylan, *The Origins of Women's Activism: New York and Boston, 1797–1840* (Chapel Hill: University of North Carolina Press, 2002), 289.

76. I believe that James Jackson Sr. actually died in April 1829 and Susan Paul was mistaken that James Jr. had lost his father before the age of two. There was a forty-two-year-old James Jackson who died April 10, 1829. His death notice appeared in the *Boston Daily Advertiser* and was reprinted in the *Boston Traveler*, the *Christian Register*, and the *Columbian Centinel*. See, "Died," *Boston Daily Advertiser*, April 9, 1829.

77. "Garrison Juvenile Society," *Liberator*, May 17, 1834.

78. "Death of a Well-Known Nurse," *Boston Evening Transcript*, January 25, 1855.

79. For instance, Elizabeth's daughter, Sarah Jackson, wrote a letter, later published in the *Liberator*, on behalf of Elizabeth and William. See "First Charge," *Liberator*, November 15, 1844.

80. "Accident and Narrow Escape," *Weekly Messenger (MA)*, February 4, 1852.

81. "First Charge," *Liberator*; "Died," *Liberator*, July 27, 1849. Reverend Samuel Snowden married the couple on July 4, 1829.

82. "Died," *Liberator*, November 9, 1833.

83. Susan Paul, *Memoir of James Jackson: The Attentive and Obedient Scholar, Who Died in Boston, October 31, 1833, Aged Six Years and Eleven Months, by His Teacher, Miss Susan Paul* (1835), edited by Lois Brown (Cambridge, MA: Harvard University Press, 2000), 67.

84. Two years after the publication of *Memoir of James Jackson*, the publisher Isaac Knapp, also a friend of William Lloyd Garrison's, advertised in the *Liberator* the many antislavery texts he had for sale, including *Gustavus Vassa*, the slave narrative of Olaudah Equiano, as well as the poems of Phillis Wheatley, an early African American poet. Alongside these texts was Susan Paul's *Memoir of James Jackson*.

85. Paul, *Memoir of James Jackson*, 89.

86. Lois Brown, "Introduction," to *Memoir of James Jackson*, 28.

87. Paul, *Memoir of James Jackson*, 79–80.

88. Paul, *Memoir of James Jackson*, 91–92.

89. Paul, *Memoir of James Jackson*, 71–72, emphasis in original.

90. "Correspondence," *Essex North Register and Family Monitor*, September 9, 1836.

91. Paul, *Memoir of James Jackson*, 83.

92. Xiomara Santamarina, *Belabored Professions: Narratives of African American Working Womanhood* (Chapel Hill: University of North Carolina Press, 2005), 15.

93. "Died," *Liberator*, July 27, 1849.

94. Lisa Wilson, *A History of Stepfamilies in Early America* (Chapel Hill: University of North Carolina Press, 2014), 2.

95. Paul, *Memoir of James Jackson*, 104.

96. Paul, *Memoir of James Jackson*, 72.

97. "Lydia Maria Child to Jonathan Phillips Esq., [January 23, 1838]," 186.

98. "Letter from B. C. Bacon," *Liberator*, May 28, 1841.

99. Brown, "Introduction," 62.

100. "Save your money and your clothes [ad]," *Boston Herald*, June 20, 1849.

101. "Marriages," *Christian Watchman (MA)*, January 17, 1861.

102. Sarah H. Southwick, *Reminiscences of Early Anti-Slavery Days* (Cambridge, MA: Riverside Press, 1893), 29.

103. Kaestle, *Pillars of the Republic*, 123.

104. Linda Van Ingen, "'One Can't Live on Air': Sarah McComb and the Problem of Old-Age Income for Single Women Teachers, 1870s–1930s," *History of Education Quarterly* 54, no. 2 (May 2014): 195.

105. "Petition of Charlotte Myers to the Massachusetts General Court [January 1865]," Yale Indian Papers Project, edited by P. Grant-Costa et al., https://yipp.yale.edu/annotated-transcription/digcoll1865011200; "House of Representatives," *Boston Daily Advertiser*, January 15, 1864; "Legislative Notes," *Boston Herald*, February 20, 1865.

106. "Mrs. Charlotte Elizabeth Meyer," Home for Aged Colored Women records, box 6, folder 4, Massachusetts Historical Society, Boston.

107. Letter from Sarah Mapps Douglass to Rebecca White, March 27, 1876, Josiah White Papers, Haverford College Library, emphasis in original.

108. "Tribute to a Veteran Teacher," *People's Advocate (Washington, DC)*, February 14, 1880.

109. "Miss Fanny M. Jackson at the 19th Street Church," *People's Advocate (Washington, DC)*, January 10, 1880.

110. "Tribute to a Veteran Teacher," *People's Advocate (Washington, DC)*, emphasis mine.

111. "Grammar Schools," in *Annual Report of the School Committee of the City of Salem February 1851* (Salem, MA: Printed at the Observer Office, 1851), 20; "Tribute of Respect," *Salem (MA) Register*, July 31, 1845.

112. William Cooper Nell, "Improvement of Colored People," *Liberator*, August 24, 1855.

113. Charlotte Forten Grimké, Journal One, October 23, 1854, in *The Journals of Charlotte Forten Grimké*, edited by Brenda Stevenson (New York: Oxford University Press, 1988), 105.

114. Charlotte Forten Grimké, Journal One, June 4, 1854, 67.

115. Charlotte Forten Grimké, Journal One, June 5, 1854, 67.

116. Charlotte Forten Grimké, Journal One, August 10, 1854, 95.

117. Charlotte Forten Grimké, Journal Three, June 15, 1858, 315–16, emphasis in original.

118. Charlotte Forten Grimké, Journal One, July 28, 1854, 92.

119. Christine Ogren, *The American State Normal School: An Instrument of Great Good* (New York: Palgrave Macmillan, 2005), 7.

120. Mary Maillard, ed., *Whispers of Cruel Wrongs: The Correspondence of Louisa Jacobs and Her Circle* (Madison: University of Wisconsin Press, 2017), 29.

121. Mary-Lou Breitborde and Kelly Kolodny, *Remembering Massachusetts State Normal Schools: Pioneers in Teacher Education* (Westfield: Institute for Massachusetts Studies, 2014), 29.

122. Charlotte Forten Grimké, Journal One, May 1, 1855, 133.

123. "Normal Schools," *Common School Journal* 1, no. 3 (February 1839): 38.

124. William Cooper Nell, "Improvement of Colored People," *Liberator*, August 24, 1855.

125. For the contents of Robert Purvis's letter to the city tax collector in Byberry, Pennsylvania, wherein he refused to pay the school tax, see "Manly Protest against Wrong," *Liberator*, December 16, 1853.

126. Charlotte Forten Grimké, Journal Two, June 18, 1857, 231.

127. Charlotte Forten Grimké, Journal Three, November 13, 1862, 398. Charlotte described her experiences in the South in two essays: Charlotte Forten, "Life on the Sea Islands," *Atlantic Monthly* 13 (May–June 1864), 587–96, 666–76.

128. Charlotte Forten Grimké, Journal Three, January 1, 1859, 352; Emma Jones Lapsansky, "Feminism, Freedom, and Community: Charlotte Forten and Women Activists in Nineteenth-Century Philadelphia," *Pennsylvania Magazine of History and Biography* 113, no. 1 (January 1989): 18.

129. "Miss Elizabeth N. Smith Dead.," *Boston Globe*, December 2, 1899.

130. Alice Miller was designated a substitute teacher. In subsequent years, a few more African American teachers would hold positions in Boston public schools; among them was Florida Ruffin Ridley, who also graduated from the Bowdoin School and the Girls' Normal and High School.

131. "Massachusetts Schools," *Boston Globe*, March 11, 1891.

132. Miss Elizabeth N. Smith Dead.," *Boston Globe*, December 2, 1899.

Conclusion

1. The Ohio Colored Teachers' Association held its first meeting, in Springfield, in December 1861. It remained active for at least two decades and perhaps longer. More research on this organization is long overdue.

Appendix C

1. All of the birthdates are approximate and based on genealogical records that might later prove to be in error. Moreover, I provide only limited genealogical information here based on the people studied in this book.

2. Peter Vogelsang married Theodosia deGrasse, who passed away in 1854. He then married Theodosia's sister, Maria.

3. Joanna Turpin attended the Young Ladies' Domestic Seminary with Serena deGrasse. Serena's brother, John, married Cordelia L. Howard, whose brother was Edwin F. Howard, Joanna's husband. The Howard siblings' parents were Peter Howard and Margaret Gardner Howard of Boston.

4. Elizabeth's brother was Benjamin F. Roberts Sr., which means that Sarah C. Roberts was Elizabeth's and Thomas's niece.

5. The Lyons and Remond families knew each other well. Maritcha Lyons was named after Maritchia Juan Remond.

6. Mary Marshall's sister, Gloriana, attended the Canterbury Female Seminary.

7. Charlotte Forten Grimké knew her Aunt Jane well and had met her cousin James Vogelsang Forten quite a few times. See Julie Winch, *A Gentleman of Color: The Life of James Forten* (New York: Oxford University Press, 2002).

Index

For an understanding of families and their names, see Appendix C.

abolitionists: Black Law resistance, 33; Christian ideology of, 31; manual labor college proposal, 25; moral suasion, 230n14; resistance to resettlement movement, 39; role in African American education, 20, 22–25, 41–42, 57, 67, 128, 206; sexism of, 54; support for African American women, 8; support for YLDS, 48; white women, Christian ideology of, 32

abolition movement, global, 54–55, 67

Act for the Admission of Inhabitants in Towns, 29

activism and activist networks, 169; Boston school petitions, 161–64, 176; goals of, 7, 206; mothers' role, 2, 164, 167–68; reaction to Canterbury situation, 1–2. *See also* teachers, African American women

Addington, Mary M., 70, 72

Afric-American Female Intelligence Society, 181, 192, 271n21

African American women: girls' portrayal, 264n45; leisure activities, 226n9; purposeful womanhood, 2, 4–5, 9, 48, 207, 225n4

African Dorcas Association, 66, 83

African Free Schools (New York), 66, 81–83

African school movement, 6, 109–10

African Woolman Benevolent Society and Hall, 86

American Anti-Slavery Almanac, 3, 44–45

American Anti-Slavery Society, 41, 54

American Colonization Society, 14, 20, 25, 56, 59

anticolonization movement, 191, 242n61

Antioch College, 166, 180

Anti-Slavery Convention of American Women, 133–34

Aptheker, Bettina, 8

archives and research, 8, 226n11, 229n29, 229n30; use of first names, 229n32

Ball, Erica, 91

Barney, Nathaniel, 128–29

Bassard, Katherine Clay, 189

Becket, David, 118–20, 256n63

Beecher, Catherine, 52, 178

Beman, Amos G., 56, 88

Benezet, Anthony, 183

Benson, George William, 20, 30, 33

Benson, Henry E., 20, 26

Bentley, William, 112–14

Bernstein, Robin, 151

Bibb, Mary E. Miles. *See* Miles, Mary E.

Bible. *See* Christian love and teachings

Black Law: constitutional argument, 236n122; Crandall arrested and jailed, 32–33; opponents of African American education, 32

black womanhood, 27, 36, 234n72

Bolster, W. Jeffrey, 110
Bolt, Henrietta, 38, 237n142
Boston: African Americans in, 143, 146;
   African Society, 143; fugitive slave
   cases, 159; racial discrimination,
   142–43
Boston, Absalom F., 122, 124–26, 134, 136,
   138, 161
Boston, Hannah Cook, 123, 136
Boston, Phebe Ann, equal school rights
   proponent, 138–39
Boston Female Anti-Slavery Society, 41, 181
Boston schools, 146; academic achievement
   recognition, 142, 146–47, 170, 172;
   African American children expelled,
   152, 160; African Americans move
   outside Boston, 149, 159; boycott
   by whites suggested, 154; character
   education, 189; equal school rights
   campaign, 149, 155, 160, 163–64, 172,
   263n27; history of, 144–45; hyperlocal
   racial integration, 262n13; petitions
   for integrated schools, 158–63; private
   schools in, 144–45; Roberts children at
   Otis School, 151–52; School Abolishing
   Party, 147; school petition for African
   Americans, 144; separate African
   schools, 145–46, 190; teachers, 145;
   Wells School for Girls, 164–65. See
   also Girls' High and Normal School;
   Roberts v. City of Boston; Smith School
Bowers, Lucretia Turpin, 76–77, 161, 174.
   See also Turpin, Lucretia
Bradley, James, 6
Breitborde, Mary-Lou, 201
Brown, Charlotte D., 132–33, 136, 259n140
Brown, Hallie Q., 103
Brown, Henry Box, 86–87, 160
Brown, Lois, 196, 226n11
Buffum, Arnold, 26, 41, 183
Burned-Over District, 51, 56, 239n15
Bustill, Elizabeth Douglass, 23, 186, 233n54

Canterbury Female Boarding School
   (CFBS), 13, 17, 19
Canterbury Female Seminary (CFS):
   African American women students, 14,
   230n12; attempt to move school, 38–39;
   Black Law and, 32; building destroyed,
   39–40; Christian love and teachings,
   31, 35, 230n14; day students, 22, 233n45;
defied racist stereotypes, 23; enrollment,
   22–23, 233n54; flourishing despite
   Crandall case, 38; goals of, 205; Harris
   "first colored scholar," 42–43; monitorial
   educational system, 24; students become
   teachers, 42, 237n142; success of African
   American women, 43; Unionist defense
   of, 33; violence directed at, 44–45;
   white abolitionist boosters, 21; white
   opposition to, 1, 28–30, 230n13
Canterbury Village: racism of, 14–16, 26;
   white opposition to African American
   seminary, 14–16, 26
Casneau, John, 174–75, 269n169
Casneau, Sarah Clarissa Roberts, 175–76,
   262n5. See also Roberts, Sarah Clarissa
character education: female education and,
   178; at home, 195; in primary schools,
   178, 184, 188, 191. See also Paul, Susan
Christian domesticity, cult of, 48, 52–53,
   72, 238n4
Christian love and teachings: Book of
   John, 16, 185, 230n14; embraced by
   African American women students,
   40–41, 204, 238n4; Gospel of Mark, 16;
   importance in curriculum, 24; Letter to
   the Romans, 16; Proverbs, 52; reaction
   of seminary students to opposition,
   30–31; resistance to white opposition, 16
Christian Reflector, 73, 119, 196
citizenship of African Americans, 36–38,
   83–84, 247n24
Clarke, Catharine, 67–68
Clarkson Society, 115
Cleveland, Chauncey, 35–38
Colchester school, 21, 144
Colored American, 53, 63, 65–66, 83–84,
   89–91, 96, 184
Colored Female Union Society, 133, 192,
   259n141
Colored School of Brooklyn, 86–88, 248n51
Committee of Vigilance, 95–97
Compromise of 1850, 97
Cooper, Arthur, 123, 126, 257n82
Cooper, Lucy, 123, 136
Cooper, Patience Harris, 133, 136, 260n143
Cornish, Samuel, 22, 57, 81–82
Cott, Nancy, 138
Crandall, Almira, 23, 32
Crandall, Prudence: abolitionist support
   for, 26; admission of Harris, 13–14;

admission of Harris to white academy, 27; African American women's education, 23; background of, 16–17; Christian love and teachings, 30, 154; citizenship focus of teaching, 37–38; female interracial solidarity, 24; founder CFBS, 19; founder CFS, 8; model for other teachers, 126; on Northern racial prejudice, 28; praise for, 32, 43; school mission redirected, 14; sexist attacks, 28–29; travel to publicize Female Seminary, 20; *Unionist* defense of, 33. *See also State of Connecticut v. Prudence Crandall*
Crandall case. *See State of Connecticut v. Prudence Crandall*
Croger brothers, 86
Cross, Whitney, 51
Crummell, Alexander, 49, 56, 80, 174

Daggett, David, 35–36, 39
Dartmouth College, 96, 144, 179, 248n47
deGrasse, George, 22, 66
deGrasse, Isaiah, 49, 56, 75, 89
deGrasse, John V., 56, 74, 161
deGrasse, Maria van Salee, 66, 83
deGrasse, Serena Leonora, 2, 47, 65, 68, 73, 75–76, 90, 161, 207; at YLDS, 47
deGrasse, Theodosia, 22, 34, 65
Dickerson, Martina and Mary Ann, 184-85
Dickerson, Stephen, 95–96
Dodge, William, 8, 113, 121
Douglass, Elizabeth: expelled from white school, 188; target of prejudice, 187
Douglass, Frederick, 94, 130, 161
Douglass, Grace Bustill, 181, 186
Douglass, Sarah Mapps, 272n48; activist in retirement, 198; activist role, 6–7; background of, 180–81; character education, 179, 184–85, 188; Christian republican faith, 272n46; didactic writings on race and slavery, 204; female seminary in Philadelphia, 58, 183, 199; frustration with students, 186; letter in *Emancipator*, 23; public letter on Canterbury situation, 1–2; on Quaker faith, 187; target of prejudice, 186–87; teacher and activist, 10, 37, 206; at Women's Antislavery Convention, 182
Downing, George T., 73, 75, 165, 168

Downing, Serena deGrasse, 92, 168. *See also* deGrasse, Serena Leonora
Draft Riots of 1863, 166, 169
Duane, Anna Mae, 82
Dunbar, Erica Armstrong, 4, 177
Dyer, Charles, 132, 176, 270n170
Dyer, Sarah C. Roberts Casneau. *See* Roberts, Sarah Clarissa

Easton, Hosea, 150, 181
Eato, Mary E., 101–2
education of African Americans: benefits of, 81–82; debate over segregated schools, 156–57; equal educational opportunities, 134; equal educational opportunities in, 81, 109; interest by African American families, 20–21; myth of black intellectual apathy, 23, 115, 194; Quakers and white philanthropists role, 81–82; state laws prohibiting, 32; struggle for opportunities, 26; treatment in white schools, 155–56; white resistance to, 21, 25, 27–28; women's activism, 23, 42–43, 45, 132, 206
education of African American women: coeducational opportunities, 57–58; domestic education, 54; lawsuit for access to public schools, 153–54; question of subjects taught to girls, 53; radical acts of, 205
Ellsworth, William, 34–37, 235n106
Emancipator, 23, 65, 73
Ennalls, Sarah, 83
equal school rights, 229n33; Boston schools, 149, 155, 160, 163–64, 172; forerunners of school desegregation fight, 10, 230n34; Massachusetts, 135–38, 143, 176; New York schools, 170; Providence schools, 165–70; public high schools, 108, 111, 128, 132; Rhode Island, 168–70; Salem, 118, 131–32, 140–41, 207
Essay on the Education of Female Teachers, An (Beecher), 178
Essays (A. Plato), 188
Everett, Elizabeth, 8, 50, 68, 72, 74–77, 91, 238n2, 243n98

Fayerweather, Sarah Harris, 42. *See also* Harris, Sarah
Female Literary Association of Philadelphia, 178, 181

female literary societies, 5–6, 180–81, 205, 225n2. *See also* Female Literary Association of Philadelphia; Garrison Juvenile Society

female seminary movement, 225n3; age range, 231n21; boarding school or academy, 232n34; class and socializing, 19–20, 50; course of study, 19; forces for, 18, 25; middle and upper-class white women, 17–18, 25–26; predominantly white and female, 232n33; racism of, 2, 4, 18–20, 57, 227n16; role in education, 8–9. *See also* Ipswich Female Academy; Miss Whitehead's School for Young Ladies of Color; Young Ladies' Domestic Seminary (YLDS)

Fenner, Amy, 38, 237n142

Field, Corinne, 37

First Annual Convention of the Free People of Color, 24–25

Fletcher, Richard, 140, 152, 163

Forbes, Abner, 147, 149–50, 152

Forten, Charlotte. *See* Grimké, Charlotte Forten

Forten, Charlotte Vandine, 39, 53, 93, 187

Forten, James, 22, 39, 93, 181, 183, 187

Forten, Jane M. Vogelsang, 79, 92–94, 97

Foster, Charlotte Williams, 145, 262n14; background of, 189; character education, 189

Fowler, Bethsheba, 155, 161

Fowler, Samuel, 151, 159, 161

free black population, 19

Freedom's Journal, 19, 66, 81–83, 109

Free Will Baptists, 73, 79, 244n124

friendship albums, 184–85

Fugitive Slave Law, 76, 97–98, 159–60, 252n117, 252n118

Gardner, Angelina Brinton, 149–50, 176

Gardner, Anna, 126–27, 136; teacher at Nantucket African School, 125–26, 129

Gardner, Oliver and Hannah Macy, 123, 125–26

Garnet, Julia Ward Williams, 77

Garnet, Sarah J. Smith Tompkins, 172

Garrison, Elizabeth, 156

Garrison, Robert, 95–96

Garrison, William Lloyd, 8; and Anti-Slavery Society, 54; and Benjamin Roberts, 155, 157; and Crandall, 20, 34, 42; editor of the *Liberator*, 14; manual labor college proposal, 25–26; and Nancy Woodson, 149; and New England Anti-Slavery Society, 180; and Sarah Mapps Douglass, 181; and Thomas Paul Jr., 156

Garrison Juvenile Society, 189–90, 192

Girls' High and Normal School, J. Imogen Howard at, 172

Glasko, Eliza, 22, 34

Glasko, Miranda, 22, 42. *See also* Overbaugh, Miranda Glasko

Goddard, Calvin, 34, 37

Gradual Emancipation Act in 1799, 54, 80

Graham, Elizabeth Jennings, 250n92. *See also* Jennings, Elizabeth, Jr.

Gray, Nathaniel, 98–99, 102

Green, Beriah, 54–57, 59

Gregory, Eliza Turpin. *See* Turpin, Eliza

Grimké, Charlotte Forten, 161, 179; background of, 199–200; eager to learn, 200–201; at Epes Grammar School, 202; target of prejudice, 200; teacher and activist, 2, 10, 39, 201–4, 276n7

Grosvenor, Cyrus P., 120–21, 186

Hall, Primus, 144, 146

Hammond, Ann Eliza, 29, 33–34, 42–43

Hammond, Elizabeth Hall, 20, 233n39

Hardesty, Jared, 143

Harris, Blanche V., 6, 227n16

Harris, Mary, 22, 42

Harris, Sarah, 2, 9, 35, 43, 230n5; admission to white academy, 27; application to Canterbury Female Boarding School, 14; church attendance, 230n2; day student at CFS, 22; domestic work racialized, 14, 25; early education, 13, 15

Hilton, John T., 146, 149–50, 155, 190

Hilton, Lucretia, 150, 263n38

Hodges, Graham, 97

Hogarth, George, 86–87, 90

Hopkins, Pauline, 63, 155, 172

Howard, Adeline T., 161, 164, 172–74, 208

Howard, Edwin Clarence, 161–62, 174–75

Howard, Edwin F., 77, 161–62

Howard, J. Imogen, 161, 171–74, 208

Howard, Joanna Turpin, 63, 161, 164. *See also* Turpin, Joanna

Hyperlocalism, 7, 21, 108, 111, 113, 206, 262n13, 267n118,

Institute for Colored Youth, 101, 183–84, 199

Ipswich Female Academy, 28

Jackson, Ann Jennette, 191–92, 197
Jackson, James, Jr., 191–95
Jackson, James, Sr., 191–92, 195, 273n76
James, Ursula, 47, 59–60, 73, 76–77, 79, 88, 90–92
Jasper, Nancy, 189, 192
Jeffrey, Julia Roy, 85
Jennings, Elizabeth, Jr., 79, 92–94, 97, 265n66
Jennings, Elizabeth, Sr., 5
Jocelyn, Simeon, 22–23, 25, 41
Johnson, Ursula James, 60. *See also* James, Ursula
Judson, Andrew T., 35–37, 206; attacks on Crandall, 29; on destruction of seminary, 40; journalists defense of, 33–34; opponent of African American seminary, 26–27; in resettlement movement, 39; sponsor of Canterbury Female Boarding School, 14, 17;

Kaestle, Carl, 178
Kantrowitz, Stephen, 37
Kelley, Mary, 20, 25
Kellogg, Hiram Huntington: abolitionist, 8; and African American education, 57; background of, 51; and Charles Wright, 64; Christian duty to abolish racial prejudice, 65; Christian domesticity at YLDS, 54; democratizing women's education, 51; different treatment from Crandall, 59; domestic learning praised, 50; embraced abolitionist goals, 67–68, 244n116; female nature at home and classroom, 52; goal to teach purposefulness, 78; leaves YLDS for Knox College, 72–74; and New York State Anti-Slavery Society, 55; reopens YLDS, 245n150; seeks financial support for African American women, 46–48; valedictory address on Christian community, 74–75; and YLDS, 9, 58–60, 71, 207, 239n6, 244n118
Kellogg, Mary Gleason Chandler, 51, 70
Kent, James, 36, 38
Know-Nothing Party, 163–64
Knox Manual Labor College, 72, 74
Kolodny, Kelly, 201

Lancastrian system of learning, 24, 109, 182
Lanson, Grace, 21, 25
Lanson, Harriet Rosetta, 22–24, 30, 40
Lasser, Carol, 6, 227n17, 227n19
Latta, Elizabeth, 6
Lawrence, Chloe Minns, 113–14, 133–34, 255n33
Lawrence, Schuyler, 113-114, 121
Laws, Sarah C. Roberts Casneau Dyer, 176, 270n175
Leach, Daniel, 166–67, 267n124
Lee, Chloe, 157
Lewis, Joel W., 149, 251n101
Lewis, (Mary) Edmonia, 174, 269n164
Liberator, 126, 155; advertisement for CFS, 20–21, 233n43; advertisements for YLDS, 74; African American student honors, 146, 165; on Canterbury School, 33; on character education, 178; on Christian domesticity, 53; essay on slavery, 24, 234n58; Female Literary Association of Philadelphia and, 180; friendship across color line, 194; fund raising for, 192; on Nantucket school integration, 139; racial prejudice incident, 186; Roberts petition drive, 157; Stewart speech on servitude, 14; Williams donation, 62
Lincoln, Abraham, 99
Loveridge, Prince, 83, 247n24
Lyons, Maritcha, 6, 101, 166–67, 169–70, 268n139
Lyons family, 166-68, 276n5

Mabee, Carleton, 163, 170
Macy family, 123, 126
Mann, Horace, 140, 144, 148, 157
manual labor college proposal, 25–26
Marshall, Gloriana Catherine, 167
Massachusetts: abolition of slavery, 109; African American education, 9, 109; English Classical School, 110; equal school rights legislation, 143, 176; equal school rights petitions, 135–38; fifty percent white blood rule, 160; history of schools in, 108–9; hyperlocal racial integration, 7, 206–7; legal recourse for access to public schools, 138–39; public high school law, 1827, 107, 116; Salem and Nantucket school segregation decisions, 111–14

Massachusetts Anti-Slavery Society, 133, 150, 259n140

Matthews, Glenna, 52

May, Samuel J.: abolitionist, 23; on Black Law, 33; on CFS move to Massachusetts, 38; CFS to close, 40; to Hammond on fine, 29; to Judson on CFS, 27; lecturer at New England Anti-Slavery Society, 191; meeting with Mary E. Miles, 46; on school segregation, 128; State Normal School administrator, 49, 76; supporter of African American women's education, 49, 239n6; trustee of CFS, 26

Meeting Street School, 42, 49

Memoir of James Jackson (S. Paul), 192–96

Miles, Mary E., 238n2, 240n31; background of, 48–49, 239n6; at CFS, 9, 22, 42, 46; educational activist, 2; first African American graduate from public normal school, 76, 201; first African American to attend YLDS, 59, 65; gender equality, 54; at YLDS, 45–47

Miner, Myrtilla, 67–68

Minkins, Shadrach, 98, 159

Minns, Chloe. *See* Lawrence, Chloe Minns

missionaries. *See* deGrasse, Isaiah; Loveridge, Prince

Miss Whitehead's School for Young Ladies of Color, 57

Morris, Harriet D., 117

Morris, Robert, 117, 152–53, 159–60

Morris, William W., 130–33, 260n145

Morrison, Margaret, 47, 60, 68–70, 207

Morrison, Rosetta: effect of slavery on, 207–8; friendships, 76; hard life despite education, 207; interracial environment, 70–72; one of few student remaining, 73; opens a select Primary School, 79–80, 87–88; teaching career of, 85; at YLDS, 9, 47, 60–61

Moss, Hilary, 2, 157

Mother Zion African Methodist Episcopal Church, 80–81

Mott, Lucretia, 39, 49, 181

Mrs. Maxon's School for Colored Children, 55

Myers, Charlotte Williams Foster, 197–98. *See also* Foster, Charlotte Williams

Nantucket: abolition of slavery in, 122; African School in, 124–25, 128; equal school rights, 130, 132–35, 138–39; formal school for African Americans, 124; free black population, 123; mixed race heritage of African Americans, 122, 124; Nantucket Anti-Slavery Society, 126; Nantucket Colored Anti-Slavery Society, 126, 130; Nantucket County Association for the Promotion of Education, 128; Nantucket Female Anti-Slavery Society, 126; Nantucket school committee lawsuit, 139; protest over segregation of schools, 130–31, 135; public schools, 124, 127; school committee seats, 134; segregation of schools, 127–28, 134–35; slaves in, 256n78

Nantucket Inquirer & Mirror, 123–25, 127, 129, 134, 257n83, 257n88

Nash, Margaret, 18

National Anti-Slavery Standard, 74, 97, 187

Neem, Johann, 110

Nell, William Cooper, 148; abolitionist, 8, 155, 159; aids fugitive slaves, 160; equal school rights advocate, 147, 170, 176; no medal for high honors, 142; petition for integrated schools, 160–61, 163, 229n29, 263n27; Smith School closed, 164; student achievements in *Liberator,* 165; student achievements praised, 172

New England Anti-Slavery Society, 64, 180–81, 191

New York Manumission Society, 81–82, 247n31

New York schools: equal school rights fight, 170; married teachers, 249n75

New York State Anti-Slavery Society, 55–56

Noel, Rebecca R., 111

normal schools: African American graduates, 76, 94, 102; character education taught, 202; prevalence of women, 116

Northern states: domestic work racialized, 48; educational struggle in, 6; hostility toward African Americans, 5, 45; racism and racial prejudice, 1

North Star Fair Association, 97–98

Oberlin College, 5–6, 41, 166, 227n17, 227n19

Ohio Colored Teachers' Association, 208, 276n1

Olney, Frederick, 38, 167

Oneida County: background of, 51; black population of, 54; equal educational opportunities in, 54; resistance to YLDS, 67; schools for African American children, 55

Oneida Institute, 59; hostility then closing, 57; interracial institution, 55–56

Orthodox Congregational Sabbath School Society, 192-196, 193

Otis School, 151–52, 158

Our Nig, or, Sketches from the Life of a Free Black (Wilson), 62

Overbaugh, Miranda Glasko, 246n22

Parker, Amy F., 165

Parker, Clementina, 165, 169, 267n117

Parker, Ransom, 165, 168, 237n142

Paul, Ann Catharine, 145, 155, 179, 197; at African School No. 2, 145; Sunday School teacher, 180

Paul, Catharine, 155–56,179, 190, 197, 262n15

Paul, Susan: abolitionist teaching, 191, 193; African American literary associations, 181; Boston Juvenile Choir, 191; character education, 191, 195; Christian teachings, 190, 196; death and obituary, 196–97; didactic writings on race and slavery, 204; educational activist, 2, 10; family and background, 179–80; George Street School, 189; helped raise Elijah Smith, 155; home responsibilities, 196; praise for, 197; published stories, 184; target of prejudice, 186; teacher, 190–91; teacher and activist, 145, 177; teaching about slavery and poverty, 193–94. *See also Memoir of James Jackson* (S. Paul)

Paul, Thomas, Jr., 265n73; 145, 156–57, 164, 196; at Dartmouth, 179; teacher, 180

Paul, Thomas, Sr., 144–45, 156, 179, 192

Peirce, Cyrus, 126, 128–29

Pennsylvania Abolition Society, 183, 236n133

Perkins, Linda, 4, 102

Peterson, Ann, 34

Peterson, Carla, 83

Peterson, Eliza Glasko, 83. *See also* Glasko, Eliza

Peterson, John, 83–84, 246n22

Philadelphia Female Anti-Slavery Society (PFASS), 39, 181, 183

Philadelphia schools: African American female seminary suggested, 39, 236n133; Association for the Free Instruc-, 183;

private African American schools, 183; segregated schools in, 182

Philleo, Prudence Crandall: select academy in Providence, 237. *See also* Crandall, Prudence

Phillips, Wendell, 158, 161, 164

Philomathean Literary Society, 66, 247n23

Phoenix High School for Colored Youth, 57

Pindall case, 160, 266n92

Plan for Improving Female Education (Willard), 178

Plato, Ann, 179, 188–89, 198, 272n51

Pollard, Sarrah Ann, 114

Pompey, Edward J., 136–37, 260n158

Prentice, Sally, 13

Price, Caroline A. Roberts Wilson, 174, 176

Primary Select School of Brooklyn, 89–92

Providence schools: equal school rights, 165–70; lawsuits, 267n118; rejection of African American students, 166–67

public high schools, 107–8; equal school rights at, 108, 111, 128, 132; few opportunities for African American women, 115–16, 118–19; in New York and Connecticut, 110–11; success of African American women, 127; teacher education for white women, 116

public schools, role of, 2; early days of, 7–8; primary, 13, 62

Public School Society, 81, 247n31

Putnam, Chloe, 113. *See also* Lawrence, Chloe Minns

Putnam, Rufus, 116–17, 119–21

Quakers: black schools founded, 81; Nantucket school, 124; schools, 16, 49. *See also* Public School Society

Quock Walker case, 109

racial uplift ideology, 4, 25, 42, 73, 205, 249n72

racism and racial prejudice, 232n33; African American teachers targeted, 186; attacks on Crandall, 33–34; good behavior of African American students, 194; Massachusetts school segregation, 107; opposition to education of African Americans and, 30–31, 43; opposition to rights, 81; Quakers and, 187; racially exclusive schools, 110; scientific racism, 232n28; white manhood and, 36–37

Randalian Seminary, 57
Ray, Charles B., 53, 65–67, 82, 84, 93, 101, 121
Reason, Charles L., 93, 101, 166
Reminiscences of Early Anti-Slavery Days, 197
Remond, Charles Lenox, 118, 132, 161, 164
Remond, John, 118, 120, 130, 132, 167, 186, 259n135
Remond, Marchita Juan, 107, 130, 161, 207
Remond, Nancy Lenox, 118, 130, 132, 161, 167
Remond, Sarah Parker, 119; all black private school Newport, 130–31; educational activist, 2, 9; equal school rights proponent, 108, 132, 141, 207; left Salem schools, 140; rejected by private schools, 110; removed from East School for Girls, 107, 118–20, 200; Salem petition, 161
Remond family, 130–31, 152, 166, 200, 276n5
resettlement movement. *See* American Colonization Society; anticolonization movement; Windham County Colonization Society
respectability, 28, 60; at Black schools, 91; character as test of, 128, 226n9; goal of teaching, 82; of middle-class African American women, 4
Rhode Island: Boston school case impact, 165; Dorr Rebellion, black military service, 165; equal school rights law, 168–70; petitions for integrated schools, 165; testimony at legislature, 165–66
Riley, Elizabeth Jackson, 192, 195, 259n141
Riley, William, 192, 195–96, 262n20
Roberts, Adeline, 151, 159, 176
Roberts, Benjamin, Jr., 151–52, 158
Roberts, Benjamin, Sr., 153, 264n46, 264n48, 265n85; sent daughter to all white school, 151; death of, 176; equal school rights proponent, 143, 159–60; move out of Boston, 159; petition for integrated schools, 163; violence over segregation, 157. *See also* Roberts v. City of Boston
Roberts, Elizabeth Augusta, 155, 197, 276n4
Roberts, Robert, 151, 197
Roberts, Sarah Clarissa, 143, 150–55, 158–59, 164, 174, 276n4
Roberts v. City of Boston, 143, 152–55, 157, 174, 176, 270n173
Ross, Eunice: about, 125; application to Nantucket High School, 127, 134; denied

admission to Nantucket public high school, 107; denied school access, 9; equal school rights activist, 108, 132, 138, 140–41, 206; lawsuit, 139; petition for integrated schools, 136–37, 169, 258n123; rejected from Nantucket High School, 129–30
Ross, Sarah, 125, 161; petitions for equal educational rights, 136–37
Rowland, Frances Bliss, 70, 79
Rowland, William F. and family, 60–61
Ruggles, David, 57, 95–96
Rush, Benjamin, 17–18
Russwurm, John, 81, 95

Salem, 140; African American protests, 120–21, 141; African Americans in, 111, 115, 130–32; African Baptist Society, 123; African School, 113–14, 121, 130, 140; African Society, 112; Anti-Slavery Society of Salem, 117; Colored Female Religious and Moral Reform Society, 115, 117, 133; East School for Girls, 107, 116–20, 122, 131; equal school rights, 118, 131–34, 140–41, 207; expulsion of African American girls from public high school, 120–21; interracial school in, 111–12, 114–15, 121–22, 132, 255n39; private schools in, 112; public high schools for women, 116; school admission of African Americans, 117–18; School for Colored Children, 121; segregated schools in, 113; Sunday Schools, 115
Salem Female Anti-Slavery Society, 133, 201
Salem Normal School, 201–2
Salem Register, 132, 140
Saunders, Prince, 21, 144
select schools, 88–92; schools for children and adults, 88
separate but equal doctrine, 143
Sernett, Milton, 56
Serrington, William, 130–31, 259n126
sexism, 43, 54; Kellogg and Crandall treatment, 59
Shaw, Lemuel, 153, 155, 158–59
Shephard, Jedidiah, 14, 35, 264n44
Sinha, Manisha, 98
Slack, Charles W., 163
Smith, Andrew R., 82
Smith, Elizabeth H., 42, 167, 243n98

Smith, Elizabeth Norton, 165, 172, 199, 203–4
Smith, Florence, 199, 203–4
Smith, Gerrit, 46, 54–55, 239n34, 240n38
Smith, Harriet, 203–4
Smith, Susan P., 197, 253n135
Smith, Thomas Paul, 155–57, 160, 197, 271n16
Smith School, 263n21; benefits of segregated schools, 156; boycott, 143, 149, 155; Chloe Lee, teacher, 157; closure of, 164; criticism of Forbes, 149–50; deficiencies, 146–47; Forbes replaced, 149–50; lawsuit to close the school, 152; student achievement, 142, 147; Susan Paul teacher, 177; Woodson assistant teacher, 147
social reform, 86, 108, 207; at YLDS, 9, 43, 48, 71–72, 74, 78
Society for Promoting Manual Labor in Liter-, 50
Society for the Propagation of the Gospel in Foreign Parts, 124, 257n88
Spurzheim, Johann Gaspar, 177, 270n2
State of Connecticut v. Prudence Crandall, 38–39, 168; Benson testimony in, 34; citizenship of African Americans, 36–38; and Connecticut Act for the Admission of Inhabitants, 29; effect on other seminaries, 58–59; guilty verdict reversed on appeal, 36–37, 39–40; Mary Barber testimony, 35; pleads not guilty, 34; Privileges and Immunities Clause, 37; students' character, 34–35; trials, 35
Stewart, Maria W., 14, 37, 43, 80, 83, 97, 181
suffrage: New York State requirements, 82–83; universal suffrage focus, 83
Sumner, Charles, 154, 158, 163; defense of Sarah Roberts, 153
Sunday Evening School for People of Color, 55

Tappan, Arthur, 33–34, 169
Tappan, Lewis, 33, 49, 169
teachers, African American women: activist network, 79–80, 85, 177–78, 208, 225n2; careers, 84–85, 184, 199, 204; on character education, 179, 188–89, 207; didactic writings on race and slavery, 187; financial troubles, 197–98; geographic limitations, 85; praise and remembrance, 197; race work, 80; racial prejudice toward, 186
Thomas, Eliza D., 75, 77, 90
Tompkins, Fanny, 79, 97–98; teaching career of, 83–84
Tompkins, Sarah J. Smith, 101, 253n135. *See also* Garnet, Sarah J. Tompkins.
"True Tale for Children, A" (Douglass), 184
Turner, Nat, 31
Turpin, Joanna, 47, 62, 72–73, 76–77, 276n3. *See also* Howard, Joanna Turpin
Turpin, Joseph, 62–63
Turpin, Lucretia, 47, 62, 65, 73
"Two School Girls" (A. Plato), 188
Tyack, David, 116

Unionist, 33
United States Telegraph, 29

Vinovskis, Maris, 112
violence: African American female seminary suggested for Philadelphia, 236n133; anti-slavery convention, mob attack, 56; arson charge at CFS, 38; at CFS, 1; New Haven rejection of African American college, 25; Seminary building destroyed, 40, 43–45; slave trade and slavery, 29; teacher at CFS assaulted, 38; threats to Hammond, 33, 43
Vogelsang, Theodosia deGrasse, 84, 92. *See also* deGrasse, Theodosia
voting rights. *See* suffrage

Walker, David, 7, 31
Washington, Augustus, 86–87, 248n47, 272n52
Weeksville, Brooklyn, 85–86
Welburn, Ron, 188
Weld, Theodore Dwight, 41, 51, 95
Weldon, Catharine Ann, 34
Wellman, Judith, 86
Wheatley, Phillis, 201
White, Rebecca, 184–85
Wilder, Ann Elizabeth, 34
Wilder, Craig Steven, 81–82
Willard, Emma, 84, 178
Williams, Julia Ward, 41–42, 134. *See also* Garnet, Julia Ward Williams
Williams, Peter H., 22, 49, 66, 161
Wilson, Harriet E., 62, 242n69

Wilson, J. Dayton, 95–96, 98, 251n101
Wilson, Lisa, 195
Winch, Julie, 100
Women's Antislavery Convention: New York, 182; Philadelphia, 182
Woodson, Nancy, 146, 176; denied City Medal, 142, 170; fired from assistant teaching position, 147–49
Woody, Thomas, 4
Wormley, Mary, 184
Wright, Adaline Turpin, 62, 64–65
Wright, Alice, 101–2
Wright, Isaac, 92, 94–100, 102–3, 251n111, 252n128
Wright, Rosetta Morrison, 2; financial troubles, 94; marriage of, 97–100, 253n146; network of educator activists, 103, 208; opens a select Primary School, 90–92. See also Morrison, Rosetta
Wright, Theodore S., 8, 22, 55, 57, 77, 82, 85, 90; effect on Kellogg, 64–65; at Princeton Theological Seminary, 64

Young Ladies' Domestic Seminary (YLDS): academics at, 68; age range, 47, 238n1; applications, 58; bonds of friendship continued, 75–77; Christian principles taught, 51, 64, 68, 76; closure of, 73–74; enrollment, 58, 238n2, 241n55, 244n118; field trips to antislavery meetings, 72; interracial Christian fellowship, 70–71; manual labor and liberal arts, 48–50, 53, 64; Miles applies for admission, 46; racially integrated female seminary, 47–49, 67, 77; reopened by Kellogg, 245n150; Rosetta Morrison at, 79; Smith's donations, 54; social reform and Christian principles, 71; students of different backgrounds at, 50; success of integration, 206; teaching career goal, 59; Turpin sisters at, 62; typical day at, 67–68
Young Men's Literary Society, 155

ABOUT THE AUTHOR

Kabria Baumgartner is the Dean's Associate Professor of History and Africana Studies as well as Associate Director of Public History at Northeastern University in Boston, MA.